THE LIGHT

and

THE GLORY

By Peter Marshall and David Manuel

The Light and the Glory
The Light and the Glory for Children
From Sea to Shining Sea
From Sea to Shining Sea for Children
Sounding Forth the Trumpet
Sounding Forth the Trumpet for Children

REVISED AND EXPANDED EDITION

GOD'S PLAN *for* AMERICA

THE LIGHT
and
THE GLORY
1492 – 1793

PETER MARSHALL *and*
DAVID MANUEL

Revell

a division of Baker Publishing Group
Grand Rapids, Michigan

© 1977, 2009 by Peter J. Marshall and David B. Manuel Jr.

Published by Revell
a division of Baker Publishing Group
P.O. Box 6287, Grand Rapids, MI 49516-6287
www.revellbooks.com

Printed in the United States of America

ISBN 978-0-8007-1942-5 (cloth)
ISBN 978-0-8007-3271-4 (pbk.)

Library of Congress Cataloging-in-Publication Data
Marshall, Peter, 1940–
    The light and the glory: 1492–1793 / Peter Marshall and David Manuel. — Rev. and expanded ed.
        p.   cm.
    "God's plan for America."
    Includes bibliographical references and index.
    ISBN 978-0-8007-3271-4 (pbk.)
    1. United States—History—Colonial period, ca. 1600–1775. 2. United States—History—Revolution, 1775–1783. 3. United States—Church history—To 1775. 4. History—Religious aspects—Christianity. 5. Providence and government of God—Christianity. I. Manuel, David. II. Title.
E189.M36 2009
973.2—dc22   2008043613

13   14   15   8   7   6   5   4   3

green press INITIATIVE

CONTENTS

Acknowledgments

The authors wish to express their gratitude to David Barton and Wall-builders Inc. of Aledo, Texas, for the timely and capable research assistance of his staff, particularly Katie Schonhoff and Sarah Freeman. We would also like to add a word of thanks to Linda Triemstra for her professional creation of a first-rate index to the book.

A GENERATION LATER . . .

Can thirty-two years have passed since the *The Light and the Glory* was first published? It seems more like a dozen since we turned in the final manuscript to the Fleming H. Revell Company and held our breath. Throughout our prayerful research and writing, God had kept us focused on our assignment. We were to give Americans a window into the rich Christian heritage that most of us did not even know our nation possessed, because secular historians often ignored it altogether. Now it was done—would anyone read it?

They did. The blessing that God placed on the book continues to this day. More than a million copies have gone out in all its permutations, which include a young readers' edition and even a children's activity book. It has become what every publisher (and author) hopes for: a continuing back-stock title.

Then why, after all these years, bring out a new edition?

When our publishers came to us with this possibility, Peter was receptive. He had always wanted to do a revision, correcting a few minor factual errors, but mostly adding new material from his ongoing research into American history. David was less receptive. It would mean at least six months' work of difficult rewriting. But in writers' workshops he had consistently taught that the number one enemy of

"Best" is "Good." Thirty-two years ago we had given God our best. But we have gotten better at our craft since then. After much prayer, we agreed.

One compelling reason for this new edition is that basic knowledge of our nation's history has been eroding at an accelerating pace. This national amnesia was a serious problem at the time of our first edition; now it is staggering. High school and college-age young people seem to know nothing of our struggle for independence from Great Britain and cannot give the dates for the Civil War. We are losing what Abraham Lincoln referred to as "the mystic chords of memory."

Why does that matter? Woodrow Wilson, who was President during World War I (1914–18), warned us: "A nation which does not remember what it was yesterday, does not know what it is today, nor what it is trying to do. We are trying to do a futile thing, if we do not know where we came from or what we have been about."

As we began working, we introduced fresh material on Columbus, Roanoke and Jamestown, the Salem Witch Trials, and Founding Fathers Patrick Henry, Samuel Adams, and George Washington. We even added a new miracle story from the War for Independence.

We had intended to leave the rest alone, but we were soon rewriting practically every sentence. Thirty-two years had given us a deeper understanding of God's hand in our nation's founding, which affected the entire book.

Thankfully, there is renewed interest in America's Founders, typified by David McCullough's superb bestsellers *1776* and *John Adams*. Most of the new books, however, have not sought to counter the prevailing (and utterly false) opinion that all of the Founders were Deists and were not orthodox Christians. There is a need to set that record straight, using the words of the Founders themselves. Within our space constraints, this version attempts to do that.

If only the problem were merely ignorance of our past. The truth is, we have lost the founding *vision* for America. We no longer seem to know who we are, much less why we are here. We are like the ancient Israelites, who lost the Word of God (the Old Testament books of Moses) in the dusty recesses of the temple archives. The Bible alerts us to the consequences of this condition: "Where there is no vision, the people perish" (Prov. 29:18 KJV).

From the beginning this book has been about the search for that original vision. If we could find God's hand in our nation's beginnings, if we could discover that her foundations had been laid by Christian men and women who were conscious of being guided by God, maybe we could help modern Americans recover our national sense of purpose and destiny.

There is an urgency now about this update. In the 1970s we were alarmed at a divorce rate claiming one in four marriages. Now it is one in two. We were appalled at the rise of homosexuality, never dreaming that the Church would ordain practicing homosexuals as ministers or that the State would approve same-sex marriage. Abortion was a holocaust back then, but while public opinion has slowly been turning against it, in too many states it has been relegated to the status of a back-burner issue. Obscenity and profanity in movies and the media today are off the charts.

Nor is the new darkness restricted to adults; it permeates all age groups. Sexually transmitted diseases among college-age young people have become epidemic. Cheating on tests is routine, even for elementary school children.

We could go on, but you get the idea. We are in desperate shape. American morality has no firm footing; it is precariously perched on the shifting sands of the latest trend in lifestyles.

At the time of the birth of our Republic, Samuel Adams, one of its chief progenitors, declared: "A general dissolution of principles and manners [meaning mores, not table manners] will more surely overthrow the liberties of America than the whole force of the common enemy. While the people are virtuous, they cannot be subdued; but once they lose their virtue, they will be ready to surrender their liberties to the first external or internal invader. . . . [Yet] if virtue and knowledge are diffused among the people, they will never be enslaved. This will be their great security."[1]

The "general dissolution" seems to be upon us. We've lost our moral compass. Just as the needle of a compass always points to the magnetic north, so the needle of America's moral compass always points to God. From the beginning our national identity and destiny have been intertwined with our relationship with God and our belief in the Bible's authority for daily living.

The Founders of this country believed that the moral future of the nation depended on her maintaining a covenant with God, which is why they always conjoined the words *morality* and *religion* whenever they referred to them. Shortly before the Declaration of Independence was voted into existence, John Adams wisely observed: "Statesmen . . . may plan and speculate for liberty, but it is religion and morality alone, which can establish the principles upon which freedom can securely stand. . . . Religion and virtue are the only foundations . . . of all free governments."[2]

Patrick Henry also linked the terms in a letter: "The great pillars of all government [are] virtue, morality, and religion. This is the armor, my friend, and this alone, that renders us invincible."[3]

Almost two and a half centuries later, the key to the moral and spiritual crisis now plaguing this country remains: *Did God have a plan for America?*

If He did, then the reason we are wandering in a moral wasteland, no longer knowing who we are, is that we have lost His plan. And if that is the case, the solution is both simple and profound: we must rediscover that plan and follow it.

THE SEARCH BEGINS

Night had fallen on the small New England harbor, where fishing boats rocked gently at anchor. In a nearby chapel a gathering of some two hundred people was illuminated by electric candles, which glowed softly against the wood paneling. The speaker came quickly to the heart of his message: "This nation was founded by God with a special calling. The people who first came here knew that they were being led here by the Lord Jesus Christ, to found a nation where men, women, and children were to live in obedience to him. . . . This was truly to be *one nation under God.*"

The speaker paused. "The reason, I believe, that we Americans are in such trouble today is that we have forgotten this. We've rejected it. In fact, we've become quite cynical about it. We, as a people, have thrown away our Christian heritage."

It was a strong statement; would he be able to back it up? One listener wondered what exactly our Christian heritage *was*—and had wondered it before: four years before, to be exact. The listener was David Manuel, who, while an editor at a major New York publishing house, had discovered to his astonishment that God was real. And not only was God real, but He loved David beyond all human comprehension and had been waiting all of David's life for him to realize it. The discovery turned David's world upside down. Not long after, he felt that God wanted him to use whatever writing or editing ability he had in the service of His Kingdom. David had several book projects in mind, one of which was to trace the spiritual legacy of our nation's founders. But that idea had lain dormant until this night; the speaker was now reopening the file.

The speaker was Peter Marshall, who had grown up in rebellion against the spiritual legacy of two famous Christian parents: the late Chaplain of the Senate, also named Peter, and his author-wife, Catherine. Peter had given up this rebellion in 1961, when he, too, entered into a personal relationship with God and before long had committed his life to serving a living, risen Savior. This service took him into the ministry and a ten-year pastorate in a small church on Cape Cod, after which he would become a wide-ranging national speaker.

That night, on the eve of the first National Day of Prayer to be called in modern memory, what made the nation's need even more compelling to Peter was the realization of how much God's hand had played a part not only in America's founding, but, indeed, in its very discovery.

"Here's what Christopher Columbus himself said about why he came to the Americas." Peter began to read a few translated excerpts from an obscure volume of Columbus's which had never previously appeared in English.

It was the Lord who put into my mind (I could feel his hand upon me) the fact that it would be possible to sail from here to the Indies. All who heard of my project rejected it with laughter, ridiculing me. There is no question that the inspiration was from the Holy Spirit, because He comforted me with rays of marvelous inspiration from the Holy Scriptures. . . .

I am a most unworthy sinner, but I have cried out to the Lord for grace and mercy, and they have covered me completely. I have found the sweetest consolation since I made it my whole purpose to enjoy His marvelous presence. For the execution of the journey to the Indies, I did not make use of intelligence, mathematics or maps. It is simply the fulfillment of what Isaiah had prophesied. . . .

No one should fear to undertake any task in the name of our Savior, if it is just and if the intention is purely for His holy service. The working out of all things has been assigned to each person by our Lord, but it all

14

happens according to His sovereign will, even though He gives advice. He lacks nothing that it is in the power of men to give Him. Oh, what a gracious Lord, who desires that people should perform for Him those things for which He holds Himself responsible! Day and night, moment by moment, everyone should express their most devoted gratitude to Him.[1]

Stunned amazement swept through the audience. Did Columbus really think that way? All we had ever read or been taught indicated that Columbus had discovered the New World by accident while seeking a trade route to the Indies. No mention had ever been made of his faith, let alone that he felt he had been given his life's mission directly by God. Nor had we any idea of what we would later discover—that he felt called to bear the Light of Christ to undiscovered lands in fulfillment of prophetic passages in the Bible and that he knew he had been guided by the Holy Spirit every league of the way.

Moreover, this was not the wishful thinking of some overly enthusiastic Christian. These were Columbus's own words—words that few Americans had ever read. To David, seated in the audience, the impact of this revelation was staggering. For it suddenly occurred to him: *What if God had conceived a special plan for America?*

What if Columbus's discovery had not been accidental at all? What if it was merely the opening curtain of an extraordinary drama? Hadn't Peter just referred to the first settlers as having been called by God to found a new nation based on the centrality of the Christian faith and God's Word?

Did God have a plan for America? Like all who have discovered the reality of the living Christ, we knew that God had a plan for each individual's life—a plan that could, with spiritual effort, be discerned and followed.

What if he dealt with whole nations in the same way?

The Bible said He did—at least once. It reveals that the Jews were His chosen people, and that He had told them that if they would obey His commandments, He would bless them *as a nation*, not just individually. The book of Deuteronomy was explicit:

For you are a people holy to the LORD your God; the LORD your God has chosen you to be a people for his own possession, out of all the peoples that

15

are on the face of the earth. . . . it is because the LORD loves you, and is keeping the oath which he swore to your fathers, that the LORD has brought you out with a mighty hand, and redeemed you from the house of bondage, from the hand of Pharaoh king of Egypt. Know therefore that the LORD your God is God, the faithful God who keeps covenant and steadfast love with those who love him and keep his commandments, to a thousand generations.

Deuteronomy 7:6–9

Throughout their history, as long as the Israelites kept their end of that covenant, God blessed them. Yet almost as soon as God did so, they would turn away from Him, often in less than a generation. Yet, because He loved them He would not wash His hands of them, no matter how sorely they tried Him. All too often, however, they left Him no choice but to lift His grace and allow drought or flood or pestilence, or war or bondage or persecution, to turn His people back to Him.

Some modern Christians believe that this idea of a corporate covenant relationship with God ceased with the coming of Jesus Christ. They feel that, with the advent of Christianity, God replaced His covenant with Israel with the Church and that God is no longer especially interested in any physical entity called Israel. They believe that humankind's relationship with God is now simply a spiritual matter.

But what if God's point of view had never changed? What if, in addition to the personal relationship with the individual through Jesus Christ, God continued to deal with nations corporately, as He had throughout Old Testament history? What if, in particular, He had a plan for those He would bring to America, a plan that saw this continent as the stage for a new act in the drama of humankind's redemption?

Could it be that we Americans, as a people, had been given a mission by almighty God? Were we meant to be "a beacon of hope," as Lincoln declared, or a "Light to lighten the Gentiles," to put it in Scriptural terms? What if God had called us to demonstrate to the world that if His children put into practice the Biblical principles of self-government, they could indeed create a society of liberty and justice for all? And was our vast divergence from this mission, after such a promising beginning, the reason why we now seemed to be sliding into a morass of moral decay, with our world growing darker by the moment?

16

The concept seemed nothing short of fantastic. But as David and Peter talked it over after the meeting that night, it began to take on a semblance of plausibility. And so, one sunny morning in May 1975, they—we—drove up to Boston, to ascertain whether research would bear out this hypothesis, perhaps even provide enough evidence for a book.

Peter had majored in history, but that had been years ago, and neither of us had ever done any serious research after our student days. For that matter, we had only the vaguest idea of how to go about finding what we were looking for and no idea of how to structure it into a book if we did find anything. All we knew was that we had prayed earnestly about it, and we felt that God would have us proceed. If He was in the project, He would guide us.

We had hoped to begin research at Harvard's Widener Library, but upon arriving there, we found that affiliation with the university was required. Not having that at the time (it was later providentially provided) we decided to try the Boston Public Library. But as we were walking back to the car, the idea suddenly occurred to us to stop in at the Harvard Book Store across the street. There, on the history shelves, was a book by Ernest Lee Tuveson entitled *Redeemer Nation*.

As Peter read the jacket copy aloud, we discovered that we were indeed on to something—and that others had felt that God had a specific and unique plan for America. Further browsing in the history section revealed that the first settlers consciously thought of themselves as a people called into a covenant relationship with God similar to the one He had established with ancient Israel.

The Pilgrims and Puritans, looking at the parallels between the ways in which God had led them to America and the Old Testament stories of God's dealings with ancient Israel, saw themselves as called to found a "New Israel" (in their phrase), which would be a light to the whole world. "A city set upon a hill" was how John Winthrop, the first governor of Massachusetts, envisioned it.

Our exuberance at this discovery was attracting a few stares. More soberly we went upstairs to the checkout counter, purchased our books, and beat a hasty retreat. But once in the privacy of our car and headed for the Boston Public Library, we were like Forty-Niners on their way to the gold fields.

The spirit of adventure stayed with us that afternoon, as David went through the card files and tracked down titles on the shelves, while Peter pored through the armloads of books that David had brought to him. A dozen musty volumes might yield one of interest. Then, by "coincidence," a book near the one we were looking for would happen to catch our eye, and we would discover a nugget like *Remarkable Providences*, edited by John Demos. Among other things, this book contained diary and letter accounts of God's "wonder-working providences" in the lives of settlers in Jamestown, Plymouth, and the Massachusetts Bay Colony.

But it was piecemeal work, and we still had no way of knowing what we might inadvertently be overlooking. And then Peter remembered that he had Nelson Burr's critical bibliography of books on religion in America. Armed with this preliminary list of titles, we could begin to properly explore the resources of Yale's huge Sterling Memorial Library, to which, as former students, we had access. Two weeks later we found ourselves making an unexpected trip back to our alma mater, the first visit for both of us since graduating.

Entering the Gothic pile of Sterling Library, where we had often studied as undergraduates, was like walking around the set of a long-forgotten movie. But going into Beinecke, the then-new rare-book library with its translucent marble walls, was the eeriest experience of all. There was a reverent atmosphere in the place, and the hushed whispers in which we instinctively spoke were not just from customary library courtesy. It was as if we were standing on holy ground. Then it struck us: for those who worshiped intellectual achievement, it *was* holy ground. There before us in thousands of ancient volumes in a six-story-high, climate-controlled glass cube, the sum and pride of human intellect was enshrined. We exchanged glances and went downstairs to the card catalog.

That afternoon in the basement reading room of the Beinecke Library, we made the discovery that would prove to be one of the most exciting of the entire project. In his journal Christopher Columbus described an incident that took place on his fourth and final voyage, after he had been made Governor of *Española* (Hispaniola) and subsequently had been forcibly removed from that command for gross mismanagement. Sick with a fever and in the depths of despair, he had a half-awake dream in which he heard a stern voice strongly rebuke him for his self-pity. The voice (quoted in chapter 3) reminded him that the Almighty had singled him out for the honor of bearing the Light of Christ to a new world, had given him all that he had asked for, and was recording in heaven every event of his life!

Now we had clear evidence that God was leading us in the project. Here, in Columbus's own words, was a concrete example of God's hand at work in the life of the person that He used to bring Europeans to the Americas.

In sum, this book is not intended to be a history textbook, but rather a search for the hand of God in key periods of our nation's beginnings. With America's destiny at stake, the need to discover the hand of God in our past is urgent.

Seeking to understand American history from a Biblical perspective, we found ourselves so caught up in the search that we felt we should occasionally share with the reader some of the issues and struggles that we faced. These comments take the form of brief chapter preludes and will be set off by this symbol:

Wherever possible, we have let the players speak for themselves, bringing their imaginative spelling and nonchalant punctuation into some conformance with modern usage. Occasionally we imagine a key conversation for which there was no eyewitness account. These have been flagged as such and presented as faithfully as possible to what the principals might have said, given the evidence at our disposal.

Our basic premise—that God had a definite and discoverable plan for America—was confirmed many times over, albeit occasionally with surprising twists. When it came to famous figures in American history, some, like Columbus, turned out to be far more dedicated to God's service than we had imagined. Others, like Thomas Jefferson, whom we had assumed research would reveal as an orthodox Christian believer, turned out quite differently.

Once it had become clear that God did have a plan for America, our search for evidence of this plan became akin to tracking a rich vein of gold through a mountain. The vein of gold had four main characteristics.

First, God had put a specific "call" on this country and the people whom He brought to inhabit it. In the virgin wilderness of America, God was making His most significant attempt since ancient Israel to create a "New Israel" of people living in obedience to biblical principles, through faith in Jesus Christ.

The Pilgrims and Puritans actually referred to themselves as God's New Israel. But it wasn't that they thought they (and the Christian Church) had *replaced* Israel. We would discover that they used the Church's traditional method of interpreting the Old Testament: typology. This meant that they saw "types" of New Testament events or persons in the Old Testament. In this practice they were in good company. Even the New Testament writers themselves understood the Israelites' crossing of the Red Sea as a prefiguring of the sacrament of Baptism in the New Testament, and the Israelites' forty years in the desert as a prefiguring or type of Jesus's forty days in the wilderness.

America's early Christian settlers, then, used typology to interpret God's dealings in their own lives. They felt that certain passages in the Bible, originally addressed to Israel, also applied to them:

> For the LORD your God is bringing you into a good land, a land of brooks and water, of fountains and springs, flowing forth in valleys and hills . . . a land in which you will eat bread without scarcity, in which you will lack nothing . . . and you shall bless the LORD your God for the good land he has given you.
>
> Deuteronomy 8:7–10

Thus, Samuel Fisher, in his *Testimony in Truth* in 1679, would write, "Let Israel be . . . our glass to view our faces in."[2]

As we shall see, the Pilgrims' pastor in Holland, John Robinson, described their migration to the New World in these terms: "Now as the people of God in old time were called out of Babylon civil, the place of their bodily bondage, and were to come to Jerusalem, and there to build the Lord's temple . . . so are the people of God now to go out of Babylon spiritual to Jerusalem (America) . . . and to build themselves as lively stones into a spiritual house, or temple, for the Lord to dwell in."[3]

A generation after that, John Higginson would sum up their view of their calling in his preface to Cotton Mather's history of New England:

> It hath been deservedly esteemed one of the great and wonderful works of God in this last age, that the Lord stirred up the spirits of so many thousands of his servants . . . to transport themselves . . . into a desert land in America . . . in the way of seeking first the kingdom of God . . . for the purpose of "a fuller and better reformation of the Church of God, than it hath yet appeared in the world."[4]

The President of Harvard, Urian Oakes, gave this simile in 1673: "If we . . . lay all things together, this our Commonwealth seems to exhibit to us . . . a little model, of the Kingdom of Christ upon Earth."[5]

A model of the Kingdom of Christ upon earth—we Americans were intended to be living proof to the rest of the world that it *was* possible to live a life together that reflected the commandments of Christ to love God with all our heart, soul, mind, and strength; and to love others as ourselves.

Second, this call was to be worked out in terms of the settlers' covenant with God and with each other. Both elements of this covenant—the vertical relationship with God and the horizontal relationship with their neighbors—were of the utmost importance to them. Concerning the vertical aspect of the covenant, they saw themselves as being called into a direct continuation of the covenant relationship between God and Abraham: "Now the LORD said to Abram, 'Go from your country and your kindred and your father's house to the land that I will show you. And I will make of you a great nation, and I will bless you'" (Gen. 12:1–2). "'And I will establish my covenant between me and you and your descendants after you'" (Gen. 17:7).

To the Early Comers (as the first New Englanders called themselves), the Bible showed them how this would work: "And this commandment we have from him, that he who loves God should love his brother also" (1 John 4:21). This meant that the more they loved God, the more they could truly love their neighbors.

This was crucial to God's plan: it was His clear intent that as these settlers lived the Christian life, they would grow into unity and become a body of believers. The apostle Paul wrote: "So we, though many, are one body in Christ, and individually members one of another" (Rom. 12:5). "If one member suffers, all suffer together; if one member is honored, all rejoice together" (1 Cor. 12:26). In this spirit the early settlers covenanted together to form their churches.

As each church-community grew and became, in effect, a town, their church covenants provided the pattern for the first successful civil governments in the Western Hemisphere. Historians and sociologists have long regarded the early New England town meetings as the purest and most successful form that democracy has ever taken. But few, if any, have acknowledged what lay at the core of *how* and *why* they worked so well. There would be many modifications, but American government owes its inception to the covenants of the first churches on her shores.

Third, God did keep His end of the bargain, on both an individual and a corporate basis. It is a sobering experience to look closely at our history and see just how highly God regarded right attitudes of heart. One finds long droughts broken by the people of a settlement deliberately praying and humbling themselves, turning back to the God whom they once trusted and had imperceptibly begun to take for granted.

The recorded beliefs of the settlers themselves confirmed this. In private diaries and public proclamations the immediate response to any disaster, human or natural, was, "Where do we need to repent?" In fact, there seemed to be a continuing, almost predictable cycle: in great need and humility a small body of Christians would put themselves into the hands of their Lord and commit their lives to one another. They would do their best to live together as He had called them to live. And He, in turn, would begin to pour out His blessing on them with health, peace, and bounteous harvests. But as they grew affluent, they would also become proud or complacent or self-righteous.

Nonetheless, the blessing would continue unabated, sometimes for a generation or more, as God continued to honor the obedience of their fathers and grandfathers (Deut. 7:9). But inevitably, because He loved them (and because even God's patience has an end), He would lift the protection from their land, just enough to cause them to turn back to Him. A drought, an epidemic of smallpox, a plague of grasshoppers, or an Indian uprising would come, and the wisest among them would remember. Like the prophets of old, they would call the people to repentance.

Few Biblical principles are more compelling than this: that God blesses repentance. And, in the early days of our history, it was frequently proven that when people began to earnestly repent, what followed was the return of God's grace.

That a drought could be broken or an Indian attack averted by corporate repentance is an idea that sounds alien to many Christians today. Yet it was central to the faith that built this country, and it is a prominent, recurring theme in the Bible. One familiar example is, "If my people who are called by my name humble themselves, and pray and seek my face, and turn from their wicked ways, then I will hear from heaven, and will forgive their sin and heal their land" (2 Chron. 7:14).

This, then, was the key to God's plan for America: that His people—three thousand years ago, three hundred and fifty years ago, or today—would see themselves, individually and corporately, in continual need of God's forgiveness, mercy, and support. And this was the secret of the horizontal aspect of the covenant as well: for only when we know that we are no better than anyone else—only then can we truly love other people.

Moreover, from this humble position, it is impossible to enter into an arrogant nationalism, a kind of "my country right or wrong" attitude. Inherent in God's call upon our ancestors to create a Bible-based society was the necessity to live in a state of constant dependency upon His grace and forgiveness—a strong antidote against pride and self-righteousness. Anyone tempted to arrogance concerning our nation's call or history need only look at how badly we have failed—and continue to fail—to live up to God's expectations for us.

The great leaders of our past warned us about this. Here is Massachusetts Senator Daniel Webster: "If we and our posterity reject religious instruction and authority, violate the rules of eternal justice, trifle with the injunctions of morality, and recklessly destroy the political constitution which holds us together, no man can tell how sudden a catastrophe may overwhelm us and bury all our glory in profound obscurity."[6]

This, then, was the fourth and final theme: at times of great crisis God raised up great leaders to protect America from destruction so that His plan for us might have a chance of success.

Instead of aspiring to fame and fortune, leaders like Bradford, Winthrop, Samuel Adams, and Washington truly wanted nothing more than to serve God's people. And because these servant-leaders were living out the example of the one who said, "I am among you as one who serves," God was able to use them mightily to change the course of American history.

In 1775 when the U.S. Marine Corps was founded, the recruiting slogan stated that it was seeking "a few good men." That is essentially what God said to Gideon in ancient Israel, when He reduced his army from thirty-two thousand to three hundred. And it was what He seemed to be saying three and a half centuries ago, as He began to gather those who were willing to give up everything for His sake in order to dwell in His "New Israel." How much of the grace that continues to cover this country today and how many of the incredible blessings that have been poured out upon this land are a direct result of their obedience and willingness to die to self? Only God knows for certain.

That grace seems to be lifting now, but as we look through our nation's history to discover God's plan, we begin to see what a great difference a few dedicated people can make—and how much is still at stake. For God's call to this country has never been revoked.

America, America. God shed his grace on thee. . . .

1

CHRIST-BEARER

*C*olumbus. . . . We were familiar enough with the heroic figure described in the textbooks we grew up with (who is much reviled in many of them today). And our research had given us a new appreciation for his extraordinary seamanship and navigational abilities. But he was still an enigma, a bronze figure on horseback, his arm outstretched, pointing westward. Would this figure become real? What was he really like, this man who had written so passionately in his journal of his desire to serve Christ and carry His Light to heathen lands? Only God knew what had been locked away in the secret places of his heart; perhaps God would show us as He guided our research.

By His grace, as we became familiar with Columbus's life, certain scenes began to come alive. We could feel the lift of the *Santa Maria*'s afterdeck beneath our feet, hear the groaning of the masts and yards far above, and taste the salt spray on our lips. Next to us stood a tall, lean man, deeply tanned, with squint lines etched at the corners of his clear blue eyes. The once-red hair was now almost white, but the hand on the taffrail was steady. The voice, issuing commands, had the timbre of authority.

We would see this man in his moments of supreme triumph and watch with him during the long nights of despair and bitterness. For in Columbus's heart, he was a sinner like the rest of us. That was our point of entry into understanding him. To know Columbus was to know one's own desire for the rewards of this world: fame and power and all manner of ego gratification. So we came to have compassion for him, and we came to wonder whether, if we had been tried and tempted as Columbus was, we would have fared half as well.

As the manuscript pages flowed from David's typewriter, it seemed that rather than creating scenes, we were merely describing what we were seeing. This had begun one afternoon, months earlier, in the darkened stacks of Yale's Sterling Library. There, in that mysterious, labyrinthine maze of tiered volumes, only the occasional echo of a distant footfall broke the silence. Peter stood in a yellow pool of light beneath an old metallic lampshade. Open in his hand was a translation of Columbus's journal of his first voyage, undertaken in the year of our Lord 1492.

Tuesday, October 9—he sailed southwestward; he made five leagues. The wind changed, and he ran to the west, quarter northwest, and went four leagues. Afterwards, in all, he made 11 leagues in the day and 20½ leagues in the night; he reckoned 17 leagues for the men. All night they heard the birds passing.[1]

According to the accounts of others, something else happened on that day. It was something unprecedented, which Columbus apparently chose to leave out of the journal: an emergency conference at sea between Columbus and the captains of the *Pinta* and the *Niña*, Martin and Vicente Pinzón.[2] The three ships had hove to into the wind, and the smaller caravels had maneuvered into position on either side of the *Santa Maria*, enabling their captains to be rowed to the flagship over a calm sea. Under different circumstances the men aloft would have exchanged greetings as the ships came together. But now there was only silence as the grim-faced Pinzón brothers strode across the *Santa Maria*'s deck.

Columbus alone seemed cheerful as he welcomed them, but in the privacy of his cabin, his smile vanished. The Pinzóns came right to the point: they had requested the meeting—no, *demanded* it—but Columbus, ever impatient at the least delay, had attempted to put them off. They were convinced that if they continued one day further on their present course, the sailors would take over their ships and turn back. After thirty-one straight days of heading almost due west from the Canaries, the crews were in an ugly mood, and no amount of cajoling or promising rewards for the first sighting or displays of confidence were going to make a difference.

More critically, Martin and Vicente Pinzón could no longer be certain of their officers if, God forbid, it came to mutiny. Their pilots and masters knew enough about dead reckoning (the art of estimating one's position solely by compass and crude measurements of one's speed through the water) to suspect that Columbus was deliberately shortening the daily estimates passed from the flagship.

When they told him this, Columbus must have reacted in great frustration and anger. They were not just asking him to cancel the voyage but to give up everything he had lived for—all his dreams, all his plans. Every maravedi he owned or could borrow had been invested in this venture, and he had suffered through eight long years of humiliation, being rejected by one royal court after another. Even Ferdinand and Isabella had been strongly advised against having anything to do with his wild scheme. If he turned back now, he—and they—would be the laughingstock of all Europe. Which meant that there would not be another chance—ever.

Columbus knew that the Pinzóns were not exaggerating. He had overheard the grumblings of his own crew. Once he had even heard one jokingly suggest that they throw their captain overboard and return with the story that he had lost his balance while taking a sight on the polestar. It was only a matter of time before it would cease to be a joke.

In anguish, he turned away from the Pinzóns. Striding to the aft window, he gazed at the dying rays of the sun on the endless expanse of sea behind them. All his dreams . . .

There was an even deeper reason for his despair, one that he had never divulged to anyone. He had long been convinced that God had given him

27

a special, almost mystical mission: to carry the Light of Christ into the darkness of undiscovered heathen lands and to bring the inhabitants of those lands to the holy faith of Christianity. His own name, Christopher, which literally means *Christ-bearer*, was to him a clear indication that God had called him to do this. Indeed, he found confirmation of his call almost everywhere he looked. He would quote in his journal such lines of Scripture as those in Isaiah that meant so much to him:

> Listen to me, O coastlands, and hearken, you peoples from afar.
> The LORD called me from the womb,
>   from the body of my mother he named my name. . . .
> I will give you as a light to the nations,
>   that my salvation may reach to the end of the earth.
>
> Isaiah 49:1, 6

It was hard to say when his sense of mission had crystallized; it may have been while he was still a teenage boy in Genoa, working in the family wool shop, as his father and grandfather had before him, and going to sea at every opportunity. Or it could have come later, in Lisbon, the seafaring capital of the world, where the year 1484 found him and his brother Bartolomeo employed in the exclusive profession of mapmaking. He would have been just thirty-three then—the year Italians call *Anno de Cristo*, the Year of the Christ. According to folk tradition, this is a year especially reserved for spiritual revelation, being Christ's age at his death.

As a mapmaker, Columbus was privy not only to the geographic knowledge of the ancients but also to the latest information being brought back from the ever-expanding limits of the known world. He would have studied the global projections of Eratosthenes, the Greek geographer who, two thousand years before, had calculated the circumference of the earth to within 10 percent of its actual dimension.

In Columbus's time the newest world map was that of Toscanelli of Florence. Based on Marco Polo's eyewitness account of Cathay (China), Chiambra (India), and the fabulous islands of Cipangu (Japan), it placed the latter only 4,700 miles west from Lisbon. But it was not until Columbus's own navigational skills had become perfected—on voyages as far north as Thule (Iceland) and as far south as Guinea on the coast of

Africa—that the dream finally came within reach. He made his own cal-
culations and arrived at the conclusion that, traversing the 28th parallel,
the distance from the Canary Islands to Cipangu was only 750 leagues, or
approximately 2,760 miles. (No matter that Columbus had compounded
the errors inherent in the accepted cosmography of his day with one or
two of his own; God knew that there *was* something waiting out there—
barely 150 leagues beyond Columbus's estimate.)[3]

Now it was not a question of *if* but *when*, and Columbus's sense of
urgency was whetted by the Danish expedition that eight years earlier
had rediscovered the barren Norse "islands" of Helluland or Markland
(Labrador) far to the north. There were other tantalizing elements: pieces
of carved driftwood found floating west of the Azores and the bodies of
two Chinese-looking men that had washed up on Flores in the Azores.
And on Corvo, the westernmost island, there was a natural rock formation
resembling a horseman pointing west across the ocean.[4] All that remained
was to convince King John II of Portugal to send him.

The cost of even a modest expedition was so far beyond the reach of
a private citizen, even a wealthy one, that Columbus's only hope was to
interest a reigning monarch. He had worked out the cost of outfitting three
of the fast, light ships called *cararvels*, which were ideal for exploring,
along with the cost of provisions for a year and wages for the ninety men
required to sail them. The total came to two million maravedis (around
1.3 million 2009 dollars)—in those days, a breathtaking amount even
for a king.

In 1484 Columbus presented his plan to John II. The King turned
the proposal over to a royal commission of scholars for their study and
recommendation. After long deliberation, they decided that the scheme
was too costly and far too risky for the sailors and the ships. They also
found Columbus to be arrogant and overbearing. Undaunted, Columbus
dispatched his brother Bartolomeo to Henry VII of England to see if he
would be interested. After brief consideration, it was the opinion of the
English court that Bartolomeo and his brother were fools and their ideas
were madness.[5]

Columbus now became convinced that God had reserved for Ferdinand and Isabella of Spain the honor of sending forth the expedition that

would bring the Gospel to undiscovered lands. Were they not renowned throughout Christendom for their devotion to the Savior? To Columbus, this explained why he had been turned down in Portugal and England, and at first he was not dismayed that he was having no success in gaining an audience with the Sovereigns of Castile and Aragon. After all, they were at Granada, preoccupied with directing the current holy war against the powerful Moors, who had invaded southern Spain more than seven centuries earlier and had held it ever since.

But weeks of delay became months. Finally, through the intercession of the Count of Medina Celi, his suit was brought to the attention of Their Catholic Majesties in May 1486. They were sufficiently interested to turn it over to their own royal commission, which took another four and a half years to reach conclusions similar to those of their Portuguese counterparts: Columbus's scheme "rested on weak foundations," so that its success seemed "uncertain and impossible to any educated person."[6]

Ferdinand and Isabella did not close the door entirely, inviting him to resubmit his proposal when the Moors were finally vanquished, but for Columbus this was the end of hope. The only major monarch left to approach was the King of France. Yet his heart was not in it. He had been so sure that God had intended it to be Ferdinand and Isabella.

Now doubt assailed him. Could it be that he was also wrong about other things? For the first time since he had conceived of his venture—God's venture—dark shadows of despair crept into the corners of his mind, while all his pride and self-esteem drained away. As he walked along the cold, deserted road that led to La Rábida, the Franciscan monastery on the Rio Tinto where he had left his young son Diego, he had probably never felt so alone or so empty.

The Abbot of the monastery was Father Juan Perez, a man of unusual wisdom. He was responsible for the spiritual well-being of the scores of monks whom God had gathered there and for transforming the little monastery into a center of learning that was gaining a reputation throughout Christian Europe.

Guiding the studies at La Rábida was Father Antonio de la Marchena, Vicar Provincial of Queen Isabella's home province of Castile. It was

Father Antonio who, as Queen Isabella's confessor, had persuaded her to heed Medina Celi's request and receive the visionary explorer from Genoa seven years before.

No record exists of what transpired that evening, but we can imagine the Abbot, the scholar, and the dejected sojourner talking far into the night. They had long been friends. Columbus regarded La Rábida as his spiritual home, and he took the things of God very seriously, to the extent that he had even taken lay orders in the Order of St. Francis. But on this occasion it seemed he could not access the solace of the Almighty, and his two friends did their best to help him.

Bit by bit Columbus unburdened himself of all the wounds, the years of snubs and dismissals that had hardened into a rock of bitterness in his chest. How many times had he visited the royal court only to hear taunts such as: "Ah, here comes our vagabond wool-carder again, with his pathetic prattling about spheres and parallels. Tell us, Cristoforo, does the world appear any rounder to you today?"

The three men walked together through the cool stone cloister of the monastery on their way to the refectory for a late supper. Entering the low-ceilinged room, they sat at the end of the long, narrow oak table, the Abbot at its head, the scholar on his left, the captain on his right. The room was dimly illuminated by wax candles in iron sconces. Nothing else adorned the walls except for a plain wooden cross to remind them of the ultimate sacrifice their Savior had made for them.

Served on pewter plates, their fare was simple—grilled halibut caught that afternoon in the Rio Tinto, a small loaf of rye bread, sliced tomatoes from the monastery's garden, drizzled with olive oil and sprinkled with oregano. In the shifting shadows, the men spoke softly as the two monks in brown robes gently and patiently sought to lift the spirits of the tall, thin captain with the hawklike nose and angular features.

"Don Cristobál," said Father Antonio in the Spanish rendering of the captain's name, "Over the years you have told us about each step of your enterprise, and we have counseled you in all your delays and setbacks. We grasp your vision and affirm your sense of call. You are indeed called by God to this great undertaking."

The captain just looked at him, hope gone from his eyes.

Now Father Juan spoke. "Read to us from your notes through the years." He nodded to the thick leather-bound notebook on the table by the captain.

But instead of responding, Columbus stared down at his plate.

"Well then, allow me to read some of it to you." The Abbot searched for a moment among the pages. "Ah, here it is: 'All that is requested by anyone who has faith *will* be granted. Knock, and it *will* be opened unto you. No one should be afraid to take on any enterprise in the name of our Savior, if it is righteous, and if the purpose is purely for His holy service.'"[7] He looked up at the captain. "Those are *your* words, Don Cristóbal." He paused. "*Is* your cause righteous? *Is* the purpose of it for His holy service?"

The captain raised his eyes and met his old friend's gaze. Almost imperceptibly, he nodded.

"Then," declared Father Juan, "we have our Savior's word: if we make our requests in faith, they *will* be granted."

Nodding in agreement, Father Antonio put it in spiritual perspective. "There are two realities, Don Cristóbal. There is the natural reality that the world knows: what we can see, touch, taste, hear, and feel. And there is the supernatural reality of God's Kingdom, which we cannot see or touch. You have been privileged to experience the latter. God's Spirit has opened to you the secrets of His Kingdom."

The captain was listening intently now.

"You have studied the Bible, both the Old and New Testaments, and especially the prophetic books of Isaiah, Daniel, and Revelation. And that study has transformed you. You have always had a marked devotion to the Father. You have always regarded the Son as your Savior and Intercessor in the court of heaven. But you have also gained an intimacy with the Holy Spirit, of the sort that is even now transforming our order."

Father Antonio smiled. "In fact, more than a few of my brother monks find it astonishing that a layman such as yourself is part of our movement, the *recognimiento*[8] that is spiritually reforming the Order of St. Francis."

Columbus's eyes brightened. Now he paged through his notes himself until he found the letter he had drafted to the Sovereigns and read from it: "I prayed to the most merciful Lord concerning my desire, and He gave me the spirit and the intelligence for it. He gave me abundant skill in the mariner's arts, an adequate understanding of the stars, and of geometry and arithmetic."

He looked at his friends and lifted his hands, palms up. With a smile he simply said, "God has equipped me for this voyage."

Turning back to the letter, he read further: "Who can doubt that this fire was not merely mine, but also of the Holy Spirit, who encouraged me with a radiance of marvelous illumination from His sacred Holy Scriptures!"

Father Juan beamed. "There! Do you hear what you wrote, Don Cristobál? Never again let the enemy of your soul convince you that you are alone, abandoned, without friends who believe in you and daily pray for you."

Father Antonio stroked his chin. "You have shared with us your conviction that God has called you to bear the Light of Christ *west* to heathen people in undiscovered lands. What exactly do you anticipate finding once you get there?"

Columbus tapped his long fingers together. "If I have heard God correctly, the unimaginable wealth that Marco Polo saw with his own eyes. I am convinced that the source of that wealth is none other than the lost mines of King Solomon."

The monks' eyes widened. Neither of them spoke.

The captain went on. "If the Enterprise of the Indies succeeds—if I can find it for Their Majesties, then King Ferdinand will become a new King David. After all, Joachim de Fiore did say that the man who would recover the Holy Land for Christendom would come out of Spain."

Father Antonio, familiar with the writings of the ancient sage who three centuries earlier had penned this prophecy, pursed his lips and slowly nodded.

"I believe King Ferdinand is that man," the captain concluded, "and that he is to rebuild the temple in Jerusalem—and thereby fulfill the prophetic conditions for the return of our Lord."[9]

With a crust of bread Father Juan swept up the last of the olive oil on his plate. "God is pleased with your humility," he mused. "You see yourself as merely a forerunner, as the Baptizer was."

The captain sighed and laughed wryly. "A forerunner of nothing, it would seem."

The Abbot rose to his feet. "This matter is *not* closed."

He turned to the other monk. "I, too, was once the Queen's confessor. Now I will write to her and ask her before God to reconsider supporting what I believe to be a voyage of destiny."

He looked at both men. "And who knows, perhaps now God will favor our request."

The three men adjourned to the chapel, where the abbot, a shepherd of shepherds, restored this lost sheep to the fold. He gently led Columbus in an act of contrition, confessing his willfulness, pride, and unbelief.

When Father Juan pronounced absolution, the captain's eyes brimmed. Then the three friends shared the Eucharist together, reuniting themselves with the One who had given His body and shed His blood for them.

Whatever *did* transpire that night at La Rábida, it marked a turning point in God's plan to use Columbus to raise the curtain on his new Promised Land.

The following morning, Father Perez dispatched a messenger to the Queen, stating that he was convinced that God's hand rested upon Christopher Columbus and urging Her Majesty to reconsider his proposal.

Columbus tarried at La Rábida, awaiting a reply, convinced that after his own arm of flesh had been exhausted and all his hope abandoned, God in his infinite mercy might yet intervene. Not only had God altered circumstances, but far more important, He had healed Columbus's hard heart of bitterness.

The Queen's answer came soon enough: Columbus was to return immediately to Santa Fé, the City of the Holy Faith, which the besieging Christian forces had raised up outside the massive walls of the Moorish fortress of Granada. There they were determined to conclude what everyone hoped would be the last crusade. What was more, in a singularly thoughtful gesture, the monarchs included with the letter a draft for personal funds. This meant that Columbus would be able to replace his worn attire and tattered cloak and could purchase a proper mount on which to return. Once again God was bestowing favor on him.

When Columbus arrived at Santa Fé at the end of 1491, there was tremendous excitement throughout the city: the Moors were about to surrender! Armor was being burnished, battle standards were being set up, women were stringing pennants and bunting from the tops of tents and houses. Finally, as the afternoon sun fired the walls of the Alhambra, the citadel at the heart of the walled city, the Moorish banner came down, and the huge gates of Granada slowly swung open. Out came the Moorish King at the head of a column of noblemen, while lining his path on either side were mounted crusaders in full armor, their white surplices with the red crosses blazing in the sun. They stood perfectly still, their lances upright. Not a sound was heard, save the hoofbeats of the Moorish horses.

At the end of the promenade, under a pavilion, waited Ferdinand and Isabella. The Moorish King dismounted, walked up to them, knelt, and kissed their hands. And the mightiest cheer ever heard in Andalusia erupted. The war was over! The last Moorish foothold in Europe had been dislodged, and Christ reigned supreme in Castile. Pandemonium broke out—as war-weary Christian soldiers wept and cried and gave thanks to God.

Full of joy himself, Columbus was nonetheless impatient to see the King and Queen. He may have been the only Christian in Granada that night not completely given over to the exhilaration of the moment. He was not kept waiting long. Exhausted as they were, Their Catholic Majesties listened attentively to Columbus. And as it turned out, there had never been a time and there would never be another time when they would have been more receptive to his proposals. God had granted them a tremendous victory, and they had not yet thought of how they might show Him their gratitude. Build a cathedral? Make a pilgrimage? Erect shelters for the poor?

And now a far more modest yet imaginative possibility presented itself. Here, back again, was the Genoese visionary, with his proposal for his own crusade: to discover new lands for the glory of God and His church, and to spread the gospel to the ends of the earth.

What if he *were* God's man, as Perez seemed to think that he was? Could this be how God would have them show their gratitude?

Turning it over in their minds, they decided that sending Columbus on this mission would be a fitting way to display their thankfulness. Promptly they summoned Columbus to tell him that they agreed to his plan.

In that moment of victory Columbus reverted to his old proud, untrusting, ambitious self. In return for his services he loftily stipulated the following demands: one tenth of all the riches that might be found in any of the lands he might discover; the unprecedented rank and title of Admiral of the Ocean Sea; and the positions of both viceroy and governor of all discovered lands.

The King and Queen were stunned. They dismissed him summarily. And were it not for the intervention of Luis de Santángel, the royal treasurer, that would have been the end of it. But this skilled diplomat, who had long been one of Columbus's few supporters at court, now interceded for him with such clarity that the Queen was persuaded to change her mind. She even offered to pledge her personal jewelry as collateral to help finance the expedition, but Santángel assured her that this would not be necessary; they would raise the money through loans from regional governments. Thereupon, a messenger was sent at the gallop to bring Columbus back.

The next eight months were probably the happiest of Columbus's life. As a result of his meticulous care in the fitting out of his three ships, the expedition would be ideally equipped—far better than many that would cross the Atlantic two centuries later. In Martin and Vicente Pinzón, he had two experienced mariners who shared his vision and his sense of urgency. Also, they were natives of the port of Palos on the Rio Tinto, less than an hour's walk from La Rábida. As it turned out, Palos had somehow earlier offended Ferdinand and Isabella, and Their Majesties now decreed that as penance the town would furnish the ships and sailors for Columbus's expedition. Many of the men of Palos were seafarers, so the Pinzóns were able to raise first-class crews. This was crucial, for if Columbus had found it necessary to raise the crews himself, he would probably have had to rely largely on convict labor.

Additionally, Martin Pinzón owned two vessels that were ideally suited for the voyage—fast, new caravels, at a time when good ships were extremely hard to come by because wealthy Jews were frantically buying up practically everything that was seaworthy. With the end of the holy war, the Spanish Inquisition, originally commissioned to seek out hidden heresy, now focused its attention increasingly on *merranos*—Jews who had "converted" to Christianity, perhaps to escape mounting persecution or to avoid having to leave their native soil. The Inquisition set out to test the faith of these converts, for now that the Moors had been banished, only the Jews remained to defile Spain's "purity."

It is ironic that Spain contained both the very best of fifteenth-century Christianity and the very worst. In monasteries like La Rábida, lives of true humility, service, and sacrifice were being lived. And some of the most revered missionaries in the history of the Christian faith—people who taught the life of Jesus not so much with words but by their own example—would come forth from these ancient walls. Similarly, Spain's convents would produce saints like Teresa of Avila, whose inspiration would change thousands of lives through the ages.

The spirit of the Inquisition was the opposite. As Lord Acton once observed, power tends to corrupt, and absolute power corrupts absolutely. The Inquisition's power was absolute. Their final solution to the "Jewish problem" was disseminated by a royal decree issued in the spring of 1492: all Jews were given three months to get out of the country. It was one of the earliest examples of ethnic cleansing and one of the most effective.

So many ships were being used to remove the Jews that Columbus had to settle for a heavier, slower flagship than he would have desired. But then came news that cheered him immensely. His royal benefactors had acceded to yet a further request: he would be permitted to invest in the expedition to the extent of one-eighth of its total funding, and he would receive that percentage of any profits. His friends, presumably including the Duke of Medina Celi and Santángel, loaned him the funds to invest.

On the morning of August 3, 1492, as Columbus and his sailors knelt on the dock in the predawn half-light to receive Holy Communion, his heart must have been soaring. The Enterprise to the Indies was about to get under way. His dream had come true.

The tide began to turn, so they boarded the ship, and Columbus assumed command crisply and confidently. In moments the *Santa Maria* had cast off her lines, set sail, and was gliding down the river with the ebbing tide.

As Columbus's ships reached the place where the Tinto joined the River Saltés, just before emptying into the ocean, a last shipload of Jews was also waiting for the tide. They too were leaving now, bound for the Mediterranean and the lands of Islam. It is doubtful that members of either expedition thought of the other beyond a routine log entry. None of that shipload of forlorn exiles could have dreamed that the other three ships on the river were leading the way to a land that would one day provide a welcome haven to their people.

Columbus's journal also mentions that as they passed below La Rábida, they could hear the monks chanting the ancient verses for the first service of the day, with its haunting refrain that ends *Et nunc et in perpetuum*— "Now and forever."[10] As the sails began to fill with the sea breeze, the great red crusaders' crosses on them were thrust forward, as if going on before. To the east, the great orb of the sun came up, seeming to ignite the surface of the water and turn it, for a moment, into a river of molten gold.

The first few days could not have gone more smoothly. Instead of heading due west as the crews might have expected, Columbus set a course of southwest by south, making for the Canaries. Therein lay the hidden key to the entire voyage. It was this inspiration—from God, Columbus would say—that would give him success where many others had failed. And some were still trying: word had reached him that John II, on the off chance the mad Genoan might have been onto something, had dispatched one of his own Portuguese mariners due west from the Azores. After days of battling incessant headwinds, the sailor had given up.

In all of Columbus's previous extensive voyages north and south, he had noted that while the winds known as the Prevailing Westerlies were constant in the northern ocean, once one dropped below the Tropic of Cancer the air currents that prevailed there, known as the Trade Winds, were uniformly out of the northeast. Columbus concluded that by dropping down to take advantage of the trades, it would be possible to have winds behind them on the voyage out, and then on the return, they would sail north and ride the westerlies home. It was a simple and apparently obvious plan. But it had never occurred to anyone else.

They reached Grand Canary Island on August 9, where they reprovisioned and made repairs, and finally launched out into the unknown on September 8.

These were beautiful days—an expansive sea under azure skies, fresh winds billowing the white sails, flying fish and petrels skimming the waves. As the three small vessels sailed on, the succession of days settled into a familiar rhythm, with each new dawn being greeted by one of the grommets, or ship's boys, singing:

> Blessed be the light of day
> and the Holy Cross, we say;
> and the Lord of Veritie,
> and the Holy Trinity.
> Blessed be th' immortal soul,
> and the Lord who keeps it whole,
> Blessed be the light of day,
> and He who sends the night away.[11]

And yet, with the light of each new day, they sailed farther and farther out into unknown waters. And gradually fear began to dog their wake. None of them had ever been farther than three hundred miles offshore; now, even by Columbus's diminished reckoning, they were well over two thousand, and they were still going.

Or maybe not. For now the Pinzón brothers, in the privacy of his cabin, had presented Columbus with an ultimatum.

2

In Peril on the Sea

eluctantly Columbus turned from the window to face the other two captains—and reality. With a sigh he nodded imperceptibly. He agreed to turn back; he had no choice, really. But he did extract a promise from them: three additional days. If they had not sighted land by the dawn of October 12, they would come about and head home. Not at all sure they had three days of goodwill remaining among their crews, the Pinzón brothers left.

We can imagine Columbus sitting alone in his cabin after their departure, staring at the last entry in his journal, the quill pen motionless in his hand. Outside, the masts groaned—*she is pulling well*, he thought. Not that it mattered anymore. It was all over. The specter of defeat seemed to stand by his side, resting a bony hand on his shoulder. Columbus shuddered. Glancing down, he noticed that he had absently written his name, Christopher—*Christo-ferens*—Christ-bearer.

He might then have recalled the legend of the giant pagan named Christopher who sought to know Christ. To please him, he lived as a hermit beside a swift river, at a place where there was no bridge or boat to carry wayfarers across. Instead, he would carry them on his shoulders, with the help of a large staff. One night, asleep in his hut, he was awakened by the voice of a small boy, asking to be carried across. Christopher shouldered his young charge easily enough, but as he went farther and farther into the current, the burden grew progressively heavier, until it seemed as if he was carrying the whole world on his back. It was all he could do to keep from going under.

When he finally reached the far bank, he fell exhausted on the ground, gasping for breath and wondering what had happened. "Marvel not, Christopher," said his small passenger then, "for indeed you have borne the world on your back, and Him who created it. I am the Christ, whom you serve by doing good. As proof, plant your staff by your hut, and in the morning it will be covered with blossoms and fruit." And it was.

Columbus rubbed his eyes. The weight of his own burden had become more than he could bear; the difference was, he couldn't see the far bank. Three more days . . . But three days were still three days. And God was still God. He was the same God who had answered his prayers so often in the past, sometimes at the last moment when all hope was gone and only a miracle could save the situation. Columbus must have prayed that night as he had never prayed before.

The next morning, his journal records that during the previous twenty-four hours they had made an incredible fifty-nine leagues, more than they had covered on all but one other day of the whole voyage. In fact, they were now sailing so fast that the men on the *Santa Maria* grew more alarmed than ever at how rapidly they were widening the distance from their homeland. For the first time the crew openly challenged their commander. According to the historian Las Casas, who personally knew Columbus: "The Admiral reassured them as best he could, holding out to them bright hopes of the gains which they would make, and adding that it was useless to complain, since he was going to the Indies and must pursue his course until, with the help of the Lord, he found them."[1]

This could hardly have been reassuring. Their mood must have been grimmer than ever. A miracle was indeed needed.

On the morning of the eleventh, as they continued to speed along, aboard the *Pinta* a great shout went up: a reed was sighted and a small piece of wood that had unmistakably been shaped by a person. Over on the *Niña* this news was answered with the sighting of a small twig with roses on it. These sure signs of land instantly transformed the mood of the sailors, who were happier than they had been in weeks.

The prize for the first person to sight land was an annuity of ten thousand maravedis, and now the men were clamoring to take turns aloft as lookouts. The ships seemed to be racing one another, with first one and then another forging into the lead. As night fell, instead of taking in sail, they elected to plunge on into the darkness at an almost reckless pace, as luminescent foam curled up from the ships' bows. At 10:00 p.m. Columbus and one of the sailors simultaneously sighted a tiny light far ahead of them.

As Las Casas retells it from Columbus's journal, "It was like a small wax candle being raised and lowered. Few thought that this was an indication of land, but the Admiral was certain that they were near land."

Whatever the light was, Columbus took it as a strong encouragement from the Lord to press on as fast as possible. At 2:00 a.m., with less than four hours remaining before the dawn of the third and final day, the electrifying cry at last rang out from the *Pinta, "Tierra! Tierra!"* The lookout had spied what appeared to be a low white cliff shining in the moonlight, and Martin Pinzón confirmed the sighting by firing a cannon as a signal. *Land!*

Immediately they took in sail and turned south, staying well offshore to avoid piling up on the barrier reefs. In the remaining hours until daybreak they felt their way along cautiously. One can imagine Columbus's prayers now, as full of passion as before, but overflowing with gratitude.

They reached the southern tip of the island just as the sun rose above the blue horizon on their larboard beam.

A new day was dawning, and with it, a new era for humankind.

The fears and aches of weeks at sea seemed like nothing now. In every heart was emerging an awareness of the enormity of what they had accomplished. At the first sighting there had been laughing and dancing, but now the sailors were silent. Every eye followed the coastline slowly unfolding before them, glowing in the morning sun.

Rounding the end of the island and making their way up the lee side, they were speechless at the lushness of the foliage and the blueness and clarity of the waters they were gliding over. It was noon before they came to a break in the reefs wide enough to permit entrance. Columbus donned the scarlet doublet he had been saving for the occasion, and the officers put on their best attire. Boats were lowered, and the landing party rowed toward shore—not all the way ashore because the tide was out, and they had to wade the last part of the way. Joyful now as they splashed through the sun-dazzled water in full armor, they called their commander for the first time by his awarded title: Admiral of the Ocean Sea.

Columbus was the first to set foot on dry land, carrying the royal standard, with the brothers Pinzón directly behind him, bearing a huge white banner with a green cross and the crowned initials of Ferdinand and Isabella on either side of it. The men kissed the white coral beach, which was almost too bright to look at in the noonday sun.

Several of the sailors scooped out a deep hole in the hot sand and firmly planted the eight-foot oak cross Columbus had brought especially for this occasion. Then the entire company gathered around it and knelt, many with tears in their eyes. The Admiral christened the island San Salvador— "Holy Savior"—and then they bowed their heads as he prayed: "O Lord, Almighty and everlasting God, by Thy holy Word Thou hast created the heaven, and the earth, and the sea; blessed and glorified be Thy Name, and praised be Thy Majesty, which hath deigned to use us, Thy humble servants, that Thy holy Name may be proclaimed in this second part of the earth."

Eyes peered at them through the screen of heavy foliage, well hidden from the view of the shining figures on the beach. (The inhabitants of the island could not bring themselves to refer to the newly arrived creatures as men, for they had skins of gleaming metal and appeared to have descended from heaven in huge canoes pulled by white clouds.)

But they seemed to be friendly gods, not angry ones, and they were obviously happy—one could hear them laughing. One at a time the timid inhabitants stepped forward and let themselves be seen. At first the white gods seemed frightened, but then they beckoned to them to come closer. And so they did.

43

Columbus was impressed at what a handsome race they were, tall and well proportioned, "with no large bellies on them," but no clothes either, and as innocent as babes when it came to the tools of war: "for I showed them swords, and they took them by the blade and cut themselves through ignorance."

The Admiral further records: "So that they might be well-disposed towards us, for I knew that they were a people to be delivered and converted to our holy faith rather by love than by force, I gave to some red caps and to others glass beads, which they hung around their necks, and many other things. . . . At this they were greatly pleased and became so entirely our friends that it was a wonder to see. . . . I believe that they would easily be made Christians, for it seemed to me that they had no religion of their own. Our Lord willing, when I depart, I shall bring back six of them to your Highnesses, that they may learn to talk our language."

Columbus had already foreseen the necessity of having interpreters, but was his plan the Lord's will? By planning to take these people forcibly from their native soil, he was establishing a precedent that would have tragic repercussions.

The second unfortunate precedent followed soon thereafter. Columbus noted that some of the natives, whom he called Indians (having no reason to believe that he had not reached the Indies), wore tiny gold ornaments in their noses. Through sign language, he began to inquire where the gold had come from. "From signs, I was able to understand that in the south there was a king who had large vessels of gold and possessed much of it. I endeavored to make them take me there, but later I saw that they had no desire to make the journey. . . . So I resolved to go southwest, to search for gold and jewels."

One can see the hand of the devil here. Unable to overcome the faith of the Christ-bearer by sowing fear and dissension in the hearts of his crew or by paralyzing him with despair, Satan had failed to keep the Light of Christ from establishing a foothold in the New World. So he now moved to destroy Columbus's mission from *within* his own ranks. And he chose the one instrument that almost never failed: the love of money.

And so the seed was planted. It would take time for it to germinate and to put down its taproot. In the meantime Columbus and his crew members were enjoying the fruit of this bountiful Eden, to which a merciful Creator had led them. They ate food that no white person had ever tasted before—sweet, juice-giving fruit, and corn, and a pulpy bread made from cassavas. Most of all, instead of the putrid and filthy water from the ships' barrels, they could now drink pure spring water.

But Columbus was anxious to go discovering—to locate Cipangu, which he thought must be nearby, or possibly to strike out for the mainland of Cathay, which he was convinced lay only a few days further west. He was eager to locate the source of the gold. And the natives, seeing how animated he became whenever he questioned them about it, told him of vast quantities of it—for they had become fond of him and wanted to please him.

Eventually Columbus came to understand that there was an island to the south that was so large that it took twenty days to get around it in a canoe. The natives called it Cuba, but it had to be Cipangu. Without further delay, the three ships departed for it, and on October 26, the sailors hoisted flags and pennants in celebration of its sighting.

But where were the fabulous cities that Marco Polo had described? Where were the temples and palaces covered with gold? As far as the travelers could see in either direction, there was nothing but a couple of rude, deserted huts on the beach. The natives had run away at the sight of them. They were met by a lone dog, which was wandering along the beach and did not even bother to look up at them as they came ashore.

Never mind—the scents of the rain forest were intoxicating, and large birds with plumage of bright reds and yellows and greens filled the air with strange songs. Columbus recorded that it was all so wonderful that he never wanted to leave. As he proceeded northwest along the coast, his opinion of what he had found changed. He now became convinced that they were tracing the eastern coast of Cathay. But before long, fierce headwinds caused him to turn back. (Apparently, it was not God's time to reveal the true mainland; Florida lay a scant ninety miles away in the direction they had been steering.)

On every island at which they stopped, Columbus had his crew erect a large wooden cross "as a token of Jesus Christ our Lord, and in honor of the Christian faith." Almost always they found the inhabitants peaceful, innocent, and trusting; the Admiral gave strict orders that they were not to be molested or maltreated in any way. He had determined that the explorers' reputation, which was obviously preceding them through the islands, must be as favorable as possible. But nowhere did they find the quantities of gold, either in its natural state or in artifacts, that the Indians had so obligingly promised.

Aboard the *Santa Maria* the native captives (or "interpreters," as Columbus referred to them) were beginning to enjoy their roles as resident experts and the prestige their position gave them over the other Indians with whom they came in contact. They now told Columbus and the others of an island called Babeque, where the inhabitants collected nuggets of gold on the beaches by firelight and hammered them into bars. At this news, gold fever ran through the little fleet. Some of the captive natives were aboard the *Pinta*, and on November 18 that ship simply sailed away from the other two. Columbus was convinced that greed had overcome Martin Pinzón, and that he had gone in search of Babeque, and in his journal the Admiral recorded that there were many other unspoken issues between him and Pinzón. The gold was beginning to do its work.

On December 5 Columbus made his own try for Babeque, but bad weather forced the ship back, and they were blown to another large island. The natives called it Bohio, but the Admiral named it Española, because of its almost dreamlike similarity to the sere plains and distant purple mountains of Andalusia. As they felt their way east along its northern coast, Columbus ran out of superlatives to describe it; not even Castile could compare with it.

And then, shortly after midnight on Christmas morning, the dream received a crushing blow. With the *Santa Maria* becalmed in a cove, all those aboard had gone to sleep except for a grommet who had been left to mind the tiller. But an unnoticed swell developed, which gently wafted the ship ever closer to shore. Suddenly the ship grounded, the boy cried out, and Columbus rushed on deck to take command of the situation. They were stuck on a coral reef! Instantly he ordered the longboat lowered to carry the anchor astern so they might quickly winch themselves off the reef before the tide went out any further. But the sailors in the longboat panicked and rowed frantically for the *Niña*, despite the shouted commands and threats of the Admiral.

Vicente Pinzón, seeing what was happening, sent his own boat to be of assistance, but it was too late: the *Santa Maria* was now solidly grounded. Worse, as the tide left and she keeled over, the sharp, unyielding coral tore open her seams, water poured in, and in a few moments she was finished.

But what initially appeared to Columbus to be an utter disaster turned out to have some compensation, for the people of this island were kind beyond belief. And here at last was the gold Columbus had been so ardently seeking—masks of gold and bracelets and necklaces and rings. The natives helped the seamen off-load the *Santa Maria*, offered to store their goods for them in their own houses, and posted guards to make sure that no one touched anything.

The treatment the sailors received from the natives was so far beyond anything they had yet experienced that Columbus became almost thankful that the shipwreck had happened where it did. It was obvious to him that God intended for them to establish a settlement there. He named the place La Navidad, for the Nativity, and they set about laying the groundwork for a fort, complete with a moat and a tower.

Thirty-nine men gladly volunteered to remain behind, and Columbus was confident that upon his return in a year's time, through diligent trading with the Indians, they would have gained a whole barrelful of gold. Moreover, he counted on them discovering the mine that was supplying the gold, so that within three years the Sovereigns of Spain would have the finances to equip the greatest expedition of all: a crusade that would finally free the Holy Land from the grip of the Moors. When Columbus had first sought Ferdinand and Isabella's support, he had shared his conviction "that all profits from this enterprise should be devoted to the conquest of Jerusalem, and your Highnesses smiled and said that such was your will, and that even without these gains, you had the same earnest desire."[2]

But that conquest was for the still-distant future. Columbus and the thirty-eight men who chose to accompany him home boarded the *Niña* and headed northeast to catch the prevailing westerlies and a fast ride home. Three days out, as they were working their way through the islands, they came across the *Pinta*. When the two captains met, there was an angry clash. Martin Pinzón had his excuses, which Columbus finally decided to accept, though he did not believe them. Las Casas wrote: "The Admiral does not know the reasons for his [Pinzón's] shameless and disloyal conduct, but the Admiral was ready to forget it, so that he should not help Satan in his evil design to do all he could to hinder the voyage, as indeed he had done up to that time."

For three-quarters of the voyage home, they could not have asked for better conditions. The log is filled with observations of peaceful seas, sunny skies, and a steady, following wind—for all of which they repeatedly thanked God. They also kept praying, because the pumps were barely able to keep ahead of the leaks.

Then, on the night of February 12, began the worst storm that any of them had ever experienced. The waves were huge, sharp, and crossing one another. This meant that at intervals cold sea water came crashing down on them from both sides at the same time, threatening to swamp the small ship. They had no choice but to abandon their course and run before the storm, letting it take them where it would.

Extra lights were hung on both caravels to help them keep track of each other, but as the wind built up even higher, the *Pinta* fell farther and farther behind. Finally, her lights disappeared entirely, and when morning came, there was no sign of her anywhere.

Aboard the *Niña*, the storm wore the sailors down till they were running on nerves and instinct. The shrieking of the wind must have seemed to Columbus like the baying of the hounds of hell. Unable to thwart the Christ-bearer's mission or keep him from finding the New World, Satan seemed to be making an all-out effort to sink the third ship and stop the word from getting back to the Old World. If he could succeed, the settlers at La Navidad, with no one left who knew of their whereabouts, would perish soon enough.

Always in the past, turning to God in great need and concerted prayer had been enough to break the power of the Evil One. But this time prayer seemed to bring no results, and an angry, bitter Columbus may have been tempted, like Job, to raise his fist at God. Was God now indifferent to the very mission He had called into being? Ironically, the story of Job, with which Columbus was thoroughly familiar, contained the answer:

> If you return to the Almighty and humble yourself,
>   if you remove unrighteousness far from your tents,
>   if you lay gold in the dust . . .
> and if the Almighty is your gold,
>   and your precious silver;
> then you will delight yourself in the Almighty,
>   and lift up your face to God.
> You will make your prayer to him, and he will hear you;
>   and you will pay your vows.
> You will decide on a matter, and it will be established for you,
>   and light will shine on your ways.
> For God abases the proud,
>   but he saves the lowly.
>
> Job 22:23–29

God might have had two reasons for permitting the storm to rage on, unabated. First, because He loved His son Christopher and was deeply concerned for the present state of his soul, He could have been doing all in His power to get him to see how proud and vain he had become as a result of the success of his mission. For already the ravenous ego, which was determined to have all that was coming to it, all that had been denied it for so many years, was enjoying fantasies of fame. If this was now the attitude of the Admiral of the Ocean Sea, the actual rewards themselves would be pure poison to him—and might well destroy Columbus's future effectiveness in God's service.

If God did have a plan for America, He surely would have wanted His grand design for the New World to get off on the right foot. God had withheld knowledge of this place from Europeans for centuries. He had stocked it with an abundance of game and fertile soil, natural resources and beauty—all that a people would ever need—as a fitting abode for the followers of His Son. And He had chosen Christopher to point the way. It was important that this same Christopher proceed in the spirit of Christ and not in self. Therefore, God may have permitted the winds to roar and the seas to heave, hoping that Christopher would look into his heart, see himself through God's eyes, and humble himself.

But if this was God's message to Columbus in the storm—that he needed to come home in an attitude of humility—then Columbus failed to grasp it. His journal records that he knew God had a reason for allowing the violence of the storm, but in his mounting frustration, rather than repenting, Columbus tried to maneuver his way out of disaster.

Calling the crew together, he suggested that they should appease God with a sacrificial offering in the form of a solemn vow jointly undertaken. If God would deliver them, one of their number would make a pilgrimage to Santa Maria de Guadalupe in Estremadura. The men quickly agreed.

So Columbus took thirty-nine dried beans, cut a cross on one of them, and put them into a hat, shaking them together. The Admiral himself drew the marked bean. Everyone marveled at this and took it as a sign that God's hand was upon him. So did Columbus—with, unfortunately, a good deal of pride. It never occurred to him that, like Jonah, he was the problem, and that through the drawing of lots the Holy Spirit might be trying to show him that he, of all the men, was at that time the most spiritually needy.

When it became obvious that the storm was not dying down, Columbus proposed another pilgrimage and a second drawing. This time the lot fell to another, and there was still no change in the weather. They agreed upon yet a third pilgrimage, and miraculously Columbus drew the marked bean for the second time—and probably took quiet pride in the fact that God was requiring more of him than of any of the others.

On struggled the little *Niña*, looking as if she would never rise to meet the next wave, until finally the whole crew got down on their knees and cried out for mercy, loud enough to be heard above the storm. They promised the Blessed Virgin that if she would only pray for them now, they would, as soon as they reached land, go barefoot and in shirtsleeves to the nearest chapel dedicated to her and there say a solemn Mass.

But the storm continued.

All that day and the next, the weather exploded about them, till they reached such a state of numbness that it seemed as if they were dreaming it all. And then toward evening, for no apparent reason, the storm gradually subsided. Not only that, but a sliver of land appeared on the northeast horizon. Some thought it was the island of Madeira off the coast of northern Africa; others were sure it was the coast of Portugal. But the Admiral correctly identified it as one of Portugal's Azores.

The pounding and slamming, the groaning of the masts and timbers, the shrieking and wailing of the wind, the constant drenching—it was all over now, as if it had never happened. Blessed silence—*it was over*. But they were too exhausted to care.

Pennants streaming to leeward, the gold and crimson standard of Spain unfurled atop her mainmast, the *Niña* turned gracefully into the wind and dropped anchor in the Azorian harbor of Santa Maria Island. She made an impressive sight for such a small ship, but the dash of her colors and the bright heraldic shields adorning her bows in no way reflected the mood of her crew. It was Tuesday, February 19, 1493, and they had hardly slept since the storm had hit them the previous Wednesday.

And Columbus least of all. He had remained on deck in the full fury of the storm, conning the ship from the sterncastle, even though his eyes were red-rimmed and his legs could barely support him. Like his sailors, he was grateful, but he was too bone-weary to do more than send a landing party ashore to make contact with the Portuguese and seek a suitable chapel for the fulfilling of their vow. Rest and peace were all they wanted, but rest and peace were not to be their portion on this island.

In the morning Columbus and his crew prepared to disembark and to celebrate the barefoot, shirt-sleeved Mass that they had promised. However, at the last minute something made Columbus decide to send his men in two groups. It was a providential decision, for the commander of the island promptly took as prisoners all those who first went ashore.

In a delicate gambit of threat, bluff, and counterthreat, Columbus finally outmaneuvered his adversary and regained his full crew intact. It was then that he learned that the commander of the island was acting under direct orders from King John in Lisbon. The King had sent word to Madeira, the Cape Verde Islands, and all other Portuguese possessions, including the Azores, that if Columbus put in at any of them on his way back to Spain from a successful voyage, he and all his men were to be detained incommunicado, while Portugal readied its own expedition. As he weighed anchor, Columbus took delight in imagining the consternation of John II when he would learn that the Admiral of the Ocean Sea had slipped his net!

But scarcely had they cleared the Azores and set their course for home than another monstrous winter storm struck them. This one sprang up so suddenly that it tore off all their sails and left them totally at the mercy of the howling gale—and God. For five straight days they were driven northeast under bare masts, their pumps slowly failing.

Once again they prayed, vowed another pilgrimage, and drew lots. For the *third* time Columbus picked the bean with the cross carved on it. (Coincidence? The odds against it were 60,880 to 1.)

Surely now he would get the message. But he did not. Every man on board knew that God was behind the storm, but none of them—saddest of all, not even Columbus—knew why.

Their vow apparently had no effect; if anything, the storm increased in its fury. On the sixth day they sighted land. This time it *was* the coast of Portugal, and Columbus alone correctly judged them to be just above the River of Lisbon. This river, less than a day's journey from the court of John II, was the last place in the world Columbus would have chosen to seek refuge from the storm.

All morning long a growing crowd on the shore watched the progress of the little vessel with no canvas as it was blown ever closer to its doom. The storm was peaking in intensity. In minutes they would be dashed to pieces on the rocky coast. With huge waves breaking on the shore, there was no way any of them would survive. One slim chance remained— if they could make it to the river's mouth. But that would mean they would have to take the wind almost broadside—a dangerous maneuver even under the best of conditions. To attempt it in this monstrous sea? Without sails? Suicide.

The crew prayed with the certain knowledge that only God could save them now.

It is easy to imagine the scene on the sterncastle of the *Niña*. With a practiced eye, the Admiral gauged their drift and ordered the helm over accordingly—as much as he dared, before she would broach to. Carefully noting their speed through the water and the action of the waves at the river's mouth, he called out constant corrections to the helmsman at the tiller as he compensated for the ship's yaw. Though he had to shout to make himself heard above the din of the storm, he was at once calm and exhilarated—for he was being challenged by a worthy opponent at the very limit of his God-given abilities.

Wiping the salt spray from his burning eyes, he peered ahead. Everything was happening much faster now; already he could hear the crashing of the breakers on the rocky coast. It seemed, in fact, as if the jagged boulders were rushing out to meet them.

It would all be decided in the next minute. One mistake now, one error of judgment, and things would compound so quickly that there could be no time for correcting. "Lean her to starboard! More! That's it—hold her there—now steady, steady as she goes. Now! Hard a-larboard! Hold her, hold her!"

The whole ship groaned and heeled over so far that the sea began to comb over her gunwales. The men screamed; it looked as if she were about to go all the way over. But she held and then slowly straightened as a giant wave lifted her and fairly hurled her into the river's mouth.

The roar of thundering waves and flying foam was stupendous, but above it Columbus heard something else—it sounded like cheering. Clearing his eyes again, he could see the men waving and dancing and yelling themselves hoarse. They had made it! He had brought them through.

3

"If Gold Be Your Almighty"

*W*ithout stopping, the *Niña* rode the tide on up to the major port of Rastelo, where the sailors finally lowered anchor. There they learned that some of the ships in the harbor had been pinned there for four months by the worst storms in Rastelo's history. Columbus recorded in his journal that twenty-five ships had gone down that winter off the coast of Flanders alone.

News of the battered caravel's triumphant return from the Indies spread rapidly. Columbus, mindful of their recent experience in the Azores, took immediate steps to ensure the safety of himself and his crew. Making use of several highly placed and trusted friends from his days in Lisbon, he sent abbreviated reports of his voyage to Ferdinand and Isabella by different routes to make sure word would get through.

That done, they could breathe more easily and begin to enjoy their growing fame. Since the continuing storm precluded their sailing for Palos, Columbus felt that he could accept the invitation that had just arrived bearing the seal of the King of Portugal.

John II was all smiles and silken words as he greeted Columbus and subsequently sought to glean morsels of useful information from Columbus's glowing but careful generalities. Though the Admiral seemed relaxed and expansive, underneath he was on guard, for this was the man who had very nearly stolen the Indies from him—twice. What happened next is best described in Las Casas's words, from his *Historia de las Indias*:

> While the King was speaking with the Admiral, he commanded that a bowl of beans should be placed on a table beside them, and then indicated by signs that one of the Indians who was there should arrange the beans in such a way as to show the many islands in that kingdom which Columbus claimed to have discovered. The Indian immediately showed him Española, Cuba, the Lucayos Islands, and others. The King watched this sullenly, and a short while later brushed the beans away, as if by accident. He then told another Indian to replace the beans, and this one arranged them as quickly, and as readily, as the first Indian had done, and went on to lay out more countries and islands, explaining all the reasons in his own language, which, of course, nobody could understand. And when the King fully realized the extent of the new discoveries, and the wealth they contained, he could not conceal his sorrow at the loss of such invaluable treasures, but beat his breast and cried out in passion: "Oh, man of little understanding! Why did you let such an enterprise fall from your hands?"[1]

For Columbus this was a moment of supreme vindication. Although in the past he had been able to forgive, as in the case of Martin Pinzón, now the temptation to drink of the cup of retribution proved too much for him. According to Columbus's biographer Björn Landström, "The Portuguese chroniclers write that the Admiral was so boastful and supercilious, saying that it was the King's fault for having rejected his proposals in the first place, that the courtiers, when they saw the Admiral so insolent and the King so unhappy, offered to kill Columbus and prevent his taking the news to Castile. But the King would not agree to that."[2]

Columbus may have gloated that night, but it is doubtful that God shared his delight. Because Christopher had dedicated his life to serving Christ, God had given him an assignment that would test him to the limit, and indeed, much of the hardest testing had come before he set sail for the Indies. For the sake of Christ, Columbus had been willing to be taken for a fool—not once or twice, but over and over again, for seven long years. And then, as the days at sea became weeks and pressure mounted on him to turn back, he had remained obedient to his call and pressed on into the dim unknown, when perhaps not another ship captain on earth would have done so.

Despite all his shortcomings, Columbus had time and again remained faithful to the point of death. He had poured himself out totally, holding nothing back. And God intended to honor his obedience.

Before the voyage had begun, Columbus had been a beggar before God, all his hopes hanging on Ferdinand and Isabella's approval. But the moment they had agreed to back him, he decided that he could not be sure that God would sufficiently reward him through them. So, he dictated to the King and Queen how they were to compensate him for his services.

Columbus chose the three things the world prizes most: money (his percentage of the wealth), position (the titles of Viceroy and Admiral of the Ocean Sea), and power (governorship over all he discovered). Though God might well have bestowed on His gifted explorer financial blessing and titles, it is unlikely that he would have been rewarded with power. For, although Columbus was immensely gifted as a navigator and explorer at sea, he was totally unsuited to govern ashore. Quick to judge others, he demanded absolute submission from his subordinates, yet he refused to come under authority himself, except for that of the King and Queen. When things went wrong, he would succumb to anger, self-pity, or unreality rather than assume any responsibility. Moreover, he was incapable of delegating authority, ashore or at sea. In the last storm, when he was too weak to stand, he had a shelter rigged on the sterncastle so that he might continue to con the ship from his bed. He had to be in total control—of his ship and of his life.

Before his discoveries, Columbus really had no choice but to trust God. But once he gained all he had sought, he decided that being in control was infinitely preferable to trusting in God. Henceforth, Columbus would trust only Columbus.

On March 15, 1493, the Franciscan brothers in the fields at La Rábida rested for a moment, leaning on their hoes and looking down at the river, where a weather-beaten little ship with spanking new sails and long pennants flying was making her way upriver to Palos. The *Niña* was coming home!

The village erupted with joy. Families were reunited and stories told, and while those whose husbands or fathers had elected to stay on Española were disappointed, the overall mood was jubilant—for word had also reached them that the *Pinta* was not lost as had been supposed. Blown nearly to Africa, she had finally reached the southern coast of Spain and was on her way home even now.

As much as Columbus might have liked to tarry, he had vows to fulfill, and he now set out on his pilgrimages.

Soon after he completed them, a letter reached him, addressed to:

DON CRISTÓBAL COLÓN,
OUR ADMIRAL OF THE OCEAN SEA,
VICEROY AND GOVERNOR OF THE ISLAND
HE HAS DISCOVERED IN THE INDIES.

He was directed to immediately commence preparations for a return expedition and then to come to Their Majesties' winter court in Barcelona as soon as possible. By return messenger he sent detailed plans for colonization, which he had drawn up on the long voyage home. Having purchased a suitable wardrobe for court, he set out for Barcelona, bringing with him several of his officers, the two Indian interpreters who had survived the voyage, and numerous artifacts and curiosities.

A grateful Ferdinand and Isabella had Barcelona decorated as if for a festival. What a splendid entrance Columbus must have made! It is easy to imagine him riding at the head of a small column, tall and erect in the saddle, one hand holding the reins, the other resting proudly on his hip. The morning sun had not yet burned away the low-lying mists, and as he emerged from the fog—first a silhouette and then a reality—the sun behind him surrounded his broad-brimmed hat and flowing cape with a corona of gold.

Word spread ahead of him, and courtiers and a mounted escort were sent forth from the Alcazar, Their Majesties' winter palace, to accompany him. Soon he was flanked by Spanish nobility and preceded by a color guard, the sun dancing on their burnished helmets.

All the way to the Alcazar the crowds lining the streets grew larger, their cheers more deafening. From upper balconies draped with colorful capes, dark-eyed senoritas showered the procession with rose petals. As the Admiral reached the entrance of the palace, a tremendous roar of acclamation went up, and he could not help raising his hand to acknowledge it.

It was a moment too vivid ever to be forgotten. Yet what transpired that evening surpassed it. As Columbus made his entrance into the grand throne room, with its marble columns softly glowing in the light of a thousand candles, the court chroniclers record that his deeply tanned complexion, white hair, long nose, and noble bearing reminded them of a Roman senator.

Respectfully he approached the throne of his beloved Sovereigns. As he did so, they did something no one had ever seen them do before: they rose to meet him. And when he knelt to kiss their hands, they raised him up and ordered that a chair be brought for him—another unprecedented honor.

At their invitation he began to tell his spellbinding story. Time and space seemed to drop away as he unfolded before them visions of dense, green rain forests with sweet exotic perfumes and parrots of startling colors and even more startling cries. He told of unbelievably blue waters, so clear that you could see schools of fish swimming at a depth of several fathoms—strange fish of bizarre shapes and colors. He told of naked natives, shy and innocent, and of an island more beautiful than the plains and hills of Castile. And he told of the loss of the *Santa Maria*, and how, largely through the friendly reception of the natives, it turned out to be such a tremendous gain.

And with that, he summoned the Indian interpreters, clothed in little more than their native attire and carrying parrots, live jungle rats two feet in length, dogs that could not bark, and strange salted fish. The courtiers were astonished.

He then had valuable trade goods brought in—aloes, cotton, and spices. But he had saved the best for last. In his narrative he had told them in passing that these naive Indians had gold ornaments, which they were delighted to exchange for hawks' bells and other worthless trinkets. Now he had a large, oaken chest brought in, which he dramatically threw open. An exclamation of amazement greeted the sight; there, gleaming in the candlelight, were crowns of gold, strange masks covered with beaten gold, necklaces and bracelets of gold, and raw nuggets of gold. The last jaded skeptics were won over—the Indies were indeed as fabulous as he had said.

As the excitement and whispering died away, a silence fell upon the court. Then, without warning, the Sovereigns fell on their knees, and all others did the same. Lifting their faces heavenward, Ferdinand and Isabella thanked God for all his bountiful mercy, and the *Te Deum* was sung. At the last line, the Sovereigns were in tears and so was Columbus: "O Lord, in Thee have I trusted, let me never be confounded."[3]

From that time forth, whenever the King went out in his carriage, Columbus was seated beside him, an honor hitherto accorded only to royalty. But gradually, imperceptibly, the Admiral began to think of it as, after all, no more than his due. After that, there was no reaching Columbus, not by circumstances, not by Father Perez, not even by God Himself.

On the surface, however, things could not have been going better. Even the Pope sent his congratulations to Their Catholic Majesties:

We heard indeed that . . . you had some time ago designed in your minds to send for and discover some islands and mainlands, remote and unknown, and hitherto undiscovered by others, in order to induce the natives and inhabitants thereof to worship our Redeemer . . . you appointed our beloved son Christopher Columbus. . . . Who, at length, by divine aid, having used diligence, discovered while navigating in the Ocean, certain very remote islands and also mainland which had hitherto not been found by others; herein dwell multitudes of people living peaceably and . . . imbued with good morals; and the hope is entertained that if they were instructed, the name of our Lord and Savior Jesus Christ might easily be introduced to the aforesaid lands and islands.

Alexander VI
to Ferdinand and Isabella, May 4, 1493[4]

The preoccupation with gold, which had subtly insinuated itself into the fabric of Columbus's first explorations in the New World, was now becoming an obsession. On May 18 he was given an outright gift of 335,000 maravedis as an expression of appreciation from a grateful country. Yet not content with the gift, on that same day Columbus claimed the 10,000 maravedis that were to be paid annually to the first person to sight land, despite the fact that in his own journal he had recorded that someone else, a crewman aboard the *Pinta*, had made the sighting. Columbus was fast losing sight of the original purpose of his mission—and his life. The verse in Job said, "If the Almighty be your gold . . ."; for Columbus, it had become reversed.

Soon he was outfitting a fleet of seventeen vessels and raising a company of twelve hundred men. This time he had no trouble getting men to sign on. Indeed, two hundred were "gentlemen volunteers" who were paying their own way in order to seek gold and adventure. Here at last was a command worthy of the Admiral of the Ocean Sea. The dream continued; he was on his way to colonize his Indies.

They departed the port of Cádiz and sailed down to the Canaries, there heading west again in perfect weather and sighting land in a remarkable twenty-two days. Even more incredible was Columbus's landfall at Dominica, the navigating target that mariners would recommend for the next four centuries. To aim further north meant possibly missing the strong trade winds; to aim farther south was to risk hitting dangerous reefs.[5] No wonder the sailors of his era considered Columbus to be the best dead-reckoning navigator of them all. By the grace of God, he was.

But the dream turned to a nightmare when they finally reached La Navidad. Every one of the thirty-nine colonists had been killed—some by each other, most of them by tribes of Indians other than those they had befriended.

When they found Indians who were not too frightened to talk to their interpreters, the story came out. No sooner had the *Niña* departed the year before, than the Spaniards who were left behind had started indulging their lust with Indian women. Nor were they satisfied with one each but took as many as they could get.

No longer did they barter for gold. They simply seized it, doing violence to any Indians who protested. Quarrelling among themselves and killing one another, they had split into factions, and were thus easily ambushed and overrun.

There was no doubting the truth of the tale that they were able to piece together. From then on, Columbus's men detested the Indians, whom they regarded as lying and devious, and against whom they constantly sought opportunities for revenge. It was only with threats of capital punishment that Columbus was able to prevent a bloodbath.

The Admiral's own authority had been seriously undermined. His men were increasingly rebellious, having lost all respect for this grandiose, mercurial Italian, who had apparently lied so blatantly about the gentleness of the Indians and the abundance of gold. So Columbus chose not to take note of many of the things that were going on—for example, turning his back on their taking native women for their pleasure—and did anything to appease and avoid open confrontation.[6]

Columbus then tried to use the hunt for gold to unite his expedition, dividing the force into several discovery parties that were assigned to establish outposts at various strategic places on the island. But from the beginning everything went wrong. The food supplies deteriorated in the heat, the mosquitoes were a deadly torment, and several of the men contracted terrible fevers.

It soon became apparent that there was no fountainhead of gold on the island. Finally, the inevitable happened, and the Viceroy of the Indies had open rebellion on his hands.

At sea, Columbus knew what to do when faced with a raging storm: get on his knees and seek God's deliverance. Now, faced with a storm on land and long out of touch with God, in panic he tried to work things out himself. The result was a fiasco that was rapidly compounding itself into a catastrophe of major proportions. Columbus was driven almost to distraction—but not back to his Savior.

Meanwhile, word of the massacre at La Navidad, of the absence of gold, and of the Admiral's gross mismanagement of the island expedition went back to Spain with the first ships to return for more supplies. Columbus was now all the more anxious to wrest some kind of victory from the dream-turned-nightmare. He had caught a terrible fever himself, and for months he was desperately sick. His two brothers, Diego and Bartolomeo, arrived, and even though he lacked the authority to do so, he immediately installed them as his lieutenants. Gradually under the care of Bartolomeo, Columbus found that his health improved, but other conditions did not.

The gold was the bitterest disappointment of all. To bring in more, he commanded that each Indian had to pay an annual tribute of gold or be punished. But there were no mines or fields on Española, which meant that the Indians had to pan for whatever gold they could find. Most were unable to meet their quota, even after it was reduced by half. As a result, they were savagely punished by Spanish tax collectors, whose own percentage depended on how much they collected. Many Indians ran away to escape them. At the same time, because the Indians were finally turning hostile, more forts were being constructed all over the island. The Indians themselves were forced to do this work and all other physical labor, having become virtually slaves on their own land. Las Casas writes:

> Since violence, provocation and injustice from the Christians never ceased, some fled to the mountains, and others began to slay Christians, in return for all the wrongs and the torture they had suffered. When that happened, vengeance was immediately taken; the Christians called it punishment, yet not the guilty alone, but all who lived in a village or a district, were sentenced to execution or torture.[7]

In two years, an appalling one-third of the entire native population of Española, originally numbering around three hundred thousand, had died or been killed. By the time another count was made eight years later, the number of those who had died had more than doubled, and four years after that it was reckoned that only twenty thousand remained alive. The nightmare holocaust went on; there was no waking up from it.

For Columbus, the memory of what Española had been like when he first came must have been too painful to recall. He dreaded returning home to the accounting he would have to give Their Majesties. But he could not think about that now; he had to put down a major Indian uprising. Finally, thanks to superior weaponry, he was successful, and a Spaniard could now walk anywhere on the island without fear.

But there was now no more putting off his return home. Leaving his brothers in charge, Columbus sailed north to catch the Prevailing Westerlies, which this time proved anything but prevailing. The crossing seemed to take forever; the sailors' food and water ran out, and they were tortured by hunger and thirst. But eventually they arrived, and the Admiral was summoned immediately to court.

To his surprise, the Sovereigns chose to believe much of Columbus's version of why everything had gone wrong, which, of course, held him nowhere at fault. He was even more surprised that they seemed far less disturbed about the lack of gold than he was. On the other hand, they were far more concerned than he was about the welfare of the Indians, whom they now considered to be their subjects, and for whose safety and protection they held themselves personally responsible before God. They remonstrated with Columbus for the way he had permitted them to be treated.

Yet while it was obvious that they had grave reservations about his ability to govern such a volatile situation, they felt morally bound by their original agreement to permit him to continue. Therefore, they shored up his authority as best they could, instituting drastic reforms in the treatment of the Indians. And because the Portuguese were preparing a major expedition of their own to the New World, they sent him back as soon as a small fleet could be readied.

Once again, nothing went right. Three-quarters of the way across, the ships were suddenly becalmed for eight days. Such was the heat that none of the crew members could bear to go below decks. The wheat was scorched, the salted meat went rotten, and Columbus and his men listened to the sound of their water and wine casks bursting. After much prayer and what seemed like an eternity of this torment, a breath of wind stirred the pennants in the rigging. Soon there was a freshening breeze, and they were on their way again. The Lord had mercifully sent the Trade Winds to them, something that never happens at that time of year in the doldrums.[8] They finally sighted an island with three mountain peaks close together, and Columbus named it Trinidad, for the Holy Trinity.

Eventually they worked their way up through the Antilles to Española, where chaos reigned. Columbus had been away for a year and a half, during which time word had reached the island that he was out of favor with Their Majesties. This so undercut the authority of his brothers that rebellion had broken out again, and it had now reached the point that there were two armed camps on the island. Columbus handled the situation by giving in to every demand of the rebels, reinstating them with full pardons and full rights, and making their leader a mayor.

Not surprisingly, the same rebellion broke out again within six months, and with even more serious ramifications. More alarming reports were sent back to Spain. Finally the Sovereigns, despite all their fondness of Columbus, felt that they no longer had any choice but to intervene for the best interests of all their subjects on Española—Spanish and Indian. They sent an old and trusted officer, Francisco de Bobadilla, to straighten out the mess, and they empowered him with whatever authority he needed. Bobadilla carried with him the following letter to Columbus:

> Don Cristobal Colón, our Admiral of the Ocean Sea: we have sent the Commendador, Francisco de Bobadilla, the bearer of this letter, to say certain things to you on our behalf. We desire you to place your full trust in him and pay him all respect, and to act accordingly.[9]

The first thing that Bobadilla saw when he landed on Española was the sight of seven Spaniards' bodies dangling from nooses. When he learned that five more Spaniards were to be executed on the following morning, he acted without further delay. Summoning all parties, Bobadilla read the proclamation that installed him as acting governor. When Columbus refused to acknowledge his authority, stating that the King and Queen had no right to depose him as Governor, Bobadilla had him and his brothers put in irons and sent them back to Spain to stand trial.

A compassionate captain offered to remove the fetters as soon as Columbus was on board, but the Admiral tearfully refused, saying that he would not permit it until the Sovereigns themselves so ordered and that he would wear them as a token of how he was rewarded for his services.

The Sovereigns were shocked to see him in irons when he reported to them in December of 1500. They ordered that the chains be removed, and they restored his house and all other properties on Española that had been confiscated. Then they listened with great understanding and compassion to his woeful tale. Yet they said nothing of his being reinstated as Governor.

Columbus went home, expecting to be ordered at any time to ready another expedition. But the months went by, and no further word was heard from the court. Finally, he turned his attention to preparing a book of prophecies gathered from the Scriptures and the writings of leaders of the early Church. Through them, he intended to prove that God had predestined Spain to be the nation that would free the Holy Land from infidels, and that none other than he himself was the man to lead the crusade.

But such a crusade would take much gold to finance it. He needed, therefore, to make one more westward voyage of discovery. After more than a year's entreaties, and possibly just to get him out of Spain, where he was becoming an increasing embarrassment to them (he was being mocked as "the Admiral of the Mosquitoes" behind his back), Ferdinand and Isabella gave him four ships and their permission to go exploring. They made only one stipulation: he was expressly forbidden to return to Española, because they feared that his presence there might spark yet another rebellion.

As soon as he departed from the Canaries, Columbus, pleading ship trouble, sailed directly for Española, where he was refused entrance at the harbor. His ship trouble now apparently no longer a problem, he sailed to Cuba and struck southwest for the mainland (Honduras, in Central America). Despite unbelievable headwinds, despite being sick and feverish (he again had his bed brought out on deck so that he could command the ship lying down), and despite the fact that God Himself seemed to be blocking him every inch of the way, such was Columbus's willfulness that he finally reached the mainland. He declared it to be the easternmost shore of the province of Chiambra (India). It had taken him thirty-eight days to cover what would normally have taken no more than three or four days, but it never occurred to Columbus to even consider that he might be defying God's will.

He decided to follow the coast to the south, expecting it to turn toward the west at any moment. And so they proceeded down the coast of what is now Honduras, Nicaragua, and Costa Rica—where he finally found the source of gold that had been eluding him for so many years. (This may explain why God's hand seemed to be set against his reaching this part of the mainland.)

Here the natives had such heavy artifacts of gold that a major source had to be nearby. The Indians took the Spaniards to the gold fields, where the mineral was right on the surface, and in a very short space of time they were able to dig out more than a thousand maravedis' worth with their bare fingers.

That discovery ushered in a drama far different from that which God had in mind for America. This new drama, which would shortly begin in earnest, was to feature such stars as Cortez, Pizarro, and a supporting cast of hundreds of Conquistadors. It would eventuate in bloody rape and conquest—and all for the love of gold. For although the Spaniards undoubtedly would have colonized Mexico and Central America eventually, it was the lust for gold that whetted the steel of the Spanish blades.

Columbus had at last found his gold; the final desire of his heart had been fulfilled. But at what a price! His health was ruined, and his sanity was nearly gone; two of his four ships would soon be too worm-eaten to go on, and he and his men would be stranded for months in the other two.

In the meantime he carried on with his exploration, enduring in the month of December 1502 the worst battle against the elements of all his voyages. He wrote:

> The tempest arose and wearied me so that I knew not where to turn; my old wound opened up, and for nine days I was as lost without hope of life; eyes never beheld the sea so high, angry and covered with foam. The wind not only prevented our progress, but offered no opportunity to run behind any headland for shelter; hence we were forced to keep out in this bloody ocean, seething like a pot on a hot fire. Never did the sky look more terrible; for one whole day and night it blazed like a furnace, and the lightning broke forth with such violence that each time I wondered if it had carried off my spars and sails; the flashes came with such fury and frightfulness that we all thought the ships would be blasted. All this time the water never ceased to fall from the sky; I don't say it rained, because it was like another deluge. The people were so worn out that they longed for death to end their dreadful sufferings.[10]

In addition to all these horrors, his son, Ferdinand, tells us that on Tuesday, December 13, a waterspout passed between the ships; "the which had they not dissolved by reciting the Gospel according to Saint

John, it would have swamped whatever it struck without a doubt; for, it draws the water up to the clouds in a column thicker than a water-butt, twisting it about like a whirlwind." Columbus's biographer, Samuel Eliot Morison, continues: "It was the Admiral who exorcised the waterspout. From his Bible he read an account of that famous tempest off Capernaum, concluding, 'Fear not, it is I!' Then, clasping the Bible in his left hand, with drawn sword he traced a cross in the sky and a circle around his whole fleet."

Yet except for shipboard crises when he automatically turned heavenward for help, nothing seemed to induce him to turn back to God in repentance, not even what would soon prove to be the greatest moment of need in his life. As the Spaniards were starting to build a settlement near the gold fields under the supervision of Columbus's brother Bartolomeo, they learned through their interpreters that the local tribe of Indians was planning an attack. So they launched a preemptive strike, taking a number of hostages, including the chief, and more than 100,000 maravedis' worth of golden ornaments.

After this adventure, they were up a nearby river, getting water and provisions, when Columbus, who had been left almost alone with the ships at the mouth of the river, heard shouts and shooting. Then there was silence, and toward evening when the tide changed, down the river floated the bodies of several of his men. Here, in his own words, is what happened next:

> I toiled up to the highest point of the ship, calling in a trembling voice, with fast-falling tears, to the war captains of our Highnesses, at every point of the compass, for succour, but never did they answer me. Exhausted, I fell asleep, groaning. I heard a very compassionate voice, saying: "O fool and slow to believe and to serve thy God, the God of all! What more did He for Moses or for His servant David? Since thou wast born, ever has He had thee in His most watchful care. When He saw thee arrive at an age with which He was content, He caused thy name to sound marvelously in the land. The Indies, which are so rich in a part of the world, He gave thee for thine own; thou hast divided them as it pleased thee, and He enabled thee to do this. Of the barriers of the Ocean Sea, which were closed with such mighty chains, He gave thee the keys; and thou wast obeyed in many

lands and among the Christians thou hast gained honorable fame. What did He more for the people of Israel when He brought them out of Egypt? Or for David, whom from a shepherd He made to be King in Judea? Turn thyself to Him, and acknowledge thine error; His mercy is infinite; thine old age shall not prevent thee from achieving great things; He has many heritages very great. Abraham had passed a hundred years when he begat Isaac and was Sarah young? Thou criest for uncertain help. Answer: who has afflicted thee so greatly and so often? God or the world? The rewards and promises which He gives, He does not bring to nothing, nor does He say, after He has received service, that His intention was not such and that it is to be differently regarded, nor does He inflict suffering in order to display His power. His deeds agree with His words; all that He promises, He performs with interest; is this the manner of men? I have said that which thy Creator has done for thee and does for all men. Now in part He shows thee the reward for the anguish and danger which thou hast endured in the service of others."

I heard all this as if I were in a trance, but I had no answer to give to words so true, but could only weep for my errors. He, whoever he was who spoke to me, ended saying: "Fear not; have trust; all these tribulations are written upon marble and are not without cause."[11]

In His infinite mercy, God stopped at nothing to reach His beloved Christopher. "Have trust," he said, and Columbus wept for his errors. Yet only a few entries further on, he writes:

I declare that I am at the fountainhead [of the gold in the New World]. Genoese, Venetians, and all who have pearls, precious stones and other things of value, all carry them to the end of the world to exchange them, to turn them into gold. Gold is most excellent. Gold constitutes treasure, and he who possesses it may do what he will in the world, and may so attain as to bring souls to Paradise.

It is doubtful that he who does what he will in the world is going to be used to bring many souls to paradise. This particular narrative goes on to reveal just how far off-center Columbus's thinking had wandered. For by the same sort of weird, convoluted reasoning that characterizes Gnosticism and so much of occult metaphysics, Columbus arrived at a monumental conclusion: he was convinced that he had found King Solomon's mines!

Columbus may have turned away from God, but God did not turn away from Columbus. By sheer grace God brought him and his remaining crew members safely home to Spain. But this time there was no royal summons inviting him to court. Queen Isabella was dying. It was the end of an era—for Castile and for Columbus. Far older than his fifty-three years and too infirm to put to sea again, Columbus spent the next two years fretting about not receiving his proper share of the Indies gold, which had finally begun to arrive in some quantity.

In the spring of 1506 what remained of his health began to fail quickly. The tall, proud old captain could no longer walk down to the harbor to see the bright sails in the morning sun or hear the latest news from the most recent landings, or mutter that "even tailors" were going discovering these days.

But we can imagine him lying in his bed and reliving with great delight his first glimpse of the moonlit cliffs of San Salvador and the joy of his sailors as they yelled with glee and danced on the decks . . . the awe of the following morning as they watched the dawning sun illuminate a new world unfolding before their eyes and realized what they had done . . . the sun gleaming on the helmets of his escort as he rode in triumph into Barcelona, the greatest hero Spain had ever known . . . and that night, as he knelt with the King and Queen and sang the *Te Deum* before their God, tears streaming down their faces.

The old man brushed away the tears at the corners of his eyes, and perhaps he spoke to God again for the first time in a long while.

"Father, it is over now, isn't it?"

Yes, son, he might have heard in his heart.

"Father, I'm afraid I have not done well in carrying the Light of Your Son to the West. I'm sorry. I pray that others will carry the Light further."

They will. You are forgiven.

"It's time now, isn't it?"

Yes.

On Ascension Day 1506 after receiving the sacraments of the Church, Christopher Columbus said these words: "Father, into Thy hands I commend my spirit," and went to be forever with the Savior whose name he bore.

4

BLESSED BE THE MARTYRS

*O*thers did carry the Light of Christ further. But so tiny were the pinpricks of illumination on a dark continent that we almost missed them entirely. In fact, the Columbus era soon deteriorated into such a debacle of rape, murder, and plunder throughout Central America that we could not conceive of what possible connection it might have with any divine plan for the establishment of a new Christian commonwealth.

Here we faced one of our first dilemmas. If God had truly been working His purpose out for America to be what the first Puritans would call the "New Israel," then how could He have let everything in the New World go to seed so badly for a whole century? Something didn't add up. This was not the Master Economist whom we knew. Where was the continuity to His work?

Once again we spelled out our concerns to the Lord in prayer. We needed answers, and we needed them urgently.

We got them. On our next trip to the Boston Public Library, we acted out a scene that would soon become routine. Ever the optimist, David would return to the reading table, arms laden with books, confident that he had unearthed new treasures of information. But Peter steadfastly maintained professional skepticism, scowling his way through the new ore samples, looking for the occasional nugget. Twin columns of rejected volumes would mount at his right elbow, while there might be four or five "keepers" at his left.

The afternoon shadows were lengthening, and it was getting close to closing time when David came up to the table with one last volume, a tall, thick book. "Thought you might get a kick out of it, just for the pictures," he said.

Peter flipped the book open to the title page of *The Pageant of America*[1] and noted the publication date: 1928. As he riffled the pages, he shook his head; full of old engravings and etchings, it had more pictures than text. But some of the illustrations toward the front of the musty volume caught our eye—etchings of long-robed priests in the wilderness accompanied by (or in some cases being tortured by) Indians. We paused then and began to read. And thus did the Lord bring to our attention one of the most crucial phases in the introduction of Christ's light into America.

The dawn of the sixteenth century saw more and more vessels approaching the New World, hull-down on the horizon, their square sails silhouetted against the rising sun. On they came, some Portuguese but mostly Spanish, bound for conquest, colonization, and gold. The Aztecs in 1519 greeted Cortez with reverence, believing him to be the reincarnation of their white god Quetzalcoatl. They ushered him with great ceremony into the capital (now Mexico City). Upon arrival, he promptly took their ruler Montezuma captive, and thus gained control over the native population in one efficient maneuver.

Pizarro did much the same thing in Peru twelve years later. Taking the Inca chief Atahualpa captive by trickery, Pizarro then demanded an impossible ransom: a large room to be filled to the ceiling with gold and silver. To the Spaniards' amazement, the Incas were able to supply the ransom, whereupon Pizarro had his hostage garroted on trumped-up charges.

This pattern continued throughout the Caribbean islands (now called the West Indies, to distinguish them from those of East Asia) and on the mainland, where the natives were forced to continually work the gold fields. In Mexico, where silver was abundant, the Indian farmers were taken from their fields and enslaved. They were set to mining silver, with no thought for the crops on which the population was entirely dependent. Widespread famine was the result, and that, plus their total lack of immunity to the Europeans' diseases, amounted to genocide of mind-numbing proportions.[2]

At first glance, it would appear that God's plan for America was doomed almost before it could be set in motion. In their wanton slaughter of the Indians, the Spanish Conquistadors were proving to be just as cruel as the Indians—those in the Caribbean who practiced cannibalism, and the "more advanced" civilizations on the mainland that derived such satisfaction from ritual murder and blood sacrifice. The murderers were now themselves being murdered, and Satan's reign in the New World remained unchallenged.

Or so, at first glance, it would appear. But there was a weakness in the fortifications, a small and unnoticed breach in the outer wall. The Conquistadors had brought monks with them, because as Cortez had put it in a message to his forces before they left Spain: "We seek not only to subdue boundless territory in the name of our Emperor Don Carlos, but to win millions of unsalvaged souls to the True Faith."[3] But these Franciscan and Dominican friars were not token chaplains just along for the ride; they loved God and were absolutely committed to serving Him, wherever He took them.

It took a particular kind of Christian to enter these orders. Not only were they relinquishing the right to own, to choose, or to marry; they were, in effect, sacrificing all for a life of service and obedience. In sixteenth-century Europe, while there were more than a few Christians, highborn and low, who had counted the cost of discipleship and were prepared to pay it, there were almost no opportunities to fulfill such a call. In fact, with the singular exception of its monasteries and convents, the Church had lapsed into a sorry state of complacency and hypocrisy. On the one hand, it was instituting Inquisitions, while on the other it was preying on the gullibility of the common people—hawking relics and selling indulgences that supposedly ensured swifter entry into heaven. By 1519, the same year in which Cortez sailed for the New World, things had reached the point where a devout young German monk named Martin Luther nailed his ninety-five theses for reformation of the Church to the door of All Saints Church in Wittenberg, taking the first step toward what would become known as the Protestant Reformation.

To a young Spaniard who wanted to serve the Lord Jesus Christ more than anything else in life, there was really only one way: the taking of holy orders. And thus, some of the most gifted young men in Spain, many from the ranks of nobility, found themselves in the plain robes of the Dominicans or the Franciscans, side by side with sons of the simplest peasant farmers. For them, the process of dying to self had begun even before they took their vows and would continue for the rest of their lives, which might indeed end in the ultimate sacrifice: death by martyrdom. But because they had chosen to live sacrificially for Christ, even death itself held no fear for them, and Satan thus found it impossible to neutralize their effectiveness. Consequently, these few humble servants of God turned out to be a greater threat to Satan's dominion on this continent than a veritable legion of do-gooders and yea-sayers.

Such was the pattern for living that God set down as He began His work in this country. It has not changed in five hundred years.

Those first friars—the Franciscans with perhaps slightly more emphasis on simplicity, the Dominicans with slightly more emphasis on study—may have been tiny pinpricks of Light, but wherever they were posted the Light grew brighter. Orphanages came into being, along with schools for the Indians and refuges for the destitute. And through the loving service of these missionaries, dozens, then hundreds, and then thousands of Indians came to realize that they had a living, risen Savior who could renew their lives as if they had been born all over again. What had first attracted them was the living example of these selfless men.

One of the things these first missionaries shared in common was a gift that God seemed to have given all of them: an intense love of this strange new land to which He had brought them. Stunned by its grandeur and majesty, which far surpassed anything they had ever seen, they were acutely aware of the hand of the Creator in its formation. More than that, they sensed that the reason He had created such breathtaking beauty was for the express purpose of delighting those who would one day call Him Father.

Imagine the sensation of being the first Christian to stand looking at the thundering falls of Niagara, to arrive at the rim of the Grand Canyon, to gaze down on the shining rocks of the Big Sur coastline, or to be suddenly confronted with the snow-capped Rockies. Is it so surprising that these missionaries' hearts were filled with the desire to see and to explore? Or that so many of these same missionaries would become known to modern American schoolchildren as those who first mapped our rivers and lakes and mountain passes?

The first European to explore territory in what is now the United States of America was the Franciscan friar Marcos de Niza. His journey into New Mexico in 1539 led to Francisco de Coronado's famous expedition in search of the Seven Cities of Cibola, whose streets were said to be paved with gold. So powerful was the impact of the legend on people's imaginations that it would eventually draw hundreds on numerous expeditons. The cities of gold were never found, but vast reaches of the Southwest were opened.

Meanwhile, back in Spain the leaders responsible for determining that country's policy in the New World gradually realized that when it came to pacifying the Indians and extending the frontier, one friar could accomplish peaceably what it might take a thousand soldiers to do forcibly. So they made it a policy to encourage these missionary efforts.

But their main method of colonization remained the *encomienda* system, whereby a Spanish overlord was allotted so many hundreds of acres and whatever Indians happened to be living on them. Officially, the native people were in his custody for the purpose of their salvation and "religious instruction." But in actuality they were little more than slaves, and the overlords tended to run their *encomiendas* like medieval serfdoms.

There was one priest, however, whom the policy makers must have always regretted having encouraged—a priest who went to Cuba not long after taking his vows. There he was assigned an *encomienda* of his own. As the labor of his Indians began to make him rich, he awoke to the insidious evil of the system. He hated what it was doing to him and especially how it was affecting his attitude toward the Indians. Renouncing all connection with the system, he dedicated the rest of his life to combatting it and exposing the plight of the Indians.

We have met this man before: he is Bartolomé de Las Casas, who was with Columbus on his third voyage and who recorded the Admiral's journal for posterity. Such was his dedication that Las Casas was eventually able to persuade Charles V to pass laws alleviating the condition of the Indians and ultimately revoking the *encomienda* system. In 1552, his history of the Indies was published, and this widely read account of what had really happened there made Spain a byword for cruelty throughout Europe.

For example, here is how he described the end of the Indian uprising on Española:

> When they saw every day how they perished from the inhuman cruelty of the Spaniards, how their people were ridden down by horses, cut to pieces by swords, eaten and torn asunder by dogs, burned alive, and subjected to all kinds of exquisite torture, those of certain provinces . . . decided to resign themselves to their fate and give themselves over into the hands of their enemies without a struggle.[4]

Historia de las Indias became justly famous, but it also secured the author's alienation from practically everyone in Spain except for his Christian brothers in the cause. Yet this one man's willingness to be vilified and all but physically martyred for the sake of his beloved Indians—his willingness to follow in Jesus's footsteps along the Way of the Cross—bought new life for much of the remaining Indian population.

The pockets of Light grew larger and brighter. More friars were outposted in New Mexico and Lower California (the Baja). Several met death at the hands of hostile Indians, but others took their place, and the Light went further to the north and the east. By 1630, Alonso de Benavides, the friar responsible for the New Mexico missions, was able to record that eighty thousand Indians had been baptized and that friars based in twenty-five missions were serving ninety Indian communities.

In 1687 Father Eusebio Kino, a Jesuit (for by this time they too were involved), refused a professorship in mathematics in his native Austria to serve the Indians in America. He founded a mission in the Sonora region of northern Mexico and soon came to love the vast solitude of the desert, with its shifting colors and awesome stillness. From his mission base he was to make more than fifty journeys of exploration, traveling on horseback across hundreds of miles of arid wasteland and ranging as far north as the Gila River and as far west as the muddy Colorado. In 1700 he founded the first mission in Arizona, San Xavier del Bac (near the present site of Tucson).

As the Lord's work progressed, the Franciscans carried the Light to California, while the Dominicans served in the Baja. Fray Junípero Serra, the hero of the settlement of California, was a Spanish professor of philosophy when he felt called to the mission field at the age of fifty-five. Among the missions he founded were San Diego, San Carlos (Carmel), and San Francisco. Just before his death, he picked the site of Santa Barbara. "Love God" was his greeting for everyone he met. He was universally loved by the Indians, his fellow friars, and even the soldiers of the Spanish garrisons.

Bit by bit the Light progressed up the West Coast and began to reach inland. The pace was slow—no gold was discovered to fire people's greed, so the only settlers interested in going there (aside from the missionaries) were a few pioneer ranchers and farmers. "God-forsaken" was what most civilized Spaniards might have called that land.

But was it? Or did God purposely withhold knowledge of the presence of gold in California for two centuries in order to ensure the kind of settlement He intended in His new Promised Land? Life in the mission towns was simple, peaceful, and centered around the churches. There, both Spaniards and Indians, guided by the example of the selfless lives of the missionaries, learned to put their trust in Him.

On the East Coast a different history was unfolding. In 1513 Ponce de León, seeking the "Fountain of Youth," whose waters were said to possess magical curative powers, sighted Florida. Over the years, a number of Spanish attempts to colonize Florida failed, due to climate, disease, and the ferocity of the Indians. Finally, in 1562 a group of French Huguenots

(Protestants), seeking a haven from religious persecution, landed at what would soon be named Saint Augustine and settled at what is now Beaufort, South Carolina. Two years later another group of Huguenots settled at the mouth of the Saint Johns River in Florida, only to be massacred by a Spanish expedition.

The Spanish then attempted to settle Saint Augustine and other sites along Florida's east coast, but their efforts were plagued by an unrelenting chain of misfortunes—a French reprisal, unending sickness, and frequent Indian raids.

Perhaps because of the blood of the innocent Huguenots, perhaps because the underlying motive for colonization was greed, or simply because it was not God's time or place and these were not the people He had chosen—the jealous, bickering, avaricious Spanish settlers in Florida were destined not to thrive or come into the mainstream of what God had planned for America.

Next upon the stage of North America were the French and a new breed of missionaries: the fabled Jesuits. If there was one word to describe the Jesuits, it would be *zeal*—in the very best sense of that maligned word. In 1540 Ignatius of Loyola, a former knight and soldier, founded the Society of Jesus—a band of brilliant young scholars and disciples who had covenanted together to live in poverty and chastity under absolute obedience to the Pope. The essence of the "Jesuits" (a derogatory nickname which they came to accept as their own) was such a soldierlike unity and companionship in the service of Christ that they all but invented the phrase *esprit de corps*. Their personal aims were threefold: purification of the soul from disordered affections and worldly standards, discovery of the divine will before choosing an area of commitment within the order, and consecration of the individual's mind and will to the service of the Creator under the lordship of Jesus Christ.

From the beginning the Jesuits had a deep commitment to the mission field, in the tradition of Francis Xavier, who with Ignatius was one of the founders of the society and who became famous for his missionary work in India and Japan. From the earliest days of the order, the mission field attracted many of the finest intellects the Church could produce. By dint of the intensive self-discipline required of them, these individuals turned out to be surprisingly well prepared for the physical hardships that awaited them. In fact, as a strong person rejoices to run a race, these Christian soldiers, superbly trained and strong in the faith, yet conditioned to prize humility, looked forward to the tests of the savage wilderness.

Like the Franciscan and Dominican orders in Spain, the very totality of the commitment the Jesuits required was appealing to gifted young men of France, who had experienced deep conversions to Christ and wanted nothing more than to serve Him totally and unreservedly.

As the Light of the Spanish missionaries began to illuminate the southwest of America, now Light began to break across the northeast corner as well. The French missionaries moved ever deeper into the uncharted wilderness, their canoes gliding silently through the early morning mists, their snowshoes leaving lonely trails through glistening pine forests. In 1534 Jacques Cartier, discoverer of the Saint Lawrence River, erected a cross thirty feet high on the western shore of its gulf. Wherever he encountered large bands of Indians, he read to them the opening verses of the Gospel of John and also read of Christ's suffering and crucifixion.

But it was Samuel de Champlain, known as the "father of New France," who undertook the most effective measures of bringing the Light to the Indians. They were living, he said, "like brute beasts, without faith, without law, without religion, without God."[5] From France he brought four gray-clad friars of the Recollets, a branch of the Franciscan order. One of these, Joseph Le Caron, pushed westward with an escort of Hurons until he reached their towns on Lake Huron's Georgian Bay, where he built a chapel and introduced the Indians to Christian worship.

Meanwhile, the Jesuits, singly or in twos, went forth in an attitude of lowliness, meeting the Indians as equals and respecting their customs but sharing with them the Gospel of Jesus Christ. Year by year the Light they imparted spread a little farther—among the Hurons around Georgian Bay, to the Algonquins north of Ottawa, to the Abenakis in Maine and Acadia (Nova Scotia), to the Iroquois south of the Saint Lawrence, and to the Chippewas, Ojibwas, Illinois, and other tribes of the upper Great Lakes and Mississippi Valley. The pace was slow, as it was on the West Coast, but it was also sure.

By way of discipline, these Jesuit missionaries were required to keep a written journal of all the significant events of the year. They then submitted their journals to their Superior, who compiled them into narratives called *Relations*, which captured the spirit and essence of what God was doing in New France. The *Relations* were then published in France and subsequently created a great stir of interest in missionary work.

Among those who were profoundly inspired by the *Relations* was a lad of seventeen from a very wealthy family. So anxious was he to become a Jesuit missionary in America that he joined the order with the full knowledge that it would take twelve arduous years of study and preparation before he could be ordained. His aptitude as a linguist finally won him an assignment to New France, first to Sault Sainte Marie and then to the southwest corner of Lake Superior. Traveling with Indians and the French pioneer furtrappers known as *voyageurs* in their birchbark canoes, he adapted himself to deep-woods living and learned how to survive on just what the land provided. So adept did he become and such was his enthusiasm that he carried the Light of Christ deeper and deeper into the wilderness, just as he had once dreamed of doing as a youth when reading the Jesuits' *Relations*. Indeed, he was to become one of the most famous of all American explorers—Father Jacques Marquette.

Called to serve the Illinois Indians, he would write in his own contribution to the *Relations*: "One must not hope that he can avoid crosses in any of our missions, and the best way to live there contentedly is not to fear them. . . . The Illinois . . . are lost sheep that must be sought for among the thickets and woods."

The seeking sometimes took him far afield, a prospect he enjoyed as much as his missionary counterparts in the Southwest, for the same reason: discovering God's magnificent handiwork in the world He had created. In 1672 he was ordered by his Superior to "seek toward the South Sea [the Gulf of Mexico] new nations that are unknown to us, to teach them to know our great God, of Whom they have hitherto been ignorant." The following May, he and Louis Joliet began their descent of the mighty Mississippi. Daily awed by the increasing size of the vast river that swept them along, they descended as far as the mouth of the Arkansas River.

Father Marquette promised the Illinois Indians at Kaskaskia that he would come back to them to found a mission. This he did, despite the fact that his health had been broken during the long and rigorous voyage. Death took him early at the age of thirty-eight; as a tribute, the Illinois brought his remains back to Jesuit headquarters in a procession of thirty canoes.

One of the most outstanding of the first Jesuit missionaries was Jean de Brébeuf. Tall, powerfully built, and possessing a commanding presence, Father Brébeuf worked for nineteen years with the Hurons, enlarging the influence of Christ and battling the devil for the souls of the native people. And it *was* a battle, for among other things, he had to overcome the lies of jealous medicine men, who said in reference to the Body of Christ in the Eucharist that the missionaries had concealed a corpse in their houses that was infecting the country.

In 1640 Father Brébeuf saw a vision in the sky of a great cross slowly approaching over the wilderness forests toward the land of the Iroquois. When asked by his companions how large it was, he replied, "Large enough to crucify us all."

The martyrdom for which he had thus mercifully been prepared, and which he had always known could be the final sacrifice of his call, came nine years later at the hands of the Iroquois. Captured with Father Gabriel Lalemant when a war party fell upon the Huron towns in which they were serving, he was subjected to every satanic torture that his captors could devise. And there can be little doubt of the source of their inspiration when one considers the nature of the tortures or the intensity of pleasure the Iroquois derived from leisurely inflicting them. For the myth of the noble savage was just that: a myth that was created a century later by romantic English poets and artists who had never crossed the ocean themselves, let alone witnessed the horrors of tribal warfare and custom. The lives of these Indians were an unending tableau of fear and hatred of other tribes and a dawn-to-dusk struggle for survival.

The first Iroquois torture was to pour boiling water over Father Brébeuf's naked body in mockery of the sacrament of baptism. When, by the grace of God, he denied them the pleasure of hearing him cry out in agony—for the pain of their victims was intoxicating to them—they tied a collar of metal hatchets, heated red-hot, around his neck. Again Father Brébeuf disappointed them by remaining silent, and so they fastened a birchbark belt filled with pitch and resin around his waist and set it afire. And still he remained mute before his tormentors, his face set like flint.

Now Father Brébeuf did speak, but not in anguish. He called out encouragement to his fellow captives. Enraged, the Indians cut off his lips and tongue and rammed a hot iron down his throat. Then they cut strips of flesh from his arms and legs and devoured them before his eyes. But as he was dying, Father Brébeuf was gaining the victory, just as his Savior had on the Cross before him, and the Indians sensed it. In the end, they cut his heart out and ate it, and drank of his blood, in the hope that they could thus gain the spirit power that had given him more courage than any man they had ever seen.

One of Father Brébeuf's companions for six years during his work with the Hurons was another Jesuit, Isaac Jogues. In 1642, while returning from a journey to Quebec to secure supplies, Father Jogues and his party were ambushed by Iroquois. He managed to escape, but when he saw that several of his companions had been taken prisoner, he surrendered himself and joined them. He said, "Could I indeed abandon them without giving them the help which the Church of my God has entrusted to me? Flight seemed horrible to me. If it must be, I said in my heart, that my body suffer the fire of earth, in order to deliver these poor souls from the flames of hell, it is but a transient death, in order to procure for them an eternal life."

The Indians tore out their captives' fingernails with their teeth, gnawed their fingers, and cut off a thumb or forefinger of each. Father Jogues was not killed outright but was kept as a slave for the purpose of their future enjoyment through torturing him—torture so cruel that he longed for Christ to release him from life and let him be with Him in heaven.

Why are some Christians called to make the supreme sacrifice? Is it because they have the faith to do so? Is it because through their example the faith of the entire body of Christ is strengthened? Or is it because a nonbeliever cannot gaze upon a cross or Indian burning-stake without asking questions that begin with *how* or *why*? Only God knows for sure. But on this we may safely speculate: of all the people on earth, those whom

Satan hates most are the Christian martyrs, because they remind him of Christ's willingness to die on the Cross out of love for humankind. It is no wonder that whenever Satan had one physically at his mercy, with servants who took such delight in inflicting pain, he provided them with tortures from the very pit of hell.

After being held captive for more than a year, Father Jogues was able to escape the Iroquois and make his way to the Dutch colony at Fort Orange (Albany) and eventually back to France, to the Jesuit college at Rennes. Word of his ordeal had preceded him, and to his surprise and acute embarrassment, he was a national hero. The Queen kissed his mangled hands, and the Pope himself paid him honor. It was all more than he could bear, and he begged to be returned to duty; his one desire was to be sent back to New France to continue to serve the Indians.

His wish was granted, and his first assignment was to act as France's ambassador to the Iroquois Nation, with whom France had just concluded a peace treaty. Father Jogues performed these duties well—the Iroquois were in awe of him—but he was more deeply concerned than ever for the state of their souls. With good reason: even while he was among them, they sacrificed a captive Algonquin woman in honor of Areskoui, their god of war. "Areskoui," they cried, "to thee we burn this victim! Feast on her flesh and grant us new victories!"[6] And they proceeded to feast on her flesh themselves. Thus, when his task was completed, Father Jogues requested to be assigned again to the Iroquois, this time as priest, to found the "Mission of the Martyrs." While he awaited reassignment, Father Jogues, well aware that his previous experience qualified him better than anyone else for the post, wrote to a friend:

> My heart tells me that if I have the happiness of being employed in this mission, I will go and not return; but I shall be happy if the Lord will complete the sacrifice where He had begun it, and make the little blood I have shed in that land, the earnest of what I would give.[7]

And it came to pass.

The first inroads of Christ's Light had been made in North America. In the span of a century and a half these tiny illuminations had become veritable spearheads of Light, thrusting deeper and deeper into the heart of a dark and murderous continent. For darkness is powerless to do anything to light except recoil before it. "The light shines in the darkness, and the darkness has not overcome it" (John 1:5).

And what of the martyrs? Other than the tremendous example of their selflessness and sacrifice, did their deaths play a part in God's unfolding plan for America? In terms of mass numbers of Indians being converted to Christ, the missionaries' impact on the continent as a whole may not at first seem to have been that significant. But God does not take the measure of people's lives by the sum of their accomplishments. Rather, in the case of the founding of America, He seems to have been more concerned with the quality and depth of commitment. Jesus said, "Unless a grain of wheat falls into the earth and dies, it remains alone; but if it dies, it bears much fruit" (John 12:24). These French and Spanish martyrs were willing to be the grains of wheat that fell into the earth and died. In soil watered with the blood of their sacrifice, God could now plant the seeds of the nation that was to become the new Promised Land.

5

THE LOST COLONY

*A*s the sixteenth century unfolded, the major powers on the European stage slowly made inroads into the unexplored North American continent. Having secured much of the Caribbean, Spain had sent explorers like de Vaca, Coronado, and de Soto deep into the American interior and had reached up both the Pacific and the Atlantic coasts, as we saw in the last chapter. Saint Augustine was Spain's first settlement on the Eastern Seaboard, and the Spaniards saw no reason to stop there. During the same time, King Francis I of France had dispatched Giovanni de Verranzano to explore between Florida and Newfoundland, and Jacques Cartier reached far up the St. Lawrence River.

But what of England? Five years after Columbus's first voyage, another visionary mariner from Genoa, Giovanni Caboto, had persuaded King Henry VII that he could open a sea route over the top of the North American continent to Cathay (China) and the Spice Islands of the Indies. John Cabot (his anglicized name) did succeed in reaching Newfoundland

and Labrador in 1497, but the polar ice cap and ice-clogged northern channels proved impassable. He died at sea without ever locating the fabled Northwest Passage. Aside from some gritty and resourceful fishing captains who had discovered the wealth of codfish on Newfoundland's Grand Banks, England was largely relegated to the sidelines. She watched with envy as Spain, thanks to the steady stream of silver and gold from mines in the New World, was rapidly becoming the wealthiest nation in Christendom.

But all of that was about to change.

From the life of Columbus we have seen how history can turn on the patience and perseverance of a single visionary. England's was Walter Raleigh.* Born in 1552, Raleigh described his breeding as "wholly gentleman, wholly soldier." Oxford-educated, Raleigh was a bit of a dandy, wearing his hair long when the fashion was short and always spending a little more than he could afford on his attire. He was also a dashing and intrepid army officer, having fought alongside the Protestant Huguenots in France and then for the English forces subduing Ireland.

It was through his half brother, Sir Humfrey Gilbert, that Walter Raleigh gained his lifelong passion for the New World. In 1578 Sir Humfrey persuaded London businessmen that the time had come to plant an English colony in the New World. His words resonated in the hearts of financier-adventurers who had long had an eye for the western horizon. These "gentlemen of the West," as they referred to themselves, were prepared to back any venture to the New World that had a reasonable chance of turning a profit. All were aware of the gold and silver that Spain was bringing home from there. Their own fishing captains, returning from navigating the coast, reported vast forests of stately oak from which Britannia's shipbuilders could fashion a mighty navy.

Sadly, the incentives drawing the imagination of Englishmen westward lacked the spiritual motivation that had originally inspired Columbus "to bear the Light of Christ west to heathen in undiscovered lands," as Pope Alexander VI had phrased it. Nor was there any evidence of the fervor of the Franciscan, Dominican, or Jesuit missionaries. Among the English

*Raleigh himself spelled his name many different ways, including Ralegh, but his widow adopted "Raleigh," and it was commonly used thereafter.

merchant-adventurers who dreamed of settlements in the New World, few sensed that God might have a plan for America and that it would behoove them to look to Him to see how they might fit into it.

That in no way diminished their enthusiasm to plant an English colony, however, and Sir Humfrey made the first attempt. He sailed with five ships, one of which was captained by young Raleigh. Headstrong and obstinate, Gilbert consistently refused the advice of the senior mariners accompanying him. He did manage to reach Newfoundland, but after running out of provisions, he had to beat a hasty retreat to England.

Walter Raleigh would, however, never forget the sense of awe and wonder he experienced at the first sighting of land on the western horizon after so many weeks at sea. From that moment on he thought of himself as an explorer-adventurer, even though circumstances conspired to keep him from setting foot on deck for many years. His passion for building an English colony in North America was born then and would never diminish.

But in those days (as now), a visionary without a benefactor was little more than an eccentric dreamer. How Raleigh found his benefactor is the stuff of legend. Impoverished but always elegant, Raleigh lived by his wits. At the art of "foining"—dueling with words—he was a master of thrust and parry. And so was his queen.

As a young sovereign, Elizabeth I was far from unattractive, but even then her most alluring feature was her nimble wit. A lover of learning, she was fluent in six languages, and for pleasure she read the classics in the original Greek and Latin. While in her conduct of formal occasions of state she could be breathtakingly regal, she also possessed a great sense of fun.

Unlike her half sister, Mary Tudor, whom she succeeded and who had married the King of Spain, Elizabeth chose not to marry, eventually becoming known as the Virgin Queen. She was, in effect, married to England, and England's future was all she cared about.

After reigning for twenty years, she was forty-six when she met Raleigh, who was twenty years her junior. She was beginning to resemble the formidable grand dame portrayed in her court portraits. But her wit was as agile as ever, and she was starved for a good match when Walter Raleigh hove into view.

The tale of how they met may be apocryphal, but the story goes that the Queen was walking out of doors after a rain, enjoying the fresh air, when the path she was following came to a particularly plashy place. She hesitated, not wanting to ruin her silk slippers. At that instant, Raleigh appeared, whipped off his new cloak (which he could ill afford), and spread it on the ground before her. Bemused by his spontaneous, flamboyant chivalry, she struck up an acquaintance with him.

Quickly they became close friends. They would tease each other and play verbal chess, each admiring the other's skill. Raleigh may have been the better player, but he was wise enough to know the one unspoken rule of the game: the Queen must never lose. She might be played to a draw, but she must not be humiliated, not even accidentally.

Each enjoyed the pleasure of the other's company. He would write her sonnets. She would tease him about his Devonshire accent, pronouncing his name "Water." Once he impulsively removed his diamond ring and scratched on a palace window: "Fain would I climb, yet I fear to fall." Instantly she took the ring and wrote, "If thy heart fail thee, climb not at all."[1]

They spent more and more time together, the Queen laughing and demanding his presence: "Where is my Water? I thirst for Water!"[2]

Gradually Elizabeth came to trust him, to the point where she would rely on his advice in all matters, from the most personal to affairs of state. So great became her reliance on his judgment that her Privy Counselor and other court advisors grew jealous of Raleigh and began to work behind the scenes to bring him down.

Her Royal Highness proved to be the consummate benefactor, giving Raleigh the use of a grand old mansion, Durham House. In addition, she gave him the right to charge every vintner in the country one English pound a year for the privilege of selling wine, and an exclusive license to export woolen broadcloth. This was the foundation of his wealth, and it assured him a steady income for the rest of his life (or his benefactor's). It also enabled him to become a major player among the gentlemen of the West.

The one thing Elizabeth denied Raleigh was to go to sea. What, go adventuring for a year or two, and perhaps become lost at sea? Never!

And to keep him at her beck and call, she made Raleigh the captain of her personal bodyguard. So in the summer of 1583, when his half brother, Sir Humfrey, outfitted his second expedition, Raleigh sadly remained behind.

It may have been a blessing in disguise. From the beginning the voyage was plagued with misfortune—some of it from bad weather, much of it from Gilbert's bad judgment. To prevent pilferage, he had all of the expedition's provisions stowed on his flagship, where he could keep a personal eye on them. Alas, his was the ship wrecked in a gale. Hastily the crew salvaged what they could. But before they could finish, a second storm arrived, more vicious than the first. It sank the ship and took the lives of all aboard, including Sir Humfrey.

When the news reached England, after a brief season of mourning, Raleigh besought the Queen to pass to him the grant to plant an English colony. In the spring of 1584 Elizabeth agreed—provided that he did not personally accompany any venture to the West.

Determined to plan well, Raleigh enlisted the aid of Thomas Harriot, an old friend from his Oxford days, whose prowess at mathematics and astronomy was widely recognized. Raleigh hired him specifically to teach his navigators, Arthur Barlowe and Philip Amadas, how to determine their exact latitude. While the magnetic compass could do this to a degree, it had fluctuating variations, particularly in the far north. Raleigh wanted something more reliable. So Harriot developed a method of shooting the sun at daybreak and worked out tables that would show a navigator exactly how far north he was on any given date (essentially the same method that is used today).

By the spring of 1584, Raleigh felt that Barlowe and Amadas were ready. He dispatched them at the helm of two ships and asked Thomas Harriot to accompany them as the expedition's surveyor and cartographer. As Columbus had done, they avoided the Prevailing Westerlies by dropping down toward the Equator. There they picked up the favorable trade winds and rode them all the way to the Caribbean. In all, their trip was unusually blessed—swift, smooth, and uneventful.

After refilling their water casks, they made their way up America's Atlantic coast, taking pains to avoid being sighted by the Spanish at Saint

Augustine. At length they arrived at the sandy Outer Banks of Cape Hatteras, where Raleigh had felt that they would find the ideal site for a settlement. For 120 miles they followed the barrier islands northward until they finally found an entry into the waters behind them.

"After thanks given to God for our safe arrival thither," Barlowe recorded, "we manned our boats and went to view the land," taking possession of it "in the right of the Queen's most excellent majesty."

Barlowe was overwhelmed by the lush beauty and abundance of the place. The gleaming white sand, the blue water, and the surf sparkling under the summer sun simply took his breath away. And there was so much game—deer, hare, and fowl of all descriptions. With lush sweet grapes to be had for the picking, red cedars taller than any they had ever seen, and flowers so fragrant as to be intoxicating, it is not surprising that he thought he must be in paradise. "I think in all the world, the like abundance is not to be found."[3]

Their first encounter with the local inhabitants bore a marked similarity to Columbus's. Gradually the landing party became aware that they were being watched. On their third day ashore three native men approached them without fear and full of curiosity. Initial communication was a matter of sign language and gestures, and although the Indians were awed by the two ships that towered over their dugout canoes, one of them was persuaded to come on board, where he was given "a shirt, a hat, and some other things." According to Barlowe's official account, this first contact was unbrokenly sunny, though he did later note that when the Englishmen demonstrated their weaponry, even the report of their small harquebus sent the locals crying out and fleeing into the woods.

Any lingering fears the Indians may have had didn't prevent them from returning the next day, led by one of their tribal elders, Granganimeo, brother to their chief, Wingina. The Indians spread a mat for the English to sit on, and Granganimeo "beckoned us to come and sit by him . . . and he makes all signs of joy, and welcome, and striking on his head, and his breast, and afterwards on ours, to show we were all one, smiling, and making show the best he could, of all love, and familiarity."[4]

And when he decided that these fair-skinned, clothed men meant no harm (even though they stank), he took them to his village on the island of Roanoke, where his wife had the women wash the men and their clothing. The island, it turned out, was ideally suited for their settlement. Twelve miles long and three wide, it was fertile, spring-fed, well stocked with game, and, best of all, hidden from view from the ocean.

In the days that followed, Barlowe began to patiently work with the natives to achieve rudimentary communication. He found that these Indians were a small tribe that belonged to a large confederation of tribes known as Algonquins.[5] Language barriers couldn't prevent a brisk trade from springing up between the sailors and the Indians. The natives were delighted to accept pieces of glass, dolls, and other trifles in exchange for animal skins. Even illiterate sailors knew that pelts had considerable value back in England, and soon they traded knives and axes for all the pelts the natives had.[6]

When the Englishmen made it clear that in addition to the wild game that was readily available they needed vegetables, the natives inundated them with onions, melons, walnuts, cucumbers, peas, and roots. Barlowe summed it up: "We were entertained with all love, and kindness, and with as much bounty, after their manner, as they could possibly devise. We found the people most gentle, loving and faithful, void of all guile and treason, and such as lived after the manner of the golden age."[7]

But then it was time to leave if they were to get home before the storms began. And Barlowe had one more bit of business to attend to. Walter Raleigh, their patron, had requested that they bring back a New World native, so they could learn his language and quiz him about the environs of their new colony.

Nearly a century after Columbus had done the same thing, Barlowe and Amadas took two tribesmen home with them—Wanchese from Roanoke, and Manteo from an Outer Banks island called Croatoan. Barlowe, elsewhere so articulate and positive, neglects to mention how these two were persuaded aboard and not allowed to leave. And here we have the first English example in America of one race making another captive. More than two centuries would pass before William Wilberforce and others persuaded Parliament to outlaw the British Empire's trafficking in slaves.

Immediately after returning to England, Thomas Harriot set about working with Wanchese and Manteo at Durham House to learn the Algonquin language, create a lexicon of Algonquin words, and work out an Algonquin alphabet of thirty-six characters. It was slow going. Manteo was cooperative, regarding the English as his hosts, but the sullen Wanchese saw them as captors. Harriot also attempted to teach them English so that he would not be the only one able to communicate with them.

Progress was made, and Harriot was able to report to Raleigh that the natives in America had no weapons of iron or of any metal. Armed with bows and arrows, clubs, and wooden swords, they would be no match for English armor and musketry should hostilities develop. Yet that meant that for their own protection the colony would need an armory, complete with muskets, pistols, powder, and musket balls.

As Harriot's list of needful things grew ever longer, Raleigh was discovering that exploration required seemingly inexhaustible funds. Though he was now well-to-do thanks to his Queen's beneficence, his finances were far from limitless. His elder half brother's expedition had bankrupted Sir Humfrey. And establishing a settlement on Roanoke would only be the beginning. Although the Gentlemen of the West were ready and willing, their combined investment would not be sufficient to plant a colony large enough to sustain itself until supply ships could return.

In Raleigh's view nothing less than state sponsorship would be required; this would have to be England's venture. That meant it would have to be the Queen's, for she saw the nation and herself as inextricably entwined.

Raleigh now asked the two men who had read everything that had been written about the New World's exploration—the brilliant Richard Hakluyt and his uncle and guardian, also named Richard—to write an appeal that would convince Her Majesty to finance their undertaking.

The younger Hakluyt presented a treatise to the Queen on bended knee. We do not know if Elizabeth got much beyond its subtitle: *Certain Reasons to Induce Her Majesty and the State to Take in Hand the Western Voyage and the Planting Therein*. But we do know that she had apparently already decided against backing this plantation. If it failed, she would be the laughingstock of Europe. Moreover, the venture was likely to cost three or four times Raleigh's estimate.

The Queen responded with a counterproposal: Raleigh could call his colony Virginia, in honor of the Virgin Queen. Phillip II of Spain would thus be put on notice that she and England intended to be a major player on this new stage. And, since the honor of England's Queen needed to be properly defended, she would confer knighthood on Raleigh. What could he do but mumble his profound thanks and reduce his expectations.

That meant cutting back severely on young Hakluyt's recommendation—which was to transport the equivalent of a large village into the wilderness. At the end of his lengthy list of necessary artisans, he had added, "There ought to be appointed one or two preachers . . . that God might be honored."[8] We have seen what happens to ventures where God is an afterthought instead of the reason for going; we are about to see it again.

Instead of the vast flotilla Raleigh had envisioned, there would now be five ships commanded by his Devonshire kinsman, the bold and intrepid Sir Richard Grenville. But now fortune smiled upon Raleigh, as he struck upon an incentive that fired the imagination. The expedition would leave at the beginning of summer, to engage, perhaps, in a bit of piracy, should one of those gold doubloon-laden Spanish galleons hove into view.

And since the Queen did not look askance at such adventuring, the pirate captains chose to think of themselves not as pirates but as privateers, sailing with the approval of the monarch. Money now poured into his coffers. The Queen herself offered the use of one of her warships, the ten-gun *Tiger*, plus all the gunpowder it could carry.

Ten days after they weighed anchor, there was a partial eclipse of the sun. Sir Richard and his captains did not think much of it, and Thomas Harriot was unconcerned. But on the eastern seaboard of America, where they were headed, the eclipse was total, and it badly frightened the Algonquins, who saw it as a portent that great evil was about to befall them.

Fortune continued to favor Grenville as he brought his ships into Hispaniola. There he was royally entertained by the island's Spanish commandant, who provided him with horses and donkeys, as well as goats, sheep, and pigs—in short, all the livestock he would need to start a colony up on the shores of Newfoundland (which was more than a thousand miles north of their actual destination). Grenville also purchased a large quantity of sugar, ginger, and pearls to ensure that he would make a handsome profit on his return to England, whether or not they encountered any Spanish treasure ships.

A fortnight later they reached the aptly named Cape Fear, where a vicious tidal rip nearly drove the *Tiger*, their flagship, onto the beach. The pilot, Simon Fernandez, who had been in these waters before, should have kept them away from it, but he soon compounded his mistake by allowing the *Tiger* to be caught by a sandbar at the southern end of the Outer Banks. And now, incredibly, the same hideous error in judgment that had devastated Sir Humfrey's expedition was about to do the same to Sir Richard's. Like his predecessor, Grenville had commanded that all their provisions be stowed aboard the flagship so he could keep an eye on them and guard them from being pilfered.

Now, as the sea pounded the stricken vessel and opened her timbers, salt water ruined their provisions and destroyed the precious seed corn that was to provide a late-season harvest. Suddenly they were at the mercy of the Algonquin. If the natives did not share their stores and food with them, they would be undone.

Grenville was a man of action, and he decided that action was what was called for now. In four small boats he led a party of some sixty men ashore to contact the natives whose help they would soon need. Among them were Ralph Lane, who was to be the Governor of the new colony once Grenville departed; Thomas Harriot, who with Manteo was needed to ensure clear communications with the Indians; and the artist John White, who would make sketches of their locale to present to Raleigh upon their return.

To make sure that no one offended the natives on whose good will they would shortly be entirely reliant, Grenville established a strict code of conduct. No sailor or colonist could do anything to violate a woman. No native could be forced to do work involuntarily. No one could strike or misuse a native or enter a native's house without permission. The punishments showed that Grenville meant business. For rape, death. For striking a native, twenty blows with a cudgel. For unwanted entry, imprisonment.

Needless to say, the men were on their best behavior as they entered the village of Pomeoic Indians. They were well received, and it was only after they had departed and returned to their boats that Grenville noticed that his personal silver drinking cup was missing. Flying into a rage, he dispatched Amadas back to the settlement with orders to burn down their houses and lay waste to their corn. It was an act of appalling stupidity. Word traveled quickly, and soon all the native tribes avoided them completely.

Back at the beach, they found that the *Tiger* had been refloated in their absence and was once again seaworthy. At Grenville's behest, Harriot reconnected with Granganimeo and arranged with him for the English to construct a small settlement on Roanoke Island. By the third week in August the fort was finished, the gun emplacements were ready, a moat had been dug, and two decent houses had been prepared for Governor Lane and Thomas Harriot. For the rest of the settlers there was a church, a storehouse, a stable, and an armory, along with shacks to shelter them from the elements.

On August 25 Grenville departed for England—and any Spanish merchantman who might happen to cross their path. He left behind 107 settlers, now under the command of Governor Lane. Most of them were ill-suited for carving a village out of the wilderness. More than a few were gentlemen who refused to work with their hands. Clearing, digging, hoeing, and planting were beneath them. About half the company was, in fact, soldiers—far too many for a successful settlement. Of the rest, many were artisans—with nothing to trade or craft. They were reluctantly willing to farm, but not in order to feed gentlemen who were not willing to do anything.

After several weeks Granganimeo's brother, King Wingina, paid a call on the settlement. Skinny, with bulging eyes and none of the customary tattoos, he wore a gleaming copper gorget around his neck as a sign of his station. He was very wary of the Englishmen—not because of the devastation they had done to the village of the Pomeoic, but because wherever they went, within a few days people began to die. Did the English have supernatural powers? To the natives it certainly seemed so. As Harriot reported, "Within a few days after our departure from every such town, the people began to die very fast . . . in some towns about 20; in some, 40; in some, 60; and in one, six score."[9] Unbeknown to the Indians (or

Harriot), the English community was bearing measles and smallpox, to which the Indians had no immunity.

Needless to say, King Wingina and his advisors leapt at the invitation of the English to join them in prayers to their God, who somehow seemed to be in charge of it all. Responding in kind, Wingina invited the English to come and sing psalms in his village, and when he thought that he was dying, he asked for the prayers of Lane and Harriot, to ensure that his spirit would go to the Englishmen's God.

Capitalizing on this new spiritual openness, Harriot took a Bible into the Indian village and started telling the people about Jesus in their native Algonquin. This caused a bit of confusion. The Indians, believing that the Bible itself was a source of power, grabbed it and rubbed it all over themselves.

That winter the Indians sustained the Roanoke settlement with food. But by spring their own supplies were running out, as was their patience. These English never stopped demanding, and now they wanted even their seed corn, without which there could be no harvest in the fall. Wingina, while remaining outwardly friendly, began to speak to other chiefs about joining with him to finish off the colonists.

Getting wind of this via Manteo, Lane decided to investigate. Taking a war party with him, he made the acquaintance of a chief named Menatonon, who confirmed it. This left the Governor with a choice: deal with Wingina as he deserved, or continue to treat him as a friend and hope for the best. Deciding on mercy over judgment, Lane returned—to find that Wingina had spread word that Lane's party had been annihilated.

With his credibility in shambles, Wingina now decided to help the settlers, teaching them how to catch fish with weirs and giving them several cleared fields, which he planted with his own seed corn. The way things turned out, Wingina qualified as a godsend without whose help the settlement surely would have perished.

Meanwhile, on his voyage home Grenville encountered a straggling Castilian ship. Loaded with gold, silver, pearls, and spices, she was the ripest plum to be picked in a long time. In one stroke, Grenville made Raleigh's backers rich and ensured that there would always be funding for westward adventures. Indeed, Roanoke was now regarded not just as a domestic settlement but as an excellent base from which marauders could prey on Spanish shipping.

This new image was further enforced by the arrival at Roanoke of Sir Francis Drake, in command of a flying squadron of twenty-three ships of the line that had wrought havoc among the Spanish settlements in the Caribbean. Having captured Santo Domingo and destroyed Saint Augustine, Drake now offered his services to Governor Lane, who regarded the timely arrival of the English fleet as a godsend of a different kind.

Sensing that the colony was growing weaker, Chief Wingina had once again shifted allegiance and was plotting the overthrow of Lane and the others. He had torn up their fishing weirs and had made ready to attack. But Lane had beaten him to it with a surprise attack on the Indians, in which Wingina was killed. With goodwill between the natives and the English now a thing of the past, he knew it was only a matter of time before the Indians regrouped and finished them.

That was the situation when Drake sailed into view. Seeing their need, Sir Francis commanded his ships to reprovision the colony to sustain them till a supply ship could reach them. But as they began off-loading, a ferocious three-day storm scattered the fleet and sank many of the provisions. At that, the heretofore steady and stable governor lost heart. It might be weeks before they were resupplied, which meant they would once again be at the mercy of the natives.

Lane abruptly announced that they were abandoning the settlement and going home with Drake. With the weather again threatening, such was their haste to get out of there that mutinous sailors at the oars of one of the small boats ferrying their goods to the fleet simply jettisoned the trunks—with all of Lane's and Harriot's journals in them and most of White's sketches.

The history of the Virginia Colony is fraught with instances of both divine connections and near misses. Just four days after their departure, the first of the supply ships Raleigh had dispatched arrived, with all the provisions they would have needed to sustain them till the harvest. Three weeks later, Grenville arrived with six ships and four hundred soldiers— a force considerably larger than was needed to defend the settlement, which indicated that Roanoke's military potential as a raiding base had not gone unnoticed.

Grenville also brought enough provisions for the entire company for a year. But when he learned of the Roanoke governor's decision to abandon, he changed his plan. Knowing that Raleigh would want to keep Roanoke going if at all possible, Grenville left a party of fifteen men with provisions for two years. But if a garrison of four hundred soldiers was far larger than necessary, fifteen was not nearly enough. With relations with the natives at an all-time low, the paucity of their number was almost a guarantee of their overthrow.

When Drake's squadron arrived back in England, the news of his extraordinary triumphs made Sir Francis an instant national hero. He was the talk of every table and every meeting place—and no one gave much thought to Lane and the ill-fated Roanoke colony. Indeed, when Richard Hakluyt eventually recorded Lane's hasty departure from Roanoke, his description was revealing and accurate: "He left all things so confusedly, as if they had been chased from thence by a mighty army, and no doubt so they were, for the hand of God came upon them for the cruelty and outrages committed by some of them against the native inhabitants of the country."[10]

What other news there was of the abandoned settlement was not good. Frustrated artisans and impoverished gentlemen spread tales of woe and hardship, till the very mention of Roanoke brought a heaviness of heart. But then, as now, the best way to counteract depressing news was with uplifting propaganda. And Thomas Harriot did his best. To encourage future backers, he wrote *A Brief and True Report*, which was neither brief nor true, as far as investment opportunities went.

One thing he promoted did catch on. The Roanoke natives smoked the dried leaves of a noxious weed they called *uppowac*, which the Spaniards called *tobacco*. The effect of inhaling the smoke directly into the lungs, according to Harriot, was "to purge . . . gross humors and open all the pores and passages of the body." It caught on, and soon smoking tobacco was all the rage in polite society. How soon could ships go back to retrieve more of this so-called sot-weed?

In the spring of the following year, as it turned out. But now Raleigh had a problem: whom to put in charge? Ralph Lane had no interest in returning. Thomas Harriot would have been the perfect choice, but he was now more interested in trying his hand at colonizing in Ireland. That left John White, the artist, who alone was anxious to return. White would be the Governor of a new settlement up on the Chesapeake, which both Lane and Harriot had convinced Raleigh was much more suitable. In addition, and perhaps most important, the natives there were friendly; indeed, they were wonderfully hospitable.

As for Roanoke, Raleigh was unwilling to give up on it entirely. He named Manteo, their trusty guide and interpreter, as the Governor of Roanoke. Manteo would rule over all the local Indians and be subject directly to Queen Elizabeth.

Finding would-be colonists was the difficulty now. Too many rumors and sordid tales were circulating about the Roanoke colony. In the end, Raleigh's agents could only fill his three ships by painting the expedition as an opportunity to escape the murder, robbery, flagrant prostitution, and virulent disease of London's crowded streets. Actually only one of his three, the *Lion*, was a proper ship of 120 tons; the other two—a pinnace and a flyboat—were so small they were referred to as boats, not ships.

Raleigh *was* successful at one innovation: for the first time, women would be accompanying the men. Fourteen couples were persuaded to make the voyage, including White's daughter Eleanora and her husband, Ananias Dare. Moreover, Eleanora was quite pregnant and was likely to bring forth the first English baby to be born in the New World.

Eight days after their departure in May of 1587, Governor White lost control of his ship and the expedition. His navigator-pilot, Simon Fernandez, who had served in that capacity under Grenville, now openly defied him. In the dark of night he deliberately abandoned the flyboat, which carried all their provisions, and refused to go back for her.

In Elizabethan times as today, the commander of a ship or an expedition had absolute power and the absolute authority to back it up. Mutiny was a hanging offense, and if Drake or Grenville or Lane had been in charge, Fernandez would soon have been dangling from the highest yardarm.

But White did not have the stomach for it, and so Fernandez became their de facto leader, at least while they were on board his ship. And it *was* his ship now, for he alone knew where they were going and how to get there. The trouble was, getting there was not Fernandez's highest priority. It took them forty-four days to reach the Caribbean, making them arrive so late in the planting season that if there were any more delays they would miss it entirely, which may have been Fernandez's plan. In his journal White accused Fernandez of deliberate and calculated sabotage, suspecting that the pilot's intention was to go hunting Spanish treasure ships.[11]

The worst came when they reached Roanoke. Fernandez now demanded that all 112 colonists get off his ship immediately, not up on Chesapeake Bay as had been planned and where Raleigh assumed they would be settling. Spineless as ever, White agreed, and the settlers were unceremoniously put ashore. As they approached the fort, they discovered that it had been demolished, and the houses were abandoned and overgrown. Nor was there any sign of the handful of men Grenville had left behind the summer before.

Trying to ascertain what had happened, they searched extensively up and down the coast, eventually coming upon the bones of one of the fifteen settlers. This led them to conclude that the entire party had been massacred—a fate that might soon be their own.

One of Manteo's kinsmen filled in the blanks. The Englishmen had indeed been ambushed by the Indians, lured out of the safety of their fort by tribesmen pretending to be on a friendly visit. In fierce combat, the Englishmen lost two men but held their own, eventually escaping to the Outer Banks, from where, scavenging for food, they simply disappeared.

The news left them all in despair, but it was lifted three days later, by the arrival of the flyboat that had been left behind at the beginning of the voyage. Here were the rest of their settlers and the rest of their supplies. God's name be praised!

Their celebration, however, was short-lived. Three days later one of their number was murdered while hunting for crabs. Obviously a major peace treaty was now imperative, and Manteo and White set about arranging it. When the local chiefs failed to appear on the agreed-upon day, White decided to do what Lane would have done: attack the Indians.

The attack failed miserably and was immediately called off when the attackers realized that they had made a horrible mistake. The tribesmen they were assaulting were Manteo's kinsmen, perhaps their last friends in the entire region. Now they desperately asked forgiveness while binding up the Indians' wounds and helping them bring in their corn harvest.

Soon, however, spirits were lifted by the happy event of Manteo's baptism into the Christian faith and his ceremonial installation as Governor of Roanoke. Five days later the struggling band of colonists welcomed Eleanora Dare's baby girl into the world, the first English child born in the New World. She was appropriately named Virginia.

Meanwhile, the *Lion* lay at anchor off the coast, with Fernandez apparently watching to see how things turned out and not the least interested in going raiding, as White had thought. His presence now raised another possibility. An inventory revealed that they did not have as many provisions as they had thought, and a careful assessment of their remaining stocks indicated that there was not enough to see them through to the next harvest.

Although White was not overly concerned, confident that supply ships were already on their way to them, the other colonists grew fearful that these ships would head for Chesapeake Bay and miss them entirely. The only solution was for one of them to go back with the *Lion* to report to Raleigh all that had happened and to redirect their supplies to Roanoke. White, the ostensible leader of the expedition, was the logical one to go. He did not want to leave, but the feeling among the others was unanimous—he had to go.

Before he departed, the governor made an agreement with them. If they should leave Roanoke for any reason, they were to carve their destination in the trunk of a tree, and if their departure was involuntary or under threat, they were to add a cross over the letters.

With a heavy heart he said his good-byes, assuring them all of his quick return. Bidding farewell to his beloved daughter and infant granddaughter who had walked with him to the boat to see him off, he waved to them from the stern all the way out to the *Lion,* until they were no longer visible.

Back in England, the island nation was now on a full war footing. Phillip II of Spain was planning to invade and was assembling a mighty armada for this purpose. Queen Elizabeth decreed that henceforth there would be no more voyaging for any reason. Every single ship would be needed for the defense of her realm.

This was the mood in London, as White urgently sought an audience with Raleigh. When Sir Walter heard that the landing had been made at Roanoke instead of Chesapeake Bay as he had specifically instructed, Virginia's champion was furious. He informed White that the first supply ship had set sail before the Queen's shipping embargo. But it was bound for the Chesapeake, not Roanoke. There was nothing to do but gather another fleet under the command of Grenville and send it directly to Roanoke along with so many provisions that resupply would no longer be an issue.

But how could that be done with the royal ban on shipping in place? Sir Walter dismissed the question. His personal projects had always fallen outside the purview of embargos and bans, and he proceeded as if nothing had changed.

This time, however, the Queen directly overruled him. Sir Richard's fleet was commandeered and put at the disposal of Sir Francis Drake, who was in charge of England's sea defenses. And Raleigh was directed to give Drake any aid that he could.

That, as it turned out, would be considerable. Sir Walter had just commissioned a magnificent privateer, the *Ark Raleigh*, which at 800 tons and 38 guns was the fastest, tightest-turning, most lethal warship afloat. For the coming battle, Sir Walter loaned her to the queen for an IOU of 5,000 pounds. Renamed the *Ark Royal*, she would serve as the Royal Navy's flagship under the command of the Earl of Nottingham, England's Lord High Admiral.

Two crumbs fell from Her Majesty's table—a pair of pinnaces belonging to Grenville, which were so small that Drake had no need of them. These were given to White to take back to Roanoke with as many provisions as he could carry.

Alas, a French pirate ship attacked the pinnaces, plundering one and sending the other scurrying. White was allowed to live, and he returned to England empty-handed, soon followed by the other pinnace.

Meanwhile, the Spanish Armada had sailed, and Sir Francis, Sir Richard, Sir Walter, Sir Martin Frobisher, Sir John Hawkins, and the other sea captains were in the fight of their lives. With their towering fore and stern castles, the Spanish galleons were like floating fortresses that hopelessly outgunned and outnumbered their enemy. All the Spanish needed to do was to get close enough to board the English ships or blow them to pieces.

But the English ships were too quick for them. Sleek, swift, and highly maneuverable, captained by seasoned warriors and manned with superb gunners, they stayed just out of range of their lumbering enemy. Or they suddenly darted in among them to wreak havoc.

The Armada itself was a terror weapon, striking fear into the heart of anyone who saw the topsails of their hundred ships coming over the horizon. But the English had a terror weapon of their own—fire ships. As the Spanish lay at anchor in the roads off Calais, their Fleet Admiral, the Duke of Medina Sidonia, warned his captains not to panic should the English use fire ships, as they had before. But it was hard not to be anxious when eight tall ships, their masts and rigging ablaze, floated towards you on the incoming tide. The Duke may have been unperturbed, but when the powder-stuffed guns on the fire ships started exploding, more than a few Spanish captains cut cable and ran for the open sea—where they were picked off by the waiting English.

Sir Walter, ever by Drake's side, could be excused if for once Roanoke was not in the forefront of his thinking. He did not return to London until March of 1589, more than a year and a half since there had been any contact with the colony. He once again tried to drum up interest in sending another expedition to America, but Virginia was becoming an increasingly hard sell.

To attract new backers, Raleigh came up with another scheme: the privilege of trading tax-free with the new "City of Raleigh" for seven years. Although some merchants were interested, there were no eager investors, and the possibility of a fresh expedition languished for another year.

Finally, at the end of March 1590 John White set sail for Roanoke—two and a half years since he had last seen his daughter and granddaughter. Captain Cocke was in command of the *Hopewell* and the *Moonlight*, and White was further frustrated by the fact that the captain was more interested in privateering in the Caribbean en route than getting to Roanoke as quickly as possible.

At last they reached Point Ferdinando, which White recognized. They were getting close. As they approached Roanoke Island, he climbed up the rigging to get a better view. From there he saw great smoke coming from the land—a sure sign of welcome. They must have been seen.

Now there was a second plume of smoke, this one from the end of the dunes on the Outer Banks. Another welcome?

White was eager to go ashore, but Captain Cocke wisely declared that all shore exploration would be put off till morning when there was better light and what he hoped would be calmer surf.

But in the morning the weather had gotten worse, not better. Captain Cocke was willing to try a landing, with thirteen good sailors at the oars and White as the other passenger. They managed to get through the opening into Pimlico Sound, but it was a near thing. A wave broke over the gunwales and nearly swamped their boat. White bailed furiously, and as he said, by the grace of God they made it into calm water, though all their furniture, victuals, matches, and gunpowder were ruined.

Now they had to watch and pray for the boat behind them to make it. Their sail was still up, and they were coming too fast. Sure enough, a breaking wave capsized them. Some of the men were trapped under the hull; others who couldn't swim clung to it to keep from drowning. Those watching from the shore, powerless to help, could only shake their heads in unbelief. Men were dying before their eyes.

Finally Captain Cocke pushed his boat back out into the water and went out to save those he could, managing to rescue four who otherwise would have perished. As it was, seven men drowned. By this time they had run out of daylight, and Captain Cocke once again wisely called a halt to further exploration.

White couldn't sleep that night. And during it there was another fire on the island. White no longer thought it was a signal fire; he did not know what to think.

When daylight arrived, they found Indian footprints on the sand near their own. So they had not been alone that night, and perhaps the fires had been set by Indians—but why?

The light of day brought no new answers. On the trunk of a tree, they found three Roman letters: C R O—but no cross, even though a hasty departure may have been the reason why they did not finish carving the name of Croatoan Island, the place of Manteo's village.

The search party reached the village of Roanoke, or what was left of it. Clearly it had been abandoned for some time. The buildings were in ruins, and there was no sign of any living soul having been there for many months. White's eye was drawn to a tree near the entrance whose bark had been stripped off. Five feet above the ground, someone had carefully carved "CROATOAN." It had not been done in haste. Nor was there a cross over it. The settlers had gone there out of choice and with deliberate planning.

A more thorough search revealed that trunks belonging to White and others, which had been buried to prevent them from being plundered, had nonetheless been located and ransacked. "Many of my things [were] spoiled and broken, and my books torn from the covers, the frames of some of my pictures and maps rotten and spoiled with rain."[12]

It was getting late, and once again the weather was deteriorating. Captain Cocke had already lost three of his four anchors, not to mention seven of his crewmen to these hostile shores. He was finished with the Outer Banks and Roanoke. And he was not about to put his ship and crew into further jeopardy by sailing down to Croatoan Island. If White wanted to search there, he was welcome to come back in the spring. But if the *Hopewell* had any hope of beating the hurricane season home, they would be leaving now. Distant thunder rumbled; it was starting to rain. The wind picked up and tore a few more pages from White's books, sending them into nearby bushes.

The rest of the landing party began leaving for the boat that would take them back to the ship. John White fell in behind them and with a shudder pulled his cloak more closely about his shoulders. At the shore, waiting his turn to get in the boat, he remembered that this was where his daughter and granddaughter had stood as he had waved good-bye to them.

Looking at the darkening sky above, his eyes filled with tears as he realized how unlikely it was that he would ever see them again. With his voice breaking, he commended them and the other Roanoke colonists "to the merciful help of the Almighty, whom I humbly beseech to help and comfort them."[13]

6

GARBOIL

*W*ith the death of the Virgin Queen in 1603, the prospects for the American colony bearing her name dimmed. Its champion had always been Sir Walter Raleigh, who now had lost his chief backer and sole means of support. James, the new King, had little use for Raleigh's clever, witty ways and foppish airs, and he despised him for introducing that filthy habit, tobacco, into English society. The King soon had Raleigh clapped in irons and relegated to the Tower of London on trumped-up charges of treason. There was a show trial, and Raleigh was condemned to death.

But the beheading would have to be put off for a season, for Raleigh was now a favorite of the people, having emerged from the victory over the Spanish Armada as one of England's intrepid sea dogs, along with Drake and Hawkins.

Interest in the Virginia Colony languished. Despite the positive published reports by Harriot and others, dark tales of colonists barely avoiding starvation in the New World had done their work. From the point of view of potential financial backers (now called Partners), the costs were prohibitive. And thus far, the returns were not simply meager—they were nonexistent.

One thing kept the New World flame flickering: the fate of the lost colonists of Roanoke. Voyagers returned to England with rumors of sightings and artifacts that indicated they were still alive—stories that made the rounds of the English taverns, gaining credibility with each retelling. Similarly a new play by Ben Johnson, *Eastward Hoe*, imagined the fate of the abandoned settlers and told of native inhabitants using jewel-encrusted chamber pots of solid gold. This was an outlandish fancy, of course, but it gained credence from the endless parade of fat Spanish galleons laden with New World gold and silver.

Ironically, Sir John Popham, the Lord Chief Justice who had presided over Raleigh's trial, now fanned the flames of interest in the New World, and by the spring of 1606 another westward adventure was gathering.

One of Raleigh's old partners, Richard Hakluyt, was especially helpful. Having outfitted the first Roanoke expedition twenty-one years before, he knew what supplies were needed. Soon crates and barrels began piling up on the London docks. Unlike his predecessor, King James was not inclined to help the partners equip the venture, so they were forced to purchase old (cheap) armor and swords left over from past European wars.

The King was inclined, however, to set the tone for the colonists in the Virginia Charter. He charged them with the "propagating of Christian religion to such people as yet live in darkness and miserable ignorance of the true knowledge and worship of God, and [that they should] in time bring the infidels and savages living in those parts, into human civility and to a settled and quiet government."

The Partners, taking their lead from the King, stated as one of their main purposes: "To preach and baptize into Christian religion and by the propagation of the Gospel, to recover out of the arms of the devil a number of poor and miserable souls wrapped up into death in almost invincible ignorance."[1]

And they piously advised the embarking colonists, "The way to prosper and achieve good success is to make yourselves all of one mind for the good of your country and your own, and to serve and fear God, the giver of all goodness, for every plantation which our heavenly Father hath *not* planted shall be rooted out."

To listen to all this wise counsel, one might assume that the leaders of this colonization effort would indeed be of one mind and one accord and that bearing the Light of Christ would be a primary concern. Unfortunately, the facts would soon demonstrate otherwise.

There were 104 men on the expedition, but only one minister, Robert Hunt. Handpicked by the aristocratic Edward-Maria Wingfield, who was the only Partner to accompany them, the Oxford-educated Hunt was chosen for what Wingfield thought would be a conventional, middle-of-the-road Anglicanism. The last thing he wanted was a clergyman tainted by that radical offshoot known as Puritanism.

As for bearing the Light of Christ to heathen, well, that was, of course, important. But this was first and foremost a commercial venture; the Partners were expecting a good return on their investment, and the sooner, the better.

Three ships would be going to Virginia. At sea, those on board the *Susan Constant*, the *Godspeed*, and the *Discovery* would be under the command of seasoned captain Christopher Newport, who had sailed those waters on John White's Roanoke rescue mission. Once they arrived, however, they would be governed by a Council whose membership would be revealed when they broke open their sealed orders.

It should be noted that while their stated purpose was to establish a plantation, no women were included. Nor were these men the heads of households, bent on carving out a homestead in the wilderness, to which they would later bring their families. The soil was known to be rich; growing English crops should not be difficult. But there were no farmers among them. Had they learned nothing from Roanoke? What there were in abundance were gentlemen, down on their luck and looking for a miraculous deliverance but without having to labor for it. Fully half their number felt it was beneath their status to work with their hands. There were others along to do that sort of thing.

Robert Hunt had a different perspective. In his first sermon at sea, he pointedly declared that "we are *all* laborers in the same vineyard." Was anyone listening? What Wingfield termed "garboil"—fractious contention—

broke out on all three ships almost immediately. For instance, Captain John Smith, a short and powerful, red-haired Lincolnshire soldier of fortune, had already packed a lifetime of adventure into his twenty-seven years. A proud man who had earned his stripes in combat on a dozen battlefronts, he had no use for Wingfield, who was in turn infuriated by Smith's lack of respect for his rank. In fact, Wingfield was hoping to see Smith hanged for supposedly wanting to seize power and run the entire expedition. While this may have been the most prominent example of contentiousness, few of the other passengers seemed interested in being of one mind and one accord.

To make matters worse, the weather was miserable. They weighed anchor on December 19 and dropped down the River Thames to the open sea, only to return two weeks later, defeated by foul weather and contrary winds. Anchoring off the coast of England, they waited out one winter storm after another, steadily consuming the provisions that were intended to see them through till their first harvest.

The garboil grew steadily more intense, setting a precedent that would hound the Jamestown settlement for years to come. According to Smith, a good deal of it was now focused against Reverend Hunt in an attempt to force him to leave the expedition, for his home was only a dozen miles away from their anchorage. How dare he tell them that their backbiting and contentiousness was sinful and wrong! The "many discontents" against him might have succeeded "had he not with the water of patience, and his godly exhortations [but chiefly by his true devoted examples] quenched those flames of envy and dissension."[2]

Finally, six full weeks after their initial departure, they set sail for the New World, arriving in late April at the south shore of Chesapeake Bay. They were astonished at the beauty of the place. One of the gentlemen, George Percy, recorded in his journal, "fair meadows and goodly tall trees, with such fresh waters running through the woods, as I was almost ravished at the sight thereof."[3]

It was springtime in Virginia. Warm, soft breezes, new greenery everywhere, dogwood trees in full blossom . . . they must have thought they had been readmitted to the Garden of Eden. They had yet to see any Indians, but the published accounts of both Harriot and Hakluyt had led them to believe that they would be warmly received.

This was not exactly the case. Venturing ashore, they were suddenly attacked by the natives, who had silently crawled toward them on all fours, their bows clenched between their teeth. Arrows flew, wounding several. But the Indians were no match for the muskets now leveled at them. The noise of these guns firing and the splinters from shattered tree limbs caused the attackers to run for their lives. Nonetheless, another unfortunate precedent had been set.

As the expedition breathed a collective sigh of relief, Robert Hunt must have wondered if they would ever get close enough to these savages to gain their trust, let alone tell them about a living, risen Savior who had died for their sins.

The garboil, meanwhile, continued unabated. At least at sea, there had been a cap on it because all acknowledged Captain Newport's authority. But now that they had arrived and Newport had claimed the land for King James, it was time to open their sealed orders. They revealed a preselected Council of seven, including Wingfield, who was elected their President, and Bartholomew Gosnold, who had sailed with Raleigh on his first expedition. A Cambridge graduate and friend of Richard Hakluyt, he knew the coast better than any of them except Newport and had even applied for a charter himself. A champion of the colony, Gosnold had recruited Wingfield and Smith. The orders also named Smith, but while he was by far the most capable, he was kept off the Council by Wingfield's outstanding charges against him. Before long, Council members, with the exception of Gosnold, were vying and contending with one another for dominance.

Robert Hunt now exercised his spiritual authority, requiring all to remain aboard for three days, to search their hearts and repent for all the backbiting and contention. When they went ashore to stay, it would be with clean hands and pure hearts. It is worth noting that they actually obeyed. For the most part, these men were churchgoing Anglicans. God might not be everything to them, as He was to the early missionaries or to the Pilgrims or Puritans who would follow them to America. But He was real to them and was a definite part of their lives. The trouble was, He was only a part.

They disembarked on April 29, 1607, and Hunt led them up a windswept dune at a place they named Cape Henry, in honor of the King's elder son. There they planted a seven-foot, rough-hewn oak cross, which they had brought with them from England.

Reminding them of the Biblical admonition from the Partners, "Every plantation which my Heavenly Father hath not planted, shall be rooted up," Hunt then prophetically declared, "From these very shores, the Gospel shall go forth to not only this New World, but the entire world."[4]

Now that they were ashore, all efforts had to be focused on finding a suitable site and establishing the plantation. They sailed up the James River until they were a good eighty miles from the ocean. That was in keeping with their instructions, which advised that they be far enough upriver to be well hidden from the prying eyes of the Spanish and French. But as Gosnold pointed out, their instructions also called for them to be far removed from swamps, on high ground with good drainage, preferably open land that would be easier to farm—and defend.

Wingfield and the majority of the Council disagreed. What was wrong, they asked, with establishing the plantation right where they were? They were tied up next to a long narrow peninsula that at high tide was almost an island. True, it was marshy and heavily wooded with no springs for fresh water, yet it had one great advantage: the riverbed there was so deep that large vessels could come right alongside, tying up to the trees.

Besides, everyone was thoroughly sick of being on board the ships and was itching to get ashore. The weather was warm and close to idyllic; even Smith was lulled into accepting the majority's decision. Thus was a third precedent set for Jamestown decision-making: if in doubt, choose the easier way.

The laborers among them now set about erecting shelters and a wall of bent boughs, while the Council debated over the proposed layout of the settlement, and some of the gentlemen opened oysters in search of pearls.

For a while, the still chilly nights of spring worked to the settlers' advantage, keeping down the mosquito population in the swamplands that surrounded them. But as summer approached and the heat and humidity grew steadily more oppressive, the true face of Jamestown began to emerge. The only drinking water came from the river. At low tide it was foul; at high tide it was brackish from ocean water creeping upriver. Looking for fresh water, they dug shallow wells too close to their waste disposal area. The "bloody flux" (typhoid fever) was inevitable.

Just as deadly were the mosquitoes. Rising in swarms from the swamps, they brought the pestilence of swamp fever (malaria), which began to take its toll on the defenseless settlers. Men became sick and began to die, and there was nothing they could do to stem the tide of illness.

To make matters worse, things were not going well with the Indians. The initial contact with members of the Paspahegh, in whose territory they had settled, seemed friendly. The Indians made it clear that their chief would soon be coming with a welcoming gift of a deer. But when he arrived, it was with a hundred armed warriors! When an Indian was caught stealing an English hatchet, its owner struck back. Another warrior retaliated against the Englishman with a wooden sword, and the English went for their guns. The Paspahegh ran away, angry. And while the English reaction was entirely understandable, there was now definite enmity between whites and Indians.

After a week of off-loading supplies, Captain Newport was ready for some exploration, so he led twenty-one men on a trip further up the James. One of those with him was George Percy, who recorded in his journal that he caught a glimpse of "a savage boy, about the age of ten years, which had a head of hair of a perfect yellow and a reasonably white skin, which is a miracle amongst savages."[5]

Was he an offspring of the lost Roanoke settlers? There was no time to go searching for him—or them. All efforts now had to be focused on building up the plantation and staying alive.

When Newport's party returned to the settlement, they learned that a force of some two hundred Indians had ambushed the remaining men outside their flimsy palisade, killing one and wounding twelve or thirteen. Only the ships' small cannons were able to drive them off. Immediately they set to work to replace the plantation's wall of bent boughs with a high palisade of sharpened stakes.

In light of the military emergency, Robert Hunt and Captain Newport persuaded the Council to drop all the charges against Smith, and he was

111

seated on the Council. The next day "Good Mr. Hunt" gathered everyone together under the shade of an old sail for the service of Holy Communion. With a plank nailed between two trees serving as the altar, he pointed out that the "common union" of the sacrament symbolized the need for them to live in harmony with one another.

With a new sense of unity supposedly established, Newport decided it was time for him to return to England, which he did on June 21, leaving the smaller pinnace *Discovery* behind for the use of the settlement. He went with the gentlemen's blessing because the ship's hold was filled with promising ore samples that they hoped would make them all rich. Anyone could see the nuggets in it. None of them recognized them for what they were: iron pyrites, more commonly known today as fool's gold.

Relations with the Indians were rapidly deteriorating, but none of the settlers stopped to think that these same Indians might soon be all that stood between them and starvation. Somehow, amid all the exploring, palisade-building, shelter-making, and Indian-fighting, they had neglected to put in a crop. In less than a month their provisions would run out, and with no harvest, they would be wholly dependent on the only food available other than shellfish or game: Indian corn. They would have to buy it, trade for it, or, if necessary, take it at gunpoint.

By August men were dying at a horrific rate, sometimes three or four in a single night. If the Indians had any idea how weak they were, they could have broken through the palisade and slaughtered them all. It was only the mercy of God (and the prayers of a few like Robert Hunt) that kept them from realizing this. As George Percy put it, "If it had not pleased God to have put a terror in the savages' hearts, we had all perished." Indeed, it could only have been God, because "our men night and day [were] groaning in every corner of the fort and most pitiful to hear."[6]

Moreover, when the Indians finally did approach, it was with gifts of food—corn bread, venison, fish, and squirrels. Immediately the men began to revive. As Smith, not a particularly spiritual man, noted, "God, the patron of all good endeavors in that desperate extremity, so changed the hearts of the savages that they brought such plenty of their fruits and provisions, as no man wanted."[7]

Still, the relief was only temporary; all too soon the dying began again. Now veteran explorer Bartholomew Gosnold passed away, and that was a grievous loss. He had been a source of stability and wisdom that simply could not be replaced.

Hunt did all he could to bring God into their lives. Already doing more than his share of the heavy manual labor, he had hoped that his example might inspire the gentlemen to come and do likewise. It didn't. There were also several services every Sunday under the sail. The gentlemen took seats on the front plank as was their due, but there is no evidence that they ever repented for their selfish attitudes.

John Smith paid tribute to Robert Hunt's ministry among them, calling him "an honest, religious, and courageous divine," saying that "our factions were often qualified [and] our wants and greatest extremities . . . comforted."[8] Though there is no further explanation, we can imagine that Hunt spent much time tending the sick, making sure they got their fair share of whatever meager rations were their lot and bringing them water when they thirsted.

Most of all, we can be certain that Hunt heard their confessions and prayed with them as their end drew near. Sometimes only great suffering, coupled with the prospect of one's imminent demise, can soften a heart toward God. With the compassion of Christ, Hunt would have listened as dying men poured out their hearts to him. And surely, some of those who previously had no particular interest in the Savior would have ended up in eternity with Him, thanks to the gentle ministrations of Robert Hunt.

By August they were on half-rations—half a pint of boiled wheat and barley per man per day. It was all that was left of their provisions. And "having fried some 26 weeks in the hold, [it] contained as many worms as grains."[9]

Just as they realized that even this pathetic supply would run out in another two weeks, Smith reports that "it pleased God [in our extremity] to move the Indians to bring us corn . . . when we rather expected they would destroy us"[10]

Many of the weak and sick men were soon back on their feet, but the deaths continued. By the middle of September, Smith counted forty-six dead.

The arrival of cooler fall weather brought relief from the mosquitoes and an added bonus: flights of migrating geese and ducks suddenly appeared on the river. For at least a few days the settlers feasted on fresh roasted fowl. But the little colony's condition remained desperate. Smith's disgust with the number of men who refused to work shows in his initial record of events: "At this time were most of our chiefest men either sick or discontented." As for the others, "they would rather starve and rot with idleness, than be persuaded to do anything for their own relief."[11]

By late fall their provisions were again almost gone. So the Council sent Smith and nine others out immediately on a trading expedition, offering the Indians trinkets in exchange for corn and oysters and bread. But although the red-bearded soldier of fortune had many virtues, patience was not one of them. When negotiations became drawn out, Smith found it quicker to draw his sword, and his trading often became raiding. Again and again he went out, often returning with an abundance of corn and oysters and bread. Some settlers might not appreciate his blunt and commanding ways, but he was often all that stood between them and starvation.

In November, after returning with supplies, Smith found that Wingfield and one of his cronies, George Kendall, had been plotting to abandon the colony and sail the pinnace home to England. Kendall was put up against the palisade and shot, while Wingfield himself was placed under arrest until he could be sent home for the other Partners to deal with.

By now Smith had learned of a great sachem, Powhatan*, who was chief over all the chiefs of that region. This was the man Smith needed to meet. But how that meeting came about was hardly the way he would have chosen.

On a corn-seeking expedition a few days after Christmas, Smith was ambushed. Thinking fast, he tied his Indian guide to him and used him as a shield from the arrows being loosed in his direction. The guide yelled at the ambushers to stop shooting, and they did. Now Smith made a run

*His name was actually Wahunsonacock, and his people were the Powhatan, but modern historical usage has him as Powhatan.

for it, only to get caught in a quagmire. Sinking, he saw that his only hope was to appeal to these same Indians who had attacked him.

But how? Then it came to him: He told their leader—who turned out to be Opechancano, Powhatan's half brother—of a magical instrument he had in his pocket, with a needle that always sought the pole star. The Indian's eyes widened. He nodded to his men, who pulled Smith out of the quicksand. When Smith pulled out his compass and demonstrated its workings to them, Opechancano was so fascinated that he decided to take it and Smith to Powhatan, whose headquarters was a village called Weromocomoco.

Their meeting took place on an unusually warm winter afternoon, with the sun filtering through the tall fir trees of the Virginia tidewater. Powhatan, whose erect and muscular stature belied his sixty-plus years, received him in a long, low building made of closely woven branches. Wrapped in a coonskin cloak, the great sachem was seated on an elevated platform at the end of the hall, with handmaidens at either side, ready at his beck and call. In front of him was a fire, and on either side were ten warriors with fiercely painted faces and feathers in their hair.

As Smith told Powhatan of the father of the sea, Newport, who would be coming back, and of all the ships the great king of England had, each with large guns that could knock down trees standing three fields away—he watched Powhatan's face closely. The sachem seemed impressed, though he did his best not to let it show.

Smith knew that Powhatan's great authority meant that he was extremely shrewd and politically skillful. What he didn't know was that some of Powhatan's elders had prophesied to him that white men would come on three separate occasions and try to plant a colony there. The first two times they would fail, but the third time they would succeed, and the native people would then be subjugated by them.[12]

To keep the vision from coming to pass, Powhatan had decided to kill Smith that very afternoon. Now he instructed his men to bind him and bend him over two half-buried boulders in the ground. Against these Smith's head would be held, while his brains were bashed out.

For once Smith's quick wit and tongue failed him. There was nothing he could do. And while his narrative makes no mention of it, the mercy of

God was still in operation. Suddenly Powhatan's favorite child, his bright and lovely twelve-year-old daughter, Pocahontas (Little Wanton), ran up to the kneeling Smith and laid her head on top of his. If her father was going to split Smith's skull, he would have to split his daughter's first.

Powhatan was shocked—and fearful. Only the Great Spirit could have inspired her to do what she had just done. For a long moment he weighed the situation. Then he announced that he was pardoning Smith, declaring eternal friendship, and sending him home with a substantial gift of corn.[13]

When he got back to the fort, Smith found only thirty-eight men left alive and Wingfield once again plotting to flee with the pinnace. Smith calmly informed him that if he should attempt it, Smith would blow him and the little ship to bits, using the cannon that were now ashore.

Fortunately, Pocahontas was determined to help them. She now came to the settlement every four or five days with her attendants, bearing sustaining gifts of venison, grain, fish, and wild game. A delightfully free spirit, she entertained the settlers by doing cartwheels through the streets. Smith acknowledged that her continuing kindness had kept them alive—"a true proof of God's love to the action."[14]

Although all of them were grateful, none of their bad attitudes had changed in the least. As long as they had enough to eat today, they would not worry about tomorrow until tomorrow. Many of the gentlemen among these early settlers were soldiers, not farmers. They didn't mind lifting a spade if they were digging for gold, but they still refused to prepare the ground for a crop. The artisans, and even those expected by the Partners to do the manual labor, were city people who knew nothing of farming and balked at chopping fields out of the forest with hand tools and no work animals. Smith put it bluntly: they "never did know what a day's work was . . . poor Gentlemen, tradesmen, serving-men, libertines, and such like, ten times more fit to spoil a Commonwealth than either begin one or help to maintain one."[15] *Twenty years* would pass before the Virginia Colony would finally plant a crop large enough to sustain itself.

New Year's Day 1608 was immediately followed by the long-awaited return of Christopher Newport. On the *John and Francis* he had brought provisions and one hundred settlers—what the company called the First

Supply—but he was greeted by only thirty-eight gaunt and miserable survivors. Nearly three-quarters of the original 144 settlers that Newport had originally brought over had died.

He arrived just in time to save John Smith's neck—literally. Smith had come back from Powhatan at the moment that the last two remaining Council members, Martin and Ratcliffe, were casting off in the pinnace to sail for England. They insisted that they were going "to fetch more supplies," though Smith doubted that Virginia would ever see either one of them again. Fast work with a fowling piece and a culverin put a stop to their departure, but they retaliated by arresting Smith and sentencing him to death by hanging for "treason against the governing authority." Smith had thus joined Wingfield under arrest, until Newport set them both free, restoring Smith (but not Wingfield) to the Council.

Sadly, the hope that Newport's added supplies had brought the colony was all too brief. On January 7 the little settlement accidentally caught fire, and in a few minutes most of Newport's provisions, the tents, blankets, bedding, clothes, and all but three houses—were destroyed. Even the palisade was burned.

Robert Hunt lost not only his clothes, but the one earthly possession that mattered to him, his small library of books. Smith, whose life may have been more touched by Hunt's example than most, marveled at his spiritual courage. "None did ever hear him repine of his loss."[16] Hunt seemed to be the only man in Virginia willing to "suffer the loss of all things in order to gain Christ."

Worst of all, since the fire had come in "the extreme frost," more lives were lost before new shelter could be erected.

Once again it was April, the planting month. The loss of food supplies in the fire had meant that throughout the winter the colony remained in desperate straits. The colonists were largely dependent on the generosity of the Indians, although a lively black market had sprung up between those who still had money and unscrupulous sailors on the *John and Francis*, who were stealing supplies from the ship's stores and selling them. Thus, a few of the English were eating quite well, while others around them were slowly starving.

The tribes of the Tidewater, busy planting the corn they would need for the next winter, were well aware of the colony's condition. As one of them said to a settler: "We can plant anywhere . . . and we know that you cannot live [without] our harvest, and that relief we bring you."[17]

The Indians undoubtedly offered to help the English grow enough of their own crops to become self-sustaining, but once again the Jamestown settlers had more important things to do. After all, Captain Smith had just successfully traded with Powhatan for a three-month supply of corn. Besides, there were fresh deposits of gold-bearing ore to be dug. Newport himself had become convinced that Jamestown was sitting on a foundation of gold, so as Smith disgustedly put it, there was "no talk, no hope, no work, but dig gold, wash gold, refine gold, load gold."[18] And once again, it would turn out to be fool's gold.

By April 10 Newport was satisfied that he had stowed enough ore on the *John and Francis*, so he set sail for England. Smith, now the only Council member still functioning, took advantage of his sole authority and got everyone busy. Soon there were work crews repairing the palisade and the storehouse, rebuilding the church, clearing fields, and planting corn. At least, they were supposed to be planting. But try as he might, he could not get the settlers to take planting seriously. The way they looked at it, more supply ships would be coming any day now.

And this one time, they happened to be right. The supply ship *Phoenix*, which had initially accompanied Newport but disappeared off the Virginia Capes, finally showed up with forty more settlers and plenty of provisions. Captain Francis Nelson had gone to the West Indies and thoughtfully loaded up the ship with food. When they added what he brought to what they already had, they estimated there was enough food for six months. "He had not any thing but he freely imparted it . . . we would not have wished more than he did for us."[19]

Thanks to the grace of God and the foresight of Captain Nelson, the people of Jamestown had been handed a temporary reprieve from their perpetual food crisis. Did they use it to plant corn? No, they saw no need to.

When it came time for the *Phoenix* to return to England, John Smith made sure that this cargo would be worth something to the Partners—a load of cedar wood. The ship also carried something quite small, but of equal value: a manuscript entitled *A True Relation*. This was the first history of Jamestown—John Smith's somewhat self-serving account of events. Though he declined to relate the most ghastly stories and reserved some of his harsher judgments for later accounts, he was honest about the garboil and made no attempt to cover up the colony's struggles.

As letters from Virginia and the returning sailors of the *John and Francis* and the *Phoenix* began to spread grim stories of failed leadership, corn raids on Indian villages that killed innocent women and children, and summary executions, the Partners frantically attempted damage control. To counteract the flow of bad news, they convinced some Church of England ministers to preach the possibilities of sharing the Good News of Christianity with the heathen natives of Virginia. From the pulpit of Paul's Cross, Crakenthorpe preached: "What glory! What honor to our Sovereign! What comfort to those subjects who shall be the means of furthering so happy a work!"[20] And Richard Crashaw admonished his flock: "Let us then believe no tales, regard no slanders . . . fear no shadows, care for no oppositions, respect no losses that may befall, nor be daunted with any discouragements whatever!"[21]

They further decided to rush into print John Smith's history, criticism and all, but to put a positive spin on it by arranging for an enthusiastic preface by none other than Thomas Harriot. Claiming that the hardest part of building a colony in Virginia was now accomplished, Harriot lauded what remained to be done as "most honorable, and the end to the high glory of God, to the erecting of true religion among infidels, to the overthrow of superstition and idolatry, to the winning of many thousands of wandering sheep into Christ's fold, who [until] now have strayed in the unknown paths of paganism, idolatry, and superstition."[22]

He never dreamed that Jamestown's darkest night was still to come.

7

"DAMN YOUR SOULS! MAKE TOBACCO!"

hen Christopher Newport finally returned to Jamestown in the fall of 1608 on the *Mary and Margaret*, he found that beneficial changes had been made. John Smith had been elected President, and he had put everyone, including gentlemen, to work repairing the storehouses and enlarging the fort. He had even overseen the planting and harvesting of a small but successful corn crop, which they harvested and stored in casks. However, when they had need of it, they found that rain had gotten into the casks and ruined it. What was more, most of the provisions from the previous supply ship, *Phoenix*, had been consumed. Worst of all, Newport had now brought seventy new settlers with him, including the first two women to arrive at Jamestown—and no food. Once again, the little colony was in crisis and on the verge of collapse.

Newport also brought with him orders from the Virginia Company Partners to bring Powhatan under control by officially crowning him as a subject king under the lordship of His Majesty, James I. As added inducements to get Powhatan to accept his subordinate position, the English were to give him a copper crown, a few scarlet robes, a washbasin and pitcher, and, best of all, a truly king-sized bed.

John Smith protested to Newport that crowning Powhatan would inflate his self-importance to the point that he would be impossible to deal with. Besides, the whole thing was a waste of good working time. Why didn't they just give Powhatan his presents and forget this coronation business? But Newport had his orders, and orders were orders.

The Captain did send Smith to Powhatan, to invite him to come to Jamestown and there receive presents from the King of England. The sachem reacted with indignation: "If your King has sent me presents, I also am a King, and this is my land: eight days I will stay to receive them. Your Father is to come to me, not I to him, nor yet to your fort." In the face of that outburst Smith felt it best not to tell Powhatan about the plans to crown him.

No one does coronations better than the English, who by 1608 had been doing them for a very long time. All must be done properly and in good order, which meant that the subject had to kneel to receive his or her crown.

Powhatan had put on his bright new red robe and was quite ready to let the English do whatever it was they were going to do, until they brought up the matter of kneeling. Though he understood nothing of the protocol of English royal coronations, he understood all too well what kneeling in front of someone meant. It was a sign of submission, and he was not about to do it.

"A foul trouble there was to make him kneel to receive his crown," wrote Smith, "he neither knowing the majesty nor meaning of a crown, nor bending of the knee, endured so many persuasions, examples, and instructions, as tired them all."

Finally, Smith and Newport decided that "the laying on of hands" was called for. "At last by leaning hard on his shoulders, he a little stooped, and three [men] having the crown in their hands put it on his head." When the deed was done, a signal pistol was fired, and the boats fired a loud salute from their cannons, which caused Powhatan to "start up in a horrible fear, till he saw all was well."[1] The English threw their hats in the air and shouted, "Long live the King!" Thus ended the first and only coronation to take place on North American soil.

The new vassal King responded with a small gift of seven or eight bushels of wheat, and Newport was able to buy an equal amount in the Indian village, but the English were heading back to Jamestown with only several days' worth of food for the colony.

In London the Partners had given Christopher Newport another order: he was to find or bring back word of "any of them sent by Sir Walter Raleigh"—the lost colonists of Roanoke. To his credit, Smith had set out on three separate exploring expeditions in 1608 to try to discover the fate of Raleigh's 1587 expedition, but he had returned with nothing but intriguing rumors.* Far southwest of Jamestown, one Indian chief and two English settlers were told that at a village called Pakerikanick there were "four men clothed" that had come from Roanoke, but they broke off their search. Smith kept hearing from the Indians about a tribe southwest of Chesapeake Bay whose people had houses built with stone walls and one story above another, "so taught them by those English."[2]

To Smith, there was a challenge far more critical than discovering the fate of the lost colonists. He had around two hundred mouths to feed now, each needing a pint of grain per day, which meant he had to find about twenty-two bushels every week. As fall turned into winter, trade with the Indians dried up because they were now demanding English weapons in exchange for their corn. It seems likely that the sailors from the *Mary and Margaret* were offering swords to the Indians for food.

The situation became desperate when they realized that there was not even enough food in the colony to provision the *Mary and Margaret* for the voyage home. Finally, just before Christmas, Smith took forty-six men with him in the pinnace to force Powhatan to resume trading, even if he had to capture the sachem to do it.

Powhatan was on guard and somewhat hostile, undoubtedly having been warned of Smith's intentions by two carpenters who had run away from Jamestown's troubles to live with the Indians. The wily old chief and Smith, both suspicious of each other, began a classic cat-and-mouse game.

---

*For further information on the fate of the lost colony of Roanoke, see Appendix One.

The chief claimed that he had no corn to spare in trade. Then he indicated that he would swap a basket of corn for one full of copper. Finally, he upped the ante by refusing to trade corn for anything except guns and swords.

When Smith curtly replied that he would do nothing of the sort, Powhatan let it drop that he knew that Smith intended to attack him, but the chief claimed that on his part he wanted no war with the English. Then he added some words of wisdom: "Captain Smith, having seen the death of all my people thrice, and not anyone living of those three generations but myself, I know the difference between peace and war better than any in my country. . . . Think you I am so simple as not to know it is better to eat good meat, lie well, and sleep quietly with my women and children, laugh and be merry with you, have copper, hatchets or what I want, being your friend, than be forced to fly from all, lie cold in the woods, feed upon acorns, roots, and such trash, and be so hunted by you that I can neither rest, eat, or sleep?"

Powhatan continued: "Let this, therefore, assure you of our love, and every year our friendly trade shall furnish you with corn—and now, also, if you would come in friendly manner and not thus, with your guns and swords as if to invade your foes . . . if you intend to be friendly as you say, send [away] your arms that I may believe you, for you see the love I bear you doth cause me thus nakedly to forget myself."[3]

Smith was not about to render himself and his men defenseless in Powhatan's village. He countered with the offer that he and his bodyguard of eight would come ashore from the pinnace the next day, unarmed. In the meantime, he arranged for a secret signal, at which his main force would suddenly swarm ashore and take Powhatan. But the canny chief was on to him and slipped away just as Smith attempted to spring his trap. Then it was all Smith and his men could do to extricate themselves from the midst of several hundred angry warriors and flee back to the pinnace, which was stuck in the low-tide mud of the river.

Powhatan was now through playing games with Smith, and he angrily determined to send his warriors to kill the captain and all his men before daylight. Once again, however, God intervened. William Simons writes: "The eternal and all-seeing God did prevent [Powhatan], and by a strange means. For Pocahontas, his dearest jewel and daughter, in that dark night came through the irksome woods, and told our Captain [that food] should be sent to us by and by; but Powhatan and all the power he could make, would after come and kill us. . . . Therefore if we would live she wished us presently to be gone . . . with the tears running down her cheeks, she said . . . [that] if Powhatan should know it, she were but dead, and so she ran away by her self as she had come."[4]

Sure enough, in less than an hour about ten of Powhatan's best warriors came with food. Smith shrewdly made the Indians taste every portion before he and his men ate, and then he sent them back to their chief. Throughout the night other Indians kept coming to check on them, but as soon as the tide was high enough to float the pinnace off the mud, Smith slipped downriver to safety.

Back in Jamestown, Smith still had no solution to the food problem. So, he launched attacks on the Paspahegh and the Chickahominy Indians— burning their dwellings, killing some and capturing others, and always taking their food supplies to feed the colony. From such raids Smith gathered enough provisions to finally outfit the *Mary and Margaret* for the voyage home to England, and Newport departed just after Christmas.

For a few winter months Jamestown's fortunes seemed to revive. Smith, now the sole authority, enforced a strict daily work schedule, and the settlers began to produce. In three months they made pitch, tar, glass, and soap to send back to England with the next ship; they also dug a well, built about twenty houses, repaired the church, made weirs and nets for fishing, built a blockhouse on the neck, and actually dug and planted thirty to forty acres.

Optimism began to rise. Did they not have 279 casks of plundered corn still in the storehouse? Maybe things were finally starting to work out for Jamestown.

It was not to be.

When it came time to think about planting a new corn crop, they went to check on their supply and found that the rats that plagued their settlement had gotten into it, and rain had finished off most of what the rats had not consumed. Staring at the soggy and putrid mess inside the casks, they realized the scope of the disaster: they had no food at all.

Drastic measures were called for. Half of the company went down to the oyster banks at the mouth of the river to attempt to live on shellfish. Another party went upriver, hoping to survive on wild berries and acorns. Still others went down to Point Comfort to fish. Typically, the fishing party could not agree on where to cast their nets, and so they never did. A number of settlers simply ran away to Powhatan, who allowed them to stay, as long as they worked for their food. Of those who did not desert to the Indians, many managed to stay alive by stealing from each other—implements, kettles, even guns—and trading them to the Indians for a capful of corn.

Even so, more than half their number perished, including good Mr. Hunt. His death meant they were now bereft of perhaps the major source of spiritual solace among them. He was sorely missed.

Just when all appeared hopeless, in July a small, well-provisioned ship arrived. Although Captain Samuel Argall's food supplies had been intended for trade with the Indians, he was gracious enough to let Smith take them for the starving settlers. They were reprieved—for the moment.

Captain Argall was the bearer of important tidings: the London merchants had reorganized the Virginia enterprise and had obtained a new charter from the King, creating a Royal Council that would hereafter appoint a governor for the colony. The Council had already chosen Baron De La Warr to be Governor, but because he was unable to go to Virginia immediately, they had sent a large fleet of nine ships under the sea command of Admiral George Somers, with Sir Thomas Gates to take over as interim Governor at Jamestown until De La Warr could come.

Argall said that Gates and Somers had sailed for Virginia in May of 1609 in the flagship *Sea Venture*, about the time Smith had sent starving men down to the oyster beds. Woefully overcrowded with some five hundred passengers, including women and children, with typical Virginia "luck," the ships sailed straight into the teeth of a hurricane in the area now known as the Bermuda Triangle.

The fleet was scattered all over the Atlantic. One ship went down; another returned to England. As for the flagship, after three days of incessant storm, she had ten feet of water in her hold, and her pumps were giving out. Just as she about to founder, out of the darkness loomed the darker silhouette of the land known as Devil's Island. ("Hell is empty, and all the devils are here!" wrote William Shakespeare of the still-vexed Bermoothes in *The Tempest*, the play inspired by this episode). In truth, Bermuda was "supposed to be enchanted and inhabited with witches and devils," wrote Somers, and "so wondrous dangerous of rocks" that none could approach it without "unspeakable hazard of shipwreck."[5]

Miraculously the *Sea Venture* was not smashed to pieces on the barrier reef but found itself wedged between two large coral formations—with the tide going out. The ship itself might not be salvageable, but everything aboard her, including her rigging and her timbers, would be. She was off-loaded with comparative ease and then dismantled. Thus, under Gates and Somers, all 150 on board were forced by an "act of God" to spend an exceedingly pleasant nine-month sojourn on a lush, uninhabited island that seemed more like paradise than hell.

In the event of a hurricane, the fleet had specific standing orders: no matter how scattered, all ships were to rendezvous at Bermuda. Had the eight surviving vessels simply followed orders, they, too, would have been abundantly blessed. Their passengers would have rapidly recovered from the plague-like disease that had spread through a number of the ships, and all would have proceeded to Jamestown with holds filled with fresh victuals, to replace those that had been ruined by the storms. They would have saved the colony then and there.

However, the sea captains chose the easier way. Continuing westward, they limped up and down the Atlantic seaboard, until six of the ships finally found their way to Jamestown in August of 1609, about a month after Argall's arrival.

But they had brought four hundred passengers. Sick, helpless, and starving, they now joined the survivors who who had consumed Argall's provisions and were once again out of food. The famished newcomers rushed ashore and ran through the cornfields, stripping the stalks bare of the still-green ears—ensuring that in the coming fall as many would die of despair as of disease.

When Smith found out that he was to be replaced but that his replacement was presumed lost at sea, he continued to exert his authority as best he could. But it soon became apparent that the new arrivals were "many unruly gallants, packed thither by their friends to escape ill destinies."

They quickly divided into squabbling factions that caused untold confusion and disorder.

Smith again sent groups of settlers in three different directions to survive on their own. One of the groups, about a hundred men under Captain David West, were sent upriver to the falls of the James to build a fort, but they ended up attacking Indians and stealing their corn. When Smith went to check on them, he found that the Indians had retaliated, killing about half of the English. The surviving Englishmen refused to obey Smith's order to move to a village he had bought from one of Powhatan's sons.

In disgust the acting Governor headed back downriver to Jamestown. On the way, a spark fell into his powder bag, and the resulting flash burn ripped open a huge ten-inch patch on his thigh. He jumped into the river to put out the fire, but the wound was so severe that it could only be properly treated back in England. And so, the man who could rightly be called the first Virginian was on his way home in early October.

When the ship bearing Smith returned from Virginia, it brought more bad news about the colony. Now the Partners were in a panic. As sincerely as possible they would declare their original intent and publish their version of what had happened in the colony. Hurriedly they drafted *A True and Sincere Declaration* and rushed it into print. They made a point of repeating that their "principal and main ends were first to preach and baptize into Christian religion, and by propagation of the Gospel, to recover out of the arms of the Devil, a number of poor and miserable souls, wrapped up unto death in almost invincible ignorance. . . . and to add our mite to the treasury of Heaven."[6]

"What a wonderful missionary endeavor!" might be the response of anyone who knew nothing of what had actually transpired in Virginia. "What a noble aspiration!"

But for anyone who knew anything of what had actually happened there, the more likely response was: "What colossal hypocrisy!"

John Smith would later render strong judgment on paper, wondering how "such wise men could so torment themselves and us with strange absurdities and impossibilities, making Religion their color, when all their aim was nothing but present profit. . . . so doting on mines of gold and the South Sea [i.e., finding a Northwest Passage through to the Pacific], that all the world could not have devised better courses to bring us to ruin, than they did themselves."[7]

Within two years, the company would be reduced to raising funds by lottery and a direct-mail campaign to mayors of small towns, urging them to invest from their municipal treasuries.

As the afternoons grew shorter and colder that fall, the corn-raiding parties had finally succeeded in alienating every last tribe up and down the James. And now they and the foragers, root-grubbers, berry-pickers, and mussel-diggers all straggled back into Jamestown. There was nowhere else to go. And with the frost having killed the mosquitoes, Jamestown was not much worse than any other place. While it was perpetually damp and marshy underfoot, at least it provided shelter from the winter winds and snow.

The Virginia Colony now entered the darkest period of its history— the time that would come to be known as "the starving time." The settlers had been hungry before—famished, in fact—and many had died of malnutrition. But never had it been this bad. All the livestock had been consumed—hogs, sheep, goats, chickens, and a few horses that had come over on the most recent ships. Next went the dogs and cats, the rats that had destroyed their corn, and field mice and snakes. The hunger continued unabated and became ravaging. The settlers dug up the roots of trees and shrubs, and they ate every bit of shoe leather on the plantation as well as leather book covers, straps, and fittings. It was not enough; the colonists grew so weak that many, having earlier traded their coats and blankets for corn, froze to death in their beds. And the hunger raged on.

At this point, George Percy, who succeeded Smith as the interim Governor when the latter returned to England, recorded that a number of the settlers dug up the fresher corpses, cut them into stew meat and boiled them. There was apparently one instance of a person hurrying another into stew-meat phase rather than waiting for nature to take its course. This settler became "unhinged," killed his wife, and salted her body. He had already begun to partake of it, when he was caught red-handed, as it were. He was summarily executed.[8]

Deliverance finally came in late May of 1610—and was labeled as such. While Percy was checking on the men he had sent to Point Comfort, sails were spotted in the bay. It was the good ship *Deliverance* and her sister ship, *Patience*, both miraculously built on Bermuda from local wood and the fittings of the *Sea Venture*.

But when Gates and Somers disembarked at Jamestown, they were horrified to be greeted by 60 shambling stick figures, moaning, "We are starved! We are starved!" Were these all that were left of the 438 that had been here the previous August?

They "found the palisades torn down, the ports open, the gates off the hinges, and empty houses [which owners' death had taken from them] rent up and burnt, rather than the dwellers [stepping] into the woods a stones cast off from them to fetch other firewood."[9]

They rang the church bell, and everyone came to the church to hear a "zealous and sorrowful prayer" from Richard Buck, the successor chaplain to Robert Hunt. But not even Buck's prayers brought forth any answers to Jamestown's condition. Gates tried his best to find a workable solution, asking advice of Somers and Percy and others, but they soon realized that the situation was truly hopeless. They had little hope of even keeping alive the new people they had brought with them, for they had assumed there would be plenty to eat at Jamestown and had not stowed on board much more food than was needed for the voyage from Bermuda.

Nor was any help available from the Indians. Powhatan had forbidden his people to trade with the settlers, and the other tribes had been so alienated by Smith's raids that they were now attacking boats on the river and any settlers who straggled out of the fort. Just before Gates's arrival, a boatload of colonists had been killed, and days later two other men had been killed near the fort.

Early in June they added up all the supplies and concluded that they had only enough food left to give everyone two cakes a day for sixteen days. That did it. Gates and the other leaders decided that the only thing to do was to abandon Jamestown and make for Newfoundland, in hopes of finding English fishing boats. Perhaps they could reprovision there and transfer some of their passengers onto ships that would eventually be returning to England.

When they announced their decision to the survivors, a ragged cheer went up, and on June 7, to the beat of a drum, everybody got on the ships.

It was all Gates and Somers could do to keep them from putting the torch to Jamestown as a parting gesture. After a farewell volley of small shot, they slipped downriver on the outgoing tide.

A day later they were lying at anchor off an island near the river's mouth when they saw a longboat coming up toward them from Point Comfort. This turned out to be, of all people, Lord De La Warr. When word had reached England of the apparent loss at sea of Gates and Somers, he had hurried to Virginia to become her Governor.

Now he gave his first command: all shall turn about and head directly back to Jamestown.

As soon as De La Warr set foot on that desolate, death-ridden piece of land, he knelt and gave thanks to God for bringing them safely there in time to save all lives.

This extraordinary coincidence of timing was viewed by the English as an act of divine providence. "If God had not sent Sir Thomas Gates from the Bermudas," exclaimed William Simons, "within four days they would have all been [dead from starvation]. If God had not directed the heart of that worthy Knight to save the fort from fire . . . if they had set sail sooner . . . this was the arm of the Lord of Hosts!"[10]

Back in London, the Company, always quick to capitalize on any opportunity, declared, "It is the arm of the Lord of Hosts, who would have his people pass through the Red Sea and the wilderness, and then possess the land of Canaan." This was from their most recent tract, *A True Declaration* (which was published after *A True and Sincere Declaration* had been soundly discredited).[11]

Clearly God had moved to preserve Virginia after human beings had abandoned her. And while more ministers were beginning to draw the analogy of a new Promised Land, none had quite the temerity to suggest that the mixed bag of convicts, down-at-the-heels gentlemen, professional soldiers without a war, and slum orphans were a new chosen people. Certainly they did not regard themselves as such—chosen for hell on earth, might be more in line with how they viewed it.

What about the timing of De La Warr's arrival? There are few instances in America's early history where God's intervention seems more apparent.

Why had He propped up such a losing venture—one in which people were so resolutely bent on doing it their own way without seeking any help or guidance from Him?

Several possibilities come to mind. From the beginning of Europe's colonization of the New World, it seemed that God had intended it to be settled by those who consciously put Him at the center of their corporate life. Had Jamestown finally been abandoned, it would have been unlikely that the Partners could have rallied enough support to try again. Perhaps the continent might even have been ceded by default to the French and the Spanish, neither of whose governments were committed to following the Christlike example of their selfless missionaries.

The Virginia Colony had to survive and be maintained right where it was. Had it not been there, the Pilgrims might have gone to South America, as they nearly did. Instead, they sailed under the Virginia Company charter, and, as we will see, it was only after they had been blocked by winds off Cape Cod for the better part of three days that they concluded that it was apparently God's will for them to start a new plantation. The Pilgrims—and the Puritans who followed them eight years later—provided a more vital perspective on how to approach God and live for Him than did the Jamestown settlers.

De La Warr proved to be more ruthless and assertive than Smith ever thought of being. First, he put the colony on a work schedule: from 6:00 a.m. until 10:00, and from 2:00 till 4:00 p.m. After each shift they would gather in church to pray, and only after that would they eat. This did not include the gentlemen, who were nonetheless expected to give counsel.[12]

Next, he put Virginia under martial law. Blasphemy or speaking "against the known articles of the Christian faith," or privately trading with the Indians, or any kind of theft at all—all of these and more were made capital offenses.

As for the Indians, he took the opposite approach of Raleigh, who had inveighed against mistreating the local inhabitants. Outdoing John Smith at his worst, De La Warr sent war parties against the nearest tribes, burning their houses and taking their Queen and her children captive. Then he had the captives murdered.

Apparently, the contradiction between honoring the Christian faith by outlawing blasphemy and totally violating it by murdering Indians never occurred to anyone. In John Smith's collection of writings on early Virginia history there is a paragraph describing the atrocities, and in the very next paragraph there is a sentence that reads: "Their daily invocating of the Name of God being thus expressed; why should not the rich harvest of our hopes be seasonably expected?"[13] Apparently God was expected to bless people who deliberately killed women and children, so long as they prayed.

Seriously ill with scurvy most of the time he was at the colony, De La Warr finally departed for England in March of 1611, less than a year after he arrived. More than two hundred settlers, nearly half those alive when he landed, had perished during his governorship. Of those who survived, fifty-five gentlemen took the occasion to leave Jamestown with him.

De La Warr's replacement, Sir Thomas Dale was, if possible, even harsher than his predecessor. A tough, hardnosed war captain, Dale enforced extreme martial discipline, taking pages from a harsh military code used with mercenaries in Europe. It was now a hanging offense to be heard speaking against authority, as it was to be absent from the daily church services three times without an excuse. For lesser offenses, Dale and his sergeants-at-arms carried bastinadoes, short sticks with which they administered corporal punishment as needed.

While his measures may have been draconian, they did produce results. Gradually order emerged from chaos, and conditions began to improve. Bricks were made, and houses built with them. A barn was constructed, and a dock was built in the river. A new village, Henrico, was started.

It now became obvious that some sort of long-term product was needed that could pay for the Virginia Company's supply ships and put the colony on a firm financial footing.

Young John Rolfe found the solution. He had sailed for Virginia on the *Sea Venture*, and when it was wrecked on the coast of Bermuda, Rolfe was fortunate enough to rescue his sea chest, which contained some small seeds of tobacco. These seeds were from the Spanish New World, which grew a strain of tobacco far superior to the tobacco native to Virginia.

Shortly after arriving at Jamestown, Rolfe planted his seeds, and by 1612 he was able to send a small amount of leaves to London for examination. The response was ecstatic, and soon many of the settlers were growing enough tobacco to enable them to buy clothes and household goods. Jamestown was developing a growing tobacco industry. Virginia had its first cash crop—and typical of the irony that shrouded the settlement, the colony's future would be secured by an addictive weed that would eventually claim countless thousands of lives.

As for relations with the Indians, little had changed. Dale had brought with him some rusty Elizabethan armor from the Tower of London, which couldn't stop musket balls but was more than enough protection against Indian arrows. Thus clad, he and his men attacked the Nansemond tribe, killing many and destroying their settlement. Though the Indians around Henrico were creating problems by shooting arrows into the palisade, most of the small surrounding tribes had either been decimated by the English attacks or pacified through trade—except for Powhatan and his people.

What Dale needed was a trump card, and he got one. His men captured Pocahontas, who was now a flashing-eyed beauty of eighteen. Dale let Powhatan know that he had Pocahontas and that he would exchange her for the eight settlers and all the English weapons Powhatan was holding. Powhatan stalled for time. For months they heard nothing from him.

Finally, Dale got tired of waiting, and he set out upriver for Powhatan's village with 150 men and Pocahontas. Along the way they found 400 armed warriors who challenged them to a fight, but Pocahontas came ashore and defused the situation. Hurt by her father's delays in redeeming her, she sent a message to her father through her brothers that if he loved her, he would give the English back their men and their weapons, and that unless he did, she would stay with the English.

At this point, Dale realized that he had a unique chance to negotiate peace, so he sent John Rolfe and Master Sparkes to Powhatan. After Rolfe left, Dale opened a letter from him and was utterly astonished. He read that the young man had fallen hopelessly in love with Pocahontas and that during the talks with Powhatan he would be asking the chief's permission to marry her. Rolfe asked Dale's blessing in the letter because he had been afraid to ask him about it face-to-face.

His motives could hardly be higher, he went on to assure Dale, for he was "striving for the good of this plantation, for the honor of our country, . . . and for the converting to the true knowledge of God and Jesus Christ an unbelieving creature, namely Pocahontas, to whom my hearty and best thoughts are, and have for a long time been so entangled and enthralled in so delicate a labyrinth. . . . But almighty God, who never faileth His who truly invoke His name, hath opened the gate."[14]

The effect of the letter was like a ray of sunlight bursting through an ominous overcast, as if God Himself might finally be smiling on the misfortune-dogged Virginia Colony. Both Dale and Powhatan were bemused by the prospect of a wedding uniting their peoples.

The sachem may have seriously been considering the annihilation of the English settlers, once and for all. But he knew that he could never permanently rid himself of them. There were simply too many, coming on too many ships. Even if most died, there were now whole fleets coming, bringing hundreds at a time. And besides, the young man seemed truly smitten with his daughter and was likely to provide well for her.

On Dale's part, he had to choose whether to bless this union or upbraid Rolfe for acting independently, outside of his authority. For once, he chose the happier way—and what had begun as a showdown in a contest of wills now brightened like blossoming wildflowers. There was going to be a wedding—the first in Virginia between a white man and an Indian bride.

Powhatan declined to attend in person (he did not trust the colonists *that* far), but he sent his brother to give his daughter away and a number of braves to act as an honor guard. It was the first time in several years that the Indians and the colonists were able to completely relax in one another's presence.

Richard Buck performed the ceremony on April 5, 1614, and thanks to Powhatan's generosity, it was a glorious feasting affair and an occasion for much rejoicing by both English and Indians. It boded well, and it marked the beginning of things going much better for Jamestown.

Soon afterward, John and Pocahontas—now called by her Christian name, Rebecca—went to England. The Partners were, of course, delighted at the newfound peace between the natives and the settlers, and they sought to exploit it for the favorable publicity value it might have.

It had much. Rebecca became the belle of London society. Dowagers and doyennes found her innocence thoroughly charming, and everyone was taken with her wit, good looks, and humility. Sir Walter Raleigh had just been released from the Tower of London, and it was John Rolfe's great delight to report to him that Virginia now had 351 men, women, and children living in six settlements, plus 144 cattle, 216 goats, and plenty of chickens. The colony was finally on the verge of being self-sufficient.

Rebecca was as taken with London as the city was with her. She had no desire to return to America, but because she and John were the only guarantee of lasting peace between their peoples, a great deal of pressure was brought to bear on them to do so.

Before they could depart, however, pneumonia struck her down and killed her. Grief-stricken, John Rolfe returned to Virginia alone.

As for Virginia's spiritual condition, by 1622 there were more than twelve hundred souls in ten widely scattered plantations, and to serve this flock there were exactly three ordained ministers. The contrast between the worldly and the spiritual was never more candidly spelled out than in an exchange between James Blair, President of the soon-to-be-founded College of William & Mary, and England's Attorney General, Edward Seymour, to whom he had to apply for a charter granted by King William and Queen Mary. Seymour thought the college was a waste of time and good money, and he said so in no uncertain terms. Whereupon Blair pointed out that the colonists of Virginia had souls that needed to be saved.

"Souls?" replied Seymour. "Damn your souls! Make tobacco!"[15]

Tobacco may have been the means, but God was the agent who preserved Virginia and who, in spite of everything, gave her yet another chance. In 1619 every one of the nonindentured men of the colony had been given at least a hundred acres of his own. In England the Company had finally collapsed and sold out its interest to ten Adventurers. They, in turn, established a system of independent rule, whereby two representatives (burgesses) from each of the ten plantations would meet to make laws and discuss mutual problems.

It was more than a new beginning for Virginia; it was the first self-governing representative assembly in North America, more than a century and a half before the fledgling United States would go to war to secure this privilege.

But Virginia was still Virginia. Of all the places they could have chosen to meet in the middle of summer, including Williamsburg, where the House of Burgesses would one day be established, they chose Jamestown. Within a week, two of the burgesses had died, and the other eighteen were sick.

Why had so much gone so wrong in Virginia when their publicly stated motives back in England had been so right? (And so convincing that even the Partners themselves were beginning to believe them?)

In an age when the leaders all acknowledged God's existence and thereby considered themselves good Christians, hardly any were living the life to which Christ calls all of us in His Gospel. Even among ministers who were extolling the need for taking the Christian faith to the heathen of undiscovered lands, hardly any were actually prepared to go there themselves.

The settlement at Jamestown had been undertaken with nominal Anglican belief in God. That might have sufficed under pleasant circumstances, but life at Jamestown proved far from pleasant. It would have taken a much deeper reliance on God to successfully bring the settlers through the horrendous ordeals they faced. God *was* there, and He *did* answer their prayers when they were accompanied with a sincere desire to amend one's life. But that attitude seemed to be in short supply in the early years at Jamestown.

Eventually God had mercy on them all, despite the fact that in 1619, when they bought twenty African indentured servants from a Dutch trader, they had introduced slavery to the North American continent.

The next group to come across the Atlantic to America had a different perspective. From hard experience, they knew that God must be at the center of their lives, or their life together would surely founder. He was the only One in whom they could put their whole trust. But if they did, He would see them through.

8

TO THE PROMISED LAND

*D*escending into the gloomy interior of the *Mayflower II*, the replica of the Pilgrims' ship, we were shocked at the closeness of the quarters. One hundred and two Pilgrims had been crammed into a space about equal to that of a volleyball court. Compound that misery by the lack of light and fresh air (all hatches had to be battened down because of the stormy weather). Add to it a diet of dried peas, dried fish, and wormy biscuits, along with the stench of an ever-fouler bilge, and multiply it all by sixty-six days at sea.

As we emerged topside, Peter shook his head. "You know, they accepted all that with very little complaining. It was part of what they were willing to endure to follow God's will." He paused. "Like the exile in Holland and their indenture in the New World."

Later that afternoon, as we climbed the dirt road that is the main street of the reconstruction of "Plimoth" Plantation, we were again struck by the enormous price these people had paid. It had been one thing to see the magnificence of the poured-out commitments of the missionaries. But these Jesuit, Dominican, and Franciscan martyrs seemed almost destined for sainthood from the moment of conversion. The Pilgrims, by contrast, were ordinary Christian families—not unlike our own.

Compared to them, our commitment to Christ seemed pale and shallow. As we became convicted of this, not as much by what the Pilgrims preached or wrote but by the lives they lived, it was a humbling experience. Considering themselves only marginally successful, they had no awareness of the spiritual impact their community would have—on the Puritans who came behind them, on the founding of a Christian nation, and on all those in subsequent ages who would be inspired by their example.

Prior to our visit to Plymouth a question had arisen: If the Pilgrims and the Massachusetts Bay Puritans were together responsible for most of the constitutional and institutional foundations of this country, why does this comparative handful of Pilgrims who never matched the achievements of their Puritan cousins a few miles to the north and were eventually absorbed by them, move the hearts of Americans on such deep levels? Why, for some people, is a visit to Plimoth Plantation more like a pilgrimage than a sightseeing tour?

Driving away from the town that afternoon, we felt we were beginning to see the answer.

On a warm, hazy July morning in 1620, three barges glided along a Dutch canal, en route from Leyden to the seaport of Delftshaven. In the distance, across the broad, low fields, a large stone windmill basked in the early morning sun, its huge white sails barely turning. It was a morning for tarrying, for taking in the fragrance of new-mown hay and the muted chirping of field crickets.

But there could be no tarrying for the congregation on these barges. For a third of them it was the beginning of a much longer voyage—a voyage from which there would be no return.

One of these was William Bradford, a young, strong, enthusiastic English farmer who was counted among their "chief men." He had been with their pastor, John Robinson, from the very beginning in Yorkshire, fourteen years before. Orphaned at an early age, he had been raised by an aunt and uncle and grandparents until the age of twelve, when he had been converted by the preaching of Richard Clyfton. The young lad's awakened conscience led him to join in spirit with the relative handful of radical Christians who had dared to separate from the Church of England. In the ensuing two years Bradford's spiritual defection had so infuriated his relatives that they threatened to disown him if he didn't return. In a letter to them, he wrote:

> Were I like to endanger my life, or consume my estate by any ungodly courses, your counsels to me were very seasonable; but you know that I have been diligent and provident in my calling, and not only desirous to augment what I have, but also to enjoy it in your company, to part from which will be as great a cross as can befall me. Nevertheless, to keep a good conscience, and walk in such a way as God has prescribed in His Word, is a thing which I must prefer before you all, and above life itself.[1]

Already at the age of fourteen Bradford was showing signs of the spiritual maturity that would make him one of America's foremost Christian leaders. When his staunchly Anglican relatives made good on their threats, the printer William Brewster took the young man into his home in nearby Scrooby.

If on the barge that morning in 1620 Bradford recalled those early years, it might have been with a sense of wonder. So much had passed into history since then. He would write it all down one day, years hence.

> It is well-known unto the Godly and judicious, how ever since the first breaking out of the Light of the Gospel in our honorable nation of England . . . what wars and oppositions ever since, Satan hath raised, maintained and continued against the saints [i.e., believers who were striving to yield their whole lives to Christ]. . . . Sometimes by bloody death and cruel torments, otherwise imprisonments, banishments and other hard usages, as being loathe [that his] kingdom should go down, the truth prevail, and the churches of God revert to their ancient purity and recover their primitive order, liberty and beauty.[2]

The churches to which Bradford was referring were those of the Church of England, presided over by the House of Bishops. The Church hierarchy had grown alarmed at the rapid growth of two movements of "fanatics." The first and much larger group claimed to be dedicated to "purifying the Church from within." That made them suspect from the start to the bishops, who saw nothing which needed purifying. These "Puritans," as they were sarcastically dubbed (and which epithet they eventually took for their own) did, however, continue to acknowledge canonical authority. Thus they could be easily kept from positions of responsibility and safely ignored.

In the bishops' eyes the much smaller but more dangerous element were the radicals who thought that the Church of England was already corrupted beyond any possibility of purification. They further believed that no person, not even the Queen, could take the title "Head of the Church." That belonged exclusively to the Lord Jesus Christ. Having separated themselves from the state Church, they now conducted their own worship as they saw fit. If allowed to continue, these "Separatists" would soon reduce worship to primitive preaching, teaching, singing, and free praying, thus doing away with sixteen centuries of established liturgical tradition.

This was the group young William Bradford had joined. At present they numbered less than a thousand, but clearly if this sort of thing were tolerated, other "believers"—who spoke enthusiastically of experiencing a personal encounter with Christ—might decide to follow their lead. Before long, little churches of fanatics would be popping up everywhere, with no semblance of order or conformity (and totally out of the bishops' control).

Queen Elizabeth had not given the bishops the free hand which they sought to suppress this contagion before it became an epidemic. She seemed to feel that occasional executions for heresy were sufficient to hold the movement in check. But now that the vain, petty (and manipulable) James I was on the throne, the bishops had their way.

The Separatists were hounded, bullied, forced to pay assessments to the Church of England, clapped into prison on trumped-up charges, and driven underground. They met in private homes, to which they came at staggered intervals by different routes, because they were constantly being spied upon. In the Midlands village of Scrooby the persecution became so intense that the congregation elected to follow other Separatists who had already sought religious asylum in Holland.

Thus they came to Leyden, where they were forged together by shared adversity. As near-penniless foreign immigrants, they qualified for only the most menial labor and had to work terribly hard just to subsist. Bradford wrote that before coming, they had, "as the Lord's free people, joined themselves by a covenant of the Lord into a church estate, in the fellowship of the Gospel, to walk in all His ways made known . . . unto them, according to their best endeavors, whatsoever it should cost them, the Lord assisting them."[3]

It cost them dearly. By 1619, after nearly a dozen years of penurious toil, they finally decided that they had to "remove."

Bradford offered four reasons for moving. First, their life (though they never complained of it) was so hard that almost no others were coming from England to join them—even after the king's edict of 1618, which decreed that all Christians unwilling to conform to ecclesiastical authority had to leave the country. Second, their life was aging them prematurely (everyone old enough to hold a job worked twelve to fifteen hours a day) and was so debilitating that, if the time came when they would have to move again, they might not physically be able to do so. Third, their children were also being worn down, and many were being drawn away by the lures of the world around them. Fourth, they had cherished a "great hope and inward zeal" of at least playing a part, if only as a stepping-stone for others, in the carrying forth of the Light of Christ to remote parts of the world.

Increasingly the Separatists came to believe that North America was the place to which God intended them to go, despite the horrors of Virginia's "starving time" which had reached their ears and the well-known savagery of the Indians. Considering that the death rate at Jamestown after twelve years was still well over 50 percent, an insidious counterproposal was raised. Might there not be an easier way? Why not go south to Guiana on the coast of South America, which Walter Raleigh had so warmly described and where the English already had a foothold? It was "rich, fruitful, and blessed with a perpetual spring, and flourishing greens, where vigorous nature brought forth all things in abundance and plenty without any great labor or art of man."[4]

Raleigh had also mentioned an abundance of gold mines.[5]

Thus does Satan ever seek to divide and sow dissension among the Christians he so hates. But the Leydenites were mature enough in their faith to know better than to reason things out with only their intellects. The crucial question in all of this was, what was God's will? Where did *He* want to send them? From hard experience they had learned that as long as they were in the center of His will, it did not matter where they were physically located.

After they had prayed and entrusted the entire undertaking into His hands, peace returned—and with it some considerations that had hitherto escaped them. Guiana was close to the Spanish Main, and the jealous Spaniards had already wiped out the French Huguenots. And if gold was there, that would only lure the Spanish more quickly. Also, the tropical climate engendered diseases that had already decimated the crews of dozens of ships passing through the Indies. The more they prayed, the clearer it became that God wanted them to go to North America. Bradford summed up their strengthening resolve:

> It was answered that all great and honorable actions are accompanied with great difficulties, and must be enterprised and overcome with answerable courages. It was granted that the dangers were great, but not desperate, and the difficulties were many, but not invincible . . . and all of them, through the help of God, by fortitude and patience, might either be borne or overcome. . . .[But] their condition was not ordinary. Their ends were good and honorable, their calling lawful and urgent, and therefore they might expect the blessing of God in their proceeding; yea, though they should lose their lives in this action, yet they might have comfort in the same, and their endeavors would be honorable.[6]

As the Leydenites worked out where they were going, their elected pastor, John Robinson, was praying for a deeper revelation of *why* they were going. Did God have a special purpose for them? To Robinson and Elder William Brewster and a few of the other leaders that purpose was beginning to come clear. As Robinson would shortly write, he perceived that God was calling them to a new Jerusalem, to build His temple anew— with themselves as its living stones: "Now as the people of God in old time were called out of Babylon civil, the place of their bodily bondage, and were to come to Jerusalem, and there to build the Lord's temple, or tabernacle . . . so are the people of God now to go out of Babylon spiritual to Jerusalem . . . and to build themselves as lively stones into a spiritual house, or temple, for the Lord to dwell in."[7]

It seemed that God had indeed chosen them and was now in the process of preparing them to become His temple in America. It was resolved then that they were going. They were already being led in a path that had once been walked by another chosen people, "for we are," wrote Robinson, "the sons and daughters of Abraham by faith."

But getting to America was another matter. The cost of transporting them there would be enormous, to say nothing of the expense of sufficient food supplies to last them until they could plant, grow, and harvest a crop. In addition to that, they would need a pinnace with which to go fishing or trading. (The French had built up a lucrative fur trade in the far north, and it occurred to the Leydenites that they might be able to do the same.)

Transports, pinnaces, a year's provisions for a hundred people—where on earth were they going to get that kind of money?

The Virginia Company was the main corporate enterprise engaged in the business of backing ventures to America. Accordingly, Robinson and Brewster drafted the seventeenth-century equivalent of a business plan and sent it to Edwin Sandys, the treasurer of the Company. A straightforward application for financing, it outlined their reasons for confidence:

1. We verily believe and trust the Lord is with us, unto Whom and Whose service we have given ourselves in many trials, and that He will graciously prosper our endeavors according to the simplicity of our hearts therein.

2. We are well weaned from the delicate milk of our mother country, and inured to the difficulties of a strange and hard land, which yet in a great part we have by patience overcome.

3. The people are, for the body of them, [as] industrious and frugal, we think we may safely say, as any company of people in the world.

4. We are knit together as a body in a most strict and sacred bond and covenant of the Lord, of the violation whereof we make great conscience, and by virtue whereof we do hold ourselves straitly tied to all care of each others good, and of the whole by everyone and so mutually.

5. Lastly, it is not with us as with other men, whom small things can discourage, or small discontentments cause to wish themselves at home again.[8]

But while Sandys was sympathetic, the hard truth was that the Virginia Company was on the brink of bankruptcy, and "now so disturbed with factions and quarrels amongst themselves, as no business could go well forward." (And so the Leydenites were providentially spared that entanglement.)

Not long after that, they were paid an unexpected visit by a London merchant named Thomas Weston. All smiles and encouragement, Weston informed them that he was an independent Adventurer, representing a group that had heard of their plight and decided to help them. The Leydenites could forget the Virginia Company (though it might be useful to sail under their charter). Instead, they could put their faith in Weston, who assured them that he felt the same way about the things of God as they did and that he would see them through, no matter what.

Englishmen who did have money to speculate on trading, exploration, and settlement were almost exclusively being attracted to the Muscovy Company or the East India Tea Company, both of which promised a 100 percent return on one's investment in six months. And so, as it seemed to be the only door open to them, with some misgivings the Leydenites entered into an agreement with Weston.

Should they have heeded the misgivings that some of them had? Should they have waited on God a little longer, trusting Him to open yet another door? If you had waited as long as they had, you might have chosen as they did. To them, it wasn't the easier way; it was the only way.

But now there was much to be done. Families who were going sold their houses and all their immovable possessions to give Weston cash with which to purchase shares in the plantation venture.

Their agreement was that each adult, sixteen years and older, would have one share, worth ten pounds sterling (almost a thousand modern dollars), and another share if he outfitted and equipped himself. Those with extra funds could, of course, buy more shares. All would continue in joint partnership for seven years (the standard period of indenture), at the end of which time all land and profits would be divided up according to the number of shares. Personal property, such as houses, home lots, and gardens, would remain wholly the property of the planters and would not be divided up. The planters were also to be given two days a week of their own.

It struck them as an eminently fair agreement, so Weston went off to London to confer with his partners and to see about hiring a ship to transport them.

The Separatists sent two of their number to London to represent them—John Carver and Robert Cushman. Carver had a stability and maturity about him that had already proven an asset. Cushman had a quick mind and a gift for eloquence, but he was immature and had difficulty accepting correction. While Carver was out of London gathering supplies for the coming voyage, Weston applied pressure to Cushman and got him to agree to certain changes in their contract.

Next on the agenda was the purchase of a pinnace, and this must have been like shopping for a used car with not enough money. Eventually they settled on an old freighter named the *Speedwell*, which would pick them up at Delftshaven and take them to Southampton. There they would join a larger merchantman, the *Mayflower*, hired by the Adventurers. But only a third of their six hundred–plus congregation could go. That meant that the man who wanted most to go, John Robinson, would have to stay behind; the main body of the flock could not be without its shepherd. So it was decided that their elder, William Brewster, would be their teacher and acting pastor until such time as Robinson could come over.

The time had come to part. Robinson declared a day of fasting and prayer to prepare them spiritually for the arduous voyage to come. At the end of the day, they had a farewell dinner, celebrating with goose and pudding and wine, and singing their favorite psalms from Ainsworth's Psalm Book in the intricate, madrigal-like harmonies that so delighted the ear.

Edward Winslow, one of the leaders, described the scene as follows: "We refreshed ourselves, after our tears, with the singing of Psalms, making joyful melody in our hearts as well as with the voice, there being many in the congregation very expert in music; and indeed it was the sweetest melody that ever mine ears have heard."[9]

The next morning, as many as could accompanied the voyagers by barge to Delftshaven. Looking back at the red-tiled roofs of Leyden receding in the distance and the great windmill with its white sails slowly turning, Bradford may have had a pang of regret. If he did, it was only temporary, for "they knew they were Pilgrims, and looked not much on those things, but lifted up their eyes to the heavens, their dearest country, and quieted their spirits."[10]

When they reached Delftshaven, they made straight for the harbor, and there was the *Speedwell*—a good deal smaller and older than most of them had pictured her. The rest of the afternoon and most of the evening were spent loading food and cargo into every conceivable cranny. Dawn on July 22, 1620, was greeted with a fair wind, and now it really was time to say good-bye. On the dock John Robinson slowly knelt, and all the others followed his lead. As he solemnly invoked God's blessing on their undertaking, tears came to all of their eyes, and even the young men wept unabashedly. Quickly they boarded the ship, and the crew cast off.

With a wind behind them, they soon reached Southampton, where they joined the ninety-ton *Mayflower*. On board were their agents, Carver and Cushman, joyously reunited with their families, and about eighty "strangers." Some of these shared the Leydenites' feelings regarding the Church of England, but others were there because they had believed Weston's enticements about the profits to be had in the wilderness.

Among the "strangers" were the rambunctious John Billington, his shrewish wife, and two rebellious teenage sons; the more-devout bootsmith William Mullins, his wife, two children, and 138 pairs of shoes and boots; and John Alden, the cooper that each ship was required by law to carry in order to tend the ship's casks and barrels. One who had asked to go with them and was turned down was none other than the feisty soldier of fortune Captain John Smith. (Here, at least, the Pilgrims' discernment regarding people was working well.)

From the Leyden group there were sixteen men, eleven women, and fourteen children—barely a third of the combined total of saints and strangers. And of these, only Bradford and William and Mary Brewster were original members of the Scrooby church. Others among the saints included the Brewsters' two sons, Love and Wrestling; John Carver and his wife, Katherine; Edward and Elizabeth Winslow; William and Dorothy Bradford (they had left their only son behind, deciding he was too young to make the initial voyage); Dr. Samuel Fuller; and Captain Miles Standish, a tough and steady veteran of the Netherlands wars, and his wife, Rose.

The Master and part-owner of the *Mayflower* was an old professional who was hired with his crew to take the Pilgrims (as they had now come to see themselves) just south of the mouth of the Hudson, within the northernmost boundary of the Virginia charter. He had agreed to stay with them long enough for them to get a start on settling in, but any time beyond that would cost them extra because it would be cutting into his earning time. The Master's name was Jones, and his Christian name was the same as that of another captain God had used to bear the light of Christ westward: Christopher.

With everything finally readied for departure, Thomas Weston chose that precise moment to present a revised contract that effectively doubled their season of indenture from seven to fourteen years. He fully expected them to object, but because they had said all their farewells and committed all their funds to the endeavor, they would simply have to sign.

To his astonishment, they refused.

In a rage, Weston stormed off to London, refusing to settle their final debts, which came to some sixty pounds. So they had to sell off several thousand pounds of butter, which happened to be their only food surplus.

And then they wrote the Adventurers in London a compromise letter, stating that "if large profits should not arise within seven years, we will continue together longer with you, if the Lord give a blessing."[11] They were, in effect, offering to extend their indentureship almost indefinitely. With their consciences now as clear as their credit balance, they were free to sail.

At this point, Brewster assembled the company to read them a letter that John Robinson had prepared for them: "We are daily to renew our repentance with our God, especially for our sins known, and generally for our unknown trespasses. . . . [For] sin being taken away by earnest repentance and the pardon thereof from the Lord . . . great shall be [a man's] security and peace in all dangers, sweet his comforts in all distresses."

Robinson went on to warn them that their "intended course of civil community will minister continual occasion of offense, and will be as fuel for that fire, except you diligently quench it with brotherly forbearance. . . . with your common employments you [should] join common affections, truly bent upon the general good."

In closing, he enjoined them, "whereas you are to become a body politic, using amongst yourselves civil government, and are not furnished with any persons of special eminency above the rest" (i.e., no gentlemen on the passenger list), they would have to choose their leaders from among equals. "Let your wisdom and godliness appear not only in choosing such persons as do entirely love and will promote the common good, but also in yielding unto them all due honor and obedience in their lawful administrations . . . [for] the image of the Lord's power and authority, which the magistrate beareth, is honorable."

For some of the strangers hearing Robinson's letter, it may have been their first realization that unlike the Jamestown colony, there were no gentry among them. Moreover, the Pilgrims were accustomed to seeking God's will in every step of the planning, as the Jamestown people had not, so He was more able to winnow out from among them any who might be unwilling to work with the rest. There could be no spectators—all had to participate.

Having finally set sail for the New World on August 5, 1620, they were barely three days out on the Atlantic before it became obvious that the *Speedwell* was in trouble. The new masts with which they had fitted her in Holland were apparently causing her seams to work open under full sail. They had no choice but to turn back to the nearest port, Dartmouth, and recaulk her.

Another week passed, and they again set forth, only to encounter the same problem. This time, it was abetted by a full gale* that initiated the Pilgrims to the rigors of seasickness. Once more they were forced to turn back, this time making for Plymouth, the home of some of the best shipwrights in England. There they searched the ship for a loose seam.

And how they searched! Holding lighted candles up close to each seam, they crept the length of the ship looking for the slightest waver in the flame that would indicate a less-than-airtight joining. Surprisingly they found nothing wrong with her hull. In spite of that, they finally made the difficult decision not to take any further chances with the *Speedwell*. They would sell her and combine her passengers and cargo with those on board the *Mayflower*.

Some historians have found hints that the Master of the *Speedwell*, anxious to get out of his contract to spend a year at the plantation, had deliberately crowded on sail to make the seams work loose. Indeed, the *Speedwell*, later rerigged, would see coastal service for many years.

But there was another explanation: God was using the *Speedwell's* problems to further separate the wheat from the chaff. As William Stoughton later put it: "God sifted a whole nation, that He might send choice grain into this wilderness."[12]

A number of them, whose hearts themselves had seams that might part if heavily worked, now began to wonder if it truly was God's will that they make this voyage. About twenty of them willingly dropped out. "Like Gideon's army," Bradford wrote, "this small number was divided, as if the Lord, by this work of His Providence, thought these few were still too many for the great work He had to do."[13] There were some surprises among their number, like Robert Cushman, "whose heart and courage was gone from them before, as it seems, though his body was with them till now he departed."

Bradford then quoted from a letter written in Dartmouth by Cushman to a friend: "For besides the eminent dangers of this voyage, which are not less than deadly. . . . Our victuals will be half eaten up, I think, before we go from the coast of England, and if our voyage last long, we shall not have a month's victuals when come [to] the country." (Indeed, by the time

---

*Gales involve winds from 50 to 80 knots; above that, it is a full-fledged hurricane.

they left Plymouth, they were already consuming the precious reserves meant to sustain them in the New World.) "Friend," concluded Cushman, "if ever we make a plantation, God works a miracle." Though he may have spoken from despair, it was the truth. God had so intended.

There was another reason for God's narrowing the company down to one ship: to make it indeed a company. It had taken years of baptism by fire to temper the spiritual core of the Pilgrims into hardened steel, but now there were only a few weeks available in which to temper these strangers and anneal them to the Pilgrims' core. For unless they were so bonded, they would soon fly apart under the pressures that awaited them on the other side of the ocean. Much could be done, but it would require tremendous heat and pressure.

The heat and the pressure began soon after they got under way: 102 Pilgrims huddled in the lantern-lit darkness of the low-ceilinged 'tween-decks. No hatches open because of continuous storms. All nonessential personnel required to stay below decks. The constant crying of small children. No chance to cook any meals.

It added up to seven weeks of ill-lighted, rolling, pitching, stinking misery—the kind that brings up sins that had lain buried for years. Anger, self-pity, bitterness, vindictiveness, jealousy, despair—all these surfaced sins had to be faced, confessed, and given up to the Lord for His cleansing. No matter how ill they felt or how grim the daily situation, they continued to seek God together, praying through despair and into peace and thanksgiving.

The weary Pilgrims were forced to endure yet another ordeal—harassment from the sailors. Several of the crew had taken to mocking them unmercifully, and their self-appointed leader had taken such a dislike to the Pilgrims that he would gloat at their seasickness and delight in telling them how much he looked forward to sewing them in shrouds and feeding them to the fish, for surely some of them would soon be dying. (Death was a familiar shipmate among landlubbers on transatlantic voyages.) And these were the puniest assortment of "psalm-singing puke-stockings" he had ever seen.

But just at the peak of his tormenting, this same crewman suddenly took gravely ill of an unknown fever and died within a single day. No one else caught this mysterious disease, and his was the first shrouded body to go over the side. Thereafter, there was no more mocking from the crew.

There was only one other death during the voyage: William Butten, a servant, ignored Master Jones's and Dr. Fuller's stern admonition about drinking a daily portion of lemon juice as a preventative for scurvy. He refused to swallow the sour stuff, and his willful disobedience cost him his life.

Another passenger nearly paid with his life for a "minor" infraction. A dozen or so days into the storm, John Howland, the servant of their governor, John Carver, could no longer stand the stench of the crowded 'tween-decks. The Master, Elder Brewster, and his own master had forbidden any of them to go topside, but if he didn't get a breath of fresh air soon, he thought he would die. Finally, he decided that he was going to get what he wanted. Up he climbed and out onto the sea-swept main deck. It was like a nightmare out there! The seas around him were mountainous; he'd never seen anything like it—huge, boiling, gray-green waves lifting and tossing the small ship in their midst, dark clouds roiling the horizon, and the wind shrieking through the rigging. Howland shuddered, and it was not from the icy blast of "fresh air" that hit him.

Just then, the ship seemed to literally drop out from beneath him—it was there, and then it wasn't—and the next thing he knew, he was falling. He hit the water, which was so cold that it was like being smashed between two huge blocks of ice. His last conscious act was to blindly reach out. By God's grace the ship at that moment was heeled so far over that the lines from her spars were trailing in the water. One of these happened to snake across his wrist, and instinctively he closed on it and hung on.

According to the U.S. Navy, if a person goes overboard into the North Atlantic in November, he or she has at most thirty minutes to live. There is no telling how long Howland was in the sea, how soon someone spotted him and raised the alarm. When they hauled him aboard, he was blue. But even though he was sick for several days, he recovered. And never again would he stick his head above deck until he was invited to do so.

The most frightening episode of the voyage occurred not long after the *Mayflower* passed the halfway mark. In a particularly violent storm, she was rolling so far over on her sides that the sole lantern seemed almost parallel with the crossbeams. Children were screaming, and more than a few Pilgrims feared she might shift her cargo and go all the way over.

Suddenly a tremendous *boom* resounded through the ship. The main crossbeam supporting the mainmast had cracked and was sagging alarmingly. Now the sailors' concern matched the Pilgrims'. They swarmed about it, trying to lever it back into place, but they could not budge it. Master Jones himself came to see. From the look on his face, it was obvious to the Pilgrims that the situation was as ominous as they had feared.

The Pilgrims helped in the only way they knew how. They prayed, "Yet Lord, Thou canst save!" Then Brewster remembered the great iron screw of his printing press. It was on board somewhere. A desperate search was begun. Finally it was located, dug out, hauled into place under the sagging beam, and cranked up. It met the beam and, to the accompaniment of a hideous creaking and groaning of wood, began to raise it—all the way back into its original position. For once the sailors joined the Pilgrims in their praises of God.

Earnestly Brewster, Carver, and Bradford questioned the Master as to the *Mayflower*'s seaworthiness. He thought about it—they were now closer to America than to England, though they would have the wind with them on the return.

"No," he decided, "she's still sound under the water, and that's the main thing! She's made many trips in weather worse than this, and I expect she'll make this one, too, without more trouble." They would go on.

At last, on November 9 the words they had waited so long to hear rang out from the lookout: "Land ho!"

Without waiting for the Master's permission, they rushed up on the main deck, where they caught their first glimpse of a long, sandy stretch of coastline, covered with dune grass and scrub pine. One of the pilots identified it as a place the fishermen called Cape Cod. Despite the seemingly endless storm, they had actually been blown less than a hundred miles off their course—north, as it turned out. It should take them only a day to round the elbow of the Cape and perhaps three more days to reach the mouth of the Hudson.

They turned south.

But at the Cape's elbow, Monomoy Point, there are fierce shoals and riptides. And with the heavy headwinds they now faced, the going became progressively more treacherous. Finally, after battling the wall of wind for two days, Master Jones said that before attempting to proceed further south, he would have to head back out to sea and wait another day.

Now Brewster, Carver, Winslow, Bradford, and several others, began to wonder if God really did want them to go to the Hudson. Perhaps He had blown them here because He intended them to remain in this place. At length, after much prayer and further discussion, they instructed Master Jones to turn about and make for the northern tip of the Cape (Provincetown). This he did, and on November 11, they dropped anchor in the natural harbor just inside the Cape.

At this point, a new question arose: if they were to settle here, they would no longer be under the jurisdiction of the Virginia Company. And since they obviously had no patent from the New England Company, they would be under—no one. This thought stirred rebellion in the hearts of some of the strangers, and the Pilgrim leaders realized that they had to act quickly and decisively to forestall the very real possibility of mutiny.

Their solution was pragmatic and expedient. It took into consideration the basic sinfulness of human nature, with which they had become all too familiar during the past seven weeks. They drafted a Compact, much along the lines of their first covenant back in Scrooby, which embodied the principles of equality and government by the consent of the governed. (Actually, this concept of equality could be traced directly back to the ancient Hebrew tradition of all men being equal in the sight of God.)

The Mayflower Compact would become cornerstone of American representative government. Although the Pilgrims had no idea of the significance for America of what they had done, it marked the first time in history since the children of Israel in the Sinai wilderness (with the exception of John Calvin's Geneva) that free and equal men had voluntarily covenanted together to create their own new civil government based on Biblical principles.

In the name of God, amen. We whose names are under-written, the loyal subjects of our dread Sovereign Lord King James by the Grace of God of Great Britain, France, Ireland, King, Defender of the Faith, etc.

Having undertaken, for the glory of God and advancement of the Christian Faith and honor of our King and country, a voyage to plant the first colony in the northern parts of Virginia, do by these presents solemnly and mutually in the presence of God and one of another, covenant and combine ourselves together into a civil body politic, for our better ordering and preservation and furtherance of the ends aforesaid, and by virtue hereof to enact, constitute and frame such just and equal laws, ordinances, acts, constitutions and offices from time to time, as shall be thought most meet and convenient for the general good of the colony. Unto which we promise all due submission and obedience. In witness whereof we have hereunder subscribed our names at Cape Cod, the 11th of November, in the year of the reign of our Sovereign King James of England . . . Anno Domini 1620.[14]

Such ringing affirmations as "We hold these truths to be self-evident, that all men are created equal" would have to wait another century and a half to be openly stated in a government document, but here was their introduction onto American soil.

It is Bradford who rightly brings this chapter to a close: "Being thus arrived in a good harbor and brought safe to land, they fell upon their knees and blessed the God of heaven, who had brought them over the vast and furious ocean, and delivered them from all the perils and miseries thereof, again to set their feet on the firm and stable earth, their proper element. And no marvel if they were thus joyful."[15] They had begun their long journey by kneeling on the dock at Delftshaven to ask God's blessing; they ended it on the sands of Cape Cod, kneeling to thank Him for that blessing.

Yet Bradford, always the realist, went on to marvel at "this poor people's present condition . . . no friends to welcome them, nor inns to entertain or refresh their weatherbeaten bodies, no houses, or much less towns to repair to, to seek for succor."

With winter storms howling around the tip of the Cape, "whichever way they turned their eyes (save upward to the heavens) they could have little solace or content in respect of any outward objects. For summer being done, all things stand upon them with a weather-beaten face; and the whole country, full of woods and thickets, represented a wild and savage hue. If they looked behind them, there was the mighty ocean which they had passed, and was now as a main bar and gulf to separate them from all the civil parts of the world. . . . Let it also be considered what weak hope of supply and succor they left behind them. . . . What could now sustain them but the Spirit of God and his grace?"

9

"GOD OUR MAKER DOTH PROVIDE"

tranger in a strange land." The phrase from Exodus seemed singularly appropriate. It *was* a strange land—bleak and wind-swept, with steep dunes and a gnarled, weather-beaten covering of underbrush that clung to the low hills in the face of what seemed to be a perpetual northwest wind.

They stood on the deck of the *Mayflower* breathing the fresh air, too exhausted to think beyond thanking God that their three-month ordeal was over. The wind was refreshing, but it had a rawness to it that foretold an ordeal of a different kind.

While sixteen men went ashore in the ship's boat to find firewood and explore, others began to reassemble the thirty-foot sailing shallop. It would be needed for exploring the inner coast of the bay as they sought the right place for settlement. With oars and a large sail, the shallop was capable of transporting more than thirty people if necessary. Its reassembly was made more difficult because some sections had been damaged in the relentless pounding of the storms.

As the afternoon light began to fail, the ship's boat returned. All passengers crowded onto the main deck of the *Mayflower*; the shore party had found something! It was an abandoned cache of corn, some thirty-six ears buried in a large iron pot. Deeply grateful to their unseen benefactors, the Pilgrims determined to repay them if and when they met them. This was their first taste of Indian corn, the staple that was to save their lives, as it had saved so many at Jamestown, and would again and again all along the eastern seaboard. It was tough eating, but it obviously kept well under the right conditions. And it looked hearty enough to grow almost anywhere. Carver and Bradford and the rest were tremendously encouraged. These men returning with corn were like the Israelites sent ahead into the Promised Land, who returned with its fruits.

It took nearly three weeks to ready the shallop and trim her out. Finally, on December 6, ten of their leaders and some seamen set out "upon further discovery, intending to circulate [circumnavigate] that deep bay of Cape Cod. The weather was very cold, and it froze so hard as the spray of the sea lighting on their coats, they were as if they had been glazed."[1]

That afternoon they saw some Indians ahead on the tidal flats cutting up a large fish that had been stranded there after a storm, but the Indians ran away before they could hail them. The second night they encamped at dusk close to the eastern corner of the bay (Eastham). They erected a barricade of cut boughs to provide shelter against the wind and protection in case of attack. During the night their sleep was interrupted by many bloodcurdling cries and howls; they were glad to be up an hour before dawn to have prayer and then breakfast.

> But presently, all of the sudden, they heard a great and strange cry, which they knew to be the same voices they [had] heard in the night, though they varied their notes, and one of the company, being abroad, came running in and cried, "Indians, Indians!" and withal, arrows came flying in amongst them. . . . two muskets were discharged at them, and two more [men] stood ready in the entrance of their rendezvous, but were commanded not to shoot till they could take full aim at them. . . . The cry of the Indians was dreadful.

The skirmish continued, with neither side gaining an advantage, until several of the Pilgrims wearing coats of mail rushed forth from the barricade and discharged their muskets together. The Indians quickly scattered, "except for one brave, who stood behind a tree within half a musket-shot, and let his arrows fly at them. He was seen to shoot three arrows, which were all avoided. He stood three shots of a musket, till one, taking full aim at him, made the bark or splinters of the tree fly about his ears, after which he gave an extraordinary shriek, and away they went, all of them."

Later, in the journal which Bradford and Edward Winslow wrote together, they added:

> Yet by the especial providence of God, none of [their arrows] either hit or hurt us, though many came close by us and on every side of us, and some coats which were hung up on our barricado were shot through and through. So, after we had given God thanks for our deliverance . . . we went on our journey and called this place "The First Encounter" [which name it bears to this day].[2]

As they sailed south along the inner shore of the lower cape, their pilot, Robert Coppin, who had been there once before, told them of a good harbor at the mouth of a creek that they should reach before nightfall. According to historian Alexander Young, this could only be the harbor at Barnstable. They would have reached it around 2:00, but about an hour before that, snow began to fall in such thick, wet flakes that they sailed right past Coppin's harbor and on around the bottom of the bay.

As the afternoon wore on, the wind began to pick up.

> The sea became very rough, and they broke their rudder, and it was as much as two men could do to steer her with a couple of oars. But their pilot bade them be of good cheer, for he saw the harbor. But the storm increasing, and night drawing on, they bore what sail they could to get in, while they could see. But herewith they broke their mast in three pieces, and their sail fell overboard in a very grown sea, so as they had like to have been [wrecked]. Yet by God's mercy, they recovered themselves, and having the [tide] with them, struck into the harbor.
>
> But when it came to, the pilot was deceived in the place and said, The Lord be merciful unto them, for his eyes never saw that place before, and

he and the master mate would have run her ashore, in a cove full of breakers, before the wind.

One of the seamen named Clark, who was steering with an oar over the stern, suddenly took charge. Shouting into the wind, he cried, "If you be men, about with her or we are all cast away!"[3]

They all rowed furiously, snatching the shallop from the very edge of the breakers. Clark continued to call out encouragement until they were able to find shelter in the lee of a small island that seemed to loom out of nowhere in the gathering dark. They named the island after Clark and spent a wet, miserable night on it.

> . . . though this had been a day and night of much trouble and danger to them, yet God gave them a morning of comfort and refreshing (as usually He doth to His children), for the next day was a fair sunshining day, and they found themselves to be on an island secure from Indians, where they might dry their stuff, fix their pieces, and rest themselves, and give God thanks for His mercies in their manifold deliverances. And this being the last day of the week, they prepared there to keep the Sabbath.[4]

Monday morning dawned crisp and clear, washed clean by the rain and glistening in the morning sun. Already a day of promise, it would be a day of discoveries, each more amazing than the one before. The first was that the little island they were on was in the middle of a perfect natural harbor, almost completely enclosed. The next was that the harbor was deep enough to take ships of twice the draft of the *Mayflower*.

Once the explorers were on the mainland, the discoveries came in quick succession. The soil was rich and fertile, capable of supporting a wide variety of crops. There was, moreover, a broad, open, gentle slope down to the water's edge. It was an ideal place to settle, with excellent drainage and an open field of fire for muskets and cannon, should they need to defend it. Finally, there were four spring-fed creeks close at hand, with the sweetest water any of them had ever tasted—so good, in fact, that they almost did not mind that their supply of beer (the common beverage, due to England's untrustworthy water) had run out.

Providentially, an open hillside contained a good twenty acres that had already been cleared and were ready to plant, though for some reason nothing had been planted there for several years. Strangely, there were a number of human bones lying about, indicating that some disaster had befallen the former inhabitants. Puzzling as this was, it seemed clear that God had brought them to this place He had provided.

Rejoicing over their good fortune, they hurried back to the *Mayflower* with the news of their extraordinary find.

News of another sort was awaiting William Bradford. His wife Dorothy had gone over the side of the ship and was drowned. No mention of this tragedy is made in any of Bradford's writings, and it is commented on only briefly elsewhere, leading modern historians to speculate that she may have taken her own life. However it happened, the young widower was now faced with a choice. He could give in to self-pity, becoming increasingly morose or passive. Or he could apply himself with more singleness of purpose than ever to the God-given task of planting the colony. He chose the latter. This thirty-year-old leader had already demonstrated remarkable maturity; now he showed even more.

The Pilgrims named the site Plymouth (and spelled it Plimoth)—not because it happened to be called New Plymouth on John Smith's map, but because "Plymouth in Old England was the last town they left in the native country; and for that they received many kindnesses from some Christians there."[5]

In desperate need of the shelter that only the *Mayflower* could provide, the elders implored Master Jones to stay on as long as he could. The captain agreed; the hearts of these humble settlers had touched him deeply. They had borne everything cheerfully, even the taunts of the bosun's mate. They never complained about their conditions or the food or the weather, and they thanked God for the merest blessings. In a few days the worst of the winter would be upon them. As they laid out the main street, erected a palisade, and began the common house, the building of shelter went slowly because their hands were so cold that they had difficulty keeping hold of axe or adze.

This time came to be known as the time of the "General Sickness," when their bodies, weakened from three long months at sea, finally succumbed to scurvy, despite what was left of the lemon juice. Often a lingering cold—contracted after wading ashore, trudging through the snow, and sleeping on the damp ground (under continuing exertion—for there was too much to be done to stop working just for a cold)—flared up into consumption or pneumonia.

The Pilgrims started dying. There were six dead in December, eight in January—they were falling like casualties on a battlefield. And in a sense, that was what they were: locked in a life-or-death struggle with Satan himself. For this was the first time that the Light of Christ had landed in force on his continent, and if he did not throw them back into the sea at the beginning, there would be reinforcements.

On Sunday, January 14, an icy wind was blowing through the cracks of the nearly completed common house, where there lay as many sick as they could crowd in. Suddenly, before anyone knew what was happening, the thatched roof above them was blazing with fire, and the place was filled with smoke. Many started to cry out in terror as burning embers fell from the roof. Had it not been for the supernatural strength given to some of the sick to take speedy action, they might have been blown to pieces, because there were open barrels of gunpowder and loaded muskets in the common house. These were quickly rushed outside. Fortunately, the timbers in the roof did not catch fire, so the building was saved. Much precious clothing was burned up, however, further exposing the sick to the elements of the New England winter.

But as they themselves had said, they were not like other people. The more that adversity mounted against them, the harder they prayed—never giving in to despair, murmuring, or any of the petty jealousies that split and divide. In contrast to the settlers of Jamestown, as their ranks thinned, they drew closer together, trusting God all the more. And still the death toll mounted. In February often two died in a day, even three on some days. The twenty-first of February claimed four lives. And at one point, in the entire company there were only five men well enough to care for the sick. One of them was Captain Standish, who tended Bradford, among others, raising his head up and cradling it in his arm to spoon him a bit of soup.

Standish, Brewster, and three or four others chopped wood, cleaned, clothed, cooked, and tended. Periodically they would show themselves at the palisade, just in case the Indians whom they had seen in the distance happened to be watching them. For the same reason, they buried their dead at night in shallow, unmarked graves so that the natives would not realize how many they had lost. In February there were seventeen deaths.

The pitched battle between love and death went on. On board the *Mayflower* the seamen, too, began to fall. One, gravely ill, promised his companion all his possessions after his death, if only he would look after him while he was still alive. His companion "went and got a little spice and made him a mess of meat once or twice, and because he died not so soon as he expected, [his companion] went amongst his fellows and swore the rogue [had swindled] him. He would see him choked before he made him any more meat! And yet the poor fellow died before morning."[6] (Shades of Jamestown!)

Gradually, almost imperceptibly, the light of Christ was gaining the victory. The bosun was stricken: "a proud young man who would often curse and scoff at the passengers, but when he grew weak, they had compassion on him and helped him. Then he confessed that he did not deserve it at their hands; he had abused them in word and deed. 'Oh!' he said, 'you, I now see, show your love like Christians indeed to one another, but we let one another lie and die like dogs.' "

March was another killing month; thirteen more died. But that was four less than the month before. And when at last the worst was finally over, they had lost forty-seven people, nearly half their original number. Thirteen out of eighteen wives died; only three families remained unbroken. Of all these first comers, the children fared the best: of seven daughters, none died; of thirteen sons, only three. And the colony, which was young to begin with, was even younger now. But compared with Jamestown's 80 to 90 percent mortality rate, they came through remarkably well.

Through it all, their hearts remained soft toward God. Whether they knew that they were being tested, as Bradford later suspected, the high point of their week remained Sunday worship. When the beat of a field drum summoned them to the morning and afternoon services, all joined the procession led by William Brewster (their spiritual leader until such time as God provided them with a minister), Governor John Carver, and Miles Standish, in charge of their defense. As they made their way up the hill, their clothes were not the somber browns, grays, and blacks of the pictures that hang in modern schoolrooms around Thanksgiving time. Miles Standish almost certainly wore his plum-red cape, and William Brewster had an emerald green satin doublet that he probably saved for Sundays. For these were Elizabethan Englishmen; it was their Puritan cousins of later settlements who would hold that "frivolous" clothes connoted a frivolous attitude.

The houses that they passed were of mud wattle and daub construction, usually with two rooms around a central fireplace and a sleeping loft atop one of the rooms. The high-peaked roofs were of thatch—especially difficult to make, because the right kind of grass grew more than a mile away. There were five such houses more or less finished, in addition to the common house at the foot of the hill, where many of them had spent the winter.

The service was held in the blockhouse at the top of the hill—an imposing building with a flat roof and a trap door—so that the house could be defended from the roof. Captain Jones had parted with one of his two huge, fifteen-hundred-pound cannons called sackers, one of his brace of twelve-hundred-pounders called minions, plus two smaller cannons called bases. From this high point it was possible to enfilade the main street, as well as cover the distant woods.

Inside on rough-hewn log benches, the men would sit on the left, the women on the right. William Brewster would preach, and he had a gift for teaching "both powerfully and profitably, to the great contentment of the hearers, and their comfortable edification; yea, many were brought to God by his ministry."[7] And elsewhere Bradford comments on the fact that God used Brewster's preaching as an instrument to bring sweet repentance to their hearts for the sins they might have forgotten about.

If any one event could be singled out to mark the turning point of their fortunes, it would be what happened on a fair Friday in the middle of March. With the iron grip of winter beginning to loosen its hold on the earth, the first shoots of green had begun to appear. The men were gathered in the common house to conclude their conference on military instruction when the cry went up, "Indian coming!"

Indian coming? Surely he meant Indians coming. Captain Standish shook his head, even as he went to look out the window—to see a tall, well-built Indian, wearing nothing but a leather loincloth, striding up their main street. He was headed straight for the common house, and the men inside hurried to the door before he walked right in on them. He stopped and stood motionless, looking at them as though sculpted in marble. Only the March wind broke the silence.

"Welcome!" he suddenly boomed, in a deep, resonant voice.

The Pilgrims were too startled to speak. At length, they replied with as much gravity as they could muster: "Welcome."

Their visitor fixed them with a piercing stare. "Have you got any beer?" he asked in flawless English. If they were surprised before, they were astounded now.

"Beer?" one of them managed.

The Indian nodded.

The Pilgrims looked at one another and then turned back to him. "Our beer is gone. Would you like . . . some brandy?"

Again the Indian nodded.

They brought him some brandy and a biscuit with butter and cheese, and then some pudding and a piece of roast duck. To their continuing amazement, he ate with evident relish everything set before him. Where had he developed such an appetite for English food? How, in fact, had he come to speak English? For that matter, who was he, and what was he doing here?

But they would have to wait, for obviously he did not intend to talk until he had finished his repast. Finally, the time for answering questions came. His name was Samoset. He was a sagamore (or chief) of the Algonquins, from what is now Pemaquid Point in Maine. He had been visiting in these parts for the past eight months, having begged a ride down the coast with Captain Thomas Dermer, an English sea captain who was known to the Pilgrims by reputation. He had been sent out to explore the coast for the Council for New England, the company to which they would now be applying for a patent. Apparently Samoset's sole motivation was a love of travel, and he had learned his English from various fishing captains who had put in to the Maine shore over the years.

Now they asked him the crucial question: What could he tell them of the Indians hereabouts?

The story he told gave every one of them cause to thank God in their hearts. This area, called Patuxet, had been the territory of a small tribe by the same name. But four years before the Pilgrims' arrival, a mysterious plague had broken out among them, killing every man, woman, and child. So complete was the devastation that the neighboring tribes had shunned the area ever since, convinced that some great supernatural spirit had destroyed the Patuxets. Hence, the cleared land on which the Pilgrims had settled belonged to no one. Their nearest neighbors, said Samoset, were the Wampanoags, some fifty miles to the southwest. These Indians numbered about sixty warriors. Massasoit, their sachem (or chief), possessed such wisdom that he also ruled over several other small tribes in the general area. It was with Massasoit that Samoset had spent most of the past eight months.

Who were the Indians out on the cape who had attacked them? Those would be the Nausets, a fierce, warlike tribe who numbered about a hundred warriors. The previous summer they had attacked Captain Dermer and killed three of his men. The Nausets hated the white people because several years earlier Captain Thomas Hunt had tricked seven of their braves into coming aboard his ship on the pretext of wanting to trade with them. He had taken them, along with twenty Patuxets, to Spain, where he sold them into slavery.

By the time he was done with his tale-telling, it was nightfall. Samoset announced that he would sleep with them and return in the morning. Captain Standish put a discreet watch on him, but Samoset slept the sleep of the untroubled. And in the morning he left, bearing a knife, a bracelet, and a ring as gifts to Massasoit.

That was the last they saw of him, until the following Thursday when he returned accompanied by another Indian who also spoke English and who was, of all things, a Patuxet.[8] This second Indian was Squanto, and he was to be, according to Bradford, "a special instrument sent of God for their good, beyond their expectation." The extraordinary chain of "coincidences" in this man's life was reminiscent of the saga of Joseph having been sold into slavery in Egypt. Indeed, in ensuing months, there was no doubt in any of their hearts that Squanto, whose Indian name was Tisquantum, was a godsend.

His story had begun in 1605, when Squanto and four other Indians were taken captive by Captain George Weymouth, who was exploring the New England coast at the behest of Sir Ferdinando Gorges. The Indians were taken to England, where they were taught English, so that Gorges could question them about the tribes populating the Atlantic coast and learn the locations of the most favorable places to establish colonies. Squanto spent the next nine years in England, where he met Captain John Smith, recently of Virginia, who promised to take Squanto back to his people as soon as he himself could get a command that would enable him to go there. Actually he did not have too long to wait. On Smith's 1614 voyage of mapping and exploring, Squanto was returned to the Patuxets at the place Smith named New Plymouth.

Commanding the other ship in Smith's expedition was Captain Thomas Hunt. One day when Smith was about to lead an exploring party, he ordered Hunt and his crew to stay behind to dry their catch of fish and trade it for more profitable beaver pelts before returning home. But Hunt had another, more lucrative cargo in mind. As soon as Smith departed, he slipped back down the coast to Plymouth, where under the pretext of barter, he lured twenty Patuxets aboard, including Squanto, and promptly clapped them in irons.

Then sailing across the bay to the outer edge of Cape Cod, he scooped up seven unsuspecting Nausets and set course for Málaga, a notorious slave-trading port on the Mediterranean coast of Spain. There he proceeded to auction them off, getting twenty pounds for each of them. (In today's money that would be over $1800 a head—which explains how the slave trade could be so tempting.) Most of Hunt's captives were bought by Arab slave traders and shipped off to North Africa.

During the auction, monks from a nearby monastery heard what was happening and bought the remaining Indians, including Squanto, "to instruct them in the Christian faith." Thus did God begin Squanto's preparation for the role he would play at Plymouth.

Squanto was too enterprising to stay long in a monastery. He attached himself to an Englishman bound for London, and there he met and joined the household of wealthy merchant Sir John Slanie. He lived on Slanie's estate until he embarked for New England with Captain Dermer in 1619. It was on this same trip that Dermer had picked up Samoset at Monhegan, one of the major fishing stations in Maine, and dropped them both off at Plymouth. At that time Dermer wrote to a friend (presumably on the New England Council): "I will first begin with that place whence Squanto, or Tisquantum, was taken away, which on Captain Smith's map is called Plymouth, and would that Plymouth [England] had the like commodities! I would that the first plantation might be here seated."[9]

When Squanto stepped ashore six months before the arrival of the Pilgrims, he received the most tragic blow of his life: not a man, woman, or child of his tribe was left alive. Nothing remained but skulls and bones and ruined dwellings. He had looked forward to coming back home to spend the remainder of his days with his people. Now, as he wandered aimlessly through the fields in which he had played as a child and the woods where he had learned to hunt, there was nothing. In despair, he trekked many miles southeast into Massasoit's camp, simply because he had nowhere else to go. And that wise chief took pity on this lonely warrior whose tribe had vanished and who had lost all reason for living.

That is, until Samoset brought news of a small colony of peaceful English families who had settled at Patuxet on the site of Squanto's old village. They were there to plant a colony, but at the moment they were hard-pressed to stay alive. It would not be long before they died of starvation, since they had little food and nothing to plant but English wheat, barley, and peas. As Squanto listened, the light began to come back into his eyes. He accompanied Samoset when the latter went to Plymouth with Massasoit, as the chief's interpreter.

It was a memorable visit. Massasoit had brought with him all sixty of his warriors, painted in startling fashion. Edward Winslow was elected to meet Massasoit and make him a gift of two more knives and "a pot of strong water." What Massasoit really wanted was Winslow's armor and sword, but before he could make this clear through Squanto, Winslow began to discourse smoothly and at length, making a long speech which said nothing, in the finest diplomatic tradition.

Eventually Massasoit nodded, smiled, and went to find Governor Carver. He was ushered into one of the partially finished houses to a fanfare of trumpet and drum, which pleased him immensely. They drank a toast to Massasoit, who lifted the pot of strong water himself and took an enormous draft, which made his eyes water and caused him to sweat profusely.

But out of that meeting came a peace treaty of mutual aid and assistance that would last for forty years until Massasoit's death. Massasoit was a remarkable example of God's providential care for the Pilgrims. He was probably the only chief on the northeast coast of America who would have welcomed the Europeans as friends. And the Pilgrims took great pains not to abuse his acceptance of them. On the contrary, the record of their relations with him and his people is a strong testimony to the love of Christ that was in them.

When Massasoit and his entourage finally left, Squanto remained behind. He had found his reason for living. These English people were ignorant of the ways of the wild. He could do something about that. The next day he went out and came back with all the eels he could hold in his hands—which the Pilgrims found to be "fat and sweet" and excellent eating. How had he caught them? He took several young men with him and taught them how to stamp the eels out of the mud with their bare feet and then catch them with their hands.

But the next thing he showed them was by far the most important, for it would prove to be a lifesaver. In April Squanto taught the Pilgrims how to plant corn the Indian way, burying fish with the kernels. The Pilgrim men cast a baleful eye on their amazing friend who seemed to have adopted them; in four months they had caught exactly one cod. No matter, said Squanto cheerfully; in four days the creeks would be overflowing with fish. He taught them how to make the weirs they would need to catch the fish. Obediently they did as he instructed, and four days later the creeks for miles around were clogged with alewives making their spring run. The Pilgrims did not catch them; they harvested them.

Now the corn was planted, with kernels of corn in the center of a six-foot square of hoed earth. Pointing spokelike at it were three fishes, their heads almost touching. Finally, said Squanto, they would have to guard against wolves. Seeing the familiar bewildered look on his charges' faces, he explained that the wolves would attempt to dig up and make off with the fish. The Pilgrims would have to guard the cornfield for two weeks until the fish had thoroughly decomposed. And so they did, and that summer, twenty full acres of corn began to flourish.

Squanto also taught them how to stalk deer, plant pumpkins among the corn, draw sap from maple trees and boil it down into maple syrup, discern which herbs were good to eat and good for medicine, and find the best berries. But after the corn, there was one additional thing he taught them that was inestimably important to their survival. What little fishing they had done was a fiasco, so any thought of them fishing commercially had to be scrapped. Squanto introduced them to the pelt of the beaver, which was then in plentiful supply in southern New England and in great demand throughout Europe. And not only did he get them started, but he guided them in the trading, making sure they got their full money's worth in top-quality pelts. Just as tobacco had been for Jamestown, this would prove to be their economic deliverance.

There were, nonetheless, moments of sadness in the midst of all these encouraging developments. In the course of planting the corn, Governor Carver was suddenly struck down with what was probably a cerebral hemorrhage. He died three days later without ever regaining consciousness. His replacement by unanimous vote was William Bradford, who would be reelected annually for the next thirty-six years of his life, except for the five years when he explicitly requested that they choose someone else.

Immediately after Carver's death, something else happened that could have thrown the colony into despair. The time had come for Master Jones to leave for England. Fearful for the Pilgrims' future, Jones had begged them to return to the mother country with him. The offer was tempting, and many had good cause to accept it. Illness had ravaged them: only four of the couples who had arrived on the *Mayflower* still had each other, and a number had lost children. Yet not one of the Pilgrims responded to Jones's entreaties.

In the midst of all the dying, something special had been born among them—they shared the love of Jesus Christ in a way that only happens when people are willing to suffer together for His cause. This was what they had come to the wilderness to find, and now none of them wished to leave it.

By the twenty-first of April, Master Jones decided he could not linger another day. The *Mayflower*'s supplies had gotten so low that he had barely enough food to get home, even though he would be returning with only half the crew with which he had left Southampton. The entire settlement gathered on the rocky shore to say good-bye, and one can imagine Jones shaking hands all around, ending with William Bradford. Then he was in the boat, and his men were rowing out the *Mayflower*.

The day was overcast, gray clouds scudding before a chilling offshore breeze. On shore the little gathering could hear his first mate's commands and the chant of the seamen as they turned the anchor windlass and slowly raised the anchor. The breeze filled the *Mayflower*'s sails, and she began to move, pointing her bow toward the harbor entrance.

As the small ship sailed away toward the horizon, a heavy silence fell over the Pilgrims. There went their last link with England, and there might be no new ones. Given the nature of their parting with Weston, they could not count on the Adventurers sending another supply ship.

They were alone.

Brewster and Bradford and others would have been sensitive to the hearts of their compatriots. Fear and discouragement, they knew, were two of Satan's most potent weapons. These could be dealt with best by the sword of the Spirit, the Word of God. If there was ever a time to sing a psalm, it was now.

As they sang, they might have marched up to the blockhouse, where Brewster might have read to them Isaiah 41:8–10:

> But you, Israel, my servant,
> > Jacob, whom I have chosen,
> > > the offspring of Abraham, my friend;
> > you whom I took from the ends of the earth,
> > > and called from its farthest corners,
> > saying to you, "You are my servant,
> > > I have chosen you and not cast you off";
> > fear not, for I am with you,

be not dismayed, for I am your God;
I will strengthen you, I will help you,
I will uphold you with my victorious right hand.

In May as the weather warmed even more and the wildflowers came into full blossom, the little community had an occasion for great joy: their first wedding. Edward Winslow had lost his wife in the General Sickness, and Susanna White had lost her husband. They both felt that God did not intend for them to carry on alone in spite of the short length of time their spouses had been gone. Governor Bradford agreed and was glad to join them together in holy matrimony, after which there was a wedding feast with much gaiety and laughter—a cleansing and healing gift from the Lord.

That summer of 1621 was beautiful. Much work went into the building of new dwellings, and ten men were sent north up the coast in the sailing shallop to conduct trade with the Indians. Once again Squanto acted as their agent, guide, and interpreter. It was a successful trip, and that fall's harvest was so bountiful that they would have enough corn to see them not only through the winter but all the way through the following summer to their next harvest.

The Pilgrims were brimming over with gratitude—not only to Squanto and the Wampanoags who had been so friendly, but to their God. In Him they had trusted, and He had honored their obedience beyond their dreams. So Governor Bradford declared a day of public thanksgiving, to be held in October.[10] Massasoit was invited and unexpectedly arrived a day early—with ninety Indians. Counting their numbers, the Pilgrims would have been tempted to give in to despair. To feed such a crowd would cut deeply into the food supply that was supposed to get them through the winter.

But if they had learned one thing through their travails, it was to trust God. As it turned out, the Indians were not arriving empty-handed. Massasoit had commanded his braves to hunt for the occasion, and they arrived with no less than five dressed deer and more than a dozen fat wild turkeys. And they helped with the preparations, teaching the Pilgrim women how to make hoecakes and a tasty pudding out of cornmeal and maple syrup.

Finally, they showed them an Indian delicacy: how to roast corn kernels in an earthen pot until they popped, fluffy and white—popcorn!

The Pilgrims in turn provided many vegetables from their household gardens: carrots, onions, turnips, parsnips, cucumbers, radishes, beets, and cabbages. Also, using some of their precious flour, they took summer fruits that the Indians had dried and introduced them to the likes of blueberry, apple, and cherry pie. It was all washed down with sweet wine made from the wild grapes—a joyous occasion for all.

All day long the feasting continued and into the evening and the following morning. Between meals the Pilgrims and Indians happily competed in shooting contests with gun and bow. The Indians were especially delighted that John Alden and some of the younger men of the plantation were eager to join them in foot races and leg wrestling. There were even military drills staged by Captain Standish. Things went so well (and Massasoit showed no inclination to leave) that their first day of Thanksgiving was extended for three days.

Surely one moment stood out in the Pilgrims' memory—William Brewster's prayer as they began their festival. They had so much for which to thank God: for providing all their needs, even when their faith had not been up to believing that He would actually do so; for the lives of the departed and for taking them home to be with Him; for their friendship with the Indians—so extraordinary when settlers down in the Virginia Colony had experienced the opposite; and for all His remarkable providences in bringing them to this place and sustaining them.

In November, a full year after their arrival, the first ship from home dropped anchor in the harbor. It was the *Fortune*, on her way to Virginia and dropping off passengers at Plymouth: thirty-five more colonists, including William Brewster's grown son, Jonathan, two brothers of Edward Winslow, and of all people, Robert Cushman. And he had with him a charter—their own charter—granted through the New England Company.

In the air of celebration that followed, no one stopped to think that these newcomers had brought not one bit of food or equipment with them—no clothing, no tools, no bedding. In the cold light of the following morning, a sobering appraisal was taken by Bradford, Brewster, and Winslow, and a grim decision was reached: they would all have to go on half-rations through the winter to ensure enough food to see them at least into the summer season when fish and game would be plentiful.

And they had a difficult matter to consider: Weston was still angry that they had refused to sign his revised agreement, and he was even angrier that they had sent the *Mayflower* back empty. "I know your weakness was the cause of it . . . more weakness of judgment, than weakness of hands. A quarter of the time you spent in discoursing, arguing, and consulting."[11]

Did Weston and the Adventurers see no difference between them and the settlers at Jamestown? A measure of the Pilgrims' spiritual maturity was that they did not respond in kind. Bradford wrote a dispassionate and honest answer, denying that they had spent any time discoursing and arguing, and pointing out that half of their number had died. He added that they would be sending goods just as soon as they were able.

But Weston's accusations were not the heaviest burden laid upon them. For the Pilgrims soon learned the real purpose of Cushman's visit. Toward the end of the *Fortune*'s two-week stay, Cushman preached on "The Sin and Danger of Self-Love":

[if thou] art not sad, churlish or discontent, but cheerful in thine heart, though thy will be crossed, it is a good sign. But if not, thou art sick of a self-will, and must purge it out. I rather press these things, because I see many men both wise and religious which are yet so tainted with this pestilent self-love, as that it is in them even as a dead fly to the apothecary's ointment, spoiling the efficacy of all their graces, making their lives uncomfortable to themselves and unprofitable to others, being neither fit for church nor commonwealth, but have even their very souls in hazard thereby, and therefore who can say too much against it.

It is reported that there are many men gone to Virginia, which, while they lived in England, seemed very religious, zealous and conscionable, and have now lost even the sap of grace and edge to all goodness, and are become mere worldlings. This testimony I believe to be partly true, and amongst many causes of it, this self-love is not the least.[12]

It was a strong sermon. He was, in effect, saying that if the Pilgrims did not give up their willfulness and self-love (sins which they shared with all men, though probably in as small measure as any group of people among America's first settlers), they were in danger of winding up in the same condition as the Jamestown settlers. The Pilgrims heeded it and sought to apply it to their lives.

Though Cushman had preached in all sincerity, it soon became apparent what specific "willfulness" he had in mind. Scarcely was his sermon over than he began to press Carver, Brewster, Bradford, and the other principals to capitulate to Weston's revised conditions.

Here is a striking example of how a loyal Christian's judgment and covenanted commitment can be subtly compromised once he or she chooses to give less than all. Cushman's crisis of faith had occurred back in Dartmouth, when the *Speedwell* was having its difficulties. He had lost his heart for the Pilgrims' undertaking and had declined to go with them aboard the *Mayflower*. Choosing the easier way, he had justified it by impressing upon them how much he was needed in London to act as their liaison with the Adventurers.

As it happened, he was probably the last one who should have been representing them. When Robinson and Brewster had written to reprimand him for accepting Weston's alterations without first checking with them, he had written a three-page reply, correcting his superiors for their avarice and willfulness. But the Pilgrims, perhaps because they did not want to hurt his feelings or simply because there was no one else to send, chose to overlook his arrogance.

Weston, however, knew exactly how to manipulate Cushman. More and more, Cushman came under the worldly influence of Weston and his powerful associates. Eventually, though he was probably unaware of it, Robert Cushman came to think of himself and the Adventurers in terms of "we," while "they" were a handful of simple farmers some three thousand miles away. Thus could Cushman, with utmost sincerity, call on the Pilgrims to repent and then challenge them to demonstrate their repentance by accepting the contractual conditions they so detested.

And the Pilgrims, their own faith momentarily shaken, again could not quite bring themselves to totally trust God to provide, despite their previous, long-standing conviction that it was His will for them to reject the agreement. All they could see was that further refusal would close their last channel for desperately needed supplies, and (for so Cushman assured them) they would be totally cut off. So they signed the agreement—thereby entering into a bondage to the Adventurers that would see them struggle for more than *twenty years* to get out from under.

The Pilgrims were mercilessly taken advantage of, at times having to borrow money at interest rates of 30 and 50 percent. Some of the most unscrupulous Adventurers, seeing that their "partners" in America were determined to pay every shilling charged to them with no questions asked, began to load them with claims so bogus that other Adventurers urged the Pilgrims not to pay, or at least to resort to the courts.

But the colonists were set on responding in the spirit of their Lord; "You have heard that it was said, 'An eye for an eye, and a tooth for a tooth.' But I say to you . . . if any one would sue you and take your coat, let him have your cloak as well" (Matt. 5:38–40). They paid every claim assessed to them, no matter how fraudulent, and they were finally able in 1645 to buy themselves clear of the Adventurers. But at a fearful cost: it took some 20,000 pounds to retire a debt of 1,800. And to do it, Bradford had to sell a large farm; Alden and Standish, three hundred acres apiece; and Winslow and Prence, their homes.

Our own first response, had we been in the Pilgrims' place, would have been to choose another verse from Matthew to follow: "Behold, I send you out as sheep in the midst of wolves; so be wise as serpents and innocent as doves" (Matt. 10:16). But on reflection, we began to see the wisdom in the harder course they so prayerfully chose: for Satan would have liked nothing better than to have drawn them into the bitter wrangling and legal disputes that were commonplace in the business dealings of that day. Nothing corrodes the soul quite so fast or effectively.

Here, too, the hand of a loving Father could be seen. For while the Pilgrims may have been out of His will when they knuckled under to Weston's demands, God was still ensuring the purity of the work that He was raising up at Plymouth. What mattered most to Him was not what was done to the Pilgrims. What mattered to God was how the Pilgrims responded to it. And He must have been pleased with their response: they kept their eyes, for the most part, on Him.

Thus did they enter their own starving time that winter of 1621–22 with all the extra people to feed and clothe and shelter, and they were ultimately reduced to a daily ration of five kernels of corn apiece. Five kernels of corn—it is almost inconceivable that life could be supported on this. And as always, they had a choice: either to give in to bitterness and despair or go deeper into Christ. They chose Christ. And incredibly, in contrast to what happened at Jamestown, not one of them died of starvation.

Then God had mercy on them, as He had so often in the past. Unexpectedly a ship put into their harbor on its way back to England from Virginia. While the captain had no extra food on board, he did have trading goods—beads, knives, trinkets, and so on—that the Pilgrims could trade for corn. His price? Beaver pelts, for which he would give them three shillings per pound. The Pilgrims well knew that he would sell the pelts at home for six times as much, but they had no choice, and they were able to thank God for seeing them through that winter.

And what of Thomas Weston? "Though the mills of God grind exceeding slow, yet they do grind exceeding fine" goes the old saying. Weston, not content to wait seven years, and acting independently of the other Adventurers, set up his own fishing enterprise, just a few miles up the coast from Plymouth at Wessagusset (now Weymouth). When the other Adventurers got wind of what he was up to, they expelled him from their consortium. About the same time, everything began to go so badly for him that to escape his creditors he disguised himself as a fisherman and sailed for the New World himself, planning on using his fishing station as a new base of operations.

But the fishing station was no more. The bunch of roughnecks he had sent there had consumed a year's supplies in four months, sold their equipment to the Indians for food, and were mainly interested in staying drunk from sunup to sundown. Moreover, they had so provoked the Indians that some renegade Massachusetts warriors were considering a general attack on all English settlers, including the Pilgrims. Warned by Massasoit, Standish and eight men promptly went to Wessagusset and thwarted the plot by killing six of the Indian ringleaders, one of whom had previously physically attacked Standish.

Then they gave Weston's rowdies an ultimatum: they could come to Plymouth or they could sail for home; either way, they were to be gone on the next tide. They sailed for England within the hour, and peace returned to Massachusetts Bay.

When Weston arrived at Charlestown, he could not believe what he had been told about his fishing station, so with another man he hired a shallop to see for himself. Bad seamanship caused their vessel to founder, and Weston was then relieved of all his belongings save his shirt by some local Indians. Having nowhere else to go, he made for Plymouth on foot. When he finally turned up on their doorstep, he presented a sorry sight, indeed.

This was a far different Weston from the imperious overlord who had bent them to his will before. He begged them for mercy and for more than that: the loan of a load of beaver skins to get him back on his feet. He promised that he would repay them in supplies as soon as the transaction was completed, and he assured them he would never be able to repay their compassion. They "pitied his case" said Bradford, "and helped him when all the world failed him"[13] and gave him the beaver skins. Eventually he did repay them—with scorn and vicious slander, and not a penny in recompense.

In November of 1622 while he was on a corn-trading expedition to Indians on Cape Cod, Squanto experienced a nosebleed. He told Bradford that among the Indians this was a sign of imminent death, and sure enough, several days later he was gone. Before his death he asked the governor to pray for him, "that he might go to the Englishmen's God in Heaven, and bequeathed sundry of his things to sundry of his English friends as remembrances of his love, of whom they had a great loss."[14]

April 1623—time once again to get the year's corn planted. But as the Pilgrims went into the fields to till the ground and plant the kernels, there was a listlessness about them that was more than just weakness from months of inadequate rations. They were well aware that they needed at least twice as large a yield as the first harvest, and they did not want a repeat of the halfhearted effort of the second summer (when they had been too busy building houses and planting gardens to give the common cornfields the attention they needed).

So the leaders of the colony decided that there would be an additional planting. For this second planting, individual lots would be parceled out, with the understanding that the corn grown on these lots would be for the planters' own private use.

Suddenly new life seemed to infuse the Pilgrims: "it made all hands very industrious, so as much more corn was planted than otherwise would have been by any means the Governor or any other could use, and saved him a great deal of trouble and gave far better content. The women now went willingly into the field and took their little ones with them to set corn, which before would allege weakness and inability, whom to have compelled would have been thought great tyranny and oppression."

Bradford made this insightful comment about their brief experiment with communism:

"The experience that was had in this common course . . . may well evince the vanity of that conceit of Plato's and other ancients applauded by some of later times, that the taking away of property and bringing in community into a commonwealth would make them happy and flourishing; as if they were wiser than God. For this community (so far as it was) was found to breed much confusion and discontent and retard much employment that would have been to their benefit and comfort."[15]

The Pilgrims had reaffirmed the Biblical teaching on the right of private property and laid the basis for what would become the American free enterprise system. A little more than 250 years later, Karl Marx's *Das Kapital* would reject Biblical economics, and reintroduce Plato's utopian ideas. The result would be the destructive madness of twentieth-century Communism.

Some time after the second planting, it became apparent that the dry spell that had begun between the two plantings was turning into a drought. Week followed week (it would continue for twelve weeks in all), and not even the oldest Indians could remember anything like it. Edward Winslow described the drought and what followed:

> There scarce fell any rain, so that the stalk of that [planting which] was first set, began to send forth the ear before it came to half growth, and that which was later, not like to yield any at all, both blade and stalk hanging the head and changing the color in such manner as we judged it utterly dead. Our beans also ran not up according to their wonted manner, but stood at a stay, many being parched away, as though they had been scorched before the fire. Now were our hopes overthrown, and we discouraged, our joy turned into mourning . . . because God, which hitherto had been our only shield and supporter, now seemed in His anger to arm Himself against us. And who can withstand the fierceness of His wrath?
>
> These and the like considerations moved not only every good man privately to enter into examination with his own estate between God and his conscience, and so to humiliation before Him, but also to humble ourselves together before the Lord by fasting and prayer. To that end, a day was appointed by public authority, and set apart from all other employments.[16]

At this point we wondered what might have caused God to visit such a judgment upon these Christians He had brought to the New World. At first we were at a loss to find anything that seemed to merit such severe, across-the-board dealing. And then it came to us: if we had been Pilgrims, how would *we* have responded after enduring months of always being hungry?

When we looked at the natural inclination of our own hearts, we found that we, too, would have been out there planting as many kernels as we possibly could. And not just to ensure that we would never be that hungry again; we would have dwelt much on what we were going to get in trade for the extra ears.

And God would have been nowhere in view; we would have been totally absorbed in looking out for our own interests. If the neighbor next door were not able to plant his plot as well as we could, well—too bad for him. In the end, we saw that the moment greed and self began to get the upper hand, there was little difference between golden kernels and golden coins. It occurred to us that the Pilgrims had not been exposed

179

to the subtle pitfalls of personal greed for a very long time. And perhaps God was using this whole episode to show them an area of self in which they had not actually overcome as much as they might have thought. For in a way, sin is like the layers of an onion: when one layer is peeled off, there are always more layers beneath.

Whatever may have brought on the drought, the sincere and deep repentance of each and every Pilgrim had a phenomenal effect. Winslow continues:

> But, O the mercy of our God, who was as ready to hear, as we were to ask! For though in the morning, when we assembled together, the heavens were as clear and the drought as like to continue as it ever was, yet (our exercise continuing some eight or nine hours) before our departure, the weather was overcast, the clouds gathered on all sides. On the next morning distilled such soft, sweet and moderate showers of rain, continuing some fourteen days (!) and mixed with such seasonable weather, as it was hard to say whether our withered corn or drooping affections were most quickened or revived, such was the bounty and goodness of our God!

Bradford says, "It came, without either wind or thunder, or any violence, and by degrees in that abundance as that the earth was thoroughly wet and soaked therewith. Which did so apparently revive and quicken the decayed corn and other fruits, as was wonderful to see and made the Indians astonished to behold."[17]

It *had* to have had a profound effect on the Indians. For although their own rain dances or the incantations of their medicine men did sometimes seem to have some effect, it is interesting to note the result, as Winslow comments: "and all of them admired the goodness of our God towards us, that wrought so great a change in so short a time, showing the difference between their conjuration and our invocation on the name of God for rain, theirs being mixed with such storms and tempests, as sometimes, instead of doing them good, it layeth the corn flat on the ground, to their prejudice, but ours in so gentle and seasonable a manner, as they never observed the like."[18] There are only two origins of supernatural phenomena, and as the Pilgrims might have said, "The proof of the pudding is in the eating."

The yield that year was so abundant that the Pilgrims ended up with a surplus of corn, which they were able to use in trading that winter with northern Indians, who had not had a good growing season. A second Day of Thanksgiving was planned, and this year there was even more reason to celebrate: their beloved Governor was to marry one Alice Southworth. Massasoit was again the guest of honor, and this time he brought his principal wife, three other sachems, and 120 braves. Fortunately, he again brought venison and turkey, as well.

The occasion was described by one of the Adventurers, Emmanuel Altham, in a letter to his brother:

> After our arrival in New England, we found all our plantation in good health, and neither man, woman or child sick . . . in this plantation is about twenty houses, four or five of which are very pleasant, and the rest (as time will serve) shall be made better . . . the fishing that is in this country, indeed it is beyond belief . . . in one hour we got 100 cod . . .
>
> And now to say somewhat of the great cheer we had at the Governor's marriage. We had about twelve tasty venisons, besides others, pieces of roasted venison and other such good cheer in such quantities that I wish you some of our share. For here we have the best grapes that ever you saw, and the biggest, and divers sorts of plums and nuts . . . six goats, about fifty hogs and pigs, also divers hens . . . A better country was never seen nor heard of, for here are a multitude of God's blessing.[19]

What Altham neglected to mention was the first course that was served: on an empty plate in front of each person were five kernels of corn—lest any should forget.

These Pilgrims were a mere handful of Light-bearers on the edge of a vast and dark continent. But the Light of Jesus Christ was penetrating further into the heart of America. William Bradford would write with remarkable discernment, "As one small candle may light a thousand, so the light kindled here has shown unto many, yea in some sort to our whole nation. . . . We have noted these things so that you might see their worth and not negligently lose what your fathers have obtained with so much hardship."[20]

10

THY KINGDOM COME

*T*he Puritans really believed it," Peter mused, breaking the heavy silence that hung over the patio.

"Believed what?" asked David, not really caring.

We were sitting in back of Peter's parents' house in Florida, where we had met for an editorial conference, and we were facing the fact that our first draft of the Puritan chapters was little more than an outline of history. Gone was all enthusiasm for the material; we sensed that we were missing the point of what God had wanted us to see.

In the aftermath of that confrontation with reality, we were well into despondency. The early morning sun was filtering down through the fronds of the palm trees, bathing everything in a soft, delicate haze. Not a hint of a breeze stirred the trees. But we were oblivious to the beauty around us as we sat staring at our coffee cups.

"They actually believed," Peter answered, speaking half to himself, "what few people have, before or since: that the Kingdom of God really could begin to come on earth, in their lifetimes. They knew that they were sinners. But like the Pilgrims, they were dedicated to actually living together in obedience to God's laws, under the lordship of Jesus Christ."

"Yes, but—" suddenly a breeze came out of nowhere and scattered several chapters' worth of manuscript across the patio. As we gathered up the pages, it occurred to David that this was the only breeze to stir a paper in the last three days. When we sat back down, he dropped the questioning. All he said was, "Go on."

Peter paused for a moment to recapture what had started coming to him. "All it needed, they felt, was the right time, the right place, and the right people. It hinged on that: if the right people were willing to commit themselves totally."

For the next hour and a half, the Holy Spirit gave us insight after insight. The Puritans were the people who, more than any other, made possible America's foundation as a Christian nation. Far from merely fleeing the persecutions of king and bishop, they determined to change their society in the only way that could make any lasting difference: by giving it a Christianity that worked. And this they set out to do, not by words but by example, in a place where it was possible to live the life to which Christ had called them: three thousand miles beyond the reach of the very church they were seeking to purify.

The Spirit also reminded us that the legacy of Puritan New England to this nation, which can still be found at the core of our American way of life, can be summed up in one word: *covenant*. We were reminded that on the night of the Last Supper, to those who were closest to him, Jesus said, "This is my blood of the covenant, which is poured out for many for the forgiveness of sins" (Matt. 26:28 KJV).

Covenant is a word almost never heard in American life today, for it speaks of a commitment to Christ and to one another that is deeper and more demanding than most of us are willing to make. As a consequence, most of us modern American Christians are of little use to God in the building of His Kingdom. For the building of that kingdom, as the Puritans demonstrated, requires total commitment.

Sitting on the patio that morning, we were convicted that our own commitment did not yet measure up to that of the Puritans.

A candle had been bravely set at Plymouth, the first to confound the darkness of New England—but what of the candles still burning in Old

England? What of the Puritans, the white lights of the Protestant Reformation? They were beginning to flicker—not through any faltering of zeal but under the combined pressure of accelerated persecution and the advanced moral decay in their society.

London in the 1620s has been romanticized almost out of reality by most modern writers. "Gay, colorful, lusty, brimming with all the drama of the Elizabethan Age"—this is the stereotype to which we have been conditioned. If one were there, one would breathe in the excitement of just being there, and one's step would be a bit springier with the zest of it all. For who knew what adventure lurked round the next corner?

The truth of early seventeenth-century London is about as far removed from the paperback notion of it as today's Manhattan is from "Fun City." To begin with, you wanted to breathe in as little of old London as possible; in fact, a well-perfumed handkerchief was more a piece of survival equipment than a mannered affectation. And as for your step being springier, it had better be, considering what came flying out of upper windows to the cry of "Gardez-loo!"

No, London was not the sort of place where you would want to take your child for a walk, even in the morning. You would have to step warily to avoid drunkards and tosspots reeling and brawling in the narrow streets. The taverns did a roaring business around the clock as the main source of public entertainment, especially if one were not in the mood for a hanging or a play, or for watching dogs bait a bear or pull a screaming ape apart.[1]

Running the taverns a close second were the trollops who hung out of windows overhead, displaying their wares and pouring out a stream of commentary on all who passed below. As for adventure lurking around the next corner, thieves abounded in the teeming streets. Though robbery was a hanging crime, life had become so meaningless that it was worth risking in order to steal money enough for a few days' oblivion in a grog shop. (No wonder there were 137 hanging offenses on the statute books. There had to be in order to maintain even a semblance of law and order.)

The real tragedy of London, however, was not confined to what was happening in its streets. It included what was happening in its heart. In the City, London's financial district, life behind the massive oaken doors of mercantile power was every bit as brutalizing, even though it was played in

184

Italian silks and fine brocade. For in a godless society, when it was possible to send out a ship and have it return with a cargo worth more than the ship itself, and interest rates of 50 percent were not uncommon, money became almost divine. The men who handled it did so with reverential respect and obeisance—loving, honoring, and worshiping it—while accumulating as much of it as possible, as quickly as possible.

If, as Paul wrote to Timothy, the love of money is the root of all evil, that might explain some of the other evils at London's heart. Graft and bribery had become an accepted part of daily business. Cheating, double-dealing, betraying one's word—or one's friend—were all part of the game. The end invariably justified whatever means were necessary to obtain it.

London was an accurate spiritual barometer for the rest of the country, for England had become a nation without a soul. A beggar could die of exposure in a merchant's doorway, and the merchant, arriving to open up in the morning would be irate at having to step over the body and would fret about how bad it might be for business until it was disposed of.

An old acquaintance might lose several ships to pirates and find himself fleeing the country ahead of his creditors or end up in a debtors' prison. In which case, the response of his so-called friends might be: "Too bad about Forsythe, his luck giving out that way. But then, he knew the risks."

In a transatlantic airliner, as the navigator plots the plane's projected course, at a certain point he will make a neat dot and draw a tiny circle around it, labeling it PNR. Once that point is passed, for the plane to attempt to go back to its point of departure would require more fuel than remains on board. The plane has just passed the point of no return. America has not quite reached that point—yet.

Elizabethan England reached it in 1628. That was the year that William Laud, the Church of England's "enforcer," was made Bishop of London, the most important bishopric in the country. That year also marked the beginning of the Great Migration, which lasted some sixteen years. More than 20,000 Puritans embarked for New England, and 45,000 other Englishmen headed for Virginia, the West Indies, and points south. That may not seem like a significant number, but today it would be like some five million Americans packing up and leaving.

Who were these Puritans, and why was migration their only option? The Puritans were a growing number of people who had entered into a deep covenant relationship with God, through the person of His Son, Jesus Christ. For each, it was the single most important decision of his or her life, changing that life permanently and irrevocably.

If life had little meaning before, now it took on enormous significance. Not only had God Himself created each life; He also cared so much for each person that He sent His only Son to die for each one's sins, to bridge that irreconcilable gap between them—sin-stained as they were—and a holy, just God. Thus, it became the redeemed person's daily response to seek the will of the Savior and do it.

The Puritans were never the least bit complacent about their salvation. As the great English Puritan theologian Richard Baxter put it: "Man's fall was his turning from God to himself; and his regeneration consisteth in the turning of him from himself to God. . . . [Hence,] self-denial and the love of God are all [one]. . . . The very names of Self and Own, should sound in the watchful Christian's ears as very terrible, wakening words, that are next to the names of sin and Satan."[2]

And Thomas Hooker, the most articulate of the New England Puritan ministers, spoke for all of them when he identified their primary adversary as not Satan but self. "Not what Self will, but what the Lord will!" declared Hooker. Self was "the great snare" and "the false Christ," "a spider's web [spun] out of our bowels, the very figure or type of hell." To "lay down god-Self," to purge "the Devil's poison and venom or infection of Self," was "to kill the old Adam in us" and to strike a blow against "Antichrist, that is, the Self in all."[3] The Puritans did not need to be overly concerned with the devil; if they directed their energies toward Christ and against self, Satan would have little enough access to them.

Since how a Puritan was faring in the battle against sin and self was more important than anything else, many of them kept spiritual journals. In England, one of the most dedicated Puritans was John Winthrop. Cambridge-educated and the owner of a sizable estate in Suffolk, Winthrop was an attorney in the Court of Wards and a Justice of the Peace. He penned these lines in 1612 at the age of twenty-four:

I desire to make it one of my chief petitions to have that grace to be poor in spirit. I will ever walk humbly before my God, and meekly, mildly, and gently towards all men. . . . I do resolve first to give myself—my life, my wits, my health, my wealth—to the service of my God and Saviour who, by giving Himself for me and to me, deserves whatsoever I am or can be, to be at His commandment and for His glory.[4]

And in 1616 he wrote:

O Lord . . . Thou assurest my heart that I am in a right course, even the narrow way that leads to heaven. Thou tellest me, and all experience tells me, that in this way there is least company, and that those who do walk openly in this way shall be despised, pointed at, hated by the world, made a byword, reviled, slandered, rebuked, made a gazing stock, called Puritans, nice fools, hypocrites, hare-brained fellows, rash, indiscreet, vainglorious, and all that naught is. Yet . . . teach me, O Lord, to put my trust in Thee, then shall I be like Mount Sion that cannot be moved.

Life was an unending battle between flesh and spirit for young Winthrop, as it is for most Christians.

Before the week was gone about, I began to lose my former affections. I upheld the outward duties, but the power and life of them was in a manner gone. . . . And still, the more I prayed and meditated, the worse I grew—the more dull, unbelieving, vain in heart, etc. so as I waxed exceeding discontent and impatient, being sometimes ready to fret and storm against God, because I found not that blessing upon my prayers and other means that I did expect. But, O Lord, forgive me! Searching my heart at last, I found the world had stolen away my love for my God. . . . Then I acknowledged my unfaithfulness and pride of heart, and turned again to my God, and humbled my soul before Him, and He returned and accepted me, and so I renewed my Covenant of walking with my God, and watching my heart and ways. O my God, forsake me not.

The American Antiquarian Society of Worcester owns the better-known of the two existing portraits of Winthrop. The viewer's first impression of the painting is that Winthrop's demeanor is a prime example of the stereotypical (and false) image that modern Americans have of the Puritans. His face is narrow and pinched, with a long nose leading to a mustache and a beard that nestles in a white ruff. His long brown hair falls below the ears, and his steadfast brown eyes gaze at us under high-arching eyebrows with solemnity. He is wearing a black doublet—which, his biographer Francis Bremer indicates, was not black because he was a Puritan, but rather was a sign that he was a man of some means. (Black was a costly color for clothes since it could not be produced by natural dyes). Both the doublet and the glove he holds in his right hand are silk, revealing his status as a successful magistrate.[5]

If one knows nothing of John Winthrop's true character and holds to the typical image of the Puritans as sour, dour, gloomy, and judgmental prudes, one might look at this portrait and conclude that the stereotype is correct. But for Winthrop, as we shall see, that conclusion would be patently false. In point of fact, throughout Winthrop's career as an attorney and a magistrate on both sides of the Atlantic Ocean, he drew criticism for being too merciful in his judgments on lawbreakers. That hardly fits the image of the Puritans as stern and uncompassionate.

Winthrop's covenant relationship with the Lord deepened through the years. His was to be a towering commitment to Christ, reminiscent of the French and Spanish missionaries before him. And as is often true of God's saints, Winthrop's union with his Savior and his corresponding compassion grew as the result of fiery personal trials. Impetuously wed at the age of seventeen to a spiritually indifferent Mary Forth, he fathered two daughters and two sons. But Mary died in June 1615 after giving birth to another daughter, who outlived her mother by only three days.

Six months later John married Thomasine Clopton, a devout Christian woman, "truly religious and industrious [who] did plainly show that truth and the love of God did lie at her heart."[6] Incredibly, tragedy again struck young Winthrop. At the end of November 1616, Thomasine gave birth to a daughter who lived only two days. Then she herself died on December 10, the day after their first wedding anniversary.

Finally, in the following year God brought him together with the lovely, gracious, and deeply pious Margaret Tyndal, who proved to be the love of his life. In one of his courtship letters to her before their marriage in 1618, he wrote: "The ground and pattern of our love is no other but that between

Christ and His dear spouse (the Church). . . . Love bred our fellowship, let love continue it. And love shall increase it until death dissolve it."[7]

During these years of Winthrop's life, the Puritan movement was gaining momentum. When the radical, life-changing experience of conversion happened to a person, the natural thing was to share it with friends. God was now blessing these lives that were being lived for Him instead of primarily for self. This, in turn, made the Puritans ever more desirous of living according to His will. Since God's will was made known to them largely through His inspired Word, they naturally wanted to get as close to a scriptural order of worship as possible. Indeed, what they ultimately wanted was to reform the spiritually stagnant Church of England and bring it back to the purity and simplicity of New Testament Christianity.

What they did not want was to tear away from the Anglican Church. They criticized the Separatists (Pilgrims) for this and pledged themselves to bring about the purification of the church within its framework by their own enlightened example. However, the bishops in charge of the church saw no need for any such purification and resented the Puritans for what they considered to be their intrusive, presumptuous, divisive, and holier-than-thou ways. The more the Puritans pushed, the more the bishops resisted, until there was open enmity.

The Puritan dilemma was similar to that of many newly regenerate Christians in our time. They faced a difficult choice: should they leave their seemingly lifeless churches to join or start a new one? Or should they stay where they were, to be used as that small candle to which William Bradford referred? Many of them felt that God had called them to walk the harder way of staying, so they stayed.

Too often, however, the attitude of their hearts was anything but submissive—and sooner or later this attitude was going to make itself known. Thus, many newly converted Puritans must have manifested—along with their contagious enthusiasm for the Christian life—a degree of self-righteousness, impatience, and spiritual superiority. As the Puritan movement came of age in the first two decades of the seventeenth century, it matured considerably. Adherents from all social classes and walks of life began to be attracted to it, including Oxford- and Cambridge-trained clergy and some of the most brilliant scholars and theologians of the age.

Now they faced their first hard testing, for Jesus had warned His disciples that the world would hate anyone who truly determined to follow Him. The Puritans were despised but were not hated as much as the Separatists, who had given up their homes, their jobs, their country—everything—to live as Jesus had called them.

Here was the core difference between the emigrating Puritans and Pilgrims: step by step God was leading the Puritans to the place where they would be willing to give up what the Pilgrims had already given up. For the Puritans had more than the Pilgrims—more money, more servants, more friends in high places, more power, more education, more business experience. They had more of everything except one thing: compassion.

Compassion is not something that can be learned, put on, or even prayed for. Compassion is produced through living out the daily sufferings and sacrifices of a life freely given to God. For the Pilgrims, compassion was the fruit of undergoing persecution so severe that they had to leave their native land or lose their lives; of twelve years of hard, penurious exile; of four months of dark, tossing, stinking, soaking torment; and four more of cold and sickly mortal suffering. It was the fruit of coming to know the depths of one's sinful nature and the cleansing of daily repentance and forgiveness. It was experiencing the peace and joy that comes from knowing that one could do absolutely nothing without the grace of God and the Lord Jesus.

It was the greater depth of Christlike compassion and humility that for a few years marked the difference between the Puritans and the Pilgrims (with such notable Puritan exceptions as John Winthrop and Thomas Hooker). Moreover, the selflessness and caring of the Pilgrims happened not in a remote, cloistered setting or far-removed missionary hospital, but in America's fields and woodlands. It is this spirit of compassion that continues to draw tourists to Plymouth in such great numbers, though perhaps not one in a thousand is consciously aware of it.

God was also bringing the Puritans into compassion and humility. For many of them it happened as He allowed the pressure of mounting persecution to come upon them. They accepted it with grace, and as persecution often does, it served to rapidly deepen and mature the movement, bonding them together in common cause and making them more determined than ever to live as God had called them.

For John Winthrop, the loss of two wives and what would turn out in the end to be a total of seven children was working not only compassion into his heart but also a genuine warmth and generosity of soul.

Now, however, there was some question as to the nature of God's call on their lives. During the reign of King James I (1603–25), the persecution of the Puritans grew. The King filled vacancies in Church dioceses with anti-Puritan bishops and began listening to the advice of bishops like William Laud, who wanted to institute harsh measures against the reforming Puritans. When Charles I took the throne in 1625, Laud and his party of anti-Puritans came into control of the Church leadership. The situation became even worse for the Puritans. No sooner had the King made William Laud the Bishop of London in 1628 than Laud presented him with a list of English clergy. Behind each name was an *O* or a *P*. If Orthodox, they were in line for promotion; if Puritan, they were marked for suppression. Within a year Laud had created a network of informants within the churches to report on Puritan ministers who refused to conform to the new edicts and regulations, such as the one requiring clergy to read divine service in the proper vestments of surplice and hood.

For a number of Puritans, this was the last straw. Reformation of the Church of England from within no longer seemed possible.

Would they now have to go underground and start worshiping in secret? If so, they might as well face the fact that they were following in the footsteps of the Separatists, and separation was against everything the Puritans believed in. They were not revolutionaries, they insisted; they believed in orderly reform. The trouble was that the King and his bishops were not living in righteousness. Together, they were leading the people away from true New Testament Christianity.

To separate or not to separate? Out of this sharpening tension grew a startling alternative, one so radical that at first it was hard to contemplate, let alone pray about it. The possibility: the Church could still be reformed—but from a nine-hundred-league remove. It could be done in America.

Why not a settlement of Puritans there, loyal to the Crown and to the Church but sufficiently removed to have a chance to live in true obedience to God? There they could start over and demonstrate what could happen when a body of Christians was allowed to live wholly and totally unto God. Surely the fruits of living that way would not only stir up the Church, they would be a beacon to all Christendom.

The right place, the right time, and the right people . . . America was obviously the right place. Virginal, wild, and as yet untainted by the godless corruption that had befouled the known world, she was peopled with savage heathens who had never heard the Gospel and whose hearts therefore were not hardened against it.

These heathen, to be sure, could be used by Satan; John Winthrop and other Puritan leaders had read the writings of John Smith and Hakluyt and knew all about Virginia's starving time and the great massacre of 1622. Perhaps they had also read of the early missionaries who were martyred by the savages they were trying to lead to Christ. But if God was with them, all the powers of hell could not prevail against them. The place, then, was America, and more specifically, New England. For the reports out of Plymouth were uniformly encouraging and reliable, in stark contrast to the gruesome accounts out of Virginia.

And the time was surely now: London was a veritable sink of depravity. And now in 1629 that the King had dissolved Parliament and announced that he would run the country by himself, it was not a question of when, but how soon.

A few farsighted Puritans could sense God's hand in a coincidence of timing that was too extraordinary to be accidental. Had Columbus landed farther north . . . Had the Spanish colonization of Florida been successful . . . Had Raleigh succeeded in settling Roanoke . . . Had Jamestown been less of a catastrophe . . . Had America's very existence not remained cloaked until the Reformation . . . Had her northeastern coast not been reserved for the Pilgrims and Puritans . . . To some, it must have seemed almost as if they were standing in the middle of a gigantic model of one of those newfangled pocket watches, with the wheels and gears of "coincidence" swinging around and meshing and turning other gears, which swung and turned others.

But they could see only behind them. Today we can see what lay ahead of them as well and sense just how extraordinary was the timing of the Puritan exodus. If Bishop Laud had not come to power and abetted King Charles in his drive to bring the Puritans to heel, or if the English Puritans' revolution of 1642 had begun ten years earlier, there might not have been a Puritan exodus of sufficient numbers to seed America with spiritual liberty. For there were not nearly enough Pilgrims to do the work that was needed, let alone withstand the concerted pressure of Church and Crown. The Puritans were the right people.

When one considers the major events swinging slowly around on the biggest gears—the American Revolution, the Age of Reason, the Industrial Revolution, the rise and wane of empires, the gradual aligning of the forces of darkness and light, and the gradual dimming of the brightest Light—time seems much compressed. It becomes apparent what the Bible means when it says that to God a thousand years is as a single day. Knowing human nature and knowing how few would freely choose His way, God knew what the twentieth century would hold in store—the totalitarian darkness that would arise out of Europe, Russia, and Asia—and knew that England alone would never have the spiritual power to stop it. And so, early in the seventeenth century He planted the seeds of Light that would make a difference hundreds of years later. The alignment of all the factors of time and place reminds one of what NASA calls a launch window—an interval of a few hours during which every predictable factor that might affect a moon shot or an outer space probe would be as favorable as it could be. Once the window passes, it might be weeks, months, or even years before conditions again line up as favorably.

The launching of the Puritan exodus to America was more awesome. From our vantage point, it looked as if in all the years of Christendom there was only one brief window, one main chance. And rather than lifting off from a stationary launch pad, it seemed as if the Puritans were a stone placed in a whirling sling and let fly just as the tiny window hove into view. Up and out they went, arcing right through it, clear to their landing place in America.

The right place, the right time, the right people. It remained to be seen if the right people would be willing to give themselves totally.

As the prospect of a Bible-based commonwealth in New England became a real possibility in the thinking of the most dedicated Puritans, events began to move quickly. First, the New England Company was reorganized as the Massachusetts Bay Company. A new, enlarged charter was routinely processed through Parliament and presented for His Majesty's signature. But the King failed to notice that there was no mention of where the company's meetings were to be held. He signed it and forgot about it. The wondrous timing of God can further be seen in the fact that less than a week later the King dissolved Parliament and took the reins of the country entirely into his own hands, thereafter jealously scrutinizing every document to ensure that his authority was in no way diminished.

The Massachusetts Bay Company's partners were privately jubilant. Now there was nothing binding them to England, nothing to prevent them from moving to New England themselves and taking their charter with them. Once removed from the suspicious eyes of Church and Crown, the company could become a self-governing commonwealth with the charter as their statement of authority. But now they would be governed by the laws of God, not merely the laws of human beings. Not since God had brought the first chosen people into the first Promised Land had a nation enjoyed such an opportunity.

The Puritans' exodus conspiracy shifted into high gear. Preparations had long been made, and soon after the new charter was secured, two ships with some two hundred people aboard sailed past Land's End. As the coast of Cornwall faded in the distance, their leader, the Reverend Francis Higginson, exclaimed to the passengers: "We will not say, as the Separatists were wont to say at their leaving of England, 'Farewell, Rome!' or 'Farewell, Babylon!' But we will say, 'Farewell, dear England! Farewell, the Church of God in England, and all the Christian friends there! We do not go to New England as Separatists from the Church of England, though we cannot but separate from the corruptions in it, but we go to practice the positive part of Church reformation, and propagate the Gospel in America!"[8]

The exodus had begun. But in order to gain the necessary momentum, it would need a Moses. The principal partners had such a man in mind—John Winthrop. But Winthrop himself was not at all sure that it was God's will that he go. On such major steps as this, he knew that God sometimes seemed to withdraw Himself in order to give the individual the opportunity to sift and sort all possibilities and move out on faith. And so he did what so many Christians have done in similar situations: he drew up a list of pros and cons (which was later published[9] and helped thousands of Puritans to clarify their own decisions).

His reasons for undertaking the intended plantation in New England included:

[It would be] a service to the Church of great consequence to carry the Gospel into those parts of the world. . . .

All other Churches of Europe are brought to desolation . . . and who knows but that God hath provided this place to be a refuge for many whom He means to save out of the general calamity. [La Rochelle, the seaport bastion in which the French Huguenots had held out for two years, had just fallen to Cardinal Richelieu, and in Germany, Wallenstein was pulverizing the armies of the Protestants.] And seeing the Church hath no place left to fly into but the wilderness, what better work can there be, than to go and provide tabernacles and food for her against [that time when] she comes thither.

This land grows weary of her inhabitants, so as man, who is the most precious of all creatures, is here more vile and base than the earth we tread upon, and of less price among us than a horse or a sheep. . . .

. . . All arts and trades are carried in that deceitful and unrighteous course, [so] it is almost impossible for a good and upright man to maintain his charge and live comfortably in any of them.

The fountains of learning and religion are so corrupted as most children are perverted [and] corrupted.

Then Winthrop went on to state objections against the plantation and provided his answers. For example:

Obj: The ill success of other plantations may tell us what will become of this.

Ans: None of the former sustained any great damage but Virginia, which happened through their own sloth. . . . There were great and fundamental errors in the former which are like to be avoided in this, for their main end

195

was carnal and not religious; they used unfit instruments, a multitude of rude and misgoverned persons, the very scum of the land; and they did not establish a right form of government.

Obj: It is attended with many and great difficulties.

Ans: So is every good action. . . . The way of God's Kingdom, which is the best way in the world, is accompanied with the most difficulties.

Thus did John Winthrop come to be persuaded that it was God's will for him to go to America. But in addition, there was an intensely personal struggle that he did not mention: on the one hand, there was his old friend and advisor, Robert Ryece, saying, "the Church and commonwealth here at home hath more need of your best ability in these dangerous times, than any remote plantation." On the other hand, the principal Partners, who were preparing to go themselves, considered his presence so essential that they gave him an ultimatum: if he would not lead them, they would not go either, and the founding of the plantation would be doomed.[10]

It was settled then: he would go. As he put it: "I have assurance that my charge is of the Lord, and that He hath called me to this work."[11]

On August 16, 1629, he met with the other principals at Cambridge, where many of them had attended university together. They put their lives where they had already put their money and their mouths (in contrast to the Virginia and Plymouth backers). The Cambridge Agreement, as it was called, stated that "It is fully and faithfully agreed amongst us . . . we will be ready in our persons . . . to embark for the said plantation by the first of March next . . . to pass the seas (under God's protection) to inhabit and continue in New England."[12]

As historian Perry Miller wrote, "Winthrop and his colleagues believed . . . that their errand was not a mere scouting expedition: it was an essential maneuver in the drama of Christendom. The Bay Company was not a battered remnant of suffering Separatists thrown up on a rocky shore; it was an organized task force of Christians, executing a flank attack on the corruptions of Christendom. These Puritans did not flee to America; they went in order to work out that complete reformation which was not yet accomplished in England and Europe."[13]

Three days after the Cambridge Agreement, the decision was approved by the general membership, and on October 20 the General Court of the Massachusetts Bay Company unanimously elected John Winthrop as their governor. He was soon burdened with the enormous headache of arranging passage for more than a thousand Puritans who were waiting to emigrate. But as was typical of Winthrop, the ships were ready on schedule.

By now a farewell sermon had become a tradition, and it was preached by a stalwart young Puritan minister named John Cotton, whose star was also destined to rise over New England. He preached on 2 Samuel 7:10 (KJV): "Moreover I will appoint a place for my people Israel, and will plant them, that they may dwell in a place of their own, and move no more; neither shall the children of wickedness afflict them any more, as beforetime."

"Go forth," Cotton exhorted, "with a public spirit," with that "care of universal helpfulness. . . . Have a tender care . . . to your children, that they do not degenerate as the Israelites did."

Samuel Eliot Morison put it thus: "Cotton's sermon was of a nature to inspire these new children of Israel with the belief that they were the Lord's chosen people; destined, if they kept the covenant with Him, to people and fructify this new Canaan in the western wilderness."[14]

Cotton concluded his sermon with these words:

What He hath planted, He will maintain. Every plantation His right hand hath not planted shall be rooted up, but His own plantation shall prosper and flourish. When He promiseth peace and safety, what enemies shall be able to make the promise of God of none effect? Neglect not walls and bulwarks and fortifications for your own defense, but ever let the name of the Lord be your strong tower, and the word of His promise, the rock of your refuge. His word that made heaven and earth will not fail, till heaven and earth be no more.

11

A City upon a Hill

*O*n June 8, 1630, John Winthrop, standing at the rail of the *Arbella*, got his first sight of New England: the fir-covered hills of Maine. He stared in wonder at pines taller than any trees he had ever seen, coming right down to the boulders on the shore. The afternoon sun was shining, and an iridescent haze hung over the hills so that the firs seemed to glisten.

It was so much grander than he had expected. It was breathtakingly beautiful, but it was wild and savage too. This was not a land to be easily cleared and settled. His heart welled within him as it occurred to him that even this forbidding wilderness was a blessing, for it would discourage any who came for selfish reasons. A fresh, clear breeze came out to them over the sun-dappled waters, bearing the scent of those majestic pines, "and there came a smell off the shore like the smell of a garden."[1]

During the next few days as they made their way down the rocky coastline, they frequently tacked in, close enough to pick out individual trees and catch their delightful fragrance. It had been a peaceful voyage. Carrying a year's food supply, they did not have to arrive before the spring planting season, so they could afford to wait out the worst of the winter storms before clearing Southampton. In fact, so calm was the ocean in May that at one point Winthrop declared a fast day, in hopes of the Lord stirring up a moderate wind.

A peaceful passage may not seem particularly noteworthy, but in those days it was considered another manifestation of God's special grace. As Edward Johnson, an amateur historian and a contemporary of Winthrop, put it in the opening words of his *Wonder-Working Providences of Sion's Saviour in New England*, "Then judge, all you (whom the Lord hath given a discerning spirit), whether these poor New England people be not forerunners of Christ's army, and the marvelous providences which you shall now hear, be not the very finger of God." The first example in his highly enthusiastic compendium of instances of divine intervention makes an interesting point. In the first half of the seventeenth century, when so many ships were going down in storms or being taken by pirates and privateers, of the 198 vessels to set sail for New England only one was ever lost.[2]

We can imagine Winthrop at the rail on the afterdeck, wishing that his wife, Margaret, were at his side to share all of this beauty with him. But she was back at Groton, their family estate in Suffolk County, closing out their affairs with the help of John Jr. She had wanted to come but was due to give birth in April, just a few weeks after the expedition was to sail, and so she accepted that it was God's will for her to wait until her husband should send for her. As they faced a lengthy separation, they agreed to pray for one another every Monday and Friday from 5:00 to 6:00 p.m.[3]

In the coming months Winthrop would write often to her, doing his best to console her:

> My trust is that He who hath so disposed it, will supply thee with much patience. . . . The Lord is able to do this, and thou mayest expect it, for He hath promised it. Seeing He calls me to His work, He will have care of thee and all ours and our affairs in my absence; therefore, I must send thee to Him, for all thou lackest. Go boldly, sweet wife, to the throne of Grace.[4]

In another letter dated September 1630 he addressed her as if she were present: "I am sorry to part with thee so soon, seeing we meet so seldom. . . . So I kiss my sweet wife and my dear children, and rest thy faithful husband."[5]

He knew that because they each were in God's will, she would have the same inner peace that he now had. Then too, young John was with her and already at age twenty-three was showing remarkable maturity and judgment. No, Winthrop's only concern at the moment was for his second eldest, Henry, who was with him on the *Arbella*. Henry was the opposite of John Jr. Seemingly determined to carve out a career as a wastrel, Henry had gone so far as to deceive his parents into permitting him to marry his cousin, with whom he was convinced that he was madly in love, by telling them that he had gotten her with child. This had turned out not to be the case, and Winthrop, after paying his son's debts, had decided to put him under firm discipline for a while, counting on the rigors of the New World to straighten him out.

On the morning of June 11, they came upon a cheerful sight: a ship at anchor with half a dozen fishing shallops around her, all bobbing up and down. A little while later the captain informed Winthrop that they had Cape Ann in sight, which meant that they would be arriving in Salem harbor on next morning's tide. Salem at last! After seventy-two days of waiting.

But the sight that greeted them the following morning was far from cheerful. Where was Salem? Surely this pitiful collection of huts and hovels and canvas shelters—surely *this* was not the first town of the Massachusetts Bay Company. It must be the remnants of their first camp, temporary housing that they had not bothered to dismantle. The main town must be further back in the woods.

But as the ship drew nearer, the truth sank in: this *was* Salem. And then the people came down to the shore, gaunt and ragged—glad to see the new arrivals, but something was wrong. It was something more than their thinness or the sorry condition of their clothing—something inside of them. They were listless, slow of movement, apathetic. The life was gone out of their expressions.

Deeply troubled, Winthrop quickly arranged for a private briefing on board ship by John Endecott, the brash, quick-tempered soldier who had acted as Governor for the now-defunct New England Company and was filling in as provisional Governor for the Massachusetts Bay Company until Winthrop should arrive as his replacement. From Endecott, Winthrop learned that of the sixty-six people who had come over with him in

1628 and the two hundred who had come with Higginson and Skelton the following year, scarcely eighty-five remained. More than eighty had died, while the rest had quit and gone back to England. Many of the remainder were intending to do the same, for "all the bread and corn among them [was] hardly sufficient to feed upon a fortnight."[6]

It is not difficult to imagine the sort of exchange that probably followed: "But my good heavens, man!" Winthrop might have exclaimed, "What's to become of the plantation? This is as bad as Jamestown. And these people aren't fortune-hunters; they're decent Puritans. You had ministers here, good ones. Is there no teaching here?"

"We have a teaching service on Thursdays," Endecott might have retorted, "and two services on Sundays." He sighed. "But it seems to do no good. They hear the words and nod—and nothing changes." His voice trailed off in the same defeat that Winthrop had noted outside.

Winthrop spent that night aboard the *Arbella*, undoubtedly availing himself of the privacy of the captain's cabin. It began to look as if the final curtain would ring down before the play could finish even the first act. Was it all for nothing? Had he not heard God, after all? Had his selfishness or pride put all their lives into jeopardy?

He might have walked over to the porthole then and looked out, recalling another time only a few weeks ago, when he had stood at this very port. . . .

Outside, a green-white wake trailed erratically behind them on the surface of the ocean, as they yawed this way and that under a lead-gray sky. He had been thinking for a long time about the plantation and the quality of life that they could have together. Now in a rush of inspiration it was all coming together in his mind. Like all people trained to work with words, he yearned to get out his writing box and ink and paper, but he restrained himself until the concepts were clearly formed.

The sea had moderated somewhat when he finally went to the chart table and took out the box. Selecting a quill, he sharpened it, dipped it into the wide-bottomed ink bottle, carefully removing the excess against the rim, and looked at the white sheet of paper before him.

What he would write next would rank in importance with the Compact that the Pilgrims had drawn up aboard the *Mayflower*. Indeed, he took their concept one step further. For while they had stated what they were about to do as a body politic of equal members—gathered by God to live for Him and to be governed by their mutual consent—Winthrop now spelled out why it would work. His definition of covenant love has seldom been equaled.

The words that went across the top of the sheet of paper read: A MODEL OF CHRISTIAN CHARITY. He went straight to the heart of the matter, beginning with some thoughts on the nature of a person's love for his or her neighbor—what it could and should be, by the grace of God.

> This love among Christians is . . . as absolutely necessary to the [well] being of the Body of Christ, as the sinews and other ligaments of a natural body are to the [well] being of that body. . . . We are a company, professing ourselves fellow members of Christ, [and thus] we ought to account ourselves knit together by this bond of love.

Then came the heart of his vision:

> Thus stands the cause between God and us: we are entered into covenant with Him for this work. We have taken out a Commission; the Lord hath given us leave to draw our own articles. . . . If the Lord shall please to hear us, and bring us in peace to the place we desire, then hath He ratified this Covenant and sealed our Commission, [and] will expect a strict performance of the Articles contained in it. But if we shall neglect the observance of these Articles . . . the Lord will surely break out in wrath against us.
>
> Now the only way to avoid this shipwreck and to provide for our posterity, is to follow the counsel of Micah, to do justly, to love mercy, to walk humbly with our God. For this end, we must be knit together in this work as one man. . . . We must hold a familiar commerce together in all meekness, gentleness, patience, and liberality. We must delight in each other, make one another's condition our own, rejoice together, mourn together, labor and suffer together, always having before our eyes our Commission and Community in this work, as members of the same body. So shall we keep the unity of the Spirit in the bond of peace. . . .
>
> We shall find that the God of Israel is among us, when ten of us shall be able to resist a thousand of our enemies, when He shall make us a praise and glory, that men of succeeding plantations shall say, "The Lord make

it like that of New England." For we must consider that we shall be as a City upon a Hill.[7]

Standing now at the port and looking out at the New England night, Winthrop knew that it was God who had brought that previous time to his mind, as if to remind him that God would not have given him this momentous revelation if He had not intended it to be put to use.

Winthrop soon learned what had happened that winter of 1628–29. They had suffered a general sickness of the same sort that had stricken Plymouth during its first winter. In fact, Endecott had written to Governor Bradford, appealing for help. Bradford's response was to send their doctor, Samuel Fuller, who had by now had abundant experience in treating cases of scurvy and constitutions gravely weakened by long sea voyages, as well as the various fevers and illnesses accompanying a sharp, cold winter.

Fuller stayed through the winter in Endecott's house and helped substantially. Indeed, Endecott was so impressed that he named their settlement *Salem*, the Hebrew word for peace. This Separatist whom he had been prepared to dislike had manifested as much Christian love as any Puritan he knew. The two men had often talked late by the fire. And the more Endecott learned, the more respectful he became of what God was doing some forty miles down the coast.

Dr. Fuller was also a deacon, and Endecott was especially interested in the structure of their church. Under the leadership of Elder Brewster, the Plymouth church was organizationally separate from the civil authority under Governor Bradford. Yet it obviously exercised decisive moral influence over it. Separatist church leadership was provided by a pastor, a teacher, and a ruling elder, but these were chosen by the members of the church (not imposed by a presbytery or hierarchy of bishops). The right to choose freely their own spiritual leadership was zealously guarded as one of the basic tenets of their Christian faith. What was more, the Separatist church was open to all who cared to worship there. But to become a member of that church (and thus to be eligible to vote in both civil and religious elections), one had to convince the elders of the church of one's personal, saving relationship with Jesus Christ and of the orthodoxy of one's faith.

Winthrop may have had some private doubts about the wisdom of giving the right to vote to those who were not landholders (the idea of servants having equal voting rights with their masters smacked of "democracy"), but he held his tongue. From all reports, whatever else the people of Plymouth were doing, they were trying to do God's will. And He seemed well-pleased with them, blessing them more abundantly each successive year.

What was more, while some of their practices might be decidedly unconventional, even radical, that was not necessarily a bad thing. For instance, they reelected their Governor every year. And every year Governor Bradford insisted that the day before the election be a holiday. They were to do nothing but pray and seek God's will as to who He would have govern them.

The more Endecott listened to Dr. Fuller, the more convinced he became that this was the church model that God intended Salem to follow as well. Thus, when the Reverends Higginson and Skelton arrived, he told them of his decision. They insisted that they were loyal to the Church of England, but since they had not decided on any particular church structure before coming, they were open to Endecott's proposals. (When one considers the combinations of timing and circumstance that produced the Congregational Church, it obviously seems to be God's handiwork.) So Higginson and Smith were duly elected pastor and teacher, though their formal installation would have to wait until the arrival of the Governor.

Of the "gathering" of this first Puritan church in America, we have a vivid contemporary account from the ebullient Edward Johnson:

> Although the number of the faithful people of Christ were but few, yet their longing desire to gather into a church was very great. . . . Having fasted and prayed with humble acknowledgement of their own unworthiness to be called of Christ to so worthy a work, they joined together in a holy Covenant with the Lord and with one another, promising by the Lord's assistance to walk together in exhorting, admonishing and rebuking one another, and to cleave to the Lord with a full purpose of heart.[8]

As Endecott was relating the account of their covenanting with God and one another, we can imagine that Winthrop interrupted him: "That's why it's not working!" he might have exclaimed.

Endecott stared at him. "I don't understand."

"Don't you see? They love God, and they've covenanted to obey Him, or they wouldn't be here. But they're not living out their covenant with one another. They don't love one another enough to exhort, admonish, and rebuke. And at Plymouth they do. That's the difference!"

"But," Endecott objected, "the Separatists at Plymouth—the First Comers, as we call them—already had been a church for years before they came, and we've only just gathered here."

"That's all the more reason why we've got to live up to our covenant with each other." Winthrop paused and looked straight at Endecott. "And it must begin with the leadership. Unless you and I demonstrate our own commitment to this plantation and to these people—unless you and I are willing to put our whole lives into the work here—we can't expect them to. Well?"

Endecott met his gaze. "You can count on it," he said.

"Good. Now, first of all, I want to get settled ashore right away. This house is large enough to accommodate both of us, is it not?"

"But Mr. Winthrop, this is your house; it belongs to the Governor. I'll find lodgings elsewhere."

"If you had room for Dr. Fuller over the winter, there is room for both of us, until we newcomers build places of our own."

Before Endecott could reply, Winthrop went on to the next thing on his mind. "An hour before noon, have every able-bodied man and boy assembled in the center of town." He thought for a moment. "And have the women come too, those who are healthy and are not needed to tend the sick." He glanced at the height of the sun. "In the meantime I will see about getting my belongings ashore and stored."

Winthrop started out the door and then turned back. "Oh, and tell the gentlemen—that would be Mr. Saltonstall, Mr. Pynchon, Mr. Nowell, and the others—that this includes them, too." He smiled. "You'd better suggest that they wear old clothes."

"Right, Mr. Winthrop," Endecott said, and nodded.

Promptly at one o'clock he came to the open space in the center of the huts and shelters that was "town." A number of people were already there, staring at their Governor in amazement. Dressed in worn boots and breeches and an old frayed shirt, he looked more like an indentured servant than a gentleman.

When most of the people had gathered, he addressed them: "The situation here is not exactly what we in England were led to expect." There was some cynical laughter but mostly silence; the people were waiting to hear what would come next. "But I think it can be rectified without too much trouble. It is, however, going to require a good deal of hard work. By the end of the summer, every one of you is going to have a proper roof over your head. As for houses of your own, until we have them for all, more than one family will have to live together for the first winter."

There was a marked current of unbelief. "How are we going to do it?" Winthrop asked the question for them. "By God's grace and by helping one another."

At that moment he was interrupted by the arrival of Richard Saltonstall and a friend, who were carrying on a conversation of their own. Saltonstall was wearing a white shirt with a ruff at the neck. Winthrop's lips compressed; then he turned back to the rest.

"First of all, who among you has had any experience fishing?" Eight men raised their hands, and Winthrop conferred with Endecott. "All right, Packham and Kenworthy, each of you take three men, and on alternate days you will take turns using the shallop for fishing."

He looked up from his lists. "Now, the women. Those of you who are able will do field work in the mornings. The rest will be under Mr. Skelton on nursing detail. Mr. Skelton? As of this moment, you are officially responsible for what you and Reverend Higginson have been unofficially doing all along: tending the sick. Only now you are going to have more help."

Here he turned to the ailing pastor who, unable to stand any longer, had lowered himself to a stump. "Considering your condition, sir, you can help us most with your prayers—and a strong word on Sunday about what it means to serve God and one another."

He returned his attention to the other minister. "Mr. Skelton, you will also be in charge of the food stores. I want an inventory taken daily, and I would appreciate your alerting me of any projected shortfalls, as far in advance as possible. Also, by the guidance of the Holy Spirit, you are to decide what the daily ration will be." He looked around the circle. "Those of you who have your own stocks will be expected to forego your ration."

He folded the lists and handed them to Endecott. "The rest of you will form into two work parties: those under forty with Mr. Endecott, and those over forty with me. Any questions?"

"I have one, John." It was Richard Saltonstall. "You don't really expect me to . . ."

"Yes, Richard, I really do."

"But—common labor, John! I brought nine men with me to look after that sort of thing. And you brought more than I."

Winthrop hesitated before replying: "Last August at Cambridge you put your name to an agreement that bound you as a Christian to be ready *in your person* to further this work. So did I. This work will not succeed unless every person is willing to give his all. We are all laborers in God's vineyard, and that does not mean that, just because we can afford to, we pay someone else to do our work for us."

Fuming, Saltonstall shook his head. "This is . . ."

"The way it's going to be, I'm afraid," replied Winthrop with a smile. "And there's something else," he added, looked around the group. "You need to know that I consider lateness to be not only impolite but a sin against God. This is His work, and He has called us to it. To steal His time is to blaspheme against what He is trying to accomplish here."

He paused, letting that sink in. "Starting tomorrow morning we will meet here promptly at two hours past sunrise for daily work assignments. And bring something with you to eat at the noon hour. We will then work until four hours past noon, and the rest of the day is entirely your own." There was laughter now.

"Any other questions?" There were none.

Without doubt, a miracle took place upon Winthrop's arrival: a nearly dead colony was resurrected. From all reports, God's single instrument in this resurrection was John Winthrop. Cotton Mather would describe Winthrop as *Nehemias Americanus*[9]—referring to the Old Testament leader who had brought the Israelites back from their Babylonian exile to the Promised Land and had directed the rebuilding of the walls of

Jerusalem. More important, Nehemiah had inspired them to resume their covenant with God.

To be sure, they endured the same general sickness that seemed to afflict every shipload of settlers. Scurvy and various fevers were common, and Winthrop said that "peas, pudding, and fish . . . were their ordinary diet."[10]

A few days after their arrival, tragedy was piled on hardship. Winthrop suffered the grievous loss of his son, Henry, who drowned in a fishing accident. The death seemed to redouble his dedication to the business of planting the colony (much as a similar tragedy had affected William Bradford before him).

Letters from colonists to friends and family back in England told of Winthrop pitching in and working as hard as any of the others, never acting as if he were above the rest because he was Governor. He was referred to as a "discreet and sober man, giving good example to all the planters, wearing plain apparel such as may well beseem a mean [ordinary] man, drinking ordinary water. When he wasn't engaged in his duties as Governor, he [put] his hand to any ordinary labor with his servants." This was confirmed by a report stating that so soon "as Mr. Winthrop was landed, perceiving what misery was like to ensue through their idleness, he presently fell to work with his own hands, and thereby so encouraged the rest that there was not an idle person then to be found in the whole plantation."[11]

By mid-July Winthrop was living in the new settlement of Charleston, and Watertown, Roxbury, Medford, Lynn, and Dorchester had been founded as well. Conditions were still severe—between April and December about two hundred people died. In late September, Winthrop and a large number of people moved to the Shawmut peninsula, where there was a good spring with much fresh water. They named the new settlement Boston.

That same month he wrote to Margaret that although they had endured "much mortality, sickness, and trouble" he believed that through it all "God had purged out corruptions, and healed the hardness and error of our hearts, and stripped us of our vain confidence in this arm of flesh, that He may have us rely wholly upon Himself."[12]

Not all the settlers were choosing to rely on God and endure hardship until their fortunes improved. Nearly half those who came over that first year returned. But more than half of the settlers stayed, and there were far fewer graves dug that winter than there might have been. John Winthrop was a rock of stability, whose faith often stood in the gap for all of them. Abandon the colony? Never!

How critically important for us Christians is this business of commitment to one another—as vital for the Body of Christ today as it was four centuries ago. There are two great steps of faith in the Christian walk, and they correspond to the two great commandments: "You shall love the Lord your God with all your heart, and with all your soul, and with all your strength, and with all your mind; and your neighbor as yourself" (Luke 10:27).

The first step of faith is the vertical commitment: when a person has discovered the reality of God and has experienced the miraculous gift of salvation in his Son Jesus Christ, he or she must also surrender his or her will to Christ as Lord and Master. Like our Lord, our attitude must be "Nevertheless not my will, but thine, be done" (Luke 22:42). And it is a covenant relationship, which means there are two parties to the agreement. As long as the Christian daily seeks to obey Christ, God will honor his or her obedience, often blessing the person beyond all imagining.

The vertical aspect of the covenant has to come first, just as the first and great commandment does. But as strong as it is, the vertical aspect alone, without a crossbar, is not the Cross of Christ.

The second step of faith is the horizontal commitment to one's neighbor, including that specific local part of the Body of Christ to whom God calls one to be a part. And the effectiveness of that congregation in the wider community will be magnified to the extent to which its members mutually dedicate themselves.

This may be one of the reasons why God permits pressures to befall the Body of Christ. For wherever there is pressure or affliction, there is a corresponding increase in commitment to one another, as well as commitment to God. This, we believe, is the reason that God allowed the persecution and long exile of the Pilgrims: the four wretched months in which Saints and Strangers shared their plight in the belly of the *Mayflower* before being disgorged onto the new Promised Land and the four more months of general sickness, so that when they finally stood on their feet, they stood together as a body. And they were thus able to pass on to the Puritans a proven model by which to build.

"Every city or house divided against itself shall not stand," Jesus told his disciples (Matt. 12:25 KJV), and with each New England church, God was building a house. As the Apostle Peter wrote to new Christians, "[Come] and, like living stones, be yourselves built [into] a spiritual house" (1 Peter 2:5 AMP).

In the rocky fields of New England, God was raising up a kingdom of stone houses, each stone in each house fitted into place by him. These stone houses were not only part of the groundwork for the Kingdom of God in America, but as we would come to see, they would lay the foundations for American constitutional government.

12

THE PURITAN WAY

*N*early everyone today seems to believe that the Puritans were bluenosed killjoys in tall black hats, a somber group of sin-obsessed, witch-hunting bigots "whose main occupation was to prevent each other from having any fun and whose sole virtue lay in their furniture."[1]

How could such a monstrous misrepresentation have been so widely and so quickly accepted? For the anti-Puritan phenomenon has arisen largely in the last hundred years. Almost no negative bias can be found among nineteenth-century historians; on the contrary, they gladly gave the Puritans the lion's share of credit for setting the direction of this nation. Why then, the sudden prejudice in so many hearts?

The answer seems to lie in the fact that never before in the four hundred years of our history has the spirit of rebellion gained such a tight hold on the minds and wills of the American people. What could be more of an anathema to such an attitude than the cheerful submission to authority, holy service, and corporate commitment that the Puritans personified? If there is one group of people in the history of the country whose example Satan hates more than any other it is the Puritans. And since rebellion is his specialty, it is no wonder that the Puritans have received such a bad press.

Thus, as social customs that have been acceptable in this country for more than three centuries are vilified and torn down, the usual withering epithet one hears attached to them is *puritanical*, whether the topic is work ethic, chastity before marriage, modesty in decorum and dress, traditional lifestyles, regulations against obscenity in the media, or legislation against immorality. The list is endless, and societal norms are crumbling under an ever-more determined onslaught.

As we investigated the Puritans, we found these much-maligned Christians to be sinners like ourselves, but we also found them to be warm and human, possessed of remarkable spiritual wisdom and discernment.

But what about their legendary self-righteousness and intolerance? Had they not banished Roger Williams, the founder of the Rhode Island Colony, simply because he spoke his mind and because his doctrine did not happen to agree with theirs? He has certainly become the hero of outspoken anti-establishment academics.

And what of Anne Hutchinson? Had the Puritans not expelled her? She now has a river (and a parkway) named after her and is enormously popular with modern feminists. The dilemma we faced was this: if such narrow-minded self-righteousness was an inevitable by-product of human attempts to establish the Kingdom of God on earth, did that not bring the whole matter of the feasibility of a Bible commonwealth into question? And if the Puritans were attempting the impossible, how much more impossible would it be today?

The scarlet letter—*A* for *adulteress*—that Hester Prynne, heroine of Nathaniel Hawthorne's famous novel, was forced to wear seared its way into the psyche of nineteenth-century America. A century later Arthur Miller's play about the Salem witch hunters, *The Crucible*, reinforced the stereotyped image of the Puritans. And countless other modern novelists and dramatists have presented the Puritans as morbidly preoccupied with sin and guilt. What is the truth?

There is no question that the Puritans took sins seriously—far more seriously than most American Christians today. But they had good reason: they knew that the very success or failure of their Bible commonwealth hung on their willingness to deal strongly with sin—in themselves first, but also in those who had been called with them to build the Kingdom. Indeed, there could be no compromise where the presence of sin was concerned. For an example of the fruit of compromise, all they needed to do was look across the Atlantic at what was happening in England. And so they did not shy away from facing up to sin or dealing with it.

One modern historian consistently exposed the popular Puritan stereotype for the false view that it is: the late Perry Miller, widely regarded as the dean of Puritan historians. For years his works sought to bring about a major revision in the thinking of serious students of American history (a lamentably minute segment of the American public).

Here is what Miller wrote concerning the Puritans' attitude toward sin:

> Puritanism would make every man an expert psychologist, to detect all makeshift "rationalizations," to shatter without pity the sweet dreams of self-enhancement in which the ego takes refuge from reality. A large quantity of Puritan sermons were devoted to . . . exposing not merely the conscious duplicity of evil men, but the abysmal tricks which the subconscious can play upon the best of men. The duty of the Puritan in this world was to know himself—without sparing himself one bit, without flattering himself in the slightest, without concealing from himself a single unpleasant fact about himself.[2]

This willingness to look unblinkingly at the worst side of their own natures made them consummate realists. It was also responsible for the extraordinary compassion that became the hallmark of such exceptional leaders among them as John Winthrop, Thomas Hooker, and Cotton Mather. For once you knew how corrupt your own nature was at its core, you would be much more readily inclined to have compassion on the sinfulness of others.

Anyone who searches their church records will find that Puritan discipline, though strict by necessity, was almost always tempered with great mercy. The reason it was strict (and enforced by civil law), was that they felt that the entire fabric of their covenant life together depended on living in proper order and in joint obedience to the laws of God. Thus, when one sinned, it affected them all.

Tryal Pore, a young girl arraigned before the Middlesex County Court in 1656, confessed that "by [my] sin I have not only done what I can to pull down judgment from the Lord on myself, but also upon the place where I live."[3] But Tryal Pore's tearful confession convinced the magistrates of her repentance, and they were more than ready to forgive her. "I have no pleasure in the death of the wicked, but that the wicked turn from his way and live" (Ezek. 33:11). Puritan magistrates, whose law book was the Bible, were generally far more anxious to see a sinner come to repentance than to mete out punishment.

In case after case, the mercy, forgiveness, and pastoral concern for the defendant stand out. Yet to any modern writer with a streak of rebellion, the discipline is all that he or she sees, and any mention of discipline these days is like waving the proverbial red flag. Rebellion, in fact, has been so romanticized in recent years that church discipline is literally unheard of. Today, if anyone were threatened with dismissal from a local church, he or she would probably shrug, laugh, and leave.

It was a different matter three centuries ago. A church was gathered together first, and then a town formed around it. Under those circumstances, excommunication was a matter of the utmost gravity. It meant that the local body of Christ, after repeatedly trying to bring a sinner to repentance so he or she could receive God's forgiveness, would finally have no choice but to break fellowship with the individual and turn the person over to his or her sin. This meant that person would be under Satan's influence, and for those who knew the reality of the devil, this was a fearsome turn of events.

That the fruit of compassion was being worked into the hearts of the Puritan elders, magistrates, and pastors is amply evidenced in the case of Ann Hibbens. Mrs. Hibbens was the wife of one of the elders of the First Church of Boston, where John Cotton was the pastor. She had accused a woodworker named Davis (also a member of the church) of overcharging her for some decorative carving that he had done at her request. He insisted that his price had been fair, and finally the church had to step in. Impartial woodworkers from another town were summoned to assess the work, and they judged that Davis's price was fair, perhaps even low. This had humbled Mrs. Hibbens for a season, and she had confessed her error with tears.

But then, like a dog worrying a bone, she started in again. Now the church strongly censured her, and she quieted down again—for a while. But she could not simply be wrong and accept her correction; she began once more to berate Davis, both to his face and behind his back. Finally, the church had no alternative left but to hold an excommunication hearing.

The purpose of the hearing was to give her one last opportunity to humble herself and admit her error, but Mrs. Hibbens airily refused, not deigning to answer more than the first few questions put to her. Finally, Pastor Cotton addressed the congregation:

> It grows now very late, and we must [ascertain whether] . . . it be the mind of the church that we shall proceed to pass the sentence of excommunication upon this Sister. We shall take our silence for your consent and approbation thereto; if any of the church be of another mind, he hath liberty to express himself. [silence] We perceive by the universal silence of the church that with one consent it is your mind [that] we should proceed. And therefore let us first seek unto God for His direction and for a sanctified use of this His ordinance, [in order] that we may proceed not out of bitterness or envy but out of tender love to her soul, and that God would give her a sight of her great and many evils and break her heart by kindly repentance [so] that she may the more speedily return to God and the church again, as now she is cast out.[4]

Following the prayer Mr. Cotton proceeded to reluctantly pronounce the dread sentence of excommunication:

> . . . for slandering . . . for raising up an evil report . . . for several lies and untruths . . . for your stopping your ears and hardening your heart against the former admonition of the church . . . for your sowing discord and jealousies . . . for these and many more foul and sinful transgressions . . . I do here, in the name of the whole church and in the name of the Lord Jesus

Christ, and by virtue of that power and authority which He hath given to His church . . . cast you out and cut you off from the enjoyment of all those blessed privileges and ordinances which God hath entrusted His church withal, which you have so long abused . . . I do from this time forward pronounce you an excommunicated person from God and His people.

Ten years later Mrs. Hibbens would be the defendant in another trial, a civil one this time. The charge: witchcraft. The sentence: the only one worse than excommunication—death by hanging. This must have brought to many minds the reminder that "Rebellion is as the sin of witchcraft" (1 Sam. 15:23 KJV).

As Pastor Cotton indicated, the purpose of excommunication was not to condemn sinners but to let the pressure of their sin bring them to repentance. In the case of Captain John Underhill, who was excommunicated for adultery, being expelled was the very thing that finally brought him to repentance. He begged to be reinstated, and at length he was given leave to speak before the congregation. Winthrop recorded the occasion as follows:

He came in his worst clothes (being accustomed to take great pride in his bravery and neatness), and standing upon a form, he did with many sighs and abundance of tears, lay open his wicked course—his adultery, his hypocrisy, his persecution of God's people here, and especially his pride (as the root of all, which caused God to give him over to his other sinful courses) and contempt of magistrates. He (then) justified God and the church and the court in all that had been inflicted on him.

Many fearful temptations he met with beside, and in all these, his heart shut up in hardness and impenitency as the bondslave of Satan, till the Lord, after a long time and great afflictions, had broken his heart, and brought him to humble himself before Him night and day with prayers and tears . . . in the end, he earnestly and humbly besought the church to have compassion on him, and deliver him out of the hands of Satan. So accordingly he was received into the church again.[5]

The skeptical reader might be inclined to wonder how sincere Underhill's repentance was, but the fact is that he did go on to become a successful military captain and hold many positions of responsibility.

The Puritans were willing to face the reality of their own sinful natures and the harm that sin caused their covenant life. And this willingness produced not only compassion for one another but also a remarkable maturity when it came to meeting the realities of life and death.

Infant mortality was a grim specter in the seventeenth century. There was no cure for smallpox, and even measles was a dread killer—of adults as well as children. Death was an ominous and ever-present possibility. And as with everything else in a Puritan's life, there were two ways to handle it: in Christ or in self.

Perhaps the most famous Puritan was Cotton Mather, whose image has been especially maligned and distorted out of any resemblance to reality. He has been painted as a witch-hunting, sadistic monster, a sort of Puritan Torquemada, when nothing could be further from the truth. Mather was an ordinary sinner and was the first to admit it, but his warm humanness made him one of the most popular preachers of his age.

True, he could be self-righteous, and he was not above playing pulpit politics. But Mather fearlessly proclaimed God's Word, and he truly hungered after God's righteousness and holiness. He also had a pastor's heart, for which his parishioners loved him.

The son of Increase Mather, the most prominent clergyman in New England (for many years president of Harvard College and later New England's special ambassador to the King), Cotton Mather was also the grandson of John Cotton and Richard Mather, two of the strongest ministers in the first generation of American Puritans. Such was his upbringing that when personal tragedy came to his family—and it came repeatedly—he instinctively turned to Christ.

There was shock and grieving, fasting and praying. But there was no self-pity, no long drawn-out remorse or bitterness, no hatred of God. Each time tragedy struck, a further work was done in him, increasing his capacity for mercy and compassion. So that toward the end of his life, his prayers and counsel were highly sought by those facing a recent or impending loss in their families. Despite all his writing (and he authored more than 450 books, tracts, and treatises), he made a point of always being available to anyone in need, and he instituted what was to become an American pastoral tradition: regular calls on his aged and ailing parishioners, as well as prisoners.

It is possible to follow his spiritual growth at key points, because starting in his nineteenth year (1681) he kept a diary, as was the custom among educated men of his time. (He had already received his B.A. and M.A. from Harvard and had begun to preach.) His first entry is a long devotional passage, full of good resolutions and signed "by Cotton Mather, feeble and worthless, yet (Lord, by thy grace) desirous to approve himself a sincere and faithful servant of Jesus Christ."[6]

Mather was to have more than a dozen children, but only two would survive him. The first to fall ill was his four-year-old daughter Mary. On October 3, 1695, as he prayed for her, "I was unaccountably assured, not only that this child shall be happy forever, but that I should never have any child, except what should be an everlasting temple to the Spirit of God; yea, that I and mine should be together in the Kingdom of God, world without end." Three days later the Lord took her. Her epitaph: GONE BUT NOT LOST.

In 1702 he began a seven-month-long struggle in prayer for the life of his wife, whom he referred to as his beloved consort.

> In the forenoon, while I was at prayer with my dying wife in her chamber, I began to feel the blessed breezes of a particular faith, blowing from Heaven upon my mind. . . . In the afternoon, when I was alone in my study, crying unto the Lord, my particular faith was again renewed, and with a flood of tears I thought I received an assurance from Heaven that she should recover. Whereupon, I begged the Lord that He would, by His good Spirit, incline me to be exemplarily wise and chaste and holy, in my whole conversation, when I should again obtain such favor of the Lord.

She did recover, only to fall ill again before her strength could be regained, and again her demise called for an all-night bedside vigil.

> But in this extremity, when I renew my visits unto Heaven, a strange irradiation comes from Heaven upon my spirit, that her life shall not as yet come unto an end.

But still she hovered near death, and six weeks later Mather wrote:

> I suspect I have been too unattentive unto the meaning of the Holy Spirit . . . about my consort's being restored to me. When she has been several

times on or near the last agonies of death, I cry to the Lord, that He will yet spare her. He tells me that He will yet do it. . . . But it may be, after the Lord has given me admirable demonstrations of His being loathe to deny me anything that I importunately ask of Him, and therefore does delay one month after another, the thing which I fear, yet I must at last encounter.

On October 30 in the midst of concern for his wife he wrote:

On this day my little daughter Nibby began to fall sick of the small-pox. The dreadful disease, which is raging in the neighborhood, is now got to my family. God prepare me, God prepare me for what is coming upon me.

The pestilence grew worse, and toward the end of November his small son, Increase, was stricken down.

The little creatures keep calling for me so often to pray with them that I can scarce do it less than ten or a dozen times in a day, besides what I do with my neighbors.

Two days later, his beloved wife died.

At last the black day arrives. I [have] never yet seen such a black day, in all the time of my pilgrimage. The desire of my eyes is this day to be taken from me. All the forenoon, she lies in pangs of death, sensible until the last minute or two before her final expiration. I cannot remember the discourses that passed between us, only [that] her devout soul was full of satisfaction about her going to a state of blessedness with the Lord Jesus Christ, and as far as my distress would permit me, I studied how to confirm her satisfaction and consolation. . . .

When I saw to what point of resignation I was now called of the Lord, I resolved, with His help therein, to glorify Him. So, two hours before my lovely consort expired, I kneeled by her bedside, and I took into my two hands a dear hand, the dearest in the world. With her thus in my hands, I solemnly and sincerely gave her up to the Lord. . . . When she was expired, I . . . prayed with her father and the other weeping people in the chamber, for the grace to carry it well.

And he did carry it well.

When it came to their closest relationships, the Puritans were realists in life as well as in death. They believed that their covenant relationship with God included their children, and because they loved them, they were no more tolerant of sin in their children's lives than in their own. They would deal with sinfulness in their children as strongly as the situation required, regardless of how the children might respond at the moment.

One has to ask: how many modern-day parents are willing to risk losing the "love" in their relationship with their children by persevering with them in matters of discipline? One important cause of the breakdown of the modern American family is that so much of what we call love, the Puritans had another name for: idolatry.

According to God's first commandment ("Thou shalt have no other gods before me"), any person, any thing, any relationship that is exalted above the Lord in one's life can be said to be an idol. Taking that one step further: any love that does not emanate from God (for God *is* love) by definition is idolatrous. No matter how noble the sentiments or how seemingly sacrificial, if it does not begin with God and have Him as its end, it is, in reality, nothing more than a subtle extension of our limitless capacity to love ourselves and to entice others to do likewise.

Unlike most modern parents, the Puritans knew that their children did not belong to them; they belonged to God. Consequently, they did not possess them but considered that their children had been entrusted into their care by God. Parents were to protect them, raise them, and teach them, training them up in the way that He would have them go. In other words, parenthood was a sacred responsibility in Christ, and if they failed to live up to it, they would be directly accountable to Him.

This did not prevent them from loving their children; they loved them very much indeed, as we have seen from the brief glimpse into Cotton Mather's heart. But they were aware that their love should originate in the heart of God. His love abounds with tenderness and compassion and joy, but it also contains discipline. "For the Lord disciplines him whom he loves, and chastises every son whom he receives" (Heb. 12:6). God loves his children too much to permit them to stay in a sin that could harm their development or to allow them to persist in willfulness when they need to learn how to submit their wills to His.

It was in this area of having one's will crossed that Puritan children (just like ours) had the hardest time understanding that this was God's love for them. Many did not make the connection until their teenage years, and some never did. Often the turning point came during the whole business of courtship. This area of Puritan life affords a classic example of how God's will-crossing love can come through parents who are willing to risk their children's anger in order to be obedient to the guidance that they feel God has given them.

As in the rest of their living patterns, Puritan courtship gradually evolved into a code of conduct that they felt was pleasing to God and that, when adhered to, resulted in stable, fulfilling marriages. Certain evenings were set aside for "calling"—and there were strict ordinances against "night-walking"—couples wandering down inviting country lanes. As a result, the premarital birthrate was negligible, and sensual temptations were kept to a minimum. Modern writers have made this constraint a point of ridicule, but when one stops to think about it, nothing clouds the wisdom and clear discernment of two people beginning to consider marriage more than the pink haze of imminent sexual gratification.

Contrary to popular opinion, the Puritans did not arrange marriages between their children; they did, however, exercise their veto. If either set of parents felt that the marriage was out of the will of God, they had no compunction about withholding their permission. From hard experience they knew that if the marriage was not in God's will and the couple went ahead and got married anyway, they could be in for a great deal of misery and suffering. Sometimes the parents simply felt that the couple was ahead of God's timing, in which case the betrothal might last several years—while the boy and/or girl matured to the point at which they were ready to take on the responsibility of raising a family.

Puritan parents were also well aware that they could never be entirely sure of always hearing the Lord's will. And so, on such an important decision as whether to permit their children to marry, they were grateful for counsel from their brothers and sisters in Christ. And because each marriage had a deep and long-lasting effect on the covenanted community as a whole, it was a matter of importance to every member.

Instead of resenting the counsel of their fellow Christians, the parents welcomed it because they were a big family. As God intended, this was one of the fruits of the horizontal aspect of the covenant. As hard as that is to imagine today, that was the way they chose, and they would not have wanted it any other way. For example, in 1636 the church in Boston renewed its covenant in the following terms:

> We do give up our selves unto that God whose name is Jehovah, Father, Son and Holy Spirit . . . and unto our blessed Lord Jesus Christ . . . promising (by the help of His Spirit and grace) to cleave unto [Him] . . . by faith in a way of Gospel obedience, as becometh His covenant people forever.
>
> We do also give up our offspring unto God in Jesus Christ, avouching the Lord to be our God, and the God of our children, and our selves, with our children to be His people, humbly adoring this grace of God, that we and our offspring with us, may be looked upon as the Lord's.
>
> We do also give up our selves one unto another in the Lord, and according to the will of God, freely covenanting and binding our selves to walk together as a right ordered congregation and church of Christ, in all ways of His worship, according to the holy rules of the Word of God, promising in brotherly love, faithfully to watch over one another's souls.[7]

Imagine the reaction that most Americans today would have at the thought that their neighbors might be watching over their souls. Even among those of us in the Body of Christ, when we say, "How are you?" and smile, we are inwardly relieved when the reply is limited to the obligatory "fine." Many of our churches are congregations of private people, surrounded by private personal spaces and wrapped up in private thought, until it is time to smile and shake the minister's hand and get into private cars.

In fact, for many of us Americans, privacy has become our religion, with the home as the foremost place of worship. As a result of increasingly temporary and artificial friendships, frequent uprootings, and growing insecurity in the world, we turn more and more for the fulfillment of our needs to family relationships. We place increasing demands on husband, wife, son, daughter, mother, father, sister, brother, or whomever the person or persons might be. They become the focal point for all our hopes, our dreams, and our thwarted ambitions.

This other person is now expected to provide the love that we are so desperate for, and we begin to draw more and more heavily on that love. To ensure no interruption in its flow, we lavish undue attention, gifts, and advice on the other persons, believing that we are really loving them. When they do not love us back to the degree or in the way that we think they should (which is humanly impossible), we feel hurt and angry—and one way or another, we let them know it.

This is what always happens with idolatry sooner or later, because it is a spiritual law that natural love, when crossed, turns to hate. For example, when we Americans exalt our children, they start to rebel against the role into which they have been cast—as love generators and love objects. With increasing resentment they come to see that what their parents regard as love is in reality a kind of smothering, possessive control, vicarious reliving, or ego projection.

Or possibly the children do not even know what it is, except that they dread going home and feel as if they are suffocating while they are there. We all know about the alarming number of teenagers who are running away from so-called nice homes because their parents are so self-loving that they do not have any time for them. But what does not make the headlines are the numbers of teenagers who flee homes where they get too much of the wrong kind of attention—idolatrous attention.

Some children are willing to play the game for the sake of their own ego gratification, even into their middle years. Their parents "lovingly" try to shield and protect them from all the knocks of life and by so doing, wind up crippling them—to the point where they can no longer make it socially on their own. It is just easier to stay home and take shelter with one's parents. For example, in a recent survey, administrators at Smith College discovered that one-third of the school's graduates were still living with their parents ten years after receiving their diplomas.

In such cases, the "love" cycle may appear to be working—for a while. But God help the future mate of such a spoiled and self-loving person, should he or she ever decide to leave home and marry. For unless the mate is willing to be enfolded and totally absorbed into that cycle, the results will be unending conflicts, divorce, and broken hearts.

The American family does indeed seem to be unraveling because of the almost universal ignorance of the idolatrous nature of godless "love." In the face of this fact, it is ironic that the larger community—which privacy so effectively seals out—is the very thing that can restore and ensure wholesome, open, and honest family relationships, provided that community is Christ-centered and covenanted.

This understanding of the corporate nature of their call—now almost forgotten—was built into the foundation of the new spiritual houses that God began to build some four centuries ago in America. As the Boston church's covenant reveals, it was at the heart of their daily life together—to the Puritan, it was so normal, such a matter of course, that no one even thought about it.

The Puritans were glad that they had been called together, and they liked nothing better than to work together as a large family. Usually a good deal got accomplished at such get-togethers. For there were certain things that a person simply could not do alone, such as raising a roof, pulling stumps, or going to a town meeting. When outdoor work was needed and the weather was decent, the womenfolk would do the cooking and make a festive occasion of it. Frequently in the evenings there would be quilting or sewing or baking or husking bees, and for the children, spelling bees.

John Winthrop pointed out that, just as the community was a large family, so each family was a small community. And the Puritans put great stock in that community being an orderly one, with the parents in undisputed authority. "If God make a covenant to be a God to thee and thine," said John Cotton, "then it is thy part to see to it that thy children and servants be God's people."[8] This was also the tone he set in his famous catechism on the Ten Commandments, which Puritan children had to memorize and recite on Saturday afternoons in preparation for the Sabbath: "Who are meant here by [Honor thy] Father and Mother?" The correct answer was: "All our superiors, whether in family, school, church, or Commonwealth."

The Puritans saw very clearly that authority—whether spiritual or temporal—invariably began in the home. "Well-ordered families naturally

THE PURITAN WAY

produce a good order in society," said Cotton Mather succinctly, and James Fitch echoed him: "Such as families are, such at last the Church and Commonwealth must be." Obviously this is every bit as true today, but in Puritan New England, the people took care to make sure that discipline and authority in the homes was all that it should be. For in the end, a lax or loose home hurt them all, being a sin against God's plan, to say nothing of a social menace. Thus, if parents ever reached the point where they were drinking heavily, or whoring, or abusing their children, the children would be taken out of their homes and put into homes where they would receive the love (including correction) that they needed.

A great deal of emphasis was put on this matter of parental responsibility. Parents of stable families were expected to take in single men and women and to raise them as part of their families, with the newcomers submitting to the heads of the house as if they were their own parents. There was even a law requiring any single person who could not afford to support a home in proper order to live with one of the town families. In almost all cases this proved to be a great blessing, providing a warm family environment that the single person did not have and sometimes had never experienced.

The Puritan way may seem foreign to our modern American family ways, but the quality of genuine Christian love and caring for one another's souls that so characterized the family lives of our ancestors may well contain the beginnings of answers to our own family problems.

"Gather my saints together unto me; those that have made a covenant with me by sacrifice" (Ps. 50:5 KJV) was one of the Puritans' favorite texts, for it referred directly to the sacrifice required of each of them by the covenant into which they had entered.

No one was more cognizant of the need for personal sacrifice than John Winthrop—nor was anyone more ready to give as generously and cheerfully. Winthrop understood clearly that to belong to Christ was to belong to one another, and their situation in the fall and winter of 1630–31 would test their covenant commitment to the utmost.

In many of the new towns the inhabitants were still living in tents and wigwams. And all the while, shiploads of impoverished would-be set-

225

tlers kept arriving—often with no supplies at all. This meant that while the winter might have started off with ample supplies, food stocks soon dwindled to the point where only emergency rations were left. According to Charlestown's records, "the people were compelled to live on clams and mussels, ground nuts and acorns, and these got with much difficulty in the winter time."[9] Once again shellfish became an emergency staple, as it had in Jamestown. Cotton Mather relates that one man, "inviting his friends to a dish of clams, at the table gave thanks to Heaven, who 'had given them to suck the abundance of the seas and the treasures of the sands.'"[10]

Winthrop now had two boats fishing at all times, setting up a competition between the crews. At low tide the women went out to dig at the clam banks. Edward Johnson reports a conversation among them. One woman said, "My husband hath travailed so far as Plymouth . . . and hath with great toil brought a little corn home with him."

A second responded, "Our last peck of meal is now in the oven at home a-baking, and many of our godly neighbors have quite spent all, and we owe one loaf of what little we have."

A third added, "My husband hath ventured himself among the Indians for corn and can get none, as also our honored Governor has distributed his so far, that a day or two will put an end to his store."[11]

Winthrop turned out to be a superb teacher when it came to bartering for corn with the Indians. "His solemnity of manner was precisely the attitude to win their respect, and he took care that relations should be on his terms, not theirs."[12]

Eventually the local Indians had only enough corn left to get themselves through the winter, so the governor dispatched a pinnace to trade with the Narragansetts. It came back with a hundred bushels, but such were their numbers that this did not last very long.

Winthrop, however, was also graced by God with an unusual gift of wisdom. As far back as September he had foreseen that their supplies would give out long before spring. He had sent the *Lyon* home to Bristol with their most reliable ship captain, William Pierce, and a long shopping list of vital supplies, accompanied by a letter to John Jr., requesting that he sell land, if necessary, to provide the necessary funds. This kind of sacrifice was to become a pattern with Winthrop, whose personal interpretation of the horizontal aspect of the covenant meant that one committed everything to the cause, even the last of one's personal funds.

When disillusioned would-be settlers (who had quit and gone back to England) began to circulate negative reports around London, the Bay Colony's sources of funds began to dry up, just as Jamestown's and Plymouth's had before them. Time and again Winthrop would dig deeper into his own coffers to pay for desperately needed supplies. During this period he was supporting the colony almost single-handedly, and he was rapidly exhausting what remained of his own wealth to do so. But never once did he make the slightest complaint, not even in his private journal.

Finally, in the middle of that winter, they declared February 6 a day of fasting and humiliation, to search their hearts for any reasons why God might be withholding his providence and to pray for a miracle. There was nothing else they could do: the corn was gone, the ground nuts had long been scavenged, and the clam banks were exhausted. The *Lyon* was so long overdue that they could only assume that she had been shipwrecked.

On the morning before the day of fasting was scheduled, "when Winthrop was distributing the last handful of meal in the barrel unto a poor man distressed by the wolf at the door," reported Mather, "at that instant they spied a ship arrived at the harbor's mouth, laden with provisions for them all."[13]

It was the *Lyon*. She had come across a dismasted ship on her way home and had towed her to port, which accounted for the long delay. Her cargo consisted of wheat, meal, peas, oatmeal, beef, pork, cheese, butter, and suet, and what was of most importance to many of the sick, casks of lemon juice. "Circumstances no longer being appropriate for a fast, the Governor and council ordered a day of Thanksgiving . . . such was the deliverance which made a profound impression on the minds of that distressed people. It was recognized as a signal providence of God. About their firesides its story was told by fathers to their children for many a day in praise of the goodness of God and His guardianship over the colony."

Winthrop's love of his neighbors, exemplary in any age, and his commitment to them rank second to none in the annals of this nation's history. One of the chroniclers of his own era summed him up: "His justice was impartial, his wisdom excellently tempered . . . his courage made him dare to do right. . . . Accordingly, when the noble design of carrying a colony of Chosen People into an American wilderness was by some eminent persons undertaken, this eminent person was, by the consent of all, chosen for the Moses."[14]

A historian from the early nineteenth century ranks him second only to Washington in terms of stature among the founders of America, and we would agree.

"Gather my saints unto me." In Puritan New England the saints gathered on the Lord's Day in the meetinghouse, the hub of their covenant life together. They came to worship the Lord and to be taught from his Word. Such was their hunger for the Word of God and for sound teaching that—surprising as it may seem by today's standards—the Puritans welcomed sermons lasting two hours or more. When he was in top form, their pastor could be counted on in the course of a sermon for at least two turns of the large hourglass that stood in plain view near the pulpit—and then another turn's worth of prayers. If a visiting preacher gave out after only three-quarters of an hour or so, they spoke of him as they might of a spavined horse that had given out between the stays.

The man who turned the hourglass was the sergeant-at-arms, the redoubtable tithing-man. In addition to turning the glass, he had other responsibilities. It was he who checked the local inns on Sunday to make sure they stayed closed. And it was he who stopped by the houses of known truants to make certain that they were in their appointed pews. Above all, it was he who was responsible for keeping the saints alert in their pews as their minister went from his thirteenth point to his fourteenth (or, heaven forfend, from his twenty-seventh point to his twenty-eighth, which had been known to happen). Drugged by a lazy summer day, with the sound of crickets mingling with the "howsomesoevers," even the most zealous Puritan had been known to nod off.

But the tithing-man, ever watchful for the saint who was "only resting his eyes," was equal to his task. He had a staff to discomfort them, usually with a foxtail or pheasant feather on one end for the ladies and a brass knob on the other for the men. It should be noted that the tithing-man was not imposed upon the congregation by some ecclesiastical or civil authority; rather, he was paid by the church members themselves. For such was their desire to learn from their pastor that they did not want to miss anything due to a betrayal of their flesh. Few Americans have better understood the meaning of Jesus's admonition to His disciples, "The spirit is willing, but the flesh is weak."

Although they were indeed serious about the importance of their spiritual life together, they were not—as the present-day image would have them—taking themselves so seriously that they were incapable of laughing at themselves. The opposite was, in fact, the case. They had a hearty appreciation of the silly incidents our foibles can cause, and laughter was a frequent visitor in their meetinghouses.

The tithing-man in Lynn had a sharp thorn on the end of his staff for those whose sleep was especially sound. We are indebted to the journal of Obadiah Turner for the following eyewitness account of what happened in church on the first Sunday in June 1646:

> As he strutted about the meetinghouse, he did spy Mr. Tomlins sleeping with much comfort, his head kept steady by being in the corner, and his hand grasping the rail. And so spying, Allen [the tithing-man] did quickly thrust his staff behind Dame Ballard and given him a grievous prick upon the hand. Whereupon Mr. Tomlins did spring up much above the floor, and with terrible force did strike his hand against the wall, and also, to the great wonder of all, did profanely exclaim, *"Curse ye, woodchuck!"* he dreaming, so it seemed, that a woodchuck had seized and bit his hand. But on coming to know where he was, and the great scandal he had committed, he seemed much abashed, but did not speak. And I think he will not soon again go to sleep in meeting.[15]

For the Puritans Sunday was the first day of the week, not the last. There was the morning service, which lasted three to four hours, after which they adjourned for a light lunch and returned for the afternoon teaching, which could run another three hours. Then came Sunday dinner, the heartiest meal of the week. A nap was often in order afterwards, to sleep off the effects of so much good food and preaching.

The Puritans respected their pastor, who was generally a graduate of Oxford or Cambridge and possessed the best classical education available. (Harvard, Yale, and other New England colleges were originally founded to provide such training to American-born ministers).

The townspeople relied on their pastor to keep them apprised of what was going on in the world. Moreover, he was expected to have spiritual insight on the news he passed along, whether it was a natural disaster or a scientific discovery or a distant war. And since the pastor was almost always the most-educated man in the community, he was counted on to bring the sum of human knowledge as well as God's wisdom into his preaching. He was unquestionably the most influential person in town.

Not all Puritan ministers were regarded with profound respect, and occasionally even those who were found themselves confronting rebellion. Sometimes the rebellion took the form of a willful choir, as in the case of one minister who, glaring at his choir, announced with much vehemence the hymn that began "And are you wretches yet alive? And do you yet rebel?"[16]

Choirs were vital to the worship service, for most New England congregations had no accompaniment, nor could they remember many tunes. Even the few well-known melodies had become so corrupted that no two individuals sang them alike, or quite together, for that matter. Hence, a congregation singing often sounded like "five hundred different tunes roared out at the same time."[17] This being the case, the main singing was from the Psalms, with an elder or deacon leading with a line and the choir dutifully repeating it.

One Puritan deacon, rising to lead an obedient choir one Sunday, found his eyesight failing him as he started to read and apologized, "My eyes, indeed, are very blind."

The choir, assuming this was the first line of a common-meter hymn, immediately sang it.

Whereupon the deacon exclaimed, "I cannot see at all!"

This the choir also sang.

Frustrated, the deacon cried out, "I really believe you are bewitched!"

And when the choir sang that, too, the deacon loudly added, "The mischief's in you all!" and sat down in disgust.

For any believer truly committed to Jesus Christ in a covenant life that demands all, humor and laughter become two of God's most precious gifts. The struggle against sin and self is often difficult. When one is angry, tired, or on the verge of self-pity, the grace and mercy of God's holy humor provide a balm of healing ointment to the soul. The Puritans appreciated God-given opportunities to relax and perhaps even be a bit foolish with one another.

One such occasion was the dedication of the Old Tunnel Meetinghouse in Lynn in 1682, which coincided with the installation of one Mr. Shepherd as its pastor. It was a double cause for celebration, and ministers from all the churches for miles around were invited as guests of honor. The town clerk recorded the events as follows:

> The dedication dinner was had in the great barn of Mr. Hood, which by reason of its goodly size was deemed the most fit place. It was greatly adorned with green bows and other hangings and made very fair to look upon, the wreaths being mostly wrought by the young folk, they meeting together both maids and young men, and having a merry time in doing the work. The rough stalls and unhewed posts being gaily begirt, and all the corners and cubbies being swept clean and well aired, it truly did appear a meet banqueting hall. The scaffolds, too, from which provender had been removed, were swept as clean as broom could make them. Some seats were put up on the scaffolds, whereon might sit such of the ancient women as would see, and the maids and children. The great floor was held for the company which was to partake of the feast of fat things, none others being admitted save them that were there to wait upon the same. The kine [cattle] that were wont to be there were forced to keep holiday in the field.

There follows a detailed account of how the fowls that were accustomed to living in the barn persisted in flying in and roosting over the table, scattering feathers and hay on the august assembly below. Finally, the new pastor's patience was at an end. Normally the pastor was the soul of dignity and decorum, but this was too much:

> Mr. Shepherd's face did turn very red, and he catched up an apple and hurled it at the birds. But he thereby made a bad matter worse, for the fruit being well aimed, it hit the legs of a fowl and brought him floundering

and flopping down on the table, scattering gravy, sauce and divers things upon our garments and in our faces . . . this did not please some, yet with most it was a happening that made great merriment.

Dainty meats were on the table in great plenty, bear-steak, deer-meat, rabbit and fowl, both wild and from the barn-yard. Luscious puddings were likewise had in abundance, mostly apple and berry, but some of corn meal with small bits of suet baked therein, also pies and tarts. We had some pleasant fruits, as apples, nuts, and wild grapes, and to crown all, we had plenty of good cider and the inspiring Barbados drink [rum]. Mr. Shepherd and most of the ministers were grave and prudent at the table [except, of course, when flinging apples at the chickens!], discoursing much upon the great points of the dedication sermon and in silence laboring upon the food before them. But I will not risk to say on which they dwelt with most relish, the discourse or the dinner.

Most of the young members of the council would fain make a jolly time of it. Mr. Gerrish, the Wenham minister, though prudent in his meat and drinks, was yet in a right merry mood. And he did once grievously scandalize Mr. Shepherd, who on suddenly looking up from his dish did spy him, as he thought, winking in an unbecoming way to one of the pretty damsels up on the scaffold. And thereupon bidding the godly Mr. Rogers to labor with him aside of his misbehavior, it turned out that the winking was occasioned by some of the hay seeds that were blowing about, lodging in his eye. Whereat Mr. Shepherd felt greatly relieved.

The new meetinghouse was much discoursed upon at the table. And most thought it as comely a house of worship as can be found in the whole colony, save only three or four. Mr. Gerrish was in such a merry mood that he kept the end of the table where he sat in right jovial humor. Some did loudly laugh and clap their hands. But in the midst of the merriment, a strange disaster did happen unto him. Not having his thoughts about him, he endeavored the dangerous performance of gaping and laughing at the same time, which he now must feel is not so easy or safe a thing. In doing this, he set his jaws open in such wise that it was beyond all his power to bring them together again.

His agony was very great, and his joyful laugh soon turned to grievous groaning. The women in the scaffolds became much distressed for him. We did our utmost to stay the anguish of Mr. Gerrish, but could make out little till Mr. Rogers, who knoweth somewhat of anatomy, did bid the sufferer to sit down on the floor, which being done Mr. Rogers . . . gave a powerful blow and then sudden press which brought the jaws into working order. But Mr. Gerrish did not gape or laugh much more on that occasion, neither did he talk much, for that matter.

No other weighty mishap occurred save one of the Salem delegates, in boastfully essaying to crack a walnut between his teeth did crack, instead of the nut, a most useful double tooth and was thereby forced to appear at the evening with a bandaged face.

There were further interruptions by invading roosters, staved off by barrages of flying nuts and apples, and in the end a few "maudlin songs and much roistering laughter." The account concludes, "So noble and savory a banquet was never before spread in this noble town, God be praised!"[18]

So much for the modern image of dour Puritans.

13

THE PRUNING OF
THE LORD'S VINEYARD

The army of Light had established its beachhead in the new Promised Land. And as reinforcements poured ashore, the Light was advancing inland up the rivers of southeastern New England. Its momentum was inexorable, and those with the eyes to see it recognized it as a miracle of God, of a magnitude seldom seen in the sixteen hundred years of the church's history.

For in spite of extreme differences of background and level of commitment, in spite of all the temptations of jealousy and strife, in spite of wave upon wave of weak, sick, and helpless newcomers, they were being "knit together" to become "as one body." In the rocky soil of New England, God was planting a new vineyard, and a surprising number of the strong-willed, independent, and self-reliant characters who would come to typify that region chose to be rooted into it as living vines.

Jesus said to his disciples: "I am the true vine, and my Father is the vinedresser. Every branch of mine that bears no fruit, He takes away, and every branch that does bear fruit He prunes that it may bear more fruit"

(John 15:1–2). The pruning began the moment that settlers had landed in this savage wilderness. The raw New England winter and times of famine had already prompted several shiploads of fruitless branches to return to England. Those that remained would be pruned severely by adversity and would bear good fruit.

With each passing season the vineyard became more established. The Vinedresser was looking for an abundant yield, and so His careful but incisive pruning of the Massachusetts Bay Colony continued. Three prominent branches fell to the pruning hook—two wild shoots and one excellent one, suitable for transplanting.

The first branch appeared in February of 1631. A passenger aboard the *Lyon*, he was known to John Winthrop, who remembered him back in England as a "godly minister," one of the most ardent in the Puritan movement. Though only twenty-eight, he was possessed of a keen intellect and a gift for lyrical and inspiring preaching that had few equals.

Such was the impact of Roger Williams on New England that Cotton Mather, in his great history of God's acts in America, *Magnalia Christi Americana*, introduced him in terms of the following allegory:

> In the year 1654, a certain windmill in the Low Countries (Holland), whirling around with extraordinary violence by reason of a violent storm then blowing, the stone at length by its rapid motion became so intensely hot as to fire the mill, from whence the flames, being dispersed by the high winds, did set a whole town on fire. But I can tell my reader that about twenty years before this, there was a whole country in America like to be set on fire by the rapid motion of a windmill in the head of one particular man.[1]

Roger Williams was that most tragic and intriguing of all zealous Christians: a purist. "Charming, sweet-tempered, winning, courageous, selfless, God-intoxicated—and stubborn,"[2] he was so obsessed with being doctrinally and ecclesiastically correct that not even the Puritans were pure enough for him. From the moment he stepped off the boat he brought anguish to the hearts of all who came to know him. Because to know him was to like him, no matter how impossible the tenets he insisted upon.

And they *were* impossible. Witness his response when John Winthrop invited him to become the Boston church's teacher. At the time the invitation actually involved assuming the pulpit, since Pastor John Wilson had gone back to England to bring over his wife. But Roger Williams did not feel that he could accept. For although the Boston church had put off all the trappings of Anglicanism and followed Plymouth's example of representative leadership and congregational autonomy, Williams would not be satisfied until the congregation publicly repented for ever having taken Holy Communion within the framework of the Church of England, which they sensibly saw no need to do.

Williams's insistence upon absolute purity in the Church grew out of his personal obsession with having to be right—in doctrine, in conduct, in church associations—in short, in every area of life. The driving need to be right colored everything he thought or did, compelling him into one untenable position after another. The alternative—facing up to his self-righteousness and repenting of it on a continuing basis—was more than he could accept.

For Roger Williams, then, Christianity became so super-spiritualized that it was removed from all contact with the sin-stained realities of daily living. In his view the saints of New England belonged to a spiritual Israel, in the same way as did all Christians everywhere. But there should be no talk of God attempting to build his Kingdom on earth through imperfect human beings. For Winthrop and the others to even suggest that God might be doing a new thing in this Promised Land of America was to "pull God and Christ and Spirit out of Heaven, and subject them unto natural, sinful, inconstant men."[3]

Williams apparently did not understand that this paradox actually described the mystery of Christ's incarnation, His life on earth, and His death on the Cross—God embracing humankind in all of its fallen humanity. Further, Jesus called all of his disciples to follow his example. Williams could not abide the tension of being called to be in the world but not of it, or of being subject to a congregation comprised of "natural, sinful, inconstant men."

Balking at subjecting himself to the circumstances of this world (which his Savior had willingly accepted), Williams chose to withdraw even more fully into a controlled environment of his own choosing. Of all those who tried to reason with him—including at different times Thomas

Hooker, John Cotton, William Bradford, and Edward Winslow—John Winthrop came the closest to reaching his heart. In fact, Williams may well have considered the compassionate Governor his closest personal friend throughout the remainder of his life.

But when it came to a matter of principle, Roger Williams would never back down. As much as he might have been tempted by Winthrop's vision to build a model of Christian charity, the covenanted kingdom that the Governor described cut across the principle that Williams held most dear: liberty of conscience ("Nobody is going to tell me what I should believe").

Liberty of conscience *is* a vital part of Christianity—as long as it is in balance with all the other parts. Taken out of balance and pursued to its extremes (which is where Williams, ever the purist, invariably pursued everything), it becomes a license to disregard all authority with which one does not happen to agree at the time. This was the boat that Williams was rowing when he landed at Boston. Since, at its extreme, liberty of conscience represented freedom from any commitment to corporate unity, Williams was not about to hear God through Winthrop or anyone else.

And so, uncomfortable with the lack of purity among the Puritans, off he went to join the Separatists' colony at Plymouth, where he hoped to find people who were as separated from religious trappings as he was. Here he was seemingly content to keep his more provocative opinions to himself. The Pilgrims were charmed by him—until he discovered that their agents in London had attended Anglican services there. That did it; he demanded that they repent or be excommunicated.

Of Williams's two years in the Old Colony, Bradford had this to say:

Mr. Roger Williams, a man godly and zealous, having many precious parts but very unsettled in judgment, came over first to Massachusetts, but upon some discontent left that place and came hither, where he was friendly entertained, according to their poor ability and exercised his gifts among them and after some time was admitted a member of the church. And his teaching [was] well approved, for the benefit thereof I still bless God, and am thankful to him even for his sharpest admonitions and reproofs, so far as they agreed with the truth. He this year [1633] began to fall into some strange opinions and from opinion to practice, which caused some controversy between the church and him, and in the end some discontent on his part, by occasion whereof he left them something abruptly. . . . [When they refused his demand that they excommunicate their agents, he had no choice but to separate himself from them, as a matter of principle.] He is to be pitied, and prayed for, and so I . . . desire the Lord to show him his errors and reduce him to the way of truth, and give him a settled judgment and constancy in the same.[4]

Both Winthrop and Bradford had essentially the same reaction to Williams: personal fondness but genuine anguish over the tragic course that he seemed implacably determined to pursue, steadfastly refusing to even consider the possibility that he might be wrong.

Had Roger Williams been able to humble himself and come to see how judgmental and self-righteous he was, he might have been a great general in Christ's army, one who would have led troops smashing through the very gates of hell. All agreed that he was tremendously gifted in intellect, preaching, personality, and leadership ability. He attracted people in large numbers. But he had one tragic flaw: he could not see his wrongness. Forever hammering home points on the truth, he was so bound up in his intellect that no one could get close to him. Trying to relate to him on a personal level was like trying to relate to cold steel that is highly polished and impossible to penetrate.

No sooner had Roger Williams broken with Plymouth than the Congregational church at Salem offered him their pulpit. He readily accepted, and now with a church behind him, Williams began to row in earnest. He immediately started preaching that the King had no right to issue a charter to the Bay Colony because the Indians (not the King) were the original owners of the land. He also charged the King with blasphemy for referring to Europe as Christendom.

This left John Winthrop, the Bay Colony's chief magistrate, no choice but to admonish him in open court, and for a while Williams actually seemed to have a change of heart.

But within six months he was back at the oars, now dueling in print with John Cotton, one of the great Puritan pastor-teachers. But before Williams's long and tedious debates were published, Cotton had asked the magistrates' permission to entreat with him privately on behalf of the Bay Colony. Here, as everywhere else, he was shown nothing but love. Essentially the attitude of his peers was, "Let him believe whatever he wants as long as he is quiet about it. In due course, time will mellow him, and God will break him and ultimately make good use of him."

Yet Roger Williams would not be quiet. His attacks on the King continued, as if he was bent on jeopardizing their charter and bringing the full weight of the Crown's wrath down upon them all. Moreover, he was now dispensing such views as the pastor of a church. When the other pastors appealed to him, he replied with a treatise prepared for publication in which he denounced the King as a liar and recommended that the people of the Bay Colony either send the charter back to England as fraudulent or return to England themselves.

Although his clerical colleagues were powerless to unseat him, the civil authorities were not. He was again hailed before the General Court, this time for willful and persistent heresy and troublemaking. Williams countered that since the churches had obviously given up the principle of congregational independence and had called upon the government to help suppress him, they were no longer pure churches. He and his congregation, therefore, would have no choice but to renounce all the other churches in Massachusetts.

Here was the sort of shining moment that Roger Williams lived for. The gallant captain, fearless and intrepid, was about to lead a charge against insurmountable odds. With a wave of his arm he stepped out in front of his troops and led them into battle. On and on he ran, never flagging, indeed seeming actually to gain strength the closer he came to the enemy positions. Yet had he looked back to see how his troops were faring, he would have received a shock: nobody was following him.

But Roger Williams never looked back.

At the time he led this particular charge, he was sick in bed with a cold and so was unable to appeal to his flock in person. He had to do so in writing, and without the force of his personality to put it over, the appeal fell flat. His congregation finally balked. Faced with this betrayal, the dictates of his principles were clear: he had no choice but to renounce his own congregation, too.

Williams was, to be sure, granted his day in court—and he reveled in it, excoriating all present, even Winthrop, and wearing his subsequent sentence of banishment as if it were a medal of honor.

In spite of all his posturing and condemning, the court, under Winthrop's leadership, was willing to postpone sentence until the following spring (1636), provided that Williams would cease and desist from his inflammatory activities. They were, in effect, putting him on probation; if he were to stop "drawing other people to his opinions," the sentence might have been mild or even rescinded.

But that was like telling a chain-smoker he ought to give up cigarettes. Williams persisted, and when the civil authorities finally were about to arrest him, he fled to Rhode Island, where he founded a colony of his own, which he named Providence.

When God has us between a rock and a hard place in order to deal with us on a level of deep-rooted sin, and we try to avoid it by escaping, we are merely forcing Him to deal with us that much harder in the next place. So now in Providence, God began to deal with Roger Williams in earnest. He had gone to England and procured a charter for his colony (apparently no longer having any scruples against accepting charters issued by the King). Populated at first by those who had remained loyal to him at Salem, Providence now became a magnet for every crackpot, rebel, misfit, and independent thinker on the Atlantic seaboard. And Williams, as President, was responsible for keeping order.

What a nightmare! A man named Verrin refused to obey any order from the government on the grounds that it interfered with his "liberty of conscience." A seductive spellbinder named Samuel Gorton, whose philosophy was so obscure that none of his adherents could even define it and who had been unceremoniously ushered out of the Bay Colony, had subsequently so stirred up things at Plymouth that he and his followers were among the few people whom the Pilgrims ever invited to leave.

Then, after being thrown out of the town of Aquidnick, Gorton finally descended upon Providence, where he was driving Williams to distraction. As Williams would write to Winthrop, who took it upon himself to maintain a warm correspondence with him (thereby keeping the door open, should Williams ever want to return): "Master Gorton, having foully abused high and low at Aquidnick, is now bewitching and bemadding poor Providence both with his unclean and foul censures of all the ministers of this country (for which I myself have in Christ's name withstood him), and also denying all visible and external ordinances."[5]

But Williams's greatest problem proved to be the Quakers. Here again, the popular modern image of a humble, quiet folk, close to the earth, devout and simple in their ways, who drew people to God by their own unique brand of "friendly persuasion" is accurate enough for the eighteenth and nineteenth centuries, once they finally accepted William Penn's offer of sanctuary and settled down. But back at their beginnings in the seventeenth century, the Quakers were the wildest and most fanatical believers in all Christendom. To their way of thinking, Puritanism was hopelessly compromised and polluted, an institution that needed to be brought down by violent activism.

And violent was the right word. One Sunday a Puritan minister had barely turned the hourglass for the first time when suddenly the door of the church burst open, and in came a fire-breathing Quaker with two bottles in his hand. Everyone held his or her breath, including the preacher. Up the aisle strode the Quaker, who then bellowed, "God will shatter you for your hypocrisy, just like *this!*" hurling the bottles on the floor. He turned on his heel and strode out before anyone could stop him. And then there was the Quaker lass who had her own way of protesting Puritan hypocrisy: in the middle of a service, she walked in without a stitch of clothing on, went up to the altar, turned around, and walked silently out.

Not surprisingly the Puritans were riled to the point of apoplexy by the mere mention of the word *Quaker*. And the Quakers seemed to love every minute of it. Like some modern cults, they apparently felt truly fulfilled only when and where they were the objects of persecution. In short, if things were peaceful, they were not living up to their faith. They stirred up such turmoil in Massachusetts that they were finally banished upon pain of death if they ever returned. Four promptly decided they would martyr themselves and return, which they did, only to find themselves completely ignored. Whereupon they raised such an unholy ruction that the authorities finally, albeit reluctantly, obliged them.

In Providence they took pernicious delight in bedeviling Williams by reading back to him his most famous quotations whenever he tried to assert his authority. Everything that Williams had ever inflicted upon the Bay Colony was now being inflicted upon him, till he cried out in anguish. (Concerning the Quakers, in the end he outsmarted them by simply refusing to take civil action against them, which made them loathe his colony. And it was Williams's book attacking the Quakers' doctrine that the Bay Puritans adopted as the ablest statement of their point of view.[6])

Meanwhile, Williams's continuing obsession with doctrinal purity had caused him to separate himself progressively further, until the only person whom he deemed fit to take communion with him was his wife, and one historian says that even she was finally found to be "impure." The great danger of such obsessive self-righteousness is progressive withdrawal from society and from other Christians. It can also lead to a dangerous, other-worldly mysticism that neutralizes any further effectiveness the believer might have in forwarding the Kingdom of God.

However, by the amazing workings of the grace of God, when Williams finally reached this point, he abruptly concluded that true purity was an unobtainable goal. In frustration he reversed himself entirely and decided to embrace everyone. The breaking process had at least begun.

Nevertheless, throughout the remainder of his life, even as his spirit mellowed, it was still of paramount importance to him that he be right. Years after his principal opponents were dead and everyone else had forgotten the issues, he would still wage phantom debates, writing wearying volumes, trying to prove that, after all, his position was the only valid one. And thus, so much of what might have worked pure gold in him where humility and inner peace were concerned, turned him to self-pity and despair. Toward the end of his life, he would write, "As to myself, in endeavoring after . . . temporal and spiritual peace, I humbly desire to say, if I perish, I perish. It is but a shadow vanished, a bubble broke, a dream finished. Eternity will pay for all."[7]

In the end, the memory of Williams evokes genuine sorrow because his life could have counted for so much more. As it was, he did accomplish far more than even he himself realized. He would have pointed with pride to the long list of books, sermons, and treatises that he published, yet even his staunchest modern defenders have to admit that these writings (the fruit of his rightness) are dull to the point of stupefaction.

Ironically his greatest accomplishment turned out to have been on the heart level—not the head. In his late-blooming humility, he befriended the hostile Narrangansetts, becoming a trusted friend of their chief and leading many of them to Christ. Because of his missionary work among them, Rhode Island was the only colony spared from Indian uprisings, and he was able to send key intelligence that saved Massachusetts from being taken by surprise in a terrible massacre.

With the passing of years, God had succeeded in humbling Roger Williams to the point where He could make significant use of him. And Winthrop, Cotton, Hooker, and the others never lost their personal fondness for the windmill that once blew among them.

If Roger Williams succumbed to one of the two great temptations for Christians—adamant, intellectual self-righteousness—Anne Hutchinson succumbed to the other: total infatuation with the experiential.

Mrs. Hutchinson and her husband arrived at Boston in 1636 and immediately joined John Cotton's church, for she had been an admirer of Cotton's when he had been preaching at Saint Botolph's in England. She admired him even more now, and for a while everything was sweetness and light. Mrs. Hutchinson had an extremely quick mind and a charming personality, in such potent combination that no one in New England had seen her like on their side of the ocean. And as for Cotton, never had he met anyone who was so enthusiastic about the Gospel or who had such a quick grasp of the deeper things of the Spirit. She, in turn, could not praise him enough for his illumination of practically every subject on which he happened to preach.

When a man is gifted with a strong intellect, as Cotton was, there is an equally strong temptation that goes along with it: pride. In Mrs. Hutchinson he had finally found someone who appreciated—who really understood—his most profound points. Not only did she understand them, but she even received insights of her own that were compatible with what he was preaching. Cotton began to look forward to his meetings with her after his sermons.

Her own enthusiasm now reached the point where she started inviting women to her home after church to discuss the high points of Cotton's sermons. The meetings grew rapidly, and now some men began coming too. Gradually, imperceptibly, Mrs. Hutchinson began sharing some of her own beliefs, which were not entirely in line with what was being taught by Cotton—or anyone else, for that matter. Not that she was concerned about any of the other New England ministers; she subtly and indirectly proceeded to put each one of them down in her comments (though never to their faces) and always denied it if anyone ever asked her about it.

Heresy begins when someone takes a basic truth and pushes it slightly out of balance with the rest of the body of truths that together comprise the essence of the Christian faith. Anne Hutchinson was teaching that a Christian was saved by faith alone. That is true, but she went on to state that therefore, no amount of sanctification or good works could be taken as proof of salvation. While that is technically true, she maintained that the corollary was also true: The absence of sanctification and good works was no sign that a person was not saved. How *could* one tell, then? According to Mrs. Hutchinson, the Holy Spirit entered bodily into a person when he or she became saved. And anyone who had the Holy Spirit in them could tell whether someone else had the Spirit in him, too.

For individuals caught up in the heady intoxication of profound spiritual experiences, it is easy to slip into error. Not that there is anything wrong with such experiences per se, but spiritual experience is only one leg of a three-legged stool. Unless it is balanced by the Word of God through Scripture and through other Christians and by the daily living of a life of self-denial, obedience, and repentance, the stool will topple.

Satan is the master counterfeiter, able to imitate every spiritual experience a Christian can have, including the "inner voice" of the Holy Spirit. Time after time we have seen cases of "anointed" personalities who will lead a flock of gullible sheep into the strangest heresies because the sheep have not yet learned to know their Shepherd's voice and follow Him. Not nearly enough has been preached under the title "Beware the Christless Pentecost."

What keeps the stool in balance? Facing the reality of our own egos, being willing to be corrected and shown where we are wrong, and choosing to stand against the demands of self. This is the Way of the Cross: to have self decrease so that Christ in us might increase. It is the only way a disciple can go, and it was a way that neither Roger Williams nor Anne Hutchinson chose to go.

Without the Cross, error could only multiply, and soon Mrs. Hutchinson was claiming that the direct revelation of what she called the Holy Spirit was superior to the ministry of the Word. This meant that whenever her personal revelation was in conflict with the ministers' interpretation of the Bible, they were wrong. Believing that she was always in direct communication with the Holy Spirit, she felt that she did not need to submit to the rest of the Body of Christ in order to hear God. On the rare occasion that anyone dared to openly question whether the inner voice she heard was indeed of God, she would grow fanatical, withering the questioner with the power and eloquence of her response.

Understandably alarmed at such increasingly bizarre teaching, the ministers of the Bay Colony were also concerned with John Cotton's attitude toward Anne Hutchinson. For Cotton, normally their spokesman, could not bring himself to censure the woman; indeed, he seemed to be under her spell. And now her Sunday meetings had sixty to eighty people attending on a regular basis, including members of their own congregations. And she, waxing bolder in her rapidly growing popularity, was now not so subtly suggesting that none of the ministers (save Cotton, of course) was fit to preach the gospel because the Holy Spirit was telling her that none of them was truly saved.

The showdown came on the day when she was summoned to appear before the magistrates to answer a charge of heresy. The courtroom was packed. Every minister within two days' ride was there, plus all the deputies, assistants, and Governor Winthrop. When she was challenged, in full confidence she exclaimed, "Take heed what you go about to do unto me . . . for I know that for this [which] you [are] about to do to me, God will ruin you! And your posterity! And this whole State!"

How, the court asked her, did she know it was God who revealed these things to her and not Satan? And with that, fire fairly blazed from her eyes, and suddenly the roles were reversed: she became the interrogator, and the court was the defendant:

MRS. H: How did Abraham know that it was God that bid him offer his
    son, being a breach of the sixth commandment?
COURT: By an immediate voice.
MRS. H: So to me by an immediate revelation!
COURT: How an immediate revelation?
MRS. H: *By the voice of His own Spirit to my soul!*[8]

And then she went on to threaten all of them with what God was telling her that He would do to them, even as she stood there in court.

The court needed only a short deliberation to decide upon banishing her and those who would not disavow her beliefs as "unfit for society." Where would she go? Where else? But by the time she departed for Rhode Island, her following had shrunk to a mere handful, and these were already arguing among themselves.

Mrs. Hutchinson's husband died the following year, and the badly deformed child that she was carrying at the time of her exile died at birth. Whereupon, she decided to leave Rhode Island and moved the rest of her family to a lonely settlement in the Dutch colony of New Netherlands, near a place called Hell's Gate (now Pelham). There, in September of 1643, she and her family were cut down on their doorstep, the first victims of a local Indian uprising.

There is a macabre footnote to the Anne Hutchinson story, which the Puritans were convinced bore out all the other evidence that she was a mouthpiece for Satan. We would not mention it, except for the fact that Winthrop himself felt that it merited a detailed account in his history of New England. In the same year that Anne Hutchinson gave birth to a deformed stillborn child, so did her chief protégée, Mary Dyer. No description of the Hutchinson child exists, and the mothers endeavored to bury both babies without entering them into the town records. But word got out about Mary Dyer's baby—that it was a monster—and Winthrop, together with another magistrate and a church elder, questioned the midwife who had been present at its birth.

Winthrop's detailed description of the creature's deformities is too revolting to reproduce here. He went on:

> The Governor, with advice of some other of the magistrates and of the elders of Boston, caused the said monster to be taken up, and though it were much corrupted, yet most of those things were to be seen, as the horns and claws, the scales, etc. When it died in the mother's body (which was about two hours before the birth), the bed whereon the mother lay did shake, and withal there was such a noisome savor, as most of the women were taken with extreme vomiting and purging and were forced to depart. And others of them, their children were taken with convulsions (which they never had before or after), and so were sent home, so as by these occasions, it came to be concealed.[9]

It should be kept in mind that this is not a horror movie; the bed-shaking, the stench, the convulsions, the vomiting and the spawn of evil itself actually happened. Governor Winthrop is too mature of a witness to suspect him of distortion or exaggeration. If anything, his presentation would be conservative. And perhaps the Puritans, who somberly regarded it as a sign of Satan's authorship of Mrs. Dyer's and Mrs. Hutchinson's teaching, were not that far wrong.

The banishment of Roger Williams and Anne Hutchinson might best be summed up in these words from the Old Testament:

> My beloved had a vineyard
>   on a very fertile hill.
> He digged it and cleared it of stones,
>   and planted it with choice vines . . .
> and he looked for it to yield grapes,
>   but it yielded wild grapes.
>
>   Isaiah 5:1–2

Thus did the Vinedresser remove two aberrant shoots that were producing wild grapes.

247

The same year in which Roger Williams left the Bay Colony, the Vine-dresser removed another branch, but this one was a cutting especially selected for transplanting.

It was a pruning that Governor Winthrop resisted at first, because he felt that the loss could hurt or even cripple the colony. The Reverend Thomas Hooker was a man of God who was in rare balance and who had been following the Way of the Cross for many years. Indeed, he had arrived at a point where he could write—and live—what amounted to the synthesis of the highest Puritan ideals.

He had much to say about the Way of the Cross, and we found ourselves wishing we had room to reprint large selections from his *Sum of Church Discipline* and *The Christian's Two Lessons: Self-Denial and Self-Trial.* This small sample will have to give the flavor of the rest:

> We must lay down self. . . . Therefore, because it is not in us to help ourselves, let us lay all at the feet of Christ, and expect nothing from self-sufficiency, but all from Christ . . . because that Christ and self-service cannot stand together, to have self in anything is to put out Christ; no man can serve two masters. . . .
>
> Thus you have seen the first means [of becoming disciples], viz, self-denial. Now we come to the second; take up the cross. You must not think to go to heaven on a featherbed; if you will be Christ's disciples, you must take up His Cross, and it will make you sweat. By Cross, we understand troubles, because the death of the Cross was the bitterest and most accursed; therefore, it is put for all misery, trouble, affliction and persecution. [A man] must take up his cross, because it is his own. . . . We must not bring misery on ourselves; there is no credit or comfort in this. The text does not say, "Let him make his cross," no, it is made already. So long as we have the world and our own corrupt hearts, and as long as there are devils in hell, there are troubles enough. . . .
>
> Shall I not drink the cup which my Father gives? There is the force of the argument. God prepares it, therefore drink it, so the Apostle [Paul] reasons . . . God would have us live. If the patient be persuaded [that] the Physician has the skill, he will be willing to receive the potions prescribed by Him.[10]

There are some Christians today who are so resistant to denying themselves anything and so committed to maintaining an atmosphere of artificial, self-generated joy that they would like to think that the man who wrote those lines must have been a pretty miserable fellow. Quite to the contrary, Thomas Hooker led an exceedingly positive and fulfilled life, and in many ways he made an even greater contribution to the birth of American democracy than Winthrop did.

Here was a man who, seeing himself as a totally needy sinner, was able to come to Christ daily with openness and humility. Thus he was a Christian who had profound inner peace and balance, to whom God could give heavy responsibility and through whom God could create a whole new vine for His vineyard. For Hooker listened to God, trusted Him, and obeyed Him.

Cambridge-educated, Thomas Hooker was an extremely gifted and compassionate pastor, probably the most popular Puritan preacher in all England. As such, he was at the top of Laud's hit list, as soon as the latter became Archbishop. Hooker barely escaped the King's soldiers when he embarked for Holland in 1630. Three years later God called him to New England, where a body of Christians who called themselves "Mr. Hooker's Company" had come over the year before and were waiting for him.

In Hooker, Winthrop found the first person he had met who fully shared his vision of what God was doing in New England. But for all his fame and popularity, Hooker had a humble spirit. Cheerfully and quickly he fitted into the work at Massachusetts Bay and was a frequent guest in the Governor's home. Winthrop saw Hooker as the ablest of all the clergy to come to America and increasingly began to rely on him.

The men enjoyed one another's company. Both were intellectually creative and could argue dispassionately, spending much of what little free time they had in discussion. We can easily imagine the sort of exchange that might have taken place in the long winter of 1633–34.

"Can you really be serious," Winthrop might have asked Hooker one evening, seated by the hearth with his wife Margaret spinning nearby (for she had joined him now), "about extending the vote? Government by the consent of the governed is one thing, and it has worked well enough for the first comers, our cousins to the south." He paused. "But every man with a vote? And all the magistrates elected?"

He got up and stood with his back to the fire. "You're inviting anarchy, Thomas, or worse. Just because an idea happens to be momentarily popular with just over half of the people does not make it necessarily right. How often are God's strong dealings that popular? If the Kingdom of God were a democracy, how long do you think God would remain in office? That's why we've set up the Bay's government so that responsible leadership will not be encumbered by irresponsible legislation."

Hooker sipped his mulled wine and looked into the fire. "I have no quarrel with government by responsible and caring men. But tell me something: where are the checks and balances in the Massachusetts Bay system to ensure against the corruption in leadership that so often accompanies absolute power? Don't you see that the people themselves must be allowed to help create the laws that govern them? Mind you," he smiled and tapped the rim of his pewter mug, "nothing would make me happier, John, than to have you continue in office until the Lord returns. But you're not going to, and we both know that. What if your successor turns out to be a bad apple? What if the magistrates start creating laws that line their own pockets or subvert the common good? How do we pluck them out before they ruin the barrel?" He looked at his host. "You know that can happen. And you know how quickly it can happen," he added, as the Governor remained silent.

Winthrop poked a log into better position, creases forming on his brow. "But I say, you cannot trust most men to have the necessary wisdom to elect governors and assistants and magistrates. You'll have them putting their cronies in office for favors or putting in golden-tongued charmers who will promise the world and deliver nothing. I tell you, you'll wind up with more bad apples in your barrel than you ever dreamed of!"

He started back to his chair. "Government is best off in the hands of a few men who are totally dedicated to the work at hand—God's work. I am not advocating an aristocracy; you know that. I do not care what a man's background is, so long as he is totally surrendered to God and really means to serve his fellow man—and has the brains and pluck to do the job."

"I know," said Hooker, looking up at him. "But it is not a question of trusting the voters' judgment; it is a question of trusting the Holy Spirit to work through them. After all, wasn't one of the main purposes of the Reformation to restore to believers the responsibility for their own spiritual government? And isn't giving every man the vote really just an extension of the Reformation into civil government?" He rubbed his chin. "I know there's a risk. Yet the risk of the alternative worries me even more."

But Winthrop balked at the thought of trusting every person with the responsibility of government. And so they reached an impasse—one that would occur again and again, until finally Hooker and his church at Newton (Cambridge) requested permission to leave the Bay Colony and settle over on the Connecticut River.

Winthrop was loath to let him go. Hooker had been of more service to the commonwealth and had provided more leadership than all the other ministers combined. And even that was not his main contribution. For Hooker was a peacemaker. He would take two people with seemingly irreconcilable differences and would gently remind them what—and who—was more important. Through his ministrations reconciliation would often come, and to Winthrop, reconciliation was a commodity more precious than a year's supply of food or a shipload of new farming equipment. Then, too, if Hooker left, how many good people would go with him?

Hooker's mode of departure was itself exemplary. He asked the Governor's permission and patiently awaited his response. And soon Winthrop came to see that if it were God's will, as Hooker seemed so sure that it was, instead of weakening the Bay Colony as he feared, it would eventually somehow strengthen it. Indeed, the two settlements could well prove to be mutually supportive.

This was, of course, what happened. God had given Hooker the vision of the next step in the evolution of American civil government, which had been born in the Reformation, actualized in the Pilgrim's church covenant and the Mayflower Compact, and further developed by Winthrop's working model of Christian charity.

Hooker felt strongly that all civil government in God's "New Israel" must be based on a voluntary submission to the same kind of covenant in civil terms that was the essence of their Puritan churches: "There must of necessity be a mutual engagement, each of the other, by their free consent, before by any rule of God they have any right or power, or can exercise either, each towards the other."[11]

251

In a letter to Winthrop in 1638, Hooker further crystallized his views on magistrates being elected for life and thus remaining virtually unchecked by the people in their exercise of authority: "I must confess, I ever looked at it, as a way which leads directly to tyranny, and so to confusion, and must plainly profess, if it was in my liberty, I should choose neither to live, nor leave my posterity, under such a government."[12]

It was not yet the final form of American representative government, but it was getting closer. A year later Hooker drafted the *Fundamental Orders of Connecticut*, which naturally evolved out of his beliefs. This constitution (for that is what it was) differed from the Bay Colony's system in four respects. First, there was no religious qualification for one to be able to vote. Second, restrictions were placed on the authority of the magistrates. Third, though the "inhabitants" (servants, etc.) could not vote for the Governor and other officers as could "freemen" (landholders), nonetheless they had the right to elect deputies to the court. Fourth, the Governor was sharply limited in power and could not seek immediate reelection.

In *The Sum of Church Discipline* Hooker took the opportunity to add his personal conviction that it was impossible to overemphasize the importance of the horizontal aspect of the covenant:

> Mutual covenanting and confederating of the saints in the fellowship of the faith according to the order of the Gospel, is that which gives constitution and being to a visible church. . . . It is free for any man to offer to join with another who is fit for fellowship, or to refuse . . . by mutual reference and dependence they are joined each to the other. . . .
>
> In all combinations there is and will be some common end. . . . [But] if each man may do what is good in his own eyes, proceed according to his own pleasure, so that none may cross him or control him by any power, there must of necessity follow the distraction and desolation of the whole, when each man hath liberty to follow his own imagination and humorous devices, and seek his particular, but oppose one another and all prejudice the public good. . . . [Therefore] mutual subjection is, as it were, the sinews of society, by which it is sustained and supported.[13]

It is hard to say whether Hooker had Roger Williams and Anne Hutchinson specifically in mind when he penned those words. In sum, he was speaking for all the Puritans. And no one had better stated the case for a covenanted society, as opposed to either aristocratic rule or the chaos of the extreme individualists. For "they had come to New England to build a City upon a Hill, not to erect a Tower of Babel."[14]

Thus would Connecticut become legendary for "steady habits," and its form of government would serve as the model for other colonies and eventually for a union of colonies (which is why Connecticut's license plates proudly proclaim it to be the Constitution State).

As for Hooker? His wise counsel was continually sought by Winthrop long after he had moved to Connecticut, and he was frequently invited to return in order to help the Bay Colony magistrates liberalize their own body of laws.

The new vine, though still young, was already producing some of the choicest grapes in God's vineyard. But as healthy as the vineyard now appeared, within the span of a generation the yield of all vines would seriously decline.

14

GOD'S CONTROVERSY
WITH NEW ENGLAND

*O*ne of the mysteries that we faced in our search was this: What finally became of the Puritans? They had seemed to be prospering in every way—the hard times were behind them. There was plenty of good land and plenty to eat. They had a lasting peace with the Indians. Everyone who had been there for any length of time had a roof over their heads, and some of the homes were quite spacious.

Spiritually, most were deeply committed and were fulfilling the terms of the covenant, and God was, in turn, keeping His end of the bargain, blessing them beyond all measure. But all the while, like a fire dying down, the spiritual light was growing dimmer. It happened so gradually that no one seemed to notice it—until by the beginning of the eighteenth century, what had been a blazing white Light of the Gospel of Christ had become only a faint red glow from smoldering embers.

What had gone wrong?

The more reading we did, the more the question plagued us, for our research was beginning to indicate that the Covenant Way was the way God had intended America to go. If that is true, then the answer to the

254

question of where the Puritans went wrong might very well provide the way back to His purpose for the nation today.

We found our answer mostly between the lines of a number of sad accounts of such compromises as the Half-Way Covenant and increasingly vehement sermons that fell on increasingly deaf ears. And we found something else: countless recorded instances of what the Puritans called divine providence—extraordinary interventions of God on behalf of His people when they were in covenant with Him. Time after time God would pour out His grace and mercy on the Puritans and protect them from dangers they could not foresee.

But we also discovered some sobering examples of divine justice, when those who had once been in covenant openly scorned their commitment by word and deed. And we gained a better understanding of the judgments of God—those major and minor calamities that a loving Father permits in order to get the attention of His wayward children and cause them to turn back to Him. For the Puritans saw God's interventions, for weal or for woe, as distinctly as had their spiritual ancestors in ancient Israel: "Behold, I set before you this day a blessing and a curse: the blessing, if you obey the commandments of the LORD your God . . . and the curse, if you do not obey the commandments of the LORD your God." (Deut. 11:26–28).

So numerous were the blessings that God showered on the people of New England who were seeking to obey His commandments that Cotton Mather's *Magnalia* devotes several hundred pages to chronicling just some of the occurrences of divine providence. One remarkable account of God's supernatural care for His children occurs in Book II of the *Magnalia*:

> For instance, an honest carpenter being at work upon a house where eight children were sitting in a ring at some childish play on the floor below; he let fall accidentally from an upper story a bulky piece of timber just over these little children. The good man, with inexpressible agony, cried out, "O Lord, direct it!" and the Lord did so direct it, that it fell on end in the

midst of the little children and then canted along the floor between two of the children, without touching one of them all. But the instances of such things would be numberless.[1]

Another instance of God's taking a personal hand in the saving of Puritan children is described by John Winthrop in his journal. It involved his two daughters, who, in February of 1632 "were sitting under a great heap of logs, plucking of birds, and the wind, driving the feathers into the house, the Governor's wife caused them to remove away. They were no sooner gone, but the whole heap of logs fell down in the place, and had crushed them to death, if the Lord, in His special providence, had not delivered them."[2] If that wind had sprung up a minute later or been blowing in any other direction, they would have been killed.

"They that go down to the sea in ships . . . these see the works of the LORD and his wonders in the deep" (Ps. 107:23–24 KJV). Thus begins one of the most intriguing sections in the *Magnalia*: eleven tales of miraculous deliverances at sea. Here are two. On September 10, 1676, Ephraim Howe, his two sons, and three other men set sail from Boston for New Haven. Contrary winds and a storm blew them far out into the Atlantic and held them captive. Their exposure to the elements was lethal, and with little food aboard, one by one they began to die.

First, Ephraim lost his two sons, as had his Biblical namesake before him. But the storm raged on, finally driving them ashore on a desolate island near Cape Sable. The other men died after a few weeks because there was nothing to eat but an occasional fish or gulls that they could shoot (they had rescued some gunpowder). Ephraim survived alone.

Month after month went by, and although he could see fishing vessels on the horizon, none ventured near.

> The good man, while thus deserted, kept many days in prayer, with fasting [*sic*], wherein he confessed and bewailed the many sins which had rendered him worthy of these calamities, and cried out to God for his deliverance. But at last it came into his mind that he ought very solemnly to give thanks unto God for the marvelous preservations which he had hitherto experienced, and accordingly he set apart a day for solemn thanksgiving unto God, his gracious preserver, for the divine favors which had been intermixed with

all his troubles. *Immediately* [italics Mather's] after this, a vessel belonging to Salem did pass by that island, and seeing this poor servant of God there, they took him in. And so he arrived in Salem, July 18, 1677. [Less than two months shy of a year from the day he had departed!][3]

Our favorite of these sea stories involves two ships in distress. The first, under the mastery of William Laiton, was out of Piscataqua and bound for Barbados when, some thousand miles off the coast, she sprang a leak that could not be staunched. Her crew was forced to take refuge in their longboat. It happened that they had a plentiful supply of bread, more than they could possibly eat, but so little water that after eighteen days of drifting, they were down to a teaspoon per man per day.

Meanwhile, another ship, captained by one Samuel Scarlet, was having its own difficulties, being "destitute of provisions, only they had water enough, and to spare." They spied the drifting longboat, but as Scarlet made ready to take them aboard, his men

desired that he would not go to take the men in, lest they should all die by famine. But the captain was a man of too generous a charity to follow the selfish proposals thus made unto him. He replied, "It may be these distressed creatures are our own countrymen, and [anyway] they are distressed creatures. I am resolved I will take them in, and I'll trust in God, who is able to deliver us all." Nor was he a loser by this charitable resolution, for Captain Scarlet had the water which Laiton wanted, and Mr. Laiton had the bread and fish which Scarlet wanted. So they refreshed one another, and in a few days arrived safe to New England.

But it was remarked that the chief of the mariners who urged Captain Scarlet against his taking in these distressed people, did afterwards, in his distress at sea, perish without any to take him in.[4]

One never tires of hearing accounts of God's wondrous faithfulness toward those who love and seek to remain faithful to Him. The same psalm with which Mather opens his sea accounts also contains these words: "Oh that men would praise the LORD for His goodness, and for His wonderful works to the children of men!" (Ps. 107:8 KJV).

But for those whose hearts had become so hardened that they had nothing but scorn for the covenant, God's intervention took the form of judgment.

And the Puritans expected no less; as a people chosen to do His work, they knew that He would deal with them more strictly because of their call.

One of the grimmest tales of God's strict justice is recorded by John Winthrop. It happened in August of 1633.

> Two men servants to one Moody of Roxbury, returning in a boat from the windmill, struck upon the oyster bank. They went out to gather oysters, and, not making fast their boat, when the flood [tide] came, it floated away, and they were both drowned, although they might have waded out on either side. But it was an evident judgment of God upon them, for they were wicked persons. One of them, a little before, being reproved for his lewdness and put in mind of Hell, answered that if Hell were ten times hotter, he had rather be there than he would serve his master.[5]

And so his wish was fulfilled.

An even more pointed example of God's judgment—and a moving, last-minute gift of repentance—took place in Boston in 1686. A condemned murderer, James Morgan, who in the days before his execution had responded to the spiritual help of Cotton Mather and given his life to Christ, turned on the gallows steps and addressed the crowd:

> I pray God that I may be a warning to you all. . . . In the fear of God, I warn you to . . . mind and have a care of that sin of drunkenness, for that sin leads to all manner of sins and wickedness. . . . When a man is in drink, he is ready to commit all manner of sin, till he fill up the cup of the wrath of God, as I have done by committing that sin of murder.
>
> I beg of God, as I am a dying man and to appear before the Lord within a few minutes, that you may take notice of what I say to you. . . . O that I may make improvement of this little, little time, before I go hence and be no more. O let all mind what I am saying now [that] I am going out of this world. O take warning by me, and beg God to keep you from this sin, which has been my ruin.
>
> [And as the noose went round his neck] O Lord, receive my spirit! I come unto thee, O Lord, *I come unto thee!*[6]

More than a few people among the onlookers were, no doubt, convicted of the need for a significant amendment of their own lives. Sad to say, the likely response of the majority of those present was one of indifference, for a subtle and dangerous change was taking place in the heart of Puritan New England.

The ministers could see it coming, and Sunday after Sunday they had warned their congregations with such passages from the Word of God as:

> Take heed lest you forget the LORD your God, by not keeping his commandments and his ordinances and his statues . . . lest, when you have eaten and are full, and have built goodly houses and live in them, and when your herds and flocks multiply, and your silver and gold is multiplied, and all that you have is multiplied, then your heart be lifted up, and you forget the LORD your God. . . . Beware lest you say in your heart, "My power and the might of my hand have gotten me this wealth." You shall remember the LORD your God, for it is he who gives you power to get wealth; that he may confirm his covenant which he swore to our fathers, as at this day. And if you forget the LORD your God and go after other gods and serve them and worship them, I solemnly warn you this day that you shall surely perish.
>
> Deuteronomy 8:11–14; 17–19

This summed up what was beginning to happen in God's "New Israel" just one generation after the arrival of the first comers. Faith was not something that could be passed on from generation to generation or imparted by baptism or the partaking of Holy Communion. For faith to come to flower, it had to be planted in the soil of gratitude.

Born into comfortable towns instead of having to carve them out of the wilderness, succeeding generations would not know the refining fire of affliction and adversity. They would grow up never knowing what it meant to be persecuted for one's faith, to be mocked and scorned or even imprisoned merely because they loved God enough to attempt to put Him and His will before all else. The sons of the fathers would never know what it was like to have no land and no work and no say in how they were governed. They would have no indelible memories etched into their minds of ten, twelve, or sixteen weeks of wet misery on the open seas, or of living in tents or holes in the ground, while cold and sickness took the lives of one in two people. They would have no memory of starving times in which they were all on their hands and knees looking for ground nuts or grubbing for mussels to stay alive—and all for the sake of their combined faith in the vision of a Promised Land.

They would, therefore, be disinclined to put all their trust in God. It was by His grace that they and their parents were being blessed. And while they might give lip service to His grace, the truth was that since they had never known anything else, they could hardly share the gratefulness of their parents.

And what of those parents? As their common condition of great need gradually receded and shifted to one of decided affluence, was their commitment to the covenant as absolute as it once had been? Or was having more than enough to eat, more than adequate shelter, and more than enough land beginning to take its toll? How quickly fade the pangs of harder times. Would America's affluence—the very gifts of a loving Father in response to the obedience of loving children—dim the light of Christ that had seemed so dazzling? As a homestead of three acres became thirty and then three hundred, would greed replace need?

It is also human nature that a generation that has gone through a time of great tribulation will do all in its power to preserve and protect its offspring from the same deprivations. As the Puritan fathers and mothers became wise in the ways of living close to the land, they passed on to their sons and daughters an endless and priceless compendium of frontier knowledge—how to shoe a horse, how to tell when the wheat is ready for harvest, how to know when the herring will run, and the finer points of carding and spinning wool.

And if, before each lesson, they forgot to stress the need to pray first and commit it all to God and to know that His grace was solely responsible for anything turning out well, the golden gift of resourcefulness would transmute itself to the leaden influence of self-reliance: *my* land, *my* team of horses, "with the might of *my* hand. . . ." As the fathers began to think this way, they raised a generation of strong, well-adapted, supremely capable—and self-reliant—Yankees.

When a man can look at his own two hands and know what they are able to do—gripping the handles of a plow or an axe or the stock of a gun—when he knows what they can fashion with an awl or a plane or an adze, when he knows that they can tell by touch how soon a mare will foal or how fertile the soil is. . . . when a man knows these things, he may well think that he does not need God as much. And then it will follow that he does not need other men either.

Thus began one of the strongest and most fevered of American traits: independence. The lone pioneer, carving out a homestead with his or her own family—that image occupies a favored place in our cultural heritage. It carries on into the present time, with the glorification of the loner, the easy rider, and the rebel. The media extol that type of hero, the older generation relives youthful illusions through the model, and their children believe in it and leave home to try to be king of the road themselves—often discovering too late that the dream is a nightmare.

It is a nightmare because God did not intend people to live alone. He intended men and women, and especially His children who are called by the name of His Son, to live as a body, to help and support one another. And God does His work of nurturing Christians primarily through other Christians. Indeed, the process of maturation (which the Bible calls sanctification) cannot be accomplished alone.

A number of the earliest Americans forgot this, as did even more of their sons and daughters. They still went to church, but their minds were often back on the spread or the plantation.

Those in church on Sunday were treated to increasingly vehement calls to repentance from the ministers. This type of sermon was preached so often that it would eventually become known as a Jeremiad, in honor of the Old Testament prophet who had thundered at a complacent Israel and from whose writings the Puritan ministers frequently took inspiration. Sunday after Sunday they inveighed from their pulpits across New England, and meetinghouse rafters rang with verses like Jeremiah 8:5–6:

> Why then has this people turned away
>   in perpetual backsliding?
> They hold fast to deceit,
>   they refuse to return.
> I have given heed and listened,
>   but they have not spoken aright;

no man repents of his wickedness,
     saying, 'What have I done?' "

A person can become hardened to such strong words. After all, the preachers had been saying the same thing for years, but the land was still fertile, the climate favorable, the Indians peaceable, and God seemed to help those who helped themselves.

And so their grandsons and granddaughters helped themselves to more land and moved further away to establish their own life on their own land. There was no bothering now to gather a church first, no adherence to the unwritten law that forbade inhabitants to live more than half a mile from the meetinghouse of a settled town, as there once had been. A person was free to go and do as he or she pleased, or as the Book of Judges puts it, "whatever was right in his own eyes."

Bradford, not surprisingly, had foreseen it before anyone else, and it had broken his heart because he knew what God had intended.

No man now [1632] thought he could live, except he had cattle and a great deal of ground to keep them; all [were] striving to increase their stocks. By which means they were scattered all over the bay quickly, and the town in which they lived compactly till now was left very thin and in a short time almost desolate. And if this had been all, it [would have] been less, though too much. But the church must also be divided, and those that had lived so long together in Christian comfort and fellowship must now part and suffer many divisions. . . . And this, I fear, will be the ruin of New England, at least of the churches of God there, and will provoke the Lord's displeasure against them.[7]

A dozen years later, as more Pilgrims were anxious to get out on Cape Cod before all the best land was taken, Bradford would write:

But such as were resolved upon removal . . . went on notwithstanding, neither could the rest hinder them. . . . And thus was this poor church left, like an ancient mother, grown old and forsaken of her children (though not in their affections), yet in regard of their bodily presence and personal helpfulness. Her ancient members being most of them worn away by death, and these of later time like children translated into other families, and she like a widow left only to trust in God. Thus she that had made many rich became herself poor.[8]

Cotton Mather, writing years later, put it more bitingly: "Religion begat prosperity, and the daughter devoured the mother."[9] And in the same blunt vein, speaking of all New England, Judge Sewall wrote to a friend, "Prosperity is too fulsome a diet for any man . . . unless seasoned with some grains of adversity."[10]

Was God wrong, then, to honor the obedience of His beloved children with blessings? Of course not. But as John Danforth preached, "to turn blessings into idols is the way to have them clapped under a blast. If the Lord loves His people, He will deliver the weapons out of their hands, that they are obstinately resolved to fight Him with. . . . Better is it that Israel be saved and prosperity lost, than that prosperity be saved and Israel lost!"

God would clap them under a blast, as events would shortly demonstrate. But with all His heart, He was reluctant to do so, being patient far beyond the patience of human beings. And meanwhile, those people who knew the heart of God tried to alert their neighbors of the dire peril that they were surely bringing upon themselves. For God was now warning them directly—with droughts, with plagues of locusts and caterpillars, with smallpox epidemics, and with all the myriad and seemingly unconnected things that start to go wrong when grace is lifted.

Perhaps the most extraordinary chastisement in this vein was the rain of caterpillars that Winthrop reported in the summer of 1646.

Great harm was done in corn (especially wheat and barley) in this month by a caterpillar, like a black worm about an inch and a half long. They eat up first the blades of the stalk, then they eat up the tassels, whereupon the ear withered. It was believed by divers good observers that they fell in a great thunder shower, for divers yards and other bare places where not one of them was to be seen an hour before, were presently after the shower almost covered with them, besides grass places where they were not so easily discerned. They did the most harm in the southern parts, as in Rhode Island, etc., and in the eastern parts in their Indian corn. In divers places the churches kept a day of humiliation, and presently after, the caterpillars vanished away.[11]

The astonishing end to this plague is borne out by the Roxbury church records: "Much prayer there was made to God about it, with fasting in divers places, and the Lord heard and on a sudden, took them all away again in all parts of the country, to the wonderment of all men. It was the Lord, for it was done suddenly."[12]

For further corroboration, we have the account of the irrepressible Johnson:

> Also the Lord was pleased to awaken us (to our sinful neglect of the Sabbath) with an army of caterpillars that, had He not suddenly rebuked them, they had surely destroyed the husbandman's hope. Where they fell upon trees, they left them like winter-wasting cold: bare and naked. And although they fell on fields very rarely, yet in some places they made as clear a riddance as the harvest-man's hand, and uncovered the gay green meadow ground. But indeed the Lord did, by some plots, show us what He could have done with the whole, and in many places cast them into the highways, that the cartwheels in their passage were painted green with running over the great swarms of them. In some fields they devoured the leaves of their peas and left the straw with the full crop, so tender was the Lord in His correction.
>
> This [re]minded all these Jacobites of the end [purpose] of their coming over, but chiefly the husbandmen, whose over-eager pursuit of the fruits of the earth made some of them many times run out so far in this wilderness, even out of the sweet sound of the silver trumpets blown by the laborious ministers of Christ, forsaking the assembly of the Lord's people, to celebrate their Sabbaths in the chimney-corner, horse, kine [cattle], sheep, goats and swine being their most dear companions.[13]

While Johnson, Winthrop, and some others had sufficient discernment to see at that early stage what was happening, and spoke of it in no uncertain terms, they were as voices crying in the wilderness. Few listened. And so God, in His great love, had to follow the caterpillars with chastenings and warnings progressively more severe. Repeatedly His people would turn back to Him, and pray and call His name and humble themselves, and He would gladly relent and return blessings. But each time they turned away again a little quicker, and each time their repentance was a little more perfunctory—going through the motions, with not everyone bothering to observe the fast days or attend the services. There may indeed have been repentance, but it did not reach deeply enough to affect an amending of lives, for their hearts were turning hard and dry like those of the people in Israel of old. And so the droughts did not lift so quickly, nor did the pests entirely disappear.

The tragedy was poignantly expressed by Bradford, who stood at the end of his life, like old Jacob weeping for his sons gone into Egypt, looking back and measuring what might have been, by what they had actually had in the beginning. In 1655, two years before he died, as he reviewed the history that he had written of the Plymouth plantation, he came to the letter that Pastor John Robinson and Elder William Brewster had written from Leyden to Edwin Sandys in London. The letter brimmed with the confidence that, although other attempts at colonization had failed miserably, their situation was unique and unprecedented because of the proven strength of their covenant relationship. Indeed, they were "knit together as a body in a most strict and sacred bond and a covenant of the Lord, of the violation whereof we make great conscience and by virtue whereof we do hold ourselves straitly tied to all care of each other's good, and of the whole by every one and so mutually."[14]

Reading that, Bradford lost his customary composure, and in a moment of rare and overwhelming anguish, poured out his heart on the back of that page in his manuscript: "O sacred bond, whilst inviolably preserved, how sweet and precious were the fruits that flowed from the same! But when this fidelity decayed, then their ruin approached. O that these ancient members had not died or been dissipated . . . or else that this holy care and constant faithfulness had still lived and remained with those that survived!"

No one, not even Bradford, was denying that the settlement of the wilderness to the west was part of God's plan. But that was the ministers' whole point: it should be carried out as part of *His plan*, in accordance with His perfect will and timing. It should not be done willy-nilly by isolated individualists who, where a new stretch of bottom land was concerned, could not care less about being in God's will. Heedless of the covenants they had sworn, without bothering to submit their decision to the elders of their churches, let alone obtain the permission of the civil authorities, they simply departed.

One preacher who responded more in anger than in sorrow was John Cotton:

> But when men thus depart, God usually followeth them with a bitter curse: either taking their lives away from them, or blasting them with poverty, or exposing them to scandal where they come, or in entertaining them with such restless agitations that they are driven to repent of their former rashness, and many times return to the church from which they had broken away.[15]

It was an awesome thing in those days for a member of the clergy to invoke such a solemn imprecation, but John Cotton's prophecy was to prove truer than even he might have expected.

Another symptom of the spiritual malaise was the fact that the younger generation was not getting converted. Members of successive generations were not coming into the same saving relationship with Jesus Christ that their parents and grandparents had known.

The brunt of the responsibility had to rest squarely on the shoulders of the Puritan parents. For they were the ones who first eased up on their commitment to the Covenant Way. The Puritans had been called as a body to be so filled with the Light of Christ in their own lives that they would be "a city set on a hill" and "a light to lighten the Gentiles." This meant that unless there was daily repentance and a humbling of oneself before God, the inevitable result might be expressed by the unspoken motto, "If you can't be good, look good." A shorter description of it is hypocrisy— the sin the Puritans seemed to hate so passionately in others yet came to practice themselves with ever-growing self-deception.

The parents were on the horns of a dilemma: if they continued to be as hard on their children's sin as they had hitherto been on their own, their hypocrisy would become manifest, and their children would have good cause to want no part of the Covenant Way. On the other hand, if they eased up on their children's sin, as they were doing on their own, they would be guilty of permissiveness, and their children would have no awareness of their own need for Jesus Christ, let alone be drawn to the Covenant Way.

In truth, there was no need for a dilemma. Had they been willing to hold themselves accountable to the terms of the covenant that they had originally accepted, God would have heard their prayers and healed their land. But once we lay down the cross He has given us to bear, our fallen nature is such that it strongly resists taking it up again.

The Puritans had laid down their cross. They stopped their ears and refused to listen to their ministers, and they ceased to correct and admonish one another and their children, instead choosing greed, privacy, and independence.

The Light of Christ now had grown so faint it was attracting hardly any of the children. And thus the Puritan churches faced a further dilemma: what to do about the children who had not been converted to Christ but who now wanted to have their own children baptized in the church?

In the end, they came up with what was dubbed the "Half-Way Covenant." This extended partial membership to such parents and enabled them to have their children baptized but did not permit them to take Holy Communion. It was the best solution they could come up with, and it well defined the place they had come to: a halfway covenant for halfway committed Christians.

The preface to the *Magnalia* sums up the first half century of God's "New Israel":

> Now one generation passeth away, and another cometh . . . and these have had the managing of the public affairs for many years, but are apparently passing away, as their fathers before them. There is also a third generation, who are grown up and begin to stand thick upon the stage of action. . . . Much more may we, the children of such fathers, lament our gradual degeneracy from that life and power of such fathers that was in them, and the many provoking evils that are amongst us. (For these evils) have moved our God severely to witness against us, more than in our first times, by His lesser judgments going before, and His greater judgments following after.[16]

Their troubles mounted to the point that in 1670 the government of Massachusetts actually conducted a special investigation to determine why God was so afflicting the people with sickness, poor crops, and shipping losses. But nothing came of it. The settlers followed their accustomed ways, and their hearts grew ever more hardened to the voices of their clergy, who were now warning that the blast John Danforth had predicted was imminent.

Actually, the government officials could have saved the time and cost of the investigation if they had read with open hearts the poem written by Michael Wigglesworth that had already become a favorite in Puritan classrooms. Aptly entitled "God's Controversy with New England," three of its thirty-one verses read as follows:

> Our healthful days are at an end
>   and sicknesses come on
> From year to year, because our hearts
>   away from God are gone.
> New England, where for many years
>   you scarcely heard a cough.
> And where physicians had no work,
>   now finds them work enough.
>
> Our fruitful seasons have béen turned
>   of late to barrenness,
> Sometimes through great and parching drought,
>   sometimes through rain's excess.
> Yea now the pastures and corn fields
>   for want of rain do languish;
> The cattle mourn and hearts of men
>   are filled with fear and anguish.
>
> The clouds are often gathered
>   as if we should have rain;
> But for our great unworthiness
>   are scattered again.
> We pray and fast, and make fair shows,
>   as if we meant to turn;
> But whilst we turn not, God goes on
>   our fields and fruits to burn.[17]

15

As a Roaring Lion

ike the drawing back of a mighty war bow, tension mounted in the early summer of 1675. One way God's blast of judgment might descend on a complacent, greedy, self-oriented people was so ominous that no one dared think about it, let alone put it into words: a general, coordinated Indian uprising.

Prior to this, the Indians' ancient tribal rivalries had run so deep that there was never a serious possibility of a massed uprising. And because God's people were living in obedience to their covenant with Him, His providential grace so covered them that such incidents as the one in 1639, which Winthrop relates, were not unusual:

> At Kennebeck, the Indians wanting food, and there being stores in the Plymouth trading house, they conspired to kill the English there for their provisions. And some Indians, coming into the house, Mr. Willet, the master of the house, [was] reading in the Bible, his countenance more solemn that at other times, so as he did not look cheerfully upon them, as he was wont to do. Whereupon they went out and told their fellows that their purpose was discovered. They asked them, how could it be?

The others told them, that they knew it by Mr. Willet's countenance, and that he had discovered it by a book he was reading. Whereupon they gave over their design.[1]

But relations between the settlers and the Indians had been deteriorating for some time. Gone were the days of peaceful coexistence so prized by Bradford, Winslow, and the Wampanoag sachem, Massasoit. When the great chief died of old age in 1662, leadership of the Wampanoag fell to his eldest son, Wamsutta, and when he died shortly thereafter, it was assumed by Massasoit's next oldest son, Metacomet, to whom the settlers had given the Christian name of Philip.

Philip, the new King of the Wampanoag, was being pressured from all sides. The Pilgrims wanted to buy more of his land, while to the west the Iroquois Confederation was pushing hostile tribes eastward. And then, the increasingly apprehensive Pilgrims demanded that the Wampanoag surrender all their weapons. Finally, the sudden rush of events in early June forced people to think the unthinkable.[2]

The arrow had been fitted to the bowstring back in January. Early one morning some men passing by a large frozen pond in the settlement of Middleborough (about fifteen miles southwest of Plymouth) happened to notice something out on the surface of the pond. It looked like a man's hat, and nearby was what appeared to be a musket. Since neither item was the sort of thing a man would leave behind him, particularly in the dead of winter, and since the ice was clearly strong enough, they went out on the pond to take a closer look.

Sure enough, it was a hat and a gun. Suddenly one of the men gave a cry: there, beneath the clear ice, was a face, its eyes open wide, staring upward, its dark hair billowed out around it. One of the men ran to get an ax. The body that they chopped out of the ice was that of John Sassamon, a Christian Indian from the nearby Indian settlement of Nemasket. Presumably he had drowned while crossing, before the ice had fully hardened.

But something was wrong. Sassamon was an Indian; he would have known better than to try something so foolhardy. Closer examination revealed an acute swelling on the side of his head, which might have come from a blow. Moreover, no water had come out of the body to indicate death by drowning. But the most telling piece of evidence was that his neck was broken. Whatever else might happen to a man going through the ice, he would not break his neck. John Sassamon had been murdered, and the crime had been made to look like an accident.

The probability of murder became more likely when one considered the facts of John Sassamon's life. Reared in a community of Christian Indians at Natick, fifteen miles west of Boston, he had studied at Harvard. But then, perhaps in a crisis of identity, he had rejoined the Indians in the wilderness, serving as the aide of King Philip. John Sassamon was a bright and quick young man, as fluent in English as in his native tongue. As such, he must have been invaluable to Philip—until Sassamon's Christian conscience began to trouble him. God's Spirit increasingly convicted him, till he finally returned to Natick and was readmitted to the congregation. He became such a model convert that he was given the responsibility of instructing other Indians. And so, when the Indian community at Nemasket sent for a native preacher, John Sassamon was the logical choice.

All of which could only have infuriated Philip, who was well known for his thinly veiled hatred of Christianity and especially of the Christian missionaries who were pulling away some of his best warriors. In this hostility he was fully supported by the *powaws*, or medicine men, who saw their own power and influence being drastically undercut by the settlers' religion. To Philip, John Sassamon would have appeared to be the vilest sort of turncoat. That much was known.

What was *not* generally known was that shortly before his death, John Sassamon had come to Governor Winslow of the Plymouth Colony and secretly informed him and his magistrates that Philip and the Wampanoag were organizing a general conspiracy against the settlers. At the time, the Pilgrims discounted the warning—after forty-four years of unbroken peace, it was simply unthinkable. Nor did they change their minds when he insisted that he was risking his life to bring them this intelligence.

But now that it had actually cost him his life, they did take it seriously.

Incredibly, an eyewitness to Sassamon's murder was found, an Indian who had observed the whole thing from the top of a nearby hill, near enough for him to recognize all three assailants, one of whom was a chief lieutenant to Philip. These men were apprehended, and the trial was set for June. To ensure the utmost fairness, there would be two juries: one composed of settlers, the other of the wisest Indians in the colony. Although the three defendants insisted upon their innocence throughout the trial, the verdict of both juries was unanimous: guilty as charged.

The sentence was death by hanging, and now the war bow was drawn fully taut. Philip was furious. He insisted that the witness was lying and was in collusion with the settlers in an obvious attempt to besmirch his honor (for if they were guilty, there could be no question who had given the order).

Such was Philip's insistence and that of the defendants—who, even as they stood on the gallows, hotly denied that they had been at all involved with John Sassamon's death—that there might have been real doubt in future years. Indeed, that would have been almost a certainty, had it not been for a reamarkable instance of divine providence. As the trap door beneath the last of the three Indians was sprung, the rope broke. The Indian fell to the ground, and in the terror of the moment he confessed that all three of them had done exactly what they had been convicted of. And though he maintained that he had only watched while the other two had done the actual killing, he was rehanged, and this time the rope did not break.

But Philip's patience did. Now large bands of armed Indians were seen moving about the countryside, causing many settlers to abandon their far-flung homesteads and move into more densely populated areas, guarded by fortified houses called strong-houses. One wonders if perhaps they were reminded of the words of 1 Peter 5:8 (KJV): "Your adversary the devil, as a roaring lion, walketh about, seeking whom he may devour."

Fear stalked the land; the tip of the arrow on the drawn war bow was seeking its aiming point. A few of the abandoned houses were looted and burned by the Indians, and armed bodies of militia went into the woods seeking the culprits, but they returned in frustration, having chased shadows. Shots were fired and returned, but the enemy was never seen. All through the first three weeks of June a terrified populace held its breath.

One can imagine the scene on the outskirts of the settlement of Swansea in the Plymouth Colony when the explosion finally came.[3] In the half-light before dawn on the cool, clear morning of June 21, the first shot was fired. It would have been guided by the feathers of a wild turkey—feathers attached not to the tail of a plump fowl but to a lean willow shaft. At the other end was an arrowhead of pointed flint, and as the silent missile flew toward its mark, from well-concealed positions more than a hundred pairs of eyes watched its flight. On and on it flew, till it landed with a thunk in the stout oak door of the home of a settler we will call Isaac Trowbridge.

Hearing that sound and no other, Trowbridge opened the door. His eyes widened when he saw the arrow, but before he could slam the door shut, a second arrow sank into his chest, and a third pierced his throat. His oldest son took the fourth as he tried to drag his father inside. At that moment the surrounding woods erupted in an unholy din, as scores of braves gave vent to stored up hatred. The middle son barricaded the door and put the family table up against the front window, while the youngest loaded their father's long-barreled flintlock. But it was futile, and the little family knew it. Before long an ugly column of black smoke was rising in the still morning air.

That day Indians from Philip's nearby base at Mount Hope burned all the houses of Swansea, slaughtering and mutilating their inhabitants. When the colonial troops finally arrived, they were shocked and sickened at the horror of the scene. The main street of the little village was strewn with the dismembered corpses of men, women, and children. So hideous was the sight that at first it did not even register that it could have been done by human beings. It seemed as if Satan himself had unleashed his fury on New England.

Dartmouth was the next settlement to come under the tomahawk, a day later, and then Taunton and Middleborough and Sudbury. Fifty people were massacred in Lancaster. Forty homes were put to the torch in Groton. Now the Indians prepared to move on Marlborough, with King Philip himself taking personal command of some fifteen hundred braves, a far greater army than the colonists had ever been able to muster.

New England was totally unprepared strategically, mentally, and spiritually. A company of local militia would be hastily called out and dispatched to the relief of a beleaguered town or hamlet, only to be cut to pieces by a well-placed ambush waiting for it. A second column would be sent to the aid of the first, only to blunder into a separate ambush set for it. And so it went, until the settlers were afraid to go into the woods, let alone vigorously pursue the enemy. Throughout New England morale sank to its nadir, as survivors made their way to towns that had not yet come under attack. Some were in hysterics, and others were dumbstruck by atrocities beyond the human mind's capacity to assimilate.

Almost immediately a fast day was declared in Massachusetts, but no sooner had the service ended than reports of fresh disasters arrived. Clearly this time God's judgment was not going to be turned aside by one day's worth of repentance.

Increase Mather and his son Cotton sounded the note that other clergymen soon picked up. They preached the most powerful sermons of their lives, based on Scriptures such as:

> Behold, I am bringing upon you . . .
>   a nation whose language you do not know. . . .
> Their quiver is like an open tomb,
>   they are all mighty men.
> They shall eat up your harvest and your food;
>   they shall eat up your sons and your daughters . . .
>   they shall eat up your vines and your fig trees;
> your fortified cities in which you trust
>   they shall destroy with the sword. . . .
> They lay hold on bow and spear,
>   they are cruel and have no mercy,
>   the sound of them is like the roaring sea . . .
>   they . . . [are] set in array as a man for battle,
>   against you, O daughter of Zion.
>
> Jeremiah 5:15–17; 6:23

It was manifestly clear to the Mathers that God was not going to be satisfied with superficial or temporary change. What He now demanded was what He had been calling for all along: nothing less than a complete amendment of life. This would necessitate a rooting out of sin and dealing with it to a degree that had not been seen on the eastern seaboard for nearly fifty years.

At first, the people, frightened and badly shaken though they were, still did not take the Mathers and their fellow ministers seriously; they had heard it all before so many times. But the war news got steadily worse. And it obviously was war now; practically every Indian tribe in New England had donned war paint and was collecting scalps.

Finally, the people began to heed their ministers. The Bay Colony's churches filled, and people who had not attended church in years stood in the aisles and joined in the prayers. For they had come to see that the battle was a spiritual one, and even the most pragmatic among them had accepted that fact.

God's patience with the colonists' hypocritical ways had come to an end. He was not about to relent and restore the saving grace that had so long protected them and that they had so long taken for granted, unless New England had a change of heart.

In the meantime, it was now the forces of light that were reeling in confusion and disarray and falling back on all fronts. As Samuel Cooke would preach a century later, "Satan, whom the Indians worshipped . . . [raised] armies of fierce, devouring beasts."[4] The Prince of Darkness had waited patiently for the seeds of greed to do their work. And now he laughed in triumph as his counterattack reached the peak of its fury, and his own obedient servants did their savage best to make up for all the ground lost and the insults taken. They fought with reckless courage, knowing that this was their last chance. For they could not be pushed any further west by the advancing settlers. Their backs were to the Hudson River, beyond which the exceedingly hostile and powerful Iroquois nations held undisputed territorial rights. The time had come to push the colonists back—all the way back into the sea.

Many of the families and settlements now being hardest hit had long ago removed themselves from the churches, physically as well as spiritually. Moreover, many of these families had incorporated themselves into towns without first gathering a church. The Mathers and like-minded ministers were making it abundantly clear that their misfortune was no coincidence. John Cotton's prophecy had come home to roost.

But where settlements, even the most isolated ones, had striven to keep faith with God and with one another, God kept faith with them. According to a history of the town of Sudbury, the reason that Sudbury rather than Concord was chosen by the Indians as their next point of attack was that the Indians feared the influence that Concord's minister, Edward Bulkeley, had with the Great Spirit. The history quotes an old Indian chronicle as follows: "We no prosper if we burn Concord," said they. "The Great Spirit love that people. He tell us not to go there. They have a great man there. He great pray."[5]

Another case in point is the siege of Brookfield. There, by the grace of God, the townspeople had time to gather into their blockhouse, where with their muskets they were able to hold off a vastly superior number of Nipmuck Indians. A scout named Ephraim Curtis was among the besieged. Three times he tried to sneak through the Indian lines to get help. On the third attempt he succeeded, crawling through the darkness on his hands and knees, expecting at any moment to be discovered and killed. He made it on foot to Marlborough, some thirty miles distant, where he collapsed, exhausted.

Meanwhile, back at the blockhouse, the Nipmucks were strengthening their siege, occupying nearby barns and pouring musket fire into the windows of the blockhouse, which continued to hold out. Now the Indians resorted to bonfires, shooting flaming arrows into the roof of the house. But the people inside cut holes in the roof and extinguished the flames before they could spread. Next the Indians piled hay against a corner of the house and set it afire, but some of the settlers were able to dash out and quench the blaze.

Frustrated, the warriors built a mobile torch, using wheels from the farm vehicles, a barrel full of combustibles, and two extremely long shafts, made of poles spliced together. But just as this contraption was about to be set in motion, a sudden downpour drenched the combustibles and rendered the fire-wagon useless.

The siege had been under way for almost forty-eight hours when word of their plight finally reached Major Samuel Willard, who was on his way to Lancaster with a strong force of mounted troopers. The force wheeled about and rode at the gallop to Brookfield, where the Indians were making such a tumult besieging the blockhouse that they did not hear the shouts or warning shots of their sentries, who had sighted the fast-approaching horsemen. After a brief, hot skirmish, the Indians vanished. And when the bullet-riddled door swung open, the troopers received the welcome of their lives.

Even in New England's darkest hour, God's judgment could be seen to be tempered with mercy on behalf of His faithful. It was a miracle that Curtis got through, another that the cloudburst came when it did, and a third that Willard's force just happened to be within reach and ready for combat when the word came.

Throughout King Philip's War, as it came to be known, there were many recorded instances of God's mercy in the form of divine providence. But perhaps none was more moving than the narrative of Mary Rowlandson, who was taken alive by the Indians when they raided Lancaster. Her husband, the local pastor, was in Boston on business when the attack came, and she and thirty-six others were in one of the village's strong-houses, which the Indians succeeded in setting on fire.

> Then I took my children and one of my sister's to go forth and leave the house, but as soon as we came to the door and appeared, the Indians shot so thick that the bullets rattled against the house as if one had taken a handful of stones and thrown them, so that we were fain to give back. . . . The Lord hereby would make us the more to acknowledge His hand and to see that our help is always in Him. But out we must go, the fire increasing and coming along behind us, roaring, and the Indians gaping before us with their guns, spears and hatchets to devour us. No sooner were we out of the house, but my brother-in-law fell down dead, whereat the Indians scornfully shouted and hallooed, and were presently upon him, stripping off his clothes. The bullets flying thick, one went through my side, and the same through the bowels and hand of my dear child in my arms. One of my elder sister's children, named William, had then his leg broken, which the Indians perceiving, knocked him on the head. Thus were we butchered by those merciless heathen, standing amazed, with the blood running down to our heels.[6]

They took her captive, but

God was with me, in a wonderful manner, carrying me along and bearing up my spirit, that it did not quite fail. One of the Indians carried my poor wounded babe on a horse. . . . I went on foot after it, with sorrow that cannot be expressed. At length, I took it off the horse, and carried it in my arms till my strength failed, and I fell down with it. [They put her and the child on a horse, until they made camp.] And now I must sit in the snow, by a little fire, and a few boughs behind me, with my sick child in my lap, calling much for water, being now through the wound fallen into a violent fever. . . . Oh, may I see the wonderful power of God, that my spirit did not utterly sink under my affliction. Still the Lord upheld me with His gracious and merciful Spirit, and we were both alive to see the light of the next morning.

For nine days Mary Rowlandson struggled on, as she was taken with the roaming band, until finally her child died. But her awesome faith in God remained undiminished: "I have thought since of the wonderful goodness of God to me, in preserving me in the use of my reason and senses in that distressed time, that I did not use wicked and violent means to end my own miserable life."[7]

This was particularly meaningful because many of the women taken captive either went mad or committed suicide. For the Indians enjoyed inflicting mental torture almost as much as physical torture, and they never missed an opportunity to torment a captive whom they suspected of having a low threshold of fear. What was more, they seemed to recognize faith in Christ for what it was, and it either provoked them into a frenzy, or they left the Christian pretty much alone, possibly fearful of the source of the Christian's inner strength. But other, less devout captives with only hope to sustain them had precious little of that commodity. All New England was plunged into darkness, the likes of which had not been seen, even in the first terrible winters.

But the light was never entirely extinguished. And the darker it became, the fiercer burned the few lights that were left. Not in twenty years had Increase Mather preached so often to such large crowds. And for the first time in even longer than that, people were listening to every word. In the face of the repeated successes of the Indians, the much-vaunted Yankee self-reliance and self-confidence melted away like a candle on a hot stove. A great many farmers and backwoodsmen, tasting fear for the first time in their lives, got down on their knees, some also for the first time. By April of 1676, there was scarcely a man or woman in all of New England who was not diligently searching his or her own soul for unconfessed or unrepented sin. In fact, it became unpatriotic not to do so—as if one were not doing one's part for the war effort.

It was a time for poets to marshal their talents for the cause, as did Peter Folger, one of whose grandsons would be Ben Franklin:

> If we then truly turn to God,
>   He will remove His ire,
> And will forthwith take this His rod
>   And cast it in the fire.
> Let us then search what is the sin
>   that God doth punish for;
> And when found out, cast it away,
>   and ever it abhor.[8]

It was time for churches to renew their covenants. As one pastor put it, "We intend, God willing, . . . solemnly to renew our covenant in our church state according to the example in Ezra's time. . . . This is a time wherein the Providence of God does, in a knocking and terrible manner, call for it."

At last God's wrath began to abate. Mary Rowlandson observed from behind enemy lines, as it were,

> the strange providence of God in turning things about, when the Indians were at the highest and the English at the lowest. I was with the enemy eleven weeks and five days. . . . [They] triumphed and rejoiced in their in-humane and many times devilish cruelty to the English. They would boast much of their victories, saying that in two hours' time they had destroyed such a captain and his company in such a place, and [would] boast how many towns they had destroyed, and then scoff and say [that] they had done them a good turn to send them to heaven so soon. . . .

Now the heathen begin to think all is their own, and the poor Christians' hopes [begin] to fail (as to man), and now their eyes are more to God, and their hearts sigh heavenward. And [they begin] to say in earnest, "Help, Lord, or we perish." When the Lord had brought His people to this, that they saw no hope in anything but Himself, then He takes the quarrel into His own hands. And though [the Indians] had made a pit in their own imaginations, as deep as hell for the Christians that summer, yet the Lord hurled themselves into it.[9]

Mary Rowlandson was miraculously released shortly before the cessation of hostilities. Not only that, but her son and daughter, held captive elsewhere, were also released, and the family was rejoined with her husband. "Thus hath the Lord brought me and mine out of that horrible pit, and hath set us in the midst of tenderhearted and compassionate Christians. It is the desire of my soul that we may walk worthy of the mercies received, and which we are receiving."[10]

The tide of war had begun to turn. Some modern historians, loath to give God credit for anything, point out that time and numbers were on the colonists' side, once they had regained their nerve. They had the weapons, and they had the supplies; all that was needed was for them to gain the courage to take the offensive. But the Puritans themselves knew from whom that courage finally came. They knew whom to thank, and they did, profusely.

In one of the exquisite ironies of divine justice, the instruments with which God chose to turn the tide were ones that had, until the coming of the settlers, belonged to Satan. These were none other than the "Praying Indians"—who had been converted to Christianity. These had remained loyal to the settlers, even though in the initial shockwave of panic they had been the focal point of much hatred, when badly frightened farmers suddenly decided that the only good Indian was a dead Indian.

Had these Praying Indians not been courageously protected by the Reverend John Eliot (who would become known as the Apostle to the Indians), Daniel Gookin, Daniel Henchman, and William Danforth, it is almost certain that there would have been counter-massacres that would have redounded to our shame for the next three hundred years. As it was, many Christian Indians were interned on Deer Island in Boston's harbor for the duration of hostilities, with almost no shelter and wholly dependent on charity for their food. But they knew how to pray, and God looked after them.

When they were finally trusted enough to be given arms and combat assignments, these Christian Indians became scouts, the eyes and ears of the colonial forces whenever they had to maneuver in heavy cover, which was whenever they sought to carry the battle to the Indians. Only now instead of stumbling about helplessly, the colonials could move swiftly and stealthily through the densest forests. The Christian Indians also taught the settlers to fight like Indians, from cover wherever possible, being content to harass and vanish until they were strong enough in numbers to risk an open confrontation. And to prefer mobility to artillery—all the dictates of guerrilla warfare that a century later would confound and frustrate the British regulars under Howe and Burgoyne.

By the summer of 1676, the tide was definitely running in favor of the colonists. Now, instead of being fearful of going into the woods after their foes, the settlers were eager to close in combat with the enemy wherever they were. For they believed they were fighting the forces of hell itself, and now that they had purged their own hearts of unconfessed sin, they called on the Lord with confidence to join with them.

"Pray for us, and we'll fight for you!" was their cheerful cry to those who had to stay behind, and the Indians noted their new aggressive spirit with dismay.

So many people had sincerely and publicly repented of their sinful ways, so many lives were truly reformed, so many broken relationships were restored, and so many churches solemnly renewed their covenants that God relented and poured out His mercy. There was a sense of freshness in the colonies, a sense of cleanness and new hope. The colonies were united in a common cause, while Satan's house again was divided against itself along the lines of the ancient tribal rivalries. Indeed, "luck" now seemed to be running so much against the Indians that they began giving themselves up, first in small bands and then in droves.

On August 26, 1676, the final decisive action took place. An embittered Wampanoag deserter, whose kinsman King Philip had ordered killed for suggesting that the Indians should make peace with the settlers, met with the Indian fighter Captain Benjamin Church. He offered to lead Church and his company, who had been pursuing Philip all across southern New England, to the place where the renegade chieftain was encamped. For Philip had stolen back to the Wampanoag settlement at Mount Hope on the peninsula of Bristol Neck, Rhode Island, near where it had all begun.

In the dead of night Church moved his forces in canoes over to the peninsula and set up an ambush. A detachment would approach the Indian settlement from the north, getting near and lying still all night. At dawn they would rise up and attack, making as much noise as possible. Meanwhile, the main body of Church's force would have formed a wide perimeter to the south. As the Indians fled in silence, their attackers yelling behind them, the circle of Church's men would be lying in wait to pick them off.

The plan went like clockwork. At the first light of dawn the tremendous uproar terrified the Indians and sent them bolting in panic. As the charging settlers shouted and whooped, the Indians ran as swiftly and quietly as deer. One, fleeter than the rest, nearly broke through the cordon before he was felled.

It was Philip. For all intents and purposes, King Philip's War was over.

Why had Philip returned to the seat of his power? Why had he, who knew as much about ambushes as any person alive, failed to post lookouts? Was it deliberate—the Indian equivalent of a soldier's honorable death? Whatever the reason, it was over. The aftermath of the war that cost proportionately more lives than any other in America's history and loaded the survivors with crippling debt, nonetheless proved salutary. Prosperity was indeed lost, but God's "New Israel" was saved—for a season.

If God was trying to build a "New Israel," Satan was doing everything he possibly could to thwart it. And the people who represented the greatest threat to him were those most dedicated to living the covenant way of obedience to the Savior who had conquered him. These were the Puritans. We have just seen how Satan waited patiently for two generations until affluence had so softened the Army of Light that he had an excellent chance to destroy them physically. But his willing servants were defeated through God's providential intervention on behalf of His own repentant servants.

Scripture tells us that until Christ returns and destroys the devil, he will continue to wage war against the Kingdom of God. Satan would bide his time for another sixteen years before launching his second and last major assault against the Puritans. This time the battle would be waged not in terms of the flesh and blood of the physical realm, but in terms of the principalities and powers of the spiritual realm. For this final offensive Satan would loose a concentrated attack of demonic spirits, which in virulence has never been equaled in American history, before or since. We would rather not give it even this much recognition, since it was an episode that spanned only a few years in more than a century of Puritan history. Yet it has been so grossly mishandled in modern treatments that it has to be included.

The Bible makes it clear that there are only two sources of supernatural power: God and Satan. And in the spiritual realm, as in geopolitics, there is no such thing as a power vacuum: where light reigns, darkness is banished. But when the light grows dim, the shades of night gather in the wings, waiting. The candle flame grows weaker still and begins to flicker; the darkness holds its breath.

Christianity is a power religion. Christ has the power to re-create a man or woman from the inside out, as anyone who has ever met Him knows. One of the earliest lessons a new Christian learns through experience is that the power of Christ is greater than the power of the Enemy. When Jesus shed His Blood on the Cross, He broke the back of Satan's power—then, now, and forever. One of the ways God teaches Christians this is by letting Satan harass them, to the point where they call out to their Savior and discover that in the name of Jesus, they have authority over the greatest powers of hell.

For that reason, Satan avoids open confrontations with seasoned Christians wherever possible. He will send his dupes and unwitting servants to do his dirty work, and he will concentrate his most cunning wiles on breaking down citadels of Light from within, on the ground of hidden sin. The only place where he can safely flaunt his power openly is where people do not know that he is a defeated foe—or where faith in Christ has grown dim.

As the seventeenth century drew to a close, the affluent Christianity of the Puritans had again become so enfeebled that the supernatural manifestations of Satan's power—occultism, witchcraft, and poltergeist phenomena (demons at mischief)—were coming out into the open. Witches began to be bolder, letting it quietly be known that they could cure warts and straighten toes and mix love potions (all white magic for the come-ons; the black magic—the hexing, the curse-laying, and the spellbinding—would come later). With the gullible, the unwary, and the hopeless turning to this source of power, more and more people began to come for advice and counsel to "the known ones."

As their influence grew, they became brazen, until there was an unacknowledged competition between them and the local pastors. All the while, demonic activity increased to the point where scarcely a village existed that did not have at least one house that was bedeviled by "haunts."

Of the several contemporary accounts of this sudden onslaught of satanic activity, Cotton Mather's is the most comprehensive. This was not because he was obsessed with the occult (as modern anti-Puritans would have us believe), but simply because he was one of the few ministers strong enough in the faith to confront Satan and remain supremely confident of victory. Because of this, everyone came to him with their supernatural problems—as if he was the only fireman in a town of straw houses.

As we went through these ancient accounts, we were stunned: cases of demonic possession or poltergeist activity were nothing new to us, but never had we heard of whole towns becoming literally infested with invisible beings, nor had we known anything to compare with the intensity of their malevolence. And God had allowed it all as a warning and to shake Christian settlers out of their acute spiritual apathy.

Typical were the goings-on in the house of William Morse at Newberry, described here by Cotton Mather:

> In the night, he [Morse] was pulled by the hair and pinched and scratched . . . and blows that fetched blood were sometimes given him. . . . A little boy belonging to the family was the principal sufferer of these molestations, for he was flung about at such a rate, they feared his brains would have been beaten out. . . . all the knives which belonged to the house were one after another stuck into his back, which the spectators pulled out. . . . The poor

boy was divers times thrown into the fire, and preserved from scorching there, with much ado. . . . once the fist beating the man was discernible, but they could not catch hold of it . . . and another time, a drumming on the boards was heard, which was followed with a voice that sang, "Revenge! Revenge! Sweet is revenge!" At this, the people being terrified, called upon God, whereupon there followed a mournful note, "Alas, alas, we knock no more, we knock no more!" and there was an end of all.[11]

The instances of possession were as violent and tenacious as any we had ever read or heard of. The thirteen-year-old daughter of John Goodwin of Boston was such a difficult case that it actually took weeks of battling to gain her deliverance. And the final struggle was won only after several ministers fasted and prayed at length together. Mather relates:

When we went into prayer, the demons would throw her on the floor at the feet of him who prayed, where she would whistle and sing and yell to drown out the voice of prayer, and she would fetch blows with her fist and kicks with her foot at the man that prayed. But still her fist and foot would always recoil when they came within an inch or two of him, as if rebounding against a wall. . . . At last the demons put her upon saying that she was dying, and the matter proved such that we feared she really was, for she lay, she tossed, she pulled, just like one dying . . . and then one particular minister . . . set himself to serve them [the Goodwin family] in the methods prescribed by our Lord Jesus Christ. Accordingly, the Lord being besought thrice in three days of prayer, with fasting on this occasion, the family then saw their deliverance perfected. And the children afterwards, all of them, not only proved themselves devout Christians, but unto the praise of God, reckoned these their afflictions among the special incentives of their Christianity.

Things finally reached the point where the Puritans felt that broad action had to be taken, as the Bible commanded that it must. Cotton Mather, in *The Wonders of the Invisible World*, comments aptly on the state of affairs:

The New Englanders are a people of God, settled in those which were once the Devil's territories, and it may easily be supposed that the Devil was exceedingly disturbed, when he perceived such people here accomplishing the promise of old made unto our blessed Jesus—that He should have the utmost parts of the earth for His possession. . . . The Devil, thus irritated, immediately tried all sorts of methods to overturn this poor plantation. . . . Wherefore the Devil is now making one attempt more upon us—an attempt more difficult, more surprising, more snarled with unintelligible circumstances than any that we have hitherto encountered. . . . The houses of the good people there are filled with the doleful shrieks of their children and servants, tormented by invisible hands with tortures altogether preternatural.[12]

One of the most diabolical things about this attack of demonic spirits was that apparently they often assumed the form of innocent people in the town as they went about their foul practices, "framing" them, as it were, giving rise to accusations against these good people, and fomenting all manner of jealousies and hatred. This became so great a problem that Increase Mather and a conclave of ministers warned civil judges throughout the Bay Colony that this "spectral evidence" should not be accepted as the basis for conviction of witchcraft. But in spite of the fact that this kind of testimony was not admissible in an English court of law, the judges did not heed the warnings.

There certainly was no doubt in any Puritan's mind that a massive frontal assault of satanic forces was indeed afoot. Mather reports that more than 120 then in custody freely confessed that the devil had appeared to them with a book in his hand for them to sign, agreeing to serve him.

In light of the modern tendency to judge the Massachusetts Bay Puritans as sin-obsessed religious neurotics who began hysterically hunting imaginary ghosts, it should be kept in mind that sober-minded pastors such as Cotton Mather carefully documented dozens of cases similar to those described above.

The climactic phase of the attacks of witchcraft on Massachusetts opened during the winter of 1692 in the town of Salem. The Reverend Samuel Parris, a failed merchant from the West Indies, was only three years into his first ministerial position as pastor of the small church on the outskirts of the town. Things were not going well. He had taken the position only on the condition that the congregation deed over to him possession of the parsonage and its two-acre lot. This had caused such anger that many church members were refusing to furnish him with firewood.

When he had arrived at Salem, Parris had brought with him two slaves—a married couple named Samuel and Tituba Indian. Without the pastor's knowledge, Tituba began spending winter evenings in his warm kitchen initiating young girls into the occult and witchcraft. By the end of January his nine-year-old daughter, Betty, would not pray when she was supposed to, refused to do chores, and threw fits of kicking and screaming. His eleven-year-old niece, Abigail, and a playmate, Anne Putnam, had developed fits and pain spasms, and all three girls crept under tables, barking, mewing, and grunting.

When a doctor found nothing physically wrong with them and asked, "Who tortures you," they said that three women were "afflicting" them, and named Sarah Good, Sarah Osborne, and Tituba. Now the same kinds of symptoms began to show up in other girls and women, and the Puritans became convinced that a massive attack of witches was indeed afoot. By late February, Salem was "alarmed to the highest degree."[13]

Soon people began to be arrested and imprisoned on charges of witchcraft, for in Puritan New England witchcraft was a civil offense, not merely a religious one. By May, when Sir William Phips brought back from England a new charter for Massachusetts that named him as Governor, he found the jails filled with accused witches. The charter gave the Governor the authority to create new courts, so he called for one—the court of Oyer and Terminer (in Latin, "hear and determine").

At her arraignment Tituba confessed to being a witch, but long after the subsequent trials had concluded, she said that Parris had flogged her and told her to confess and implicate the other women named by the girls—perhaps to lure the attention of the court away from him.

Throughout the summer, as Tituba remained chained to the wall of a rat-infested dungeon, dozens of suspects were brought to trial for witchcraft. In a complete collapse of the centuries-old procedures of the English system of justice, the court adopted a policy of convicting those who protested innocence and acquitting those who confessed to witchcraft, regarding the confession as a sign of hope that the accused would repent and come back to God.

Since the testimonies were taken under oath, innocent women were not about to swear before God that they had been involved in witchcraft when they had not. Yet the judges refused to listen to professions of innocence, choosing instead to accept the testimonies of demon-ridden accusers who were under the influence of the Father of Lies.

So horrifying was it all to Judge Nathaniel Saltonstall that he resigned from the court, saying, "I am not willing to take part in further proceedings of this nature."[14]

Months later one of the bewitched girls admitted to authorities in the colony that the judges had told her that if she would not confess to being a witch, she would be put into a dungeon and then hanged, but if she did confess and name others, her life would be spared.

Not even multiple testimonies to one's innocence swayed the judges. In August fifty residents of Andover wrote a letter to the court protesting that the local women accused of witchcraft were blameless. They said that "confessing was the only way to obtain favor" with the court, and that "might be too powerful a temptation for timorous women to withstand."[15] Their plea was ignored.

As the trials wore on, suspicion and dread gripped the colony, with many suspects being tortured until they confessed. Mary Clements of Haverhill confessed, but after the trials she recanted her confession before Puritan minister Increase Mather.

On September 22 eight persons were hanged for witchcraft—the last to be put to death in the Salem Witch Trials, and the last ever sentenced to death for witchcraft in America. On that same day the witch court adjourned, and in early October the governor disbanded it. In all, a total of twenty people had been executed, but the witch hunt was now over.

The trials had constituted a grievous failure to uphold the Puritan standards of the New England Way, a failure that would continue to prick the American conscience in future centuries. As tragic as they were, however, they should be judged in the perspective of what was happening in Europe at this time. During that same year, literally hundreds of witches were put to death. Between the fourteenth and eighteenth centuries, more than 100,000 Europeans were executed annually for witchcraft.[16] In the light of this reality, the Massachusetts Puritans' response might actually be considered conservative.

The witch trials had ended, but the judges had yet to become convinced that they had done anything wrong. Now public opinion was turning against them, and people were actively questioning the evidence against the accused. Thomas Brattle wrote: "There are several about the Bay, men for understanding, judgment, and piety . . . that do utterly condemn the said proceedings" and went on to name former Governor Simon Bradstreet, former Deputy Governor Thomas Danforth, the Reverend Increase Mather, the Reverend Samuel Willard, and Judge Nathaniel Saltonstall.[17]

A month later the sense that grievous wrongs had been committed in the trials had mounted to the point that the Governor's Council called for a fast day on October 26, so that all Massachusetts "may be led in the right way as to the witchcrafts." God was at work.

Samuel Sewall, one of the judges on the Oyer and Terminer court, observed a personal day of prayer and fasting on November 22. In his diary he recorded that he had prayed: "God, pardon all my sinful wandering, and direct me for the future. God, save New England as to enemies and witchcrafts, and vindicate the late judges [of the Court of Oyer and Terminer] with fasting [and] with your justice and holiness."[18]

Sewall was still praying that the judges' decisions would be vindicated, but he was also now entering a period of fervent Bible study and prayer that would last for five years. During that time God would radically change his heart.

Three days later Governor Phips established the Superior Court of Judicature and gave Samuel Sewall a seat on it. This was the first court in America to be independent of all other government institutions—a major step toward the separation of powers, which would become a hallmark of American government. That court is now the Supreme Judicial Court of Massachusetts, the oldest continually functioning court in the Western Hemisphere.

As the months passed, Judge Sewall seemed to have an increasing sense of remorse. In August 1693 his wife Hannah gave birth to a daughter, but the baby died in September. Fourteen months later she almost died at her next childbirth, and in May of 1696 Sewall laid in the grave a stillborn son, the seventh child he had buried. That same month he was the only member of the General Court not invited to a wedding between prominent Salem families, and he became aware that he was the subject of gossip about the Salem Witch Trials.

During this time his daughter Betty was heavily convicted of her need of God's grace. She told her father that she could not read the Bible without weeping, and six months later she burst into tears in his presence, crying that she was "a reprobate," who "loved not God's people as she should."[19]

By the fall of 1696 everyone in New England seemed to be strongly in need of God's grace. Bad weather had ruined the harvest, and grain was at its highest price ever. Many ships were being lost at sea, and the Indians and French were regularly raiding frontier towns. Moreover, the memory of the "late tragedy raised among us by Satan," as the General Court termed it, hung over the colony like an oppressive fog.

Finally, the Governor and the General Court ordered a day of prayer and fasting for January 14 of the next year, the subject of which was to be the Witch Trials.

A little over a week before Christmas, two-year-old Sarah Sewall got sick. She was dead by December 22. Two days later during family devotions, Samuel Sewall, Jr. chose to read out loud Matthew 12:7: "If you had known what this means, 'I desire mercy and not sacrifice,' you would not have condemned the guiltless." This Scripture was deeply impressed on Judge Sewall's mind, and he wrote that the verse "did awfully bring to mind the Salem tragedy."[20]

Church attendance on days of prayer and fasting in Puritan New England was mandatory—these meetings were not to be skipped. So, on January 14, 1697, when Bostonians trudged to their churches through the snow and ice to the beat of the town crier's drum, Judge Samuel Sewall took his family to Third Church. Taking their accustomed seats in the front benches, his wife Hannah, still in mourning clothes for her daughter's death, sat with their three daughters on one side of the center aisle, and Samuel and their two sons sat on the other.

When the minister, Samuel Willard, strode up the aisle to start the service, Judge Sewall handed him a note. After an opening prayer, Willard nodded to Sewall, and the judge rose to his feet and stood with his head bowed. To a hushed congregation the Puritan pastor read aloud Sewall's confession of sin and heartfelt repentance.

> Samuel Sewall, sensible of the reiterated strokes of God upon himself and family, and being sensible that as to the guilt contracted upon the opening of the late Commission of Oyer and Terminer at Salem, he is, upon many accounts, more concerned than any that he knows of, desires to take the blame and shame of it, asking pardon of men, and especially desiring prayers that God, who has unlimited authority, would pardon that sin and all his other sins, personal and relative. And according to His infinite benignity and sovereignty, not visit the sin of him or of any other, upon himself or any of his, nor upon the land. But that He would powerfully defend him against all temptations to sin for the future, and vouchsafe him the efficacious, saving conduct of His Word and Spirit.[21]

Judge Samuel Sewall did the only thing a committed Christian under deep conviction of sin can do: He publicly asked forgiveness of God and the people of the colony. He bowed deeply before resuming his seat.

It was done.

The prevailing attitude among modern historians tends to be that the Salem Witch Trials were the natural result of a mixture of Puritan religious fanaticism, superstition, and mob hysteria. The fact is that the tragedy of the Witch Trials was due to a failure of both the church and the colony's judicial system—or, as we might say today, a failure on the part of both Church and State.

Had the Puritan ministers been operating in their usual close fellowship and pastoral oversight of the churches, they never would have allowed Samuel Parris to become the minister of the church at Salem. His unprecedented demand to own the parsonage property before he accepted the pastorate of the church was a clear indication that he did not have the right attitude of heart to be a minister of Christ. Had he and his slave Tituba not been welcomed at Salem, it is unlikely that the witchcraft troubles would have gotten out of hand.

On the other hand, the Oyer and Terminer judges were not following proper English court procedure. Several ministers registered strong objections with them during the trials, but the judges ignored them. When the demon-possessed girls were given the opportunity on the witness stand to accuse people of witchcraft, they did what the lying spirits oppressing them prompted them to do—they lied.

Long after the trials, Anne Putnam, one of the chief accusers of innocent people, was delivered of demonic influence through prayer. In 1706, now twenty-six years old and wishing to "lie in the dust" for what she had done, she publicly admitted that she had been deceived by Satan.

Finally, after a number of public statements of repentance like those of Samuel Sewall and Anne Putnam, the pall of guilt and gloom lifted from Massachusetts. It was as if the colony had awakened from a bad dream.

In the next decades, unparalleled commercial prosperity would come to the Puritans, and Salem would develop into a major seaport rivaling Boston. But spiritually, New England would close her eyes and go back to sleep again. The voices of the Mathers and a few others did their best to get her to bestir herself, but she would not budge.

As the years passed, the voices grew fainter, until at last they died away. A new generation of ministers who knew their theology, but for the most part did not know their Lord, would be content to let her sleep.

16

A SUNBURST OF LIGHT

*I*n our search for evidence of God's hand in our nation's history, one thing puzzled us: the prolonged lull that seemed to settle over America between the end of the Puritan era and the first stirrings of independence. The only significant spiritual development in this span of more than half a century was the sunburst of light that historians call the Great Awakening. The problem was, that this tremendous outpouring of the Holy Spirit, which Richard Niebuhr referred to as our national conversion,[1] seemed to be viewed by most historians as a flash in the pan—which came and then died away after just a few years.

If God is indeed the Great Economist, and if He indeed had a plan and a timetable for the establishment of His "New Israel," where was the continuity in His handiwork? How did this nova of light connect with the dying embers of the Puritan era on the one hand and the unlit torch of the War for Independence on the other?

We came to believe that the Great Awakening was actually a *reawakening* of a deep national desire for the Covenant Way of life. This yearning did not die with the passing of the Puritan era; it only went dormant.

It was a desire that would produce a new generation of clergymen who would help to prepare America spiritually for the fight of her life.

It is a hunger so deeply engrained in the American national psyche that it can never die, although it can go fast asleep and lie dormant for years. God reawakened that desire in the 1740s (and what He reawakened once, He can reawaken again).

Around the inner southern perimeter of Cape Cod Bay, vast sand flats extending more than a mile are exposed at low tide. Once a year or so, a summer lightning storm will pass over these flats. Quickly the sky grows dark, and low, heavy clouds are tinged with an ominous yellow-green. Then the wind picks up, flattening the dune grass. Suddenly the sky is illuminated by a jagged bolt of lightning, streaking earthward and blasting the wet sand of the flat. A cracking burst of thunder follows immediately, for the lightning is close to shore. Another bolt arrows down, and another and another, until the thunderclaps cannot be separated, and the ground fairly shakes under the multiple impacts.

Similar lightning storms of the Spirit of God have fallen in different places throughout history. And God has said that He would do it again:

> And in the last days it shall be, God declares,
> that I will pour out my Spirit upon all flesh,
> and your sons and your daughters shall prophesy,
> and your young men shall see visions,
> and your old men shall dream dreams;
> yea, and on my menservants and my maidservants in those days
> I will pour out my Spirit
>
> Acts 2:17–18

In 1734 the spiritual lightning began to strike New England—and nothing short of a series of divine lightning bolts could have awakened this slumbering Christian giant who had eaten so much prosperity pudding, washed down with the wine of self-satisfaction.

The place chosen for the first bolt to fall was Northampton, Massachusetts, the little town of the most learned and respected theologian America had yet produced. Jonathan Edwards was a brilliant but reserved and dry preacher, who delivered his sermons in a monotone, his eyes never straying from the back wall of the church.

Perhaps God chose Edwards's parish because he had recently been preaching ever-bolder sermons against the popular notion that a person by his or her own efforts could accomplish the purposes of God, rather than solely by the enabling of God's grace. Possibly it was because the world would be forced to take seriously Edwards's account of what was about to happen. Other theologians could not put it down to an overactive imagination; anyone who knew Edwards personally would know these phenomenal events could not have been the product of his personality.

For whatever reason, the lightning did strike, and no one was more astonished than Edwards himself. Nevertheless, he was a well-trained observer, and he did a first-class job of reporting God's lightning storm in his *Narrative of Surprising Conversions*:

> And then it was, in the latter part of December, that the Spirit of God began extraordinarily to . . . work amongst us. There were, very suddenly, one after another, five or six persons who were, to all appearance, savingly converted, and some of them wrought upon in a very remarkable manner.
>
> Particularly I was surprised with the relation of a young woman, who had been one of the greatest company-keepers in the whole town. When she came to me, I had never heard that she was become in any ways serious, but by the conversation I then had with her, it appeared to me that what she gave an account of was a glorious work of God's infinite power and sovereign grace, and that God had given her a new heart, truly broken and sanctified. . . .
>
> God made it, I suppose, the greatest occasion of awakening to others, of anything that ever came to pass in the town. I have had abundant opportunity to know the effect it had, by my private conversation with many. The news of it seemed to be almost like a flash of lightning upon the hearts of young people all over the town, and upon many others. . . .
>
> Presently upon this, a great and earnest concern about the great things of religion and the eternal world became universal in all parts of the town and among persons of all degrees and all ages. The noise of the dry bones

waxed louder and louder. . . . Those that were wont to be the vainest and loosest, and those that had been the most disposed to think and speak slightly of vital and experimental religion, were not generally subject to great awakenings. And the work of conversion was carried on in a most astonishing manner and increased more and more; souls did, as it were, come by flocks to Jesus Christ. . . .

This work of God, as it was carried on and the number of true saints multiplied, soon made a glorious alteration in the town, so that in the spring and summer following, Anno 1735, the town seemed to be full of the presence of God. It never was so full of love, nor so full of joy . . . there were remarkable tokens of God's presence in almost every house. It was a time of joy in families on the account of salvation's being brought unto them, parents rejoicing over their children as new born, and husbands over their wives, and wives over their husbands.

The goings of God were then seen in His sanctuary, God's day was a delight and His tabernacles were amiable. Our public assembles were then beautiful; the congregation was alive in God's service, everyone earnestly intent on the public worship, every hearer eager to drink the words of the minister as they came from his mouth. The assembly in general were, from time to time, in tears while the word was preached, some weeping with sorrow and distress, others with joy and love, others with pity and concern for their neighbors.

There were many instances of persons that came from abroad, on visits or on business . . . [who] partook of that shower of divine blessing that God rained down here and went home rejoicing. Till at length the same work began to appear and prevail in several other towns in the country.

In the month of March, the people in South Hadley began to be seized with a deep concern about the things of religion, which very soon became universal. . . . About the same time, it began to break forth in the west part of Suffield . . . and it soon spread into all parts of the town. It next appeared at Sunderland. . . . About the same time it began to appear in a part of Deerfield . . . Hatfield . . . West Springfield . . . Long Meadow . . . Enfield . . . Westfield . . . Northfield. . . . In every place, God brought His saving blessings with Him, and His Word, attended with His Spirit . . . returned not void. [2]

When God pours out His Spirit in a major way, He seldom concentrates on just one area. In 1733 an eager and ebullient English lad of nineteen named George Whitefield, whose widowed mother kept an inn in Gloucester, went down to Oxford to begin the first year of his advanced education. Determinedly devout, George was busily engaged in visiting prisoners and poorhouses to earn God's approval. At Oxford he was drawn to the circle of pious believers around John and Charles Wesley, and they, in turn, welcomed this good-humored and charmingly innocent young fellow into their "Holy Club." Under John Wesley's dour and often imperious leadership, the club put great emphasis on a disciplined spiritual life. Due to what their critics considered to be their methodical ways, they were dubbed Methodists. And as the Puritans had done before them, they appropriated this slur for their own name.

In his quest for a closer relationship with Christ, George Whitefield was led to an obscure, slim volume, *The Life of God in the Soul of Man*, by a forgotten Scot named Henry Scougal. Whitefield was nonplussed to discover that all of the good things that he had been doing to earn God's favor were of no account. What he needed, he learned, was to have Christ formed within him; in short, he needed to be born again.

He thereupon embarked on a rigorous program of self-imposed asceticism, giving up everything he enjoyed, even the Holy Club, to bring himself closer to Christ. Nothing he tried seemed to work, yet he drove himself harder and harder, until at last his health began to give away. His friends were deeply concerned, but nothing would dissuade him from his determined course. In the end, when nothing he could do, or pray, or think seemed to make any difference, he threw himself on his bed and cried out, "I thirst!" According to John Pollock, in his superb, popular biography of George Whitefield, it was the first time in his life that he had ever called out in utter helplessness. Pollock goes on to describe what happened next:

> He became aware that he was happy, as he had not been happy for nearly a year. Instinctively he knew why. He had thrown himself, at long last, blindfolded and without reserve, without struggle or claim, into God's almighty hands. And Someone seemed to say, "George, you have what you asked! You ceased to struggle and simply believed—and you are born again!"
>
> The sheer simplicity, almost the absurdity, of being saved by such a prayer made George Whitefield laugh. At that laugh, the flood-gates burst. "Joy—joy unspeakable—joy that's full of, big with glory!"[3]

He rushed out of the room to share the Gospel that Jesus Christ had come for sinners and that all a sinner needed to do was repent, accept Jesus's atoning death, and spiritually throw himself or herself into God's hands.

Thus began the ministry of the greatest evangelist of the eighteenth century, one of the handful of people in the history of Christendom to be used by God to change the course of nations through the power of His Spirit.

George Whitefield was ordained on June 20, 1736, at the age of twenty-two. In the first three cities in which he preached—Bath, Bristol, and Gloucester—revival broke out in the wake of his sermons. But Whitefield did not tarry to continue the harvest that God had begun.

His call, he felt, was to General Oglethorpe's new colony in America, where the Wesleys had already gone and were now urging him to come over and join them. He embarked with visions of evangelizing the Indians, and he arrived to find even more enthusiasm for his message of the New Birth. Before long it seemed that all Georgia was vibrating to the deep, resonant, far-carrying tones of the remarkable "boy preacher," who had the ability to capture the hearts as well as the minds of his hearers.

In the meantime, John Wesley, who had returned to England disillusioned, had his famous experience in Aldersgate Street, London. He felt his heart "strangely warmed. I felt that I did trust in Christ, Christ alone, for salvation; and an assurance was given to me that He had taken away my sins, even *mine*."[4]

The lightning had struck again. And now another Methodist pastor was enthusiastically proclaiming the message of the New Birth (though his ministry would never attract the throngs that Whitefield's did).

Whitefield himself returned to England after a few months, but only temporarily, to implore the trustees of the Georgia colony to provide land and approval for an orphanage, for he now regarded America as his home. Back in England he found that the revival his preaching had ignited in the Bristol-Gloucester area was continuing unabated. It cut across all class distinctions, and Whitefield was now invited to address the nobility in some of the most exclusive drawing rooms in England. The results of this, however, were mixed; while many lords and ladies truly repented and received Christ, at least as many more were outraged at the suggestion that they were sinners and that they might have as much need of a Savior as the common people.

Whitefield felt compelled to eventually return to America, the mission field to which God had called him. But someone was needed in England to be God's agent for the furthering of the revival. He urged Wesley to assume this role, and the latter readily agreed.

Now they ran into the first of many obstacles, and God showed them how He would overcome them. As Whitefield attempted to speak for the New Birth revival, he now found the pulpits of Bristol closed to him by jealous pastors who deplored his "enthusiasm." God's solution: preach in the open.

His first open-air congregation was made up of coal miners on the outskirts of Bristol—and very much on the outskirts of society. For the colliers were almost more animals than men. Wholly uneducated and cruelly exploited, they perfectly fit the dictum of Thomas Hobbes, in that their lives, which were ruled by "continual fear and danger of violent death . . . [were] solitary, poor, nasty, brutish and short."[5] Respectable citizens were terrified by their violent ways, and they shocked even hard-bitten sailors by digging up the corpse of a murderer whose suicide had robbed them of public execution—and then holding a high festival around it.

Whitefield felt a deep burden for them. They had no church—indeed, had never heard a preacher—and he was determined to bring them the Gospel of Jesus Christ. Accordingly, he found some high ground near the exit of the mines, and as the miners began to appear, he began to preach on the Sermon on the Mount. Before long several hundred miners were standing before him, listening to his words about a Savior who came not for the righteous but for sinners. He told them of Jesus's love for them—so great a love that He gave himself over to His persecutors to be crucified, and that as the nails were driven into His hands and feet, His only thought was for *them*—for each person standing there that day. As they raised Him up, and as He hung there hour after hour in unspeakable agony, He was suffering for them, so that they might be forever freed from their sins. He did this because He loved them that much.

Suddenly Whitefield noticed pale streaks forming on faces black with grime—on that of a young man on the right, an old bent miner on his left, and two scarred, depraved faces in front—on more and more of them, as he preached on, "white gutters made by their tears down their black cheeks."[6]

Three days later he was summoned before the chancellor of the diocese, who forbade him to preach in Bristol again. But the next day he was back preaching to the colliers, and this time there were two thousand listening. The following Sunday there were ten thousand, for by now there were far more townspeople than colliers. And on Sunday, March 25, 1739, the crowd was estimated by *Gentleman's Magazine* at twenty-three thousand.

The Spirit led Whitefield all over England that summer, and wherever he went, storms of holy lightning followed, until by the time he sailed for Philadelphia on August 15, "George Whitefield had preached to more people than any man alive, probably more than any one man in history." But he was anxious to get back to America, for "he dared to trust that his preaching might help create one nation under God—thirteen scattered colonies united with each other."[7]

Whitefield's reception in Bristol was almost cool in comparison with the welcome that awaited him wherever he rode or sailed, up and down the eastern seaboard. We have seen what vast crowds Billy Graham's crusades have drawn and the real conversions of so many thousands of Americans in the major cities in which they were held. We have seen a million and a half men gathered on the Mall in Washington, responding to the urging of Promise Keepers to Stand in the Gap. And we have read the old-time reports of cities being won for Christ by Billy Sunday and Alfred Price. Even so, we were not prepared for the impact of George Whitefield on America.

The lightning had already begun to strike in several locations on this side of the Atlantic. In New Jersey and Pennsylvania, William Tennent and his four sons were enthusiastically carrying the word of the New Birth to the Presbyterians. Fed up with the resistance of the administrations of Yale and Harvard to the enthusiasm of the new evangelical preachers (known as the "New Lights"), Tennent had founded a school to train preachers. Derisively dubbed the "Log College," it would lead to the formation of what is now Princeton University. His son Gilbert became the most famous American-born evangelist of the Great Awakening.

In New Jersey, Theodore Frelinghuysen was proclaiming the light throughout the Dutch Reformed Church. In Virginia and the Carolinas, it was borne by the Presbyterian minister/evangelist and hymnwriter Samuel Davies. In the backwoods of Pennsylvania, Connecticut, and New Jersey, the lightning was falling among the Indians, its conductor being a missionary named David Brainerd. Riding on horseback, under the auspices of the Presbyterian Church, Brainerd was in open awe of the power of God that fell on village after village as he preached. Indians would change so dramatically that skeptical colonists would come to the meetings to mock, only to be converted themselves.

Best of all, the Indians would tell their friends, and the light spread on its own—an "irresistible force of a mighty torrent or swelling deluge," Brainerd would write. He drove himself unmercifully, often preaching three times a day for hours at a stretch, and he tragically died of tuberculosis at the age of twenty-nine, while engaged to Jonathan Edwards's daughter Jerusha. His future father-in-law's biography of him made him an example to all who were considering a call to the mission field, and it was by far the most popular book Edwards ever wrote. Of him, Wesley said, "Find preachers of David Brainerd's spirit, and nothing can stand before them. . . . Let us be followers of him, as he was of Christ, in absolute self-devotion, in total deadness to the world, and in fervent love to God and man."

These early reformers did yeoman's service within their denominations or geographic locales, but it was Whitefield whom God used to tie it all together. Everywhere he went, revival accompanied him. And those who had been bearing the Light before he arrived unanimously welcomed him as an answer to prayer. In Northampton, where the revival of 1735–37 had died down, Jonathan Edwards offered him his pulpit and was moved to tears by his preaching. Edwards's wife Sarah wrote to her brother in New Haven: "It is wonderful to see what a spell he casts over an audience by proclaiming the simplest truths of the Bible. . . . Our mechanics shut up

301

their shops, the day laborers throw down their tools to go and hear him preach, and few return unaffected."[8]

In Philadelphia, William Tennent saw Whitefield as the prophet who would fan the embers that he had lit so long before, while Whitefield regarded the elder Tennent as "the aged standard-bearer who had been through the battle and had more to teach, if he [Whitefield] could find the time to listen."[9]

That first night in Philadelphia, Whitefield preached from the courthouse steps, with William Tennent standing by his side. The streets were jammed, but the people stood perfectly still.

"Father Abraham!" cried Whitefield. "Whom have you in heaven? Any Episcopalians?"

"No!" Whitefield called out, answering his own query.

"Any Presbyterians?"

"No!"

"Any Independents or Seceders, New Sides or Old Sides, any *Methodists*?"

"No! No! No!"

"Whom have you there, then, Father Abraham?"

"We don't know those names here! All who are here are *Christians*—believers in Christ, those who have overcome by the Blood of the Lamb and the word of His testimony."

"Oh, is that the case? Then God help me, God help us all, to forget having names and to become *Christians* in deed and in truth!"

Whitefield met another person in Philadelphia who remained a confirmed agnostic, despite all Whitefield's persuasion. Nevertheless, Ben Franklin became his fast friend. Then in his thirties, the well-known writer and publisher of *Poor Richard's Almanac* was astonished by "the extraordinary influence of [Whitefield's] oratory on his hearers." On one occasion Franklin found himself putting four gold sovereigns, all the money he had on him, in the collection plate, when he had firmly intended to part with no more than a shilling. (Wherever he spoke, Whitefield raised money for the orphanage in Georgia.) After that, though he always invited the evangelist to stay with him when he returned to Philadelphia, Franklin was careful to empty his pockets of sovereigns before going to hear Whitefield preach.

"It was wonderful to see the change soon made in the manners of our inhabitants," Franklin recorded. "From being thoughtless or indifferent about religion, it seemed as if all the world were growing religious, so that one could not walk through the town in an evening without hearing psalms sung in different families of every street."

Franklin, the first truly scientific observer of lightning, listened to Christ's twenty-five-year-old lightning rod preaching from the courthouse steps and was amazed at the carrying power of his voice. Retracing his steps backward down Market Street until he could at last no longer hear him, the amazed Franklin computed that in an open space, Whitefield's words could be heard by thirty thousand people.

And on more than one occasion, they were. Even when he came unexpectedly to a town, there was an astonishing turnout. For example, there was the time he felt that God wanted him to change his itinerary at the last minute and preach at Middletown, Connecticut. The moment they knew he was coming, riders galloped down all the roads ahead of him, spreading the word that the man who had preached in Philadelphia "like one of the old apostles" would soon be preaching in front of the meetinghouse. Farmers dropped their hoes, left their plows, grabbed their wives, and mounted their horses. One observer described a sound like distant thunder, and he saw a great cloud rising along the road—everyone was riding as fast as possible down the dirt roads to Middletown. When Whitefield arrived, several thousand horses had been tethered in long lines at the back of a vast crowd of dust-covered farmers. It looked as if an entire cavalry division had dismounted and was awaiting him.

"If George Whitefield wished to set America ablaze for God, he must win New England,"[10] writes Pollock, and that meant Boston. Of New England's chief city, Whitefield wrote on October 12, 1740:

Boston is a large populous place, and very wealthy. It has the form of religion kept up, but has lost much of its power. I have not heard of any remarkable stir for years. Ministers and people are obliged to confess that the love of many is waxed cold. Both seem too conformed to the world. . . . I fear many rest in head-knowledge, are close pharisees, and have only a name to live. It must needs be so, when the power of Godliness is dwindled away, where the form only of religion is become fashionable amongst people.[11]

Whitefield laid the blame squarely on the clergy: "I am persuaded [that] the generality of preachers talk of an unknown and unfelt Christ. The reason why congregations have been so dead is because they had dead men preaching to them. How can dead men beget living children?"[12]

That aroused a storm of antipathy, and he was roundly denounced from one famous pulpit after another (though it seemed to have no diminishing effect on the huge numbers of people who flocked to hear him). But other ministers who went to his meetings heard God Himself in what he said, and no less than twenty ministers in Boston alone openly acknowledged George Whitefield as the instrument of their conversion.

Whitefield's heart responded to the people of Boston, even as theirs did to him: "Yet Boston people are dear to my soul. They were greatly affected by the Word, followed night and day, and were very liberal to my dear orphans. . . . I promised, God willing, to visit them again, when it shall please Him."[13]

It was around this time that a New England sailor, as drunk as he could be (and still walk), happened upon him one evening. "Well, Mister Whitefield! S'good to see you again! I (*hic*) . . ."

"I do not know you, sir," replied Whitefield, bemused.

"Don't *know* me! Why, you converted me at _____ ten years ago!"

"I should not wonder. You look like one of *my* converts. If the Lord had converted you, you would have been a sober man!"[14]

And so it went, year after year, up and down the East Coast and as far inland by canoe and horseback as civilization extended. For Whitefield loved the frontier, and next to actually preaching, he was happiest in the saddle, seeing new terrain and meeting new people. In the summer of 1754 he wrote to Charles Wesley,

> My wonted vomitings have left me, and though I ride whole nights and have frequently been exposed to great thunders, violent lightnings, and heavy rains, yet I am rather better than usual, and as far as I can judge am not yet to die. O that I might at length begin to live! I am ashamed of my sloth and lukewarmness, and long to be on the stretch for God.[15]

It is a true mark of his spirit that George Whitefield should be ashamed of his sloth in the same year in which he preached a hundred times in six weeks, riding the main roads and throughout the backwoods of New England, covering nearly two thousand miles in five months. It is a miracle that he did feel so healthy, because, as any evangelist knows, preaching two, three, and sometimes even four times a day (and usually for more than an hour or two per sermon) is a punishing schedule. And to do so, straight through for six weeks . . . !

But this was the measure of how given to Christ George Whitefield was. He had cheerfully elected to go the Way of the Cross, and he counted it nothing but gain to have the privilege of picking up his cross daily. He drove himself unmercifully, and it did exact a fearful toll on his health. But no matter how sick he was, as long as he had the strength to stand and the breath to speak, he would preach and would trust God to sustain him through the sermon and to provide the power and the anointing.

The Lord never failed him. Friends would beg him to stay in bed, but Whitefield would have none of it; like his Lord, he set his face toward Jerusalem. Some might say that this was not good stewardship of God's gift of health. But the power of the Holy Spirit of God fell practically every time he preached, and one wonders if it was not given to him in response to his obedience and his willingness to put himself "on the stretch for God." Had he driven himself any less hard, had he gone easy on himself (as most of us might have under similar circumstances), would the tremendous work that God purposed through him have been accomplished?

For the Lord, through the preaching of this covenanted man, was uniting the thirteen colonies—on a level so deep that few people even realized at first what was happening. But wherever Whitefield went, he was preaching the same Gospel. The same Holy Spirit was quickening his message in people's hearts, and Presbyterians, Congregationalists, Baptists, Episcopalians, Catholics, Quakers, Moravians—all were receiving the same Christ in the same way. In so doing, as Pollock points out, Whitefield "was the first man to cut across denominational barriers. He rejected the solution of earlier reformers, who encouraged followers to drop previous loyalties and form a 'purer' sect—and thus increase the barriers that divide."[16]

In Charleston people were discovering that Jesus died for their sins, that He could and would forgive sin, and that they need not continue any longer under the bondage of sin. In New Haven, Providence, Peekskill, and Baltimore, they were making the exact same joyous discovery. And because this was so important—more important than anything else in their lives—geographical barriers became no more significant than denominational ones. They were still there, but they were inconsequential alongside the magnitude of their shared experience.

They were beginning to discover a basic truth that would be a major foundation stone of God's new nation, which by 1776 would be declared self-evident: that in the eyes of their Creator, all people were of equal value. By the sovereign acts of almighty God, and through the obedience of a few dedicated people, the Body of Christ was forming in America.

Through the universal, simultaneous experience of the Great Awakening, Americans began to become aware of themselves as a nation. They began to see themselves as God saw them: as a people chosen by Him for a specific purpose—to be not only "a city upon a hill," but a veritable citadel of light in a darkened world. The Pilgrims had seen it, especially Bradford; so had such Puritans as Winthrop and Hooker and the Mathers. But they had all died away, and the vision of the covenant relationship had seemed to die with them.

Now, through the shared experience of coming together in large groups to hear the Gospel of Jesus Christ, Americans were rediscovering God's plan to join them together by His Spirit in the common cause of advancing His Kingdom. Furthermore, they were returning to another aspect of his plan—they were not to operate as lone individualists but in covenanted groups.

Still another facet of this Great Awakening was its emphasis on action—to believe in Jesus Christ meant not merely discussing theology but making life-changing decisions and acting on them. As Jonathan Edwards emphasized about David Brainerd, the true Christian is the one who spends his or her life acting in service to the common good. Thirty years later this understanding would become a vital necessity.

By a divine lightning storm, the land had been awakened again. Only now it was not just a sprinkling of settlers strung along the Atlantic Coast;

now the land was a young giant. It was a growing giant, and here again we marveled at the depth of wisdom reflected in God's timing. It would need a full thirty years—time enough to raise up a whole new generation of evangelical ministers and laity to carry the Light to the westernmost settlements—before the young giant was spiritually tough enough to face its supreme test.

Far from there being a prolonged lull after the initial sunburst of Light, the watchword of this period was action. Whitefield and the others would ride and ride, and they would preach till their lungs nearly gave out. (All told, Whitefield preached more than eighteen *thousand* sermons between 1736 and 1770.)

We wondered, as we came to the closing pages of Whitefield's story, if part of the tremendous urgency he felt at the end of his life was Spirit-given—if indeed God was requiring of him a superhuman effort to spread the Light as far and as quickly as possible. In 1770, his health now broken and his breathing tormented by asthma attacks, he drove himself as never before. He reached Boston on his last visit, on August 15, five months after British troops had fired into a mob of civilians, killing five and igniting a fury of protest. That incident, known there-after as the Boston Massacre, had helped to create a hunger in the city for Whitefield's preaching. Never had the crowds been larger, nor "the word received with greater eagerness than now. All opposition seems, as it were, for a while to cease."[17]

The next month found him up in New Hampshire, where the ministers of Exeter begged him for a sermon. But when the time came, he could barely breathe, and one of them said to him, "Sir, you are more fit to go to bed, than to preach."

"True, sir," gasped Whitefield. Then, glancing heavenward he added, "Lord Jesus, I am weary *in* Thy work, but not *of* it. If I have not finished my course, let me go and speak for Thee once more in the fields, and seal Thy truth, and come home and die!"

And the Lord granted his request. The entire district seemed to have converged on the Exeter green that Saturday afternoon. At first Whitefield could hardly be heard, and his words were rambling, as if he could not focus his mind.

He stopped and stood silent. Minutes passed. Then he said, "I will wait for the gracious assistance of God. For He will, I am certain, assist me once more to speak in His name."

Then, according to Jonathan Parsons, the minister of Newburyport, he seemed to be rekindled by an inner fire. His voice now strong and clear, he preached for an hour with such tremendous power that Parsons could write, "He had such a sense of the incomparable excellencies of Christ that he could never say enough of Him." On and on he went, into the second hour, and seeming to look right into heaven "he felt the pleasures of heaven in his raptured soul, which made his countenance shine like the unclouded sun."

Nearly two hours had passed when he cried out: "I go! I go to rest prepared. My sun has arisen and by the aid of Heaven has given light to many. It is now about to set. . . . *No!* It is about to rise to the zenith of immortal glory. . . . O thought divine! I shall soon be in a world where time, age, pain and sorrow are unknown. My body fails, my spirit expands. How willingly I would ever live to preach Christ! But I die to be *with* Him!"

That night he was put to bed in the parson's home and had a fitful sleep. In the early morning, despite a crushing pain in his chest, he nonetheless pulled himself out of bed and made his way over to the window to see the dawn's early light. George Whitefield died just as the first rays of the sun caught the waters of the bay below.

The new day would soon break across the nation. His dream had come true: America was a nation now—one nation under God.

17

WHEN KINGS BECOME TYRANTS

*W*hen does tyranny become tyranny? Is there a time when it is not only morally correct but the will of God for one to resist legally constituted authority? When does the "Lord's anointed" lose his or her anointing? When did it become God's will for America to throw off the yoke of Britain? Was it God's will at all?

Pacifist Christians have argued that America never should have taken herself out from under the mother country's authority and certainly not by the violence of war. To be sure, if God did intend this land to be a divine experiment in self-government, then each major step in the implementation of this plan would have to conform to His righteousness. A holy end, no matter how sublime, could never justify unholy means.

Unable to resolve this apparent conflict through discussion, we earnestly prayed for clear answers. And that very morning, in Peter's parents' home in Boynton Beach, Florida, where the Holy Spirit had shown us the true nature of the Puritans' call, He went on to show us why America had to resist—why for them to do anything less would have been the gravest disobedience. This part of the revelation began with a verse of Scripture coming to Peter's mind: Galatians 5:1. When we looked it up, it proved to be the key to all that followed: "For freedom Christ has set us free; stand fast therefore, and do not submit again to a yoke of slavery."

One nation under God—this was the political as well as the spiritual legacy of the Great Awakening. All of America had now in some measure experienced the scriptural truth that in Christ, all men and women are brothers and sisters. Highborn or commoner, merchant or poor farmer, magistrate or soldier—all were equal at the foot of the Cross. Eternal heaven was open to all who accepted Jesus as their Lord and Savior; it mattered not what their station in life was, how wealthy they were, or who their parents were.

The same things were true wherever God's Kingdom began to be established on earth. As the equality of believers was emphasized more than ever in American churches, it was only natural that it would extend into civil government as well. Here, then, was the seed of the democratic principle that would be embodied in the Constitution of the United States: all men were equally entitled to the vote; in the sight of God, a farmer was as good as King George. For God was no respecter of persons: His laws applied equally to all.

It is difficult for us, with ten generations of representative government behind us, to appreciate how radical were the words of the Declaration of Independence: "All men are created equal." Never before in history had the world actually believed in the equality of human beings. That is why, beginning with the Mayflower Compact a century and a half earlier, the American system of government under God had been unique.

Under God—that was the key. Democracy would be subsequently tried in many places through the next three centuries, but only in nations where the one true God was worshiped would it succeed. Any experiment with democracy without the unifying hand of almighty God inevitably degenerates into chaos and anarchy.

"The Brotherhood of Man"—which tries to make sinful men brothers without the fatherhood of God and the healing, cleansing love of Christ—is one of the most destructive lies Satan has ever perpetrated. A decade after the American Revolution, the French, and their so-called enlight-ened Age of Reason philosophers, attempted to establish their version of the Brotherhood of Man. *Liberté, égalité, fraternité* (liberty, equality, brotherhood) was their motto, but these ideals are God's alone to give; they cannot be proclaimed or taken by force. The French Revolution soon became a blood-soaked, guillotine-punctuated nightmare that horrified the entire world. And within a generation, France was back under the yoke of tyranny, bowing to Emperor Napoleon.

But these same ideals, once given by God, must be preserved and protected, and defended with one's lifeblood if necessary. This was the concept that began to form in America during the Great Awakening. Its fruit had appeared on American vines before—specifically the Puritan one—but it could not come into full maturity until the colonies were truly united, no longer functioning as separate entities.

The first Christian settlers who came to America had known that they were separated unto God, that He had called them out for a special purpose. We have seen how carefully they guarded the privilege of self-governing autonomy and how liberally they interpreted the rights of self-regulation granted them by the Crown. They took care not to provoke the Crown into action that might in any way diminish their precarious autonomy. Although they claimed the rights of English citizens whenever it was convenient to do so and paid lip service to the Crown, from the beginning they thought of themselves as citizens of America, not England.

Some contemporary historians dispute this, emphasizing how much the colonies depended upon England for their very survival, especially in the beginning. As we have seen, that was true in Virginia. But the attitude in New England was to the contrary. For example, in 1634 one visitor was incensed that he could not find the English flag flying anywhere in Boston.[1] Reports were constantly coming back to England about how independent the Puritans were in thought, word, and deed.

The reason for this independence was that they understood that their ultimate dependence was on God, not on England. And thus it was that the Pilgrims, who had come with scant provisions and possessions, learned in their first year that God would see them through anything. And the Puritans, who were a little better off, from the beginning trusted God to show them how to take care of themselves. Nor did He ever fail them. By contrast, early Virginia never did put her trust in God, with the result that she was totally dependent on England for almost forty years.

Another factor contributed to the Yankees' legendary independence. Within thirty years of their founding, these colonies were being run by people who had been born in America. They had never experienced what it was like to live under a king and had, indeed, never known anything but representative government in its purest, town-meeting form.

The colonial tradition of independence had been an established reality for more than a century before England decided to put an end to it. The colonists' resistance would only surface when England applied pressure. Indeed, what made it so unique in humankind's long history of resistance and revolution was the amount of wisdom mixed with it.

The colonists tried to do nothing to incite England, avoiding all antagonism and complying wherever possible. Yet they also did nothing to encourage the military presence of England on their side of the ocean. Even when King Philip's War broke out and it became obvious that the Indians intended to drive them back into the sea, they did not do the obvious thing and beseech the mother country for help. The war took a fearful toll in lives and burdened them with horrendous debts, yet they knew they had to fight it out alone. To invite British troops onto their soil could well mean they would never be rid of them.

Interestingly, in the late seventeenth and early eighteenth centuries, most of New England's ministers were solidly behind the discreet resistance of the colonies. They firmly believed that acceptance of the Church of England's official doctrine of passive submission to monarchy would be nothing less than a repudiation of all that God had been building in America ever since He had first called them to His new Canaan.

At this point we had to face the nagging question of American independence: if Jesus Himself and Saint Paul both taught the importance of submission to civil authority, how could the American Revolution be justified? Romans 13:1–2 could hardly be clearer:

Let every person be subject to the governing authorities. For there is no authority except from God, and those that exist have been instituted by

God. Therefore he who resists the authorities resists what God has appointed, and those who resist will incur judgment.

Other minds in the eighteenth century must have been similarly troubled, because the ministers themselves (we found, as we read their sermons) had begun providing the answers. America was a new event in the history of the human race. Never before had God taken a body of Christians and planted them in a land where there was no immediate civil authority and where, by the guidance of the Holy Spirit, they were to establish their own civil authority. This was why the Spirit-inspired pattern of the early Pilgrim church was so important.

"For freedom Christ has set us free; stand fast therefore, and do not submit again to a yoke of slavery." That would be exactly what the new Americans would be guilty of, if, having been given their freedom by God, they voluntarily gave up their right to govern themselves. It would be as if the Israelites—after all God had done for them to bring them out of Egypt—turned around and invited Pharaoh to bring his troops to Canaan and put them back under servitude.

Their resistance did not go unnoted. Nearly a century before the American Revolution, Charles II's advisors warned him that "the ministers were preaching freedom" and urged him either to regulate them or to replace them with Anglican priests. The matter came to a head in 1682: Charles II demanded that Massachusetts swear allegiance to the Crown, administer justice in the King's name, repeal their restrictions on suffrage (only church members could vote), and allow Episcopal clergy to form churches—or relinquish its charter. As tactfully as possible, the Bay colonists informed him that they would not do the former and could not do the latter. For them, to surrender their charter would be to "give up the ark of the Lord!"[2]

Informed of this, Charles II demanded the return of the charter, decreeing in 1683 that Massachusetts "make a full submission and entire resignation of their charter to his pleasure."[3]

Now they were really in trouble. There was no way the Bay Colony alone could conceivably stand up to the mightiest military power on earth. The Yankees faced the darkest crisis since the general sickness had struck the

.Old Colony and the Bay Colony in their first winters. There seemed to be no alternative but to give up all that their parents and grandparents had lived and died for, all that they themselves had been taught to revere ever since they were old enough to understand.

At this pivotal moment the leadership of Puritan New England gravitated, as it had eight years before during the Indian uprising, to one person: Increase Mather. And as he had previously, he turned directly to heaven for his guidance. Then he carefully prepared his decision.

> To submit and resign their charter would be inconsistent with the main end of their fathers' coming to New England. . . . [Although resistance would provoke] great sufferings, [it was] better to suffer than sin (Hebrews 11:26, 27). Let them put their trust in the God of their fathers, which is better than to put confidence in princes. And if they suffer, because they dare not comply with the wills of men against the will of God, they suffer in a good cause and will be accounted martyrs in the next generation, and at the great day.[4]

Early in January 1684, Mather attended an emergency town meeting in Boston, convened to consider what Boston's response would be to the King's declaration. One can imagine the Old South Meetinghouse packed to the doors with freemen, the crowd standing shoulder to shoulder in the aisles, as the stern, upright Puritan ascended to the pulpit. He then outlined the scriptural references supporting resistance, recalling the story of Jephthah and Naboth, who refused to give away the inheritance of their fathers, and of David, who wisely chose to fall "into the hands of God, rather than into the hands of men." If we refuse to submit, argued Mather, we keep ourselves in God's hands, and who knows what He may do for us? He closed by declaring that to give up the charter would be a sin against God, and he asked who "would dare to be guilty of so great a sin."

The entire assembly was moved to tears and proceeded immediately to the vote. The decision to defy the King was unanimous! Boston's unequivocal stand strongly influenced the other towns in the colony to do likewise.

When word of the decision reached Charles II, he flew into a rage. He determined to send Colonel Percy Kirk and five thousand troops to bring Massachusetts to heel once and for all, and his choice sent shudders through even the King's advisors. "Bloody Kirk," the notorious Governor of Tangier, was known to stop at nothing to crush opposition.

As this news preceded the dispatching of Kirk, New England was plunged into despair. Increase Mather reported that when the news reached him in February of 1685, he shut himself in his study and spent the day on his knees in fasting and prayer about the colony's burdens. At length, the heaviness that he had felt in his heart left him and was replaced by joy. Without any proof except the inner conviction of his spirit, he knew that God was assuring him that Massachusetts would be delivered.[5]

Two months later word arrived that Charles II had died of apoplexy. His brother, James II, had succeeded him, and Kirk would not be coming after all. The joyous news spread throughout the colonies. When Mather worked back the date of Charles's death and found it to be the very day that he had spent in prayer and fasting, his jubilant attitude turned to awe.

Though James II did not send Kirk, he did send Sir Edmund Andros, who sought to impose the authority of the Crown in no uncertain measures. His orders were to strike at the heart of the resistance that had become ingrained in the New England colonists. And since even the Crown recognized that the resistance had begun with their religion, that was where it had to be broken. Accordingly, one of Andros's first official acts was to order that Church of England services be held in the Old South Meetinghouse.

Had there ever been any doubt among the Puritans that "resistance to tyranny was obedience to God,"[6] that doubt was now removed. It was clear to even the most undiscerning Puritan that passive, docile submission to English rule would mean reimposition of the oppressive authority of the Church of England from which God had delivered their ancestors.

The struggle was spiritual. But political freedoms were also involved, for Andros peremptorily revoked the charters of all the Crown colonies. His agents arrived to collect Connecticut's charter at the meetinghouse in Hartford one evening after dark. In the candlelit room the cherished document was laid out on a table. At the moment the King's men formally ordered that the charter be handed over to them, the candles were suddenly snuffed out. There was a great hubbub, and when light was restored, the charter had disappeared. It had been secreted away and hidden in the hollow trunk of an old oak tree. (Andros never did find the document, though he proceeded to carry out his orders without it.)

His next measure was the strict enforcement of the Navigation Acts of 1651 and 1663, which required all colonial trade to be carried exclusively in British ships manned by British crews. This meant, in effect, that the colonies could trade only with England, and it was the first of a series of increasingly oppressive, greed-motivated measures that Britain would impose on the colonies in the ensuing century.

When does tyranny become tyranny?

By Scripture, it happens when a ruler breaks the commandment of 2 Samuel 23:3 (KJV): "He that ruleth over men must be just, ruling in the fear of God."

By the teaching of the greatest theologian in the Middle Ages, Thomas Aquinas: "If the prince's authority is not just but usurped, or if he commands what is not just, his subjects are not bound to obey him."

By Puritan interpretation, constructed before the first Pilgrims and Puritans embarked for America, tyranny is when a ruler knowingly and deliberately contravenes the will of God. In this they were following Protestant Reformer John Calvin, who had written: "If princes forbid us to serve and honor God, if they command us to sully our conscience with idolatry . . . then they are not worthy to be . . . recognized as having any sort of authority."

By the Magna Carta, which established English common law, it is when a ruler ceases to act under that law and denies his or her subjects their rights, as guaranteed by that law.

By pronouncement of King James I: "A king ceases to be a king, and degenerates to a tyrant, as soon as he leaves off to rule according to his laws."[7]

By the interpretation of Parliament, it is when English citizens have measures imposed upon them, such as taxation, without their consent or even representation.

By every one of these definitions, James II's attitude toward the colonies was tyrannical. As the Puritans saw it, he was the rebel, for he was using the power of his office not to serve the people but to oppress them. Therefore he was in direct disobedience to the will of God, as delineated in both Testaments of the Bible.

Yet the personal experience of living under God's discipline, a thoughtful reading of history, and the careful study of Scripture teach the absolute necessity for submission to authority—to God, of course, but also to those civil and spiritual leaders whom He has placed in authority over us. Since all authority originates with God (however perverted it might subsequently become), a case can be made for blind submission, no matter what. On the other hand, when should a person not submit?

Like so much of the Christian walk, there is no clear-cut, a priori answer; it is a matter of the guidance of the Holy Spirit and the application of Scriptural principles to each particular situation. In the case of a people submitting to a tyrannical ruler, this is how it finally seemed to us to settle out: resistance is a matter of the utmost gravity and should be entered into only after every other recourse—legal, political, and diplomatic—has been exhausted. Moreover, a very sizable segment of the Body of Christ involved should be convinced in their hearts that resistance is now the only remaining way in which it is possible to continue in God's will. This attitude is the key: resistance should be entered into only with the greatest reluctance.

Two excellent biblical examples of this reluctance are the attitudes of David and Daniel. Insanely jealous of David's good standing with God and his people, Saul pursued him through the length and breadth of Israel. And David, of course, resisted Saul's desire to kill him by fleeing. Twice God allowed Saul to fall into David's hands. On both occasions David, though continuing to resist Saul's authority, refused to slay the man whom God had once raised up to be king of Israel. "The Lord forbid that I should . . . put forth my hand against him, seeing he is the Lord's anointed" (1 Sam. 24:6).

When Darius became king of the Medes and Persians, he made Daniel, who was obviously more capable and more submitted to him than was anyone else, the chief administrator of the land. The other satraps and administrators were so jealous that they sought high and low to find something with which to discredit Daniel to the King. But his record of service was impeccable.

Nevertheless, they were able to devise a scheme to destroy him. Knowing Daniel to be a devout believer in God, they tricked Darius into issuing an edict that stated that anyone praying to any god or man other than Darius would be thrown into the lions' den.

When Daniel learned of the edict, he was faced with a difficult choice, for to resist it could cost him his life. But his life had been given to him by God in the first place to be used as God saw fit. If God now required it of him as a pledge of his faith, so be it; in God he trusted. And so he disobeyed the command of his earthly authority in order to keep the commandment of his Ultimate Authority. It is interesting that at this point Darius was as reluctant as Daniel—and both were overjoyed and praised God when He delivered Daniel untouched from the lions' den.

In 1689 word reached the colonies that the mills of God were still grinding: James II had been overthrown by William and Mary in the "Glorious Revolution." Andros was apprehended while trying to escape capture disguised in women's clothes. Five weeks later William and Mary's Declaration of Indulgence arrived in America. Although it did not reinstate New England's charters, it did return the people's rights as freeborn English citizens—albeit under Crown-appointed governors, who were to accept the advice and counsel of the colonies' elected representatives.

With England preoccupied with its European wars, peace of a sort returned to her American colonies and lasted until well after the Great Awakening—until the coming to power of George III.

18

"No King but King Jesus!"

George III—here was a monarch whose ego demanded total submission to the throne. For a long time he had been waiting for an opportunity to deal with the independent spirit of America. Scarcely had England concluded a peace treaty with France in 1763, than George decided that the time had come. His first step was to increase the size of the British force garrisoned in America, left there to discourage a fresh outbreak of the French and Indian War. The king more than doubled it, from 3,100 troops to 7,500. The colonies saw no need for this increase, but the colonies had no say in the matter.

The cost of garrisoning these troops would be approximately 200,000 pounds sterling per annum—a staggering sum. And since it was for the protection of the colonies, the Crown decided that the colonies should pay for it, through the imposition of various acts and duties. First, the old Navigation Acts were strictly enforced. Customs commissioners were sent to the colonies to collect duties, but these commissioners turned out to be appallingly corrupt. All revenues raised went to pay the salaries of their large staffs of political cronies. The cost of garrisoning had not even begun to be met.

Then new tariffs were imposed. The most galling was the Stamp Act of 1765, which declared that every legal document had to have a stamp of the British government on it in order to be official. But infuriating as this was, it was nothing compared to the Townshend Acts of 1767, imposing duties on glass, lead, tea, paper, and so forth. Nor was there now any pretense of paying the cost of the British garrison; these revenues went toward paying for England's global adventures.

The commissioners reported that the mood in America was ugly and getting uglier—to the point where they now began to fear for their physical safety. At their request, General Thomas Gage and two more regiments were dispatched to Boston in 1768.

As usual, American opinion on this mounting crisis was largely shaped by the ministers. These men of God who were American-born and not in Crown colonies (such as Georgia and Virginia) were becoming nearly unanimous in their support of resistance. Thanks to the Great Awakening, there was now a whole new generation of committed clergy salted throughout America, many of them ministers of considerable spiritual depth and maturity.

As the list of "intolerable acts" mounted, so did the remonstrations against them—almost as if the ministers had George III in the front row of their congregations and were trying to make him see the error of his ways. Many of their sermons were duly printed in town newspapers, but if the King saw them, he took no notice. Like Pharaoh, to whom many sermons likened him, his heart was hard and growing harder.

Americans were now being taxed for the mother country's own revenue, while at the same time being denied the basic right of all English citizens to representation in the government levying the taxes. For the King to ignore this right, guaranteed by the Magna Carta, meant that he was literally putting himself above the law.

Still, despite the exhortations of firebrand Patriots like Samuel Adams of Boston and Patrick Henry of Virginia, the colonists' resistance remained reluctant and minimal. People of wisdom on both sides of the Atlantic could foresee the inevitable fruit of the Crown's present policy, but they were praying that this fruit would not come to pass.

Even among the hierarchy of the Anglican Church, which stood only to gain from the suppression of American resistance, there were people of conscience who were courageous enough to risk all in order to speak out on behalf of the Americans. Jonathan Shipley, bishop of Saint Asaph, had this to say to his colleagues in the House of Lords in 1774:

> At present we force every North American to be our enemy, and the wise and moderate at home must soon begin to suffer by the madness of our rulers. . . . It is a strange idea we have taken up, to cure their resentments by increasing their provocation. . . . Now the spirit of blindness and infatuation is gone forth. We are hurrying wildly on, without any fixed design, without any important object. We pursue a vain phantom of unlimited sovereignty which was not made for men, and reject the solid advantages of a moderate, useful and intelligent authority. That just God, whom we have all so deeply offended, can hardly inflict a severer national punishment than by committing us to the natural consequences of our own conduct. Indeed, in my opinion, a blacker cloud never hung over the island.[1]

In America, as noted, resistance to oppression had been a favorite topic in Yankee pulpits for more than a century. Indeed, a quarter of a century before Paul Revere's night ride, one of its most articulate (albeit increasingly liberal) proponents, Jonathan Mayhew of Boston, preached:

> "It is blasphemy to call tyrants and oppressors God's ministers. . . . When [magistrates] rob and ruin the public, instead of being guardians of its peace and welfare, they immediately cease to be the ordinance and ministers of God, and no more deserve that glorious character than common pirates and highwaymen."[2]

Fifteen years later, the hated Stamp Act brought forth this response from Mayhew:

> The king is as much bound by his oath not to infringe the legal rights of the people, as the people are bound to yield subjection to him. From whence it follows that as soon as the prince sets himself up above the law, he loses the king in the tyrant. He does, to all intents and purposes, unking himself by acting out of and beyond that sphere which the constitution allows him to move in, and in such cases he has no more right to be obeyed than any inferior officer who acts beyond his commission. The subject's obligation to allegiance then ceases, of course, and to resist him

is no more rebellion than to resist any foreign invader . . . it is making use of the means, and the only means, which God has put into their power for mutual and self-defense.[3]

And when the Stamp Act was repealed shortly thereafter, Mayhew had more to say:

> God gave the Israelites a king in His anger, because they had not sense and virtue enough to like a free commonwealth, and to have Himself for their king. That the Son of God came down from heaven to make us "free indeed," and that "where the Spirit of the Lord is, there is liberty," this made me conclude that freedom was a great blessing. . . . And who knows, our liberties being thus established, but that on some future occasion, when the kingdoms of earth are moved and roughly dashed one against another . . . we, or our posterity, may even have the great felicity and honor to "save much people alive," and keep Britain herself from ruin!

Nor was Mayhew the first to prophesy that one day Americans might be the salvation of the mother country that was seeking to oppress them. Cotton Mather had put it in spiritual terms in his *Magnalia*:

> But behold, ye European churches, there are golden candlesticks in the midst of this outer darkness; unto the upright children of Abraham, here hath arisen light in darkness. And let us humbly speak it, it shall be profitable for you to consider the light which from the midst of this outer darkness is now to be darted over unto the other side of the Atlantic Ocean.[4]

As George III and his ministers relentlessly increased the pressure that was calculated to bring the colonists to their knees, the rhetoric from American pulpits had also increased. In 1767 Josiah Quincy's sermon was printed in the Boston *Gazette*: "In defense of our civil and religious rights, with the God of armies on our side, we fear not the hour of trial; though the hosts of our enemies should cover the field like locusts, yet the sword of the Lord and Gideon shall prevail."[5]

The tempo had been steadily building. The rest of the world watched with fascination the battle shaping up between Britain and the foremost jewel in her crown of empire. As Du Chatelet, France's ambassador in

England, wrote privately to his minister of foreign affairs in March of 1768:

> I please myself with the thought that [open conflict] is not so far off as some imagine. . . . The ties that bind America to England are three-fourths broken. It must soon throw off the yoke. To make themselves independent, the inhabitants want nothing but arms, courage and a chief. . . . Perhaps this man exists; perhaps nothing is wanting but happy circumstances to place him upon a great theatre.[6]

Even as these words were being penned, in Virginia a veteran colonel and gentleman farmer named George Washington had quietly stated at Mount Vernon, his beautiful home on the Potomac, "Whenever my country calls upon me, I am ready to take my musket on my shoulder."

And in the following month, from New York, had come this word from a well-known attorney named William Livingston:

> Courage, Americans. . . . The finger of God points out a mighty empire to your sons. The savages of the wilderness were never expelled to make room for idolators and slaves. The land we possess is the gift of heaven to our fathers, and Divine Providence seems to have decreed it to our latest posterity. . . . The day dawns in which the foundation of this mighty empire is to be laid, by the establishment of a regular American Constitution. . . . before seven years roll over our heads, the first stone must be laid.

Livingston's words appeared in the New York *Gazette* in April 1768; exactly seven years later "the shot heard round the world" was fired on Lexington Green.

In September 1768 it was the Boston *Gazette*'s turn: "If an army should be sent to reduce us to slavery, we will put our lives in our hands and cry to the Judge of all the earth. . . . Behold—how they come to cast us out of this possession which Thou hast given us to inherit. Help us, Lord, our God, for we rest on Thee, and in Thy name we go against this multitude."[7]

Several years later the Townshend Acts were mercifully repealed, and for the next three years there was something akin to peace. The vast majority on both sides were hoping that it would last. Yet it was not a real peace born of a desire for reconciliation or the resolution of points of difference. It was as fleeting and deceptive as the calm before the storm.

In reality, nothing had changed. In 1772, a Rhode Islander traveling in England wrote to his friend Ezra Stiles, rector of Yale College: "You will often hear the following language, 'Damn those fellows! We shall never do anything with them, till we root out that cursed Puritanic spirit!' "[8]

All over New England, town meetings were issuing declarations in a veritable litany of protest. Nor had smallness of size mitigated against boldness of sentiment. In December 1772, tiny Chatham, out on the "elbow" of Cape Cod, declared that its townspeople held their "civil and religious principles to be the sweetest and essential part of their lives, without which the remainder was scarcely worth preserving."[9]

In like spirit, the new year of 1773 was rung in by the people of Marlborough proclaiming unanimously that "Death is more eligible than slavery. A free-born people are not required by the religion of Jesus Christ to submit to tyranny, but may make use of such power as God has given them to recover and support their laws and liberties. . . . [We] implore the Ruler above the skies, that He would make bare His arm in defense of His Church and people, and let Israel go."

It is interesting to note that no longer were exhortations coming exclusively from the pulpits and a few zealous Patriots; the broad mass of the people had taken up the torch and were carrying it forward on their own.

And now even a governor, Jonathan Trumbull of Connecticut, had spoken out in defense of freedom: "It is hard to break connections with our mother country, but when she strives to enslave us, the strictest union must be dissolved. . . . 'The Lord reigneth; let the earth rejoice; let the multitudes of isles be glad thereof'—the accomplishment of such noble prophecies is at hand."[10]

Nearly all the Crown-appointed governors, however, remained submitted to their king, and one had written to the Board of Trade in England: "If you ask an American, who is his master? He will tell you he has none, nor any governor but Jesus Christ."[11] Which may have given rise to the cry that was soon passed up and down the length of America by the Committees of Correspondence: "No king but King Jesus!"[12]

The Committees of Correspondence were a sort of networking organization, conceived almost simultaneously by Samuel Adams of Massachusetts and Richard Henry Lee of Virginia as a way for the Patriots in different colonies to communicate with one another. Adams further described their purpose as setting forth "the rights of the colonists . . . as men, as Christians, and as subjects," and added that these rights were "best understood by reading and carefully studying . . . the New Testament."[13]

Samuel (he did not appreciate being called Sam) Adams had been born into a strict Calvinist family and imbued with a strong Christian faith. He certainly didn't look the part of a hero. It would have been difficult to find him in a crowd—he was of average height and appearance and wore plain, simple clothes. John Adams, who was not given to hyperbole, wrote glowingly of his cousin that "he was a man of refined policy, steadfast integrity, exquisite humanity, genteel erudition, obliging, engaging manners, real as well as professed piety, and a universal good character."[14]

After graduating with honors from Harvard College in 1740, Samuel seemed headed for the ministry, but that plan fell by the wayside when his brewmaster father turned the brewery over to him.

Fortunately for America, Adams had no heart or talent for making beer. But when the crisis with Britain began to ferment, he found his true calling as a Patriot leader and political writer. His speechmaking abilities were mediocre at best, but as a political strategist and writer, he was brilliant. When he argued on paper for American rights against British oppression, he was powerful, logical, and convincing. As the struggle against Great Britain intensified, Adams followed the spiritual example of his Puritan forebears by regularly taking days of prayer and fasting "to seek the Lord," as he put it.

They bore fruit—more and more articles and pamphlets were produced under different pseudonyms. After nightly family devotions, when his wife Elizabeth had gone to bed, Adams wrote by candlelight. Often she was awakened in the middle of the night by the sound of his quill pen scratching.

Samuel Adams was humble about his writing, believing that "political writing was to be as selfless as politics itself, designed to promote its cause, not its author."[15] He would have been amazed to learn that one day Americans would bestow on him the title Father of the American Revolution.

The British were quick to recognize the threat of his leadership, and they came to call him "the chief rabble-rouser." They considered Adams the primary agitator for American independence in the northern colonies, just as Patrick Henry and Richard Henry Lee were in Virginia. Later, after Lexington and Concord, when Military Governor Thomas Gage would make a last-ditch attempt to avert all-out war by announcing a general pardon for all who would reaffirm their allegiance to the Crown, he exempted two men. Under no circumstances would Samuel Adams or John Hancock be given a pardon. And when the news reached England of the outbreak of hostilities, people referred to the conflict as "Mr. Adams's War."

Samuel Adams's leadership of the Patriot cause in Boston had begun to create serious problems for Governor Hutchinson in 1765. The British colonial ministry, learning that Adams was poor, suggested to Hutchinson that he attempt to bribe Adams into quietude. The Governor responded to the ministry: "Such is the obstinacy and inflexible disposition of the man, that he can never be conciliated by any office or gift whatever."[16]

Yet despite the networking efforts of the Massachusetts and Virginia Patriots, the colonies remained disjointed and compartmentalized in terms of any concerted action. A political cartoon of the day reflected this, picturing a snake in thirteen sections, with the caption DON'T TREAD ON ME!

This is exactly what a willful, obtuse, and vindictive Crown did. The Patriots needed only one major crisis to unite America in resistance to British oppression. That crisis turned out to be the tempest that was brewing in American teapots.

When the hated Townshend Acts had been repealed in 1770, the one commodity left untouched was tea. Americans were still paying a tax of three pence for every pound that was imported. So popular was tea drinking in the colonies that Patriot orator James Otis was afraid that people might "part with all their liberties, and religion, too, rather than renounce it." Instead of renouncing it, the colonists smuggled in Dutch tea and avoided British tea altogether. When Britain's largest tea distributor, the

East India Company, was brought to the brink of bankruptcy, Parliament granted it a monopoly on the tea trade. In turn, the East India Company slashed the price of tea to a point well below what Americans were paying for Dutch tea. But the three-pence tax remained in force.

And this tax was the problem for Samuel Adams and other Patriot leaders. If the colonists paid the duty, they would be acknowledging the right of Parliament to levy taxes on them, which they were not about to do.

Vehement protest meetings erupted in Pennsylvania and New York, whose merchants had smuggled vast amounts of tea from the Dutch. In Massachusetts an agitated citizenry issued defiant statements and wrote fiery articles for the papers. Women formed Daughters of Liberty groups and pledged that they would not drink English tea.

The issue was forced when the *Dartmouth* sailed into Boston harbor on November 28 and docked at Griffin's Wharf with a cargo of English tea. It was soon followed by tea ships *Eleanor* and *Beaver*. The Sons of Liberty, another band of Patriots created by Samuel Adams, posted an armed guard around the ships to prevent British customs officials from unloading them.

Samuel Adams was hoping that the ship captains would simply sail back to England, but British law was clear that they could not do that unless the proper duties had been paid on the cargoes, even if those cargoes were never unloaded. Furthermore, if the duties were not paid within twenty days, the governor could order the British troops stationed in the harbor to seize the cargoes and turn them over to the customs officials to be sold.

In the next two weeks the town twice asked Governor Hutchinson to return the ships to England. Thinking that he had finally gained the upper hand over his archenemy, Samuel Adams, he responded each time that he would be happy to do so once the duties were paid.

He had underestimated Adams. On December 16 the renowned Patriot convened a town meeting in Faneuil Hall. When more than five thousand people showed up, the meeting was moved to historic Old South Meeting House, the same church in which Increase Mather had preached defiance of Charles II a century earlier. The captain of the *Dartmouth* was sent for the third time to Governor Hutchinson, to ask permission to take his cargo of tea back to England.

Hours passed, filled with speeches that kept the crowd in a fever of excitement. At last, just as darkness was falling, the captain came through the church doors and announced that the Governor had once again denied his request.

Samuel Adams arose immediately, and in ringing tones proclaimed: "This meeting can do nothing more to save the country!"

At that prearranged signal, forty or fifty Sons of Liberty, thinly disguised as Mohawk Indians, gave a few war whoops and quickly left for Griffin's Wharf, followed by most of the people at the meeting. As they filed out of the church, the voice of prominent merchant John Rowe rang out: "Who knows how tea will mix with salt water?"

While the townspeople watched, the "Indians" and about a hundred other men climbed on board the three ships. For the next four hours, working in total silence, they opened 342 boxes of tea and dumped their contents in the harbor. Going home that night, they grimly joked that they had turned Boston harbor into a teapot.

It had all been done in perfect order; the Patriots even replaced the locks they had broken before the ships sailed for home.

When the news of the Boston Tea Party reached England, a furious Parliament ignored those who were counseling caution and retaliated. The Port Act closed the port of Boston to all commerce as of June 1, 1774, which in effect promised to ruin Boston financially by imposing near-siege conditions. Customs houses were shut down, local courts were suspended, and British warships were dispatched to blockade Boston harbor.

Then, in a series of laws, meant as a warning to all the colonies of what would happen to those who resisted the Crown's authority, Parliament authorized British troops to seize empty buildings for their quarters and refused to allow American courts to try British soldiers.

These Intolerable Acts, as they came to be known, soon had precisely the opposite effect that Parliament intended. Stunned outrage swept America. The first colony to send physical aid was South Carolina, which shipped two hundred barrels of rice to the port closest to Boston and pledged eight hundred more. In North Carolina the sum of two thousand pounds was raised in a few days. A vessel was donated to carry provisions, and the crew volunteered to sail her without pay. Lord North, the British Prime Minister, had scoffed at the idea of Americans uniting, likening their attempt at union to a rope of sand. "It is a rope of sand that will kill him," declared the citizens of Wilmington, North Carolina.

Windham, Connecticut, sent 258 sheep, and in Delaware plans were made for sending relief annually. Maryland and Virginia contributed liberally. George Washington personally subscribed fifty pounds (more than $13,000 in 2009 dollars).[17]

By August, the men of Pepperrell, Massachusetts, had already sent many wagonloads of rye. Their leader, William Prescott, undoubtedly summed up the feelings of numerous Americans when he wrote to the men of Boston:

> We heartily sympathize with you, and are always ready to do all in our power for your support, comfort and relief, knowing that Providence has placed you where you must stand the first shock. We consider that we are all embarked in [the same boat] and must sink or swim together. We think if we submit to these regulations, all is gone. Our forefathers passed the vast Atlantic, spent their blood and treasure, that they might enjoy their liberties, both civil and religious, and transmit them to their posterity. Their children have waded through seas of difficulty, to leave us free and happy in the enjoyment of English privileges. Now if we should give them up, can our children rise up and call us blessed? . . . Let us all be of one heart, and stand fast in the liberty wherewith Christ has made us free. And may He, of His infinite mercy, grant us deliverance out of all our troubles.[18]

Samuel Adams quickly reported on the events in Massachusetts to Committees of Correspondence throughout the colonies and was delighted by the supportive responses he received. "The Boston Port bill suddenly wrought a union of the Colonies which could not be brought about by the industry of years," he noted.

Adams wrote a resolution urging economic sanctions against Britain, which prompted another attempt to bribe him into inaction. General Gage, who had replaced Hutchinson as governor, sent Colonel Fenton to Adams with the message that any benefits Adams might request would be granted to him if he would just stop creating resistance to the royal government. He was reminded that the governor had the power to have him arrested and sent to England to stand trial for treason (the penalty for which was hanging) and that he could avoid that unpleasantness and make himself quite rich in the bargain if he would just cease and desist.

After listening politely to Colonel Fenton, Samuel Adams replied: "I have long since made my peace with the King of kings! No personal consideration shall induce me to abandon the righteous cause of my country. Tell Governor Gage, it is the advice of Samuel Adams to him, no longer to insult the feelings of an already exasperated people."[19]

American resistance to British tyranny was stiffening, and it was firmly anchored in the trust that the God who had brought the Pilgrims and Puritans to the New World would not abandon their descendants. On March 6, 1774, Patriot leader John Hancock gave what had become the annual memorial speech on the anniversary of the Boston Massacre. Hearing him, one can see why he was the other Patriot for whom there could be no British pardon:

> I have . . . confidence that the present noble struggle for liberty will terminate gloriously for America. And let us play the man for our God, and for the cities of our God; whilst we are using the means in our power, let us humbly commit our righteous cause to the great Lord of the Universe . . . let us joyfully leave our concerns in the hands of Him who raises up and puts down the empires and kingdoms of the earth as He pleases.[20]

New York called for another General Congress, similar to the Stamp Act Congress of 1765, at which nine of the thirteen colonies had been represented. This time, with the crisis at the boiling point, all the colonies sent delegates, except Georgia, which was facing trouble with Creek Indians on her borders and needed help from British soldiers.

Samuel Adams was an obvious choice to represent Massachusetts at the First Continental Congress in Philadelphia, and he was quickly chosen, along with his cousin John Adams, Robert Treat Paine, James Bowdoin, and Thomas Cushing. Adams's friends, aware that his shabby attire would not reflect well on the Bay Colony, prepared a surprise for him. One night there was a knock at the door as the Adams family was eating dinner. When

Samuel opened the door, he found a well-known tailor asking to take his measurements but unwilling to reveal who had sent him. The tailor was followed by a cobbler, a shirtmaker, and other shopkeepers; and several days later a large trunk was delivered to the Adams's home. When the Congress convened in Philadelphia on September 5, 1774, Samuel Adams entered the meeting sporting a handsome suit, new shoes, a brand new wig, a cocked hat, a gold-handled cane, and a red cloak.[21]

The other fifty delegates who gathered in Carpenters Hall had been equally well chosen. Virginia, for instance, was represented by George Washington, Peyton Randolph, Patrick Henry, Richard Henry Lee, Benjamin Harrison, and several others. Here was assembled the cream of American leadership—people such as William Livingston of New Jersey, Roger Sherman of Connecticut, Stephen Hopkins of Rhode Island, John Sullivan of New Hampshire, John Jay of New York, Caesar Rodney of Delaware, William Hooper of North Carolina, John Dickinson of Pennsylvania, Henry Middleton of South Carolina, and Samuel Chase of Maryland.

On the second day, Thomas Cushing, a descendant of Massachusetts Puritans, made a motion that Congress be opened with prayer. What happened next was recorded in a letter from John Adams to his wife, Abigail:

> It was opposed by Mr. Jay of New York and Mr. Rutledge of South Carolina, because we were so divided in religious sentiments—some Episcopalians, some Quakers, some Anabaptists, some Presbyterians, and some Congregationalists—[they thought] that we could not join in the same act of worship."

What immediately followed seems to the authors to be the hand of God at work:

> Mr. Samuel Adams arose and said that he was no bigot, and could hear a prayer from any gentleman of piety and virtue who was at the same time a friend to his country. He was a stranger in Philadelphia, but had heard that Mr. Duché deserved that character, and therefore he moved that Mr. Duché, an Episcopal clergyman, might be desired to read prayers

to Congress tomorrow morning. The motion was seconded, and passed in the affirmative.

Samuel Adams's wise counsel had cut through all possible sectarian conflicts and united the delegates before the throne of God. Duché did, in fact, appear the next morning and read Psalm 35, the appointed reading in the Anglican lectionary. The Founding Fathers' reverence for the Bible was revealed by John Adams's next comment: "I never saw a greater effect produced upon an audience. It seemed as if Heaven had ordained that Psalm to be read on that morning." (Perhaps due to a false rumor that the British had bombarded the town of Boston).

Adams's letter continued:

> After this, Mr. Duché, unexpected to everybody, struck out into extemporary prayer which filled the bosom of every man present. I must confess I never heard a better prayer or one so well pronounced with such fervor, such ardor, such earnestness and pathos, and in language so elegant and sublime. . . . They prayed fervently for America, for Congress, for the Province of Massachusetts Bay, and especially for the town of Boston. It has had an excellent effect upon everybody here.[22]

When those who would come to be called our Founding Fathers met to deal with the mounting conflict with Great Britain, their first act was to seek the guidance of God.

Before adjourning, the Congress passed a Declaration of Rights and agreed to meet again in May 1775 unless the colonies' grievances had been redressed by that date.

In October, Massachusetts held a Provincial Congress. Its President, John Hancock, who would represent his colony at the Second Continental Congress, declared:

> We think it is incumbent upon this people to humble themselves before God on account of their sins, for He hath been pleased in His righteous judgment to suffer a great calamity to befall us, as the present controversy between Great Britain and the Colonies. [And] also to implore the Divine Blessing upon us, that by the assistance of His grace, we may be enabled to reform whatever is amiss among us, that so God may be pleased to continue

to us the blessings we enjoy, and remove the tokens of His displeasure, by causing harmony and union to be restored between Great Britain and these Colonies.[23]

Two things stand out here: First, the basic Puritan response of seeking for sin at the outset of hard times was still intact among the members of the Massachusetts Provincial Congress, who had truly given themselves to God. Second, these same leaders were still hoping and praying for a peaceful resolution and would enter into active resistance only with the greatest reluctance.

Once committed, however, their dedication would be total. That same Congress addressed the inhabitants of Massachusetts Bay as follows: "Resistance to tyranny becomes the Christian and social duty of each individual. . . . Continue steadfast, and with a proper sense of your dependence on God, nobly defend those rights which heaven gave, and no man ought to take from us."[24]

In their resistance to British tyranny, the Massachusetts Patriots were so confident that they were defending their God-given rights, and thereby were justified in His eyes, that the famous Liberty Tree flag bore the inscription "An Appeal to God," and the flag of the Massachusetts navy would proclaim "An Appeal to Heaven."

As the pivotal year of 1775 unfolded, the second Virginia Revolutionary Convention gathered in March at St. John's Church in Richmond with Peyton Randolph presiding. All of Virginia's leading Patriots were present, including thirty-nine-year-old Patrick Henry.

Brought to faith in Jesus Christ under the powerful preaching of Samuel Davies, the Presbyterian evangelist of Virginia and the Carolinas during the First Great Awakening, Patrick Henry was a faithful and devout Christian and an outstanding lawyer. Henry's insights into human nature gained from his faith, combined with a rare gift of oratory, gave him great influence over juries. His first biographer, William Wirt Henry, wrote that he was "beyond doubt, the ablest defender of criminals in Virginia."[25]

Two groups of Virginia citizens were unfortunately regarded as criminals and were mistreated as such—Baptists and Quakers. Because the Anglican Church was the official established church in the colony, authorities looked the other way when Baptists and Quakers were assaulted by mobs, stoned, and whipped. Dissenter preachers were even arrested and imprisoned for merely proclaiming the Gospel.

As a lover of liberty, Patrick Henry could not stand idly by in the face of vicious religious persecution. He became one of the dissenters' staunchest defenders, once riding fifty miles out of his way to volunteer his services to some Baptists jailed in Spotsylvania. Walking into the courtroom on the day of the trial, he listened to the judges present the charge of disturbing the peace and then asked to see the indictment.

Glancing at it, he looked up in astonishment. "Did I hear it distinctly, or was it a mistake of my own?" he asked the court. "Did I hear an expression, as of a crime, that these men, whom your worships are about to try for misdemeanor, are charged with"— he peered closely at the indictment, —"what? With preaching the Gospel of the Son of God?"

He held the document aloft and waved it around three times. Then lifting his arms toward heaven, Henry simply said, "Great God!" And then he exclaimed, "Great God!" Finally, he thundered, "Preaching the Gospel of the Son of God—*Great God!*"

In the wake of the prosecution's inability to make any response, the case was dropped.[26]

As incidents of British tyranny mounted in the colonies, Henry became an outspoken Patriot, notably denouncing Parliament in 1765 during what was termed a "most bloody debate" over the Stamp Act Resolves he had authored. Thomas Jefferson said his eloquence was "such as I never heard from any other man. He appeared to me to speak as Homer wrote."[27]

In subsequent years, Henry's agitation for American independence in the Virginia Assembly made him an obvious choice for the colony's delegation to the First Continental Congress in Philadelphia. There he quickly established a reputation as one of America's most ardent advocates of independence.

Now, after several days of discussion, as the Virginia Convention met at St. John's Church on the morning of March 23, Henry proposed a motion that the colony "be immediately put into a posture of defense" and draw up a plan for arming a "well-regulated militia." Although the motion was quickly seconded by Richard Henry Lee, several delegates denounced it vehemently, saying that it went too far.

Finally, Henry rose to address the Convention in defense of his motion. According to eyewitness accounts of what followed, Henry began his speech calmly.[28]

> The question before the house . . . is nothing less than a question of freedom or slavery. . . . Mr. President, it is natural to man to indulge in the illusions of hope . . . [but] I wish to know what there has been in the conduct of the British ministry, for the last ten years, to justify those hopes with which gentlemen have been pleased to solace themselves and the house. . . . We have petitioned . . . we have supplicated—we have prostrated ourselves before the throne, and have implored its interposition to arrest the tyrannical hands of ministry and parliament. . . . Our petitions have been slighted . . . our supplications have been disregarded; and we have been spurned, with contempt, from the foot of the throne. . . . *There is no longer any room for hope.*

Every eye in the house was riveted upon Patrick Henry. He now began speaking with an intensity of passion and power that has seldom been equaled in American oratory:

> If we wish to be free . . . we must fight! I repeat it, sir, we must fight! An appeal to arms and to the God of Hosts, is all that is left us! They tell us, sir, that we are weak, unable to cope with so formidable an adversary. But when shall we be stronger? . . . Shall we gather strength by irresolution and inaction? . . . We are not weak.

The tendons on his neck stood out as Henry's voice rose.

> Three millions of people armed in the holy cause of liberty . . . are invincible by any force which our enemy can send against us. Besides, sir, we shall not fight our battles alone. There is a just God who presides over the destinies of nations, and who will raise up friends to fight our battles for us. The battle, sir, is not to the strong alone; it is to the vigilant, the active, the brave. . . . Is life so dear, or peace so sweet, as to be purchased at the price of chains and slavery?"

As his voice clearly hurled this challenge, Henry stood with head bowed and wrists crossed as if manacled, slumped in the attitude of a condemned slave.

After a pause he lifted up his eyes and chained hands and cried aloud toward heaven: "Forbid it, Almighty God!"

Then, kneeling with his hands still crossed, he bent toward the floor, seemingly weighed down with additional chains of British oppression. After remaining in that posture for a long moment, he stood proudly to his feet, and struggling against his bonds, spat out the words through clenched teeth: "I know not what course others may take, but as for me . . ."

Throwing his arms wide open as if to hurl the binding chains from him, with a radiant face Henry thundered, "Give me liberty!"

When the echo of his words had died, he let his left hand fall limply to his side, and with clenched fist, as if holding the point of a dagger to his breast, pronounced fearlessly, "Or give me death!"

As he spoke the last word, he smote his breast with his fist, as if driving the dagger into his heart.[29]

For many seconds no one spoke; the delegates hardly dared to breathe. An observer noted that had Henry but given the word, the entire assembly would have rushed out of the building into battle. Thomas Marshall, father of the future Chief Justice of the United States, spoke for every person who heard the speech when he praised it as "one of the most bold, vehement, and animated pieces of eloquence that [has] ever been delivered."[30]

19

"IF THEY WANT
TO HAVE A WAR . . ."

*A*s we began to delve into the events of the War for Independence, looking for examples of God's intervention, we found ourselves up against the generally accepted modern view: that the British, weary of the prolonged drainage of money and lives, had decided to cut their losses and pull out of the American segment of their empire. This popular assessment refuses to consider the possibility that God had anything to do with the war.

Yet if it was God's will for America to break forcibly from her mother country, there should be ample evidence of His hand in it—not only supporting her endeavors but miraculously intervening on her behalf as dramatically and conclusively as He had in the Old Testament. For the Bible teaches that God honors obedience with His blessing and does not honor disobedience.

We did find this evidence—in such abundance that the word *coincidence* seemed laughably inapplicable. We found that even the British began to rue the fact that Divine Providence appeared to be favoring the American cause. But we will let the evidence speak for itself. (There is, ironically, even one episode in which America played the part of the invading aggressor—and God seemed to act on behalf of the British.)

Sergeant William Munroe of the Lexington militia pulled his cloak tighter about him against the chill breeze of the night. At least the rain had stopped, he thought, glancing at the now-clear sky. There could be worse nights for his twelve-man squad to stand guard duty. Behind him, the house for which he and his men were responsible—the home of Lexington's minister, Jonas Clark—was dark and silent, all its occupants asleep.[1]

There was good reason for the militia to be there. Thanks to their Tory* friends, the British were well acquainted with Clark. They knew that he preached independence, and they were aware that he had not only moderated the town's debates on the issue but had also written position papers on it. Patriots throughout eastern Massachusetts were on the alert to expect word at any time that the Redcoats had left Boston and begun marching northwest to Concord to confiscate the weapons, gunpowder, and military supplies stored in the armory. The quickest road went right through Lexington, and that meant Clark's house was directly in their path.

This night the Patriots had additional cause for concern. Clark's home was a frequent meeting place for Patriot leaders, because John Hancock, a distant cousin of Clark's wife, often visited them and sometimes brought other Patriot leaders with him. In fact, he had been staying with the Clarks for the past twelve days, and Samuel Adams had joined him a week ago. The British would like nothing better than to capture Adams and Hancock engaged in treasonable activity.

Shortly after midnight on April 19, Sergeant Munroe and his comrades heard the hoofbeats of a rider coming fast up the Bedford road from the town green, called the common. In a few moments, Paul Revere reined in his foam-specked and panting horse, whose flanks were bleeding from the cuts of Revere's old-fashioned silver spurs.

"The Regulars are coming out," he yelled at Clark's house.

---

*The term refers to the one-third of the American population who remained loyal to the British Crown.

Sergeant Munroe did not know Revere and tried to shut him up, admonishing him that he was waking everyone up.

"You'll have noise soon enough," retorted Revere, brushing past the sergeant. "The Regulars are on their way."

He banged loudly on the front door of the parsonage. Instantly, window sashes flew up all over the house, as Jonas Clark, many of his twelve children, and both Adams and Hancock stuck their heads out to see what was happening.

Hancock instantly recognized the alarm rider. "Come in, Revere, we're not afraid of you!"

Revere relayed all the information he had, and shortly afterward alarm rider William Dawes, who had come by another route, arrived at the house. Urgently the men discussed the situation, one of them asking Clark if the men of Lexington would fight if they were fired upon. The minister responded: "I have trained them for this very hour."

Several hours later they all walked down to Buckman Tavern on the common to confer with members of the militia, some of whom had been spending the night there. It was decided that Revere and Dawes, weary as they were, should ride the seven miles over to Concord in order to alert the town of the British plans.

As Adams, Hancock, and Clark returned to the parsonage, the tolling of Lexington's church bell summoned the rest of the militia to muster on the common. Hancock sat at the Clarks' table, sharpening his sword and insisting that he was going to join the town's militia to fight the British. After Clark, Adams, and Revere (who had returned after being detained by a British patrol) argued at length with Hancock that he was of more use to the Patriot cause as a leader than a soldier, they finally convinced him. He, Adams, and Revere piled into Hancock's carriage and rode off toward Woburn shortly before the Redcoats arrived.[2]

"Stand your ground!" Captain John Parker called out to the seventy-odd members of the militia* who were hastily forming a line on the Lexington

---

*Minutemen were special units of highly trained militia, usually under twenty-five years of age, in good physical shape, and excellent marksmen. In Lexington, however, none of the militia had been formed into Minuteman units.

common. "Don't fire, unless fired upon. But if they want to have a war, let it begin here!"[3]

A few men must have cheered, but probably most did not look up from their preparations. They were tamping down powder charges with wadding, rolling musket balls down the three-foot-long barrels of their muskets, and securing them with more wadding. With the exception of the church bell that was still sounding the alarm and the drummer boy who was beating "to arms," it was strangely quiet. They were too busy to talk.

Jonas Parker, the Captain's first cousin, took his position. With deliberation he put his tricornered hat on the ground in front of him and filled it with musket balls and flints. He had told his friends that he was resolved "never to run from before the British troops," and he was about to prove it. On his left, Isaac Muzzey was topping up his powder horn from the open keg that was being brought down the line. On his right, Jonathan Harrington was trying to look relaxed, conscious that his young wife was watching him from the upstairs window of their house by the common.

The light of early dawn played through the limbs of shade trees just beginning to bud, their red-tipped branches throwing thin shadows across the green toward the men. It was starting off to be a chilly but beautiful day, with a clear sky and somewhat blustery winds.

"Here they come!" cried someone, and all eyes turned to the east corner of the triangular common. Coming up the road in the distance could be seen the first ranks of a column of British Regulars—marching in double time directly toward them. There were far more than Captain Parker had anticipated—seven hundred, in fact, outnumbering them at least ten to one. From his experience in the French and Indian Wars, he knew what they had to do. "Disperse, you men!" he commanded up and down the line. "Do not fire. Disperse!"

To make a stand now in the face of such overwhelming odds would be nothing but a stupid, pointless waste. Instead, they would fall back, melt away into the countryside, and beat the British to Concord. Revere and the other alarm riders would have already roused all the towns within three hours' march, and by the time they got to Concord, there would be enough Minutemen and militia to make a fight of it.

So Captain Parker and most of his band turned away from the oncoming British and started to leave the common.

But now bloodlust swept through the British forces. Months of bitter frustration, combined with supreme arrogance, exploded at the sight of these rebel bumpkins daring to oppose them. Venting their rage in long battle shouts and huzzahs, the Redcoats broke ranks and charged onto the green, redoubling their efforts as they saw most of the Americans turning away, apparently full of fear.

Major John Pitcairn, the British officer in command, sensed that he was losing control of his troops. Spurring his horse forward, he yelled out to them: "Soldiers, don't fire! Keep your ranks. Form and surround them." Then to the militia, he shouted, "Throw down your arms, and you'll come to no harm."

But other, younger British officers were caught up in the same excitement that gripped their troops. A pistol shot rang out and then another (the only pistols on the green that day were carried by British officers). Two or three nervous shots followed, mixed with confused cries of "Fire" and "Hold your fire."

Finally, a junior officer in the vanguard of the charge yelled, "Fire, fire, damn you, fire!" and waving his sword in a sweeping circle around his head to signal a volley, he pointed it at the militia.

A volley crashed across the common, and everyone stopped. It was as if both sides were startled by this development, and each looked at the other to see what had happened. None of the men of Lexington were hit, which was not surprising, considering that the British had not stopped to take aim. And the Redcoats themselves were obscured behind a cloud of powder smoke. The British regulars, composed of light infantry and grenadiers, the fastest and strongest of Gage's expeditionary force, were seasoned professionals. They were the first to come to their senses, and now they quickly formed into crisp, even lines and reloaded.

"Throw down your arms, damn you!" A British officer on horseback called out to the militia. "Why won't you rebels lay down your arms?"

As if in answer, several militia fired then, and the officer, standing in his stirrups, swung his sword and shouted to his men, "Fire, by God, *fire!*"

A second volley, this one well aimed, tore into the militia. Jonas Parker, who had stood his ground, fell. Badly wounded and unable to get up, he struggled to reload his musket where he lay. On his left, Isaac Muzzey was killed instantly; on his right, Jonathan Harrington was hit in the chest. He stumbled away toward his house, fell, got up, and fell again. He crawled the rest of the way, gushing blood from the hole in his chest. His horrified wife ran downstairs to help him in. As she opened the door, he reached out to her and died at her feet. Behind him, Jonas Parker was run through with a bayonet as he tried to raise his musket.

The only Patriots left on the common were the dead and the wounded. Some of the light infantry, out of control, were chasing fleeing members of the militia. The main body of British, however, gave three triumphant huzzahs to celebrate their victory and then marched down the road toward Concord. As the sound of their fifes and drums receded in the distance, quiet returned to the common, broken only by the muffled sound of women weeping.

The Battle of Lexington had lasted less than a quarter of an hour. But for the British, a long day—the first of an eight-year ordeal—was just beginning.

Down the country lanes pounded the alarm riders, urging their horses onward. And in the fields, farmers would stop their plowing and listen to the approaching hoofbeats. Then the rider, covered with dust, his horse lathered, would appear. "To arms, to arms! The war's begun. They're heading for Concord," was all he had time to shout as he passed. Farmers to the north and east for miles around left their plows in mid-furrow, grabbed their muskets and powder horns, filled their pockets with musket balls, and raced down the road to their assembly points.

Less than an hour after the British fired on the Lexington militia, word reached Concord, where the town's militia was already mustered. William Emerson, Concord's minister, turned out on the common in his black robe to stand with the militia. While the men nervously awaited the arrival of the British troops, the townspeople hastily hid the stores of the armory in basements, fields, and attics. Emerson noticed that one of his flock, an eighteen-year-old named Harry Gould, was trembling. In clear tones he reassured him: "Stand your ground, Harry! Your cause is just, and God will bless you."[4] Thus encouraged, Gould went on to distinguish himself in the actions of the day.

The seven hundred British Regulars had been moving fast, covering the seventeen miles from Cambridge to Concord in seven hours—including the action at Lexington. Soon thereafter, the town militia decided to pull back across North Bridge, next to Emerson's home. Reaching Concord an hour before noon, the main body of Redcoats stayed in the town, while search parties went off in different directions looking for the contents of the armory. But, except for finding some gun carriages, they were unsuccessful.

The largest British contingent continued on up the road toward North Bridge, where they left a hundred men behind and went on. Scarcely were they out of sight than the Patriot column that had been shadowing them from across Concord River now filed down toward the bridge. Hastily pulling back across the bridge toward the town, a few of the British panicked and fired, and the officer in charge ordered a volley. This cut down several of the militia, who finally fired a volley of their own, dropping four Redcoats.

The British soldiers were shocked. These farmers had not scurried away at the first volley, as those at Lexington had seemed to. Here they stood their ground and calmly returned fire. And they could shoot.

As the first British squad knelt to reload, the second took aim behind them. At that instant the second squad became aware that there was no third squad behind them. The third squad had run. Immediately the second and first squads ran after them, including a number of men who had led the charge across Lexington green. Panic now gripped them as strongly as excitement had at the beginning of the day. Their officers tried to rally them, but it was no use; their withdrawal soon became a footrace to see who could get back to Concord the fastest.

William Emerson had accompanied the militia as far as his home when they crossed North Bridge, but there he had stopped to assist his wife in sheltering and feeding women and children who were fleeing from the town. After the exchange of musket fire at the bridge, he intervened to keep a wounded British soldier from being bayoneted. (Emerson's actions that day so inspired one of the Concord militiamen that he would later name his two sons William and Emerson).

When the British squads rejoined the main body of their troops in Concord, the officers decided to get everyone back to Charlestown as fast as they could, hoping that the reinforcements, requested after the resistance they had encountered at Lexington, had been dispatched. From that point on, they were running the bloodiest gauntlet that British troops had ever experienced—or would experience, until the Charge of the Light Brigade at Balaklava. All along the way the militia and Minutemen kept up a steady fire on both their flanks from well-concealed positions behind stone walls, hedges, and screening woods. The increasingly frustrated British hardly ever saw more than a dozen in one body.

The well-trained Minutemen operated in small units, taking cover ahead of the British, aiming carefully and firing, reloading while lying down, and then running ahead to set up another ambush. The British were forced to send out large bodies of flankers to sweep the woods and fields on either side of the road. Now the Minutemen and militia began to take casualties, too. But the flankers, who had to push through underbrush and ford creeks, quickly tired and had difficulty keeping up with the column.

Exhaustion was also taking its toll in the ranks. The British had gotten no sleep the night before and had been making a forced march all day—twenty miles to Concord, and thus far, nine miles back. With their canteens long since empty, they had been running the gauntlet of hot musket fire for the last three hours. Redcoats were now dropping by the wayside, knowing that the rebels were scooping up stragglers but unable to take another step.

The most critical concern of the British officers was that the troops were no longer responding to orders that did not suit them. And more ominous, they were starting to abandon their wounded. As they approached Lexington, where nine long hours earlier they had raised their shouts of triumph, the harassing fire became so intense that the column slowed almost to a halt. Maddened by a foe they could not see, with their ammunition nearly expended, the British regulars were close to the "every-man-for-himself" stage. If that happened, their senior officers knew that the retreat would become a rout.

The officers were all on foot now, their horses having been been shot out from under them. In desperation, they ran to the front of the column and threatened the troops with sword and pistol to keep them from breaking and scattering. If they could be held, they would at least block the way of the others. Just beyond the Lexington green, under the heaviest fire of the day, the troops sullenly began to form into a line of defense, letting the remainder of the column pass through. Among them, they had perhaps three volleys left.

And then, the faint skirl of bagpipes reached them over the musket fire.

"It's the first brigade," came the shout from the rear. "We're saved!"

All heads turned, and there, coming up the road from Cambridge was the relief column with Brigadier General Percy at the head of a thousand men. Stunned by the conditions that he found, Percy ordered the two field-pieces he had brought with him to the head of the column, where they were immediately discharged into the thickening Minutemen and militia.

This stopped their pursuers, who had never faced cannon before. Percy took the opportunity to form a defensive square, in the middle of which the exhausted light infantry and grenadiers lay on the ground, panting and trying to get their breath back. Percy gave them forty minutes and then ordered the column back to Charlestown, where they would have the cover of the British warships in the harbor. The harassing fire continued, stinging like hornets. But the fresh troops were now sent out as flankers, and the cannon kept the rebels at bay.

The fiercest fighting of the retreat was at Menotomy, where about two thousand Minutemen and militia awaited the staggering British column—more than they had seen all day. The road through the town was a mile long, with houses lining both sides. Percy was not about to lead his men into this death trap without clearing out the houses, so the British forced every house. In many of the houses, the combat was hand to hand.

The hero of the day was eighty-year-old Sam Whittemore, who was not at all cowed by some fifteen hundred Redcoats. When he was informed that the British were coming through the town, he prepared his own private arsenal: two pistols, a musket, and his old cavalry saber. Telling his wife that he was going to fight the British, he positioned himself behind a stone wall about 150 yards off the road and waited for the enemy. When the column approached, Sam opened fire with such accuracy that they sent a large unit to find him. Sam stayed hidden until they were almost upon him, and then he jumped up and dropped a Redcoat with his musket. Then firing both pistols, he killed two more. He was drawing his saber when a musket ball hit him in the face and knocked him down.

The British proceeded to bayonet Sam Whittemore over and over until they were satisfied they had killed him.

Only they hadn't.

With half his face shot away and at least thirteen bayonet wounds in him, Sam lived to be ninety-eight years old, and he vowed that if he ever had the chance, he would do it all over again.[5]

It was well after dark before the British finally reached Bunker Hill and safety. That day over 250 of their men had been killed or wounded. (And in those days, a wound by a three-quarter-inch musket ball often proved fatal.) Minutemen and militia had suffered nearly a hundred casualties themselves, but the victory was clearly and gloriously theirs.

The last word on the day proved to be prophetic. The Reverend Jonas Clark declared: "From this day shall be dated in future history the liberty or slavery of the American world."[6]

The effect of Lexington and Concord on the Americans was to send their confidence soaring. They had stood up to the best British troops and had given them a fearful drubbing. Of its roughly 400,000 population, Massachusetts estimated that, counting every man from sixteen to sixty, they should be able to field 120,000. In which case, the war would be over in time to get the crops in! And as express riders fanned out through the colonies, the rest of America joined Massachusetts in her exuberance.

No sooner did word reach New Haven than a young, aggressive, and ambitious captain of militia named Benedict Arnold assembled his troops and headed for Concord, the seat of the Massachusetts Provincial Congress. He had a daring plan: the taking of Fort Ticonderoga, which controlled Lake George and Lake Champlain. The fort's brass cannon would provide the American forces around Boston with the one vital ingredient they lacked, and Massachusetts warmly welcomed him and his men. They made Arnold a colonel, and authorizing him to recruit up to four hundred men, they dispatched him immediately.

At the same time, however, other leaders in Connecticut had also decided to take Fort Ticonderoga, to block a possible thrust down Lake Champlain by British General Guy Carleton in Canada. Captain Edward Mott and his band of militia were sent from Hartford to commission Ethan Allen and his Green Mountain Boys—foresters and roustabouts roaming the New Hampshire Grants—to take the fort.

By the time Colonel Arnold had caught up with Colonel Allen on May 9, the latter was already leading a force of some 240 men. Arnold insisted that he should have sole command, but Allen ignored him. Finally they reluctantly agreed to share the command. At the shore of Lake Champlain, boats were assembled and carried some eighty-three men over in the first crossing, including both colonels. Allen decided not to risk losing the advantage of surprise by waiting for the rest. As they crept forward through the gray fog of early morning, to their astonishment they saw that the wicket gate of the fort was open. In rushed Allen and Arnold, side by side, the rest following as fast as they could. A startled sentry raised his musket, aimed it at Allen at point-blank range, and pulled the trigger, but the gun did not fire.

A few Redcoats appeared and were quickly overwhelmed, while Allen stormed up the stairs that led to the quarters of the fort's commander, Captain Delaplace. He thumped on the door, and (according to a British witness) bellowed a stream of backwoods profanity at the fellow he heard moving about inside. Eventually Delaplace opened the door, to look up at a six-foot-four giant who roared at him: "Deliver this fort instantly!"

"By what authority?" Delaplace pluckily replied.

"In the name of the great Jehovah and the Continental Congress," Allen thundered, and he raised his sword over Delaplace's head. The captain ordered his forty-man garrison to lay down their arms, and the gateway to New York was now securely in American possession.[7]

The reader at this point may well wonder where God's hand was in all this. It was there—in the fort's main gate being inexplicably left open and the sentry's weapon misfiring, so the fort was taken without the loss of a single life.

But the wine of victory is sweet—and heady. Under its influence, nothing is easier to forget than God. And the next glass would prove to be the headiest of all.

Whenever His people begin to take pride in their own strength or accomplishments, God will move heaven and earth to call them back to Himself before their hearts harden. As He has since the dawn of recorded history, He usually does this through concerned believers—the prophets of old and some of the most outspoken (and therefore least popular) Christian leaders.

In 1775 no one was more concerned than the committed clergy. For all their patriotic enthusiasm, the most mature among them never lost sight of the importance of submitting to God's will and giving Him all the thanks and all the glory. As long as Americans remained in that attitude, they were safe; God would continue to surprise them with His blessings and protection.

A large number of the rank and file also knew this. For example, Amos Farnsworth, a Yankee farmer turned militiaman, would write in his journal about an exchange with the British on one of the islands in Boston harbor:

> About fifteen of us squatted down in a ditch on the marsh and stood our ground. And there came a company of regulars on the other side of the river. . . . we had hot fire, until the regulars retreated. But notwithstanding the bullets flew very thick, there was not a man of us killed. Surely God has a favor towards us. . . . thanks be unto God that so little hurt was done us, when the balls sung like bees round our heads.[8]

On May 31, three weeks after the taking of Fort Ticonderoga, the Reverend Samuel Langdon, President of Harvard College, was invited to address the Provincial Congress of Massachusetts on election day. Knowing that his sermon would be printed and read throughout America, Langdon framed his text carefully. No matter how unpopular his message might be, he was determined to say what he felt God was impressing upon him:

We have rebelled against God. We have lost the true spirit of Christianity, though we retain the outward profession and form of it. We have neglected and set light by the glorious Gospel of our Lord Jesus Christ and His holy commands and institutions. The worship of many is but mere compliment to the Deity, while their hearts are far from Him. By many the Gospel is corrupted into a superficial system of moral philosophy, little better than ancient Platonism.

What Langdon was specifically aiming at was the drift toward Deism, which was undermining the bedrock of a Trinitarian understanding of Christianity. This trend would ultimately lead to Unitarianism, a watered-down belief in God as an impersonal higher being who was the God of nature, which denies the deity of Christ, let alone the necessity of His atoning sacrifice on the Cross.

Now Langdon turned his attention to the war.

Wherefore is all this evil upon us? Is it not because we have forsaken the Lord? Can we say we are innocent of crimes against God? No, surely it becomes us to humble ourselves under His mighty hand, that He may exalt us in due time. . . . My brethren, let us repent and implore the divine mercy. Let us amend our ways and our doings, reform everything that has been provoking the Most High, and thus endeavor to obtain the gracious interpositions of providence for our deliverance. . . .

If God be for us, who can be against us? The enemy has reproached us for calling on His name and professing our trust in Him. They have made a mock of our solemn fasts and every appearance of serious Christianity in the land. . . . May our land be purged from all its sins! Then the Lord will be our refuge and our strength, a very present help in trouble, and we will have no reason to be afraid, though thousands of enemies set themselves against us round about.

May the Lord hear us in this day of trouble . . . we will rejoice in His salvation, and in the name of our God, we will set up our banners.[9]

20

"THE GREAT SPIRIT PROTECTS THAT MAN!"

A fortnight later, across the Charles River from Boston, the Patriots were setting up their banners atop the newly dug earthworks on the southern projection of Bunker Hill known as Breed's Hill. Providentially they learned of General Gage's intent to occupy these heights and those on Dorchester peninsula to the south. The following day, after a prayer service conducted by Dr. Langdon, they moved swiftly and quietly onto the heights and proceeded to lay out and dig extensive interconnected trenches. All through the night they worked to prepare the fortifications that would greet the British on the sunrise of June 17, 1775.

When Gage received a report of what the rebels had done, he was enraged, and he immediately ordered a massive frontal assault. Now the cowards who had behaved so despicably on the Lexington-Concord road were going to have to stand still and fight like men, European style, instead of skulking about through the woods like a pack of savages. They were about to discover why the Royal Army was regarded as the finest, best-disciplined in the world. Once these farmers had tasted cold steel—eighteen inches of bayonet at the end of "Brown Bess," the standard army musket—they would lose all appetite for further rebellion, and this uprising would be over!

Gage's officers fairly rubbed their hands together in anticipation, as did their troops. Many were still smarting from the humiliation they had received two months before, which had affected the attitudes of even the Tory women toward them. Quite a few old scores were going to be settled that afternoon.

Gage, perhaps even more than the American leaders, sensed how important the impending engagement was.[1] He could not be certain how many men the Americans actually had—spies and sympathetic Loyalists indicated that, spread out in a wide perimeter around Boston, there were perhaps as many as fifteen thousand—and their numbers were increasing all the time. Because Boston was situated on a peninsula, Gage could hold the city against a superior force by heavily fortifying the landward approach over Boston Neck and relying on the heavy guns of the British fleet to protect his flanks. A decisive victory now would obviously take the wind out of the rebels' sails. If, on the other hand, they did *not* win a major victory . . . but that did not bear thinking about.

Gage committed twenty-two hundred men to the action—a full third of his entire force, which now included two thousand newly arrived reinforcements. As field commander he named his own second-in-command, Sir William Howe, who had fought on the Plains of Abraham at Quebec under Wolfe, the conqueror of Canada.

At about two in the afternoon, the cannon fire from the British ships in the harbor intensified, setting the village of Charlestown on fire. On the Boston side of the Charles, long columns of Redcoats were queuing up and embarking in a flotilla of small boats.

In charge of the thousand men in the redoubt on top of Breed's Hill was William Prescott of Pepperell. Even though his troops had been digging all night, he had them keep at it, deepening and strengthening the redoubt until it was a veritable fortress of earth.

The bombardment from the ships increased as the British came ashore and began to form into long-lined detachments. General Howe stationed himself in front of his corps on the right wing, calling to his soldiers, "I do not expect any one of you to go any further than I am willing to go myself."[2] And with that, as the Charlestown church bells struck three, he unsheathed his sword and started up the long undulating hill toward the Patriot position. Behind him two lines of Redcoats, stretching all the way across the peninsula, began to advance up the open slope.

They were observed from Copp's Hill in Boston by General John Burgoyne, affectionately known to his friends and troops as "Gentleman Johnny." He was as elegant in prose as he was in dress:

> And now ensued one of the greatest scenes of war that can be conceived. If we look to the heights, Howe's corps, ascending the hill in the face of the entrenchments, and in a very disadvantageous ground, was much engaged. To the left, the enemy poured in troops by the thousands, over the land, and in the arm of the sea our ships and floating batteries cannonaded them. Straight before us a large and noble town was in one great blaze— the church steeples, being timber, were great pyramids of fire above the rest. Behind us [in Boston], the church steeples and heights of our own camp covered with spectators; the enemy all in anxious suspense; the roar of cannon, mortars and musketry. . . . [Howe's forces looked] exceedingly soldier-like. . . . in my opinion, it was perfect.[3]

On and on came the thin red lines, supremely confident but puzzled by one thing: the silence on the part of their foes. The rebels weren't shooting, even though they were well within range. What were they waiting for?

What they were awaiting was the command to fire. Colonel Prescott, a veteran of the French and Indian Wars, had sternly admonished his troops: "Don't fire until you see the whites of their eyes. No one fires until I give the command."

Finally, he gave it, and the whole top of the hill erupted in a sheet of flame. The effect was devastating: great swaths were cut in the ranks of the Redcoats. Those left standing withdrew in disorder. As Howe struggled to re-form his lines, company after company in the front rank reported losses of six, eight, even nine out of ten.

In remarkably short order, Howe managed to get his lines ready, which spoke well of both his generalship and the truly impressive discipline of the British regulars. Once again the drums beat out the call to advance, and once again the thin red lines began to move. Back up the hill they marched, their ranks tight and even, their eyes straight ahead as they stepped over the bodies of their comrades that covered the hillside.

This time Prescott let them get twice as close as before—barely thirty yards away—before swinging down his sword and crying out, "Fire!"

Practically the entire British front rank was destroyed in the first volley. And again, after stubbornly hanging on in the face of the subsequent murderous fusillade, the British broke and ran down the hill to the boats. Prescott told his men that their enemies "could never be rallied again, if they were once more driven back."[4]

Although several of his aides had been shot dead on his right and left, Howe was nevertheless calm and collected as he sent for reinforcements and prepared to mount a third attack. But now he changed his tactics. Feinting another wide frontal attack, he ordered a bayonet charge on the redoubt, first having his soldiers discard their 120-pound field packs.

Up in the redoubt, Prescott's men had gotten so low on powder that they broke open old artillery shells and shared what scanty amount there was. The third assault was a repeat of the first two, but this time the powder did not hold out. Though the British line was stunned and staggered, it did not break and fall back as before.

Now the Redcoats came on the run, bayonets leveled, and the ragged fire of the last few Yankee rounds was not enough to stop them. As the first wave came over the parapet, Prescott shouted to all those of his troops who had bayonets to meet them, while those who had any powder left were to go to the rear of the redoubt, where they would have room to take aim. Those with neither bayonets nor powder used their muskets as clubs.

Finally, as they were about to be overwhelmed, Colonel Prescott gave the order for retreat and was himself one of the last to leave. Burgoyne later attested in a letter to British authorities that "the retreat was no rout; it was even covered with bravery and military skill."[5]

Two enlisted men also wrote accounts of that action. The first was our friend Amos Farnsworth, who was now a corporal in the Massachusetts militia and whose diary entry for that day reads:

We within the entrenchment . . . having fired away all [our] ammunition and having no reinforcements . . . were overpowered by numbers and obliged to leave. . . . I did not leave the entrenchment until the enemy got in. I then retreated ten or fifteen rods. Then I received a wound in my right arm, the ball going through a little below my elbow, breaking the little shellbone. Another ball struck my back, taking a piece of skin about as big as a penny. But I got to Cambridge that night. . . . Oh, the goodness of God in preserving my life, although they fell on my right hand and on my left! O may this act of deliverance of thine, O God, lead me never to distrust thee; but may I ever trust in thee and put confidence in no arm of flesh![6]

The other account is also by a believer, who knew how much God's hand had been in the afternoon's proceedings and who had an equally grateful heart. This is by Peter Brown in a letter to his mother:

The enemy . . . advanced towards us in order to swallow us up, but they found a chokey mouthful of us, though we could do nothing with our small arms as yet for distance, and had but two cannon and nary a gunner. And they from Boston and from the ships a-firing and throwing bombs, keeping us down till they got almost round us. But God, in His mercy to us, fought our battle for us, and although we were but few and so were suffered to be defeated by them, we were preserved in a most wonderful manner, far beyond expectation, to admiration.

Had Howe pressed on after the retreating New Englanders, he could easily have taken Cambridge (which lay only two miles away) and imprisoned thousands of Patriots. Everyone expected him to follow through, and General Sir Henry Clinton urged him to do so, but Howe concluded he should not pursue any further. His men were "too much harassed and fatigued to give much attention to the pursuit of the rebels," he later reported to General Gage.[7] (British blindness in missing golden opportunities to turn costly victories into decisive routs would become a hallmark of their military operations during the Revolution.)

Though the British wound up in possession of the hill at the end of the day, they paid a fearful price. Of the 2,200 British soldiers engaged, nearly half—1,054 officers and soldiers—had been killed or wounded. "A dear-bought victory," General Clinton observed. "Another such would have ruined us." And Gage himself admitted, "The loss we have sustained is greater than we can bear."[8]

On the other hand, the Americans, who had lost 441 men out of around 3,000 who saw combat, knew just as surely that they had won. Wrote Sam Adams to James Warren: "I dare say you would not grudge them every hill near you, upon the same terms."[9] They had proven to the British—and more importantly to themselves—that they could stand and fight with the best of them, trading volley for volley and giving as good as they got.

But if the wine of victory had caused America to get a bit tipsy before, now it very nearly ruined her.

A mature, sober head and a steady hand was badly needed to assume the leadership of the military, and as always, God had just the man in mind. Fortunately, John Adams of Boston had made the same choice. Adams was known to be a shrewd judge of character, and along with Ben Franklin, he was one of the most persuasive members of Congress. The man he wanted in charge of the new Continental Army was the only man qualified who did not want the job. As Adams put it, "Mr. Washington, who happened to sit near the door, as soon as he heard me allude to him, from his usual modesty darted into the library room."[10] But to Adams's mind, that very selflessness and abhorrence of position were two of the things that most recommended him.

The motion was formally presented, and George Washington was unanimously chosen. In accepting the position, he declared that he would serve without pay. Characteristically, he closed his brief acceptance remarks with: "I beg it to be remembered by every gentleman in this room that I this day declare with the utmost sincerity that I do not think myself equal to the command I am honored with."

On the morning of June 23, as word of the victory of the Battle of Bunker Hill spread throughout Philadelphia, a throng of admirers assembled around Washington, who was about to leave to take command of the Continental army at Cambridge. His extraordinary popularity with ordinary people would remain constant throughout his life in public service. He was a quiet man, not given to easy, backslapping friendships. And his popularity, when he was made aware of it at all, invariably astonished him—which only made him the more appealing.

This humility and popularity, coupled with a truly supernatural gift of wisdom, would evoke jealousy from colleagues in Congress and the military. But the affection of the people never wavered, and this morning, the tall, blue-eyed Virginian was positively resplendent in his brand-new general's uniform with its blue coat and cream-colored breeches and waistcoat. Embarrassed at the fuss being made over him by the gathering of officers and delegates and the band playing in his honor, Washington quickly swung into the saddle, waved good-bye, and set off at a brisk trot.

Who was this statuesque horseman riding off into the destiny of every American? Those present at his departure would have seen a large-boned, firm-jawed, well-muscled man, who was described by Captain George Mercer, Washington's aide in the Virginia militia, as "straight as an Indian . . . [with] a pleasing and benevolent though a commanding countenance."[11]

Years after the Marquis de Lafayette first met Washington, he would write, "I thought then, as now, that I had never beheld so superb a man." And Abigail Adams, after being introduced to the Virginian, commented to her husband, John: "You had prepared me to entertain a favorable opinion of him, but I thought the one half was not told me." And his step-grandson, George Custis, recalled that "he rode, as he did every thing, with ease, elegance, and with power."

Power was a word that easily came to mind when people encountered George Washington's physical strength. Noted artist Charles Willson Peale remembered a visit to Washington's home at Mount Vernon in 1772, when he and several other young men were competing to see who could toss an iron bar the farthest. Washington appeared and asked them to point out the mark of their best toss. "Then smiling, and without putting off his coat, held out his hand for the missile. [His toss landed] far, very far beyond our utmost limits." As he walked away, he left this parting comment: "When you beat my pitch, young gentlemen, I'll try again."[12]

Controversy among modern historians has swirled about him, but in the hearts of ordinary Americans, he has shared the place of top affection with only one other president—Abraham Lincoln. Surprisingly little is known about Washington's boyhood, and stories like the one about the cherry tree seem to be apocryphal attempts to fill the void.

The authors were particularly interested in sorting out the arguments about his religious views, which began shortly after his death. Enthusiastic Christians have traditionally claimed that Washington was a committed Christian, while secular historians have pointed out that these enthusiasts are prone to claim that anyone who ever alluded to God was a believer. They have argued that Washington's indirect references to God smack of the Deism that was at that time popular with people like the pamphleteer Thomas Paine.

Was George Washington a Deist?

It is a serious question, because in the three centuries of American history that this book covers, only four other people played as pivotal a role as Washington—Columbus, Bradford, Winthrop, and Whitefield. In the lives of all four, the measuring rods of their ability to carry out their divine callings had been trust in the God of the Bible, sacrifice, and selflessness.

In the thirty-two years between the first and second editions of this book, the authors have carefully researched the spirituality of the man who would be called the Father of His Country—and reached the conclusion that he was not a Deist.

Deists believed in a God who was impersonal and absent from his creation, but Washington mentioned the providential activity of God in history some 270 times. For Washington, the word *Providence* was interchangeable with a personal God and did not denote some impersonal force. For example, in a letter to the Hebrew congregation of Savannah, Georgia, he wrote:

> May the same wonder-working Deity . . . whose Providential agency has lately been conspicuous in establishing these United States as an independent nation, still continue to water them [the Jews] with the dews of Heaven and to make the inhabitants of every denomination participate in the temporal and spiritual blessings of that people whose God is Jehovah.[13]

357

Washington obviously saw God as the Jehovah of the Old Testament, who directly intervened in the affairs of human beings. In a letter to his friend Reverend William Gordon of Boston, he declared: "No man has a more perfect reliance on the all-wise, and powerful dispensations of the Supreme Being than I have, nor thinks His aid more necessary."[14] (Only a God personally involved in His creation "gives aid.")

Deists did not believe in the divinity of Christ, but Washington explicitly referred to Jesus as "the Divine Author of our blessed religion."

Deism rejected God's revelation of truth in the Bible, whereas Washington stated that America was richly blessed by "the benign light of Revelation" and referred to the Bible more than two hundred times.

Further, there is no record of Washington ever using the words *Deism* or *Deist*.

A less well-known confirmation of his Christian orthodoxy occurred in 1769, when Washington, as a member of the Virginia House of Burgesses, was named to the Committee on Religion. Also serving on the committee were Patrick Henry and Richard Henry Lee, both outspoken Christians.[15] The Burgesses had formed the Committee on Religion because they were concerned about the inroads that Deism was making in the colony through the teachers at the College of William & Mary. Bishop William Meade wrote that there were some Virginia Patriots "who had unhappily imbibed the infidel principles of France; but they were too few to raise their voices against those of Washington, Nicholas, Pendleton, Randolph, Mason, Lee, Nelson, and such like."[16] Surely the burgesses would not have put George Washington on this committee had he been a Deist.

Those who have argued that Washington was not an orthodox Christian have pointed out that he rarely used the names of Jesus or God, instead employing euphemisms and indirect references to the Deity. But in point of fact, he used the word *God* more than a hundred times and made explicit reference to Jesus Christ at least twice. His reluctance to use the names of Jesus or God was typical of eighteenth-century Virginia Anglicans, even among the clergy. The avoidance was not out of unbelief, but from a reverence for the sacred names and a desire to keep them from being profaned.[17] Indeed, Martha Washington, a devout Christian, almost always used other names for God or Jesus, even in her private correspondence.

Compounding the difficulty of making categorical statements about Washington's spirituality is the fact that for Virginia Anglicans of this period, any "enthusiasm" about Christian belief was considered unseemly, even rude. Outward displays of religious fervor were not part of the Anglican way. A gentleman was expected to hide his devotion as well as his emotions.[18]

Washington certainly conformed to these standards, and he was also an intensely private man. Throughout his adult life, he made a conscious effort to avoid personal expressions of his religious faith. His biographer Benson Lossing said: "It was a peculiar trait of his character to avoid everything, either in speech or in writing, that had a personal relation to himself."[19] And more than three decades after Washington's death, Bishop William White wrote in 1832: "I knew no man who so carefully guarded against the discoursing of himself, or of his acts, or of anything that pertained to him. . . . His ordinary behavior, although exceptionally courteous, was not such as to encourage obtrusion on what he had on his mind."

Even the British noted this trait. During Washington's presidency, British diplomat Edward Thornton would write to the British Foreign Office: "He possesses the two great requisites of a statesman, the faculty of concealing his own sentiments, and of discovering those of other men."[20]

Cumulative historical evidence leads to the conclusion that George Washington was a low-church, orthodox, eighteenth-century Virginia Anglican, who confessed a Trinitarian Christianity, anchored by his belief that the Holy Son of God, Jesus Christ, died for his sins on the Cross and rose from the dead to win for him eternal life.

No less a witness than the renowned Bishop Francis Asbury would pay tribute to Washington's Christian faith at the time of his death: "Matchless man! At all times he acknowledged the providence of God, and never was he ashamed of his Redeemer."[21]

His mother, Mary Ball Washington, had been a strong source of spiritual life in his early years. On the day he left home to begin a lifetime of serving his country, she said to him: "Remember that God only is our sure trust. To Him, I commend you." Then she added, "My son, neglect not the duty of secret prayer."[22] His discipline of private prayer was to stand him in good stead in the years to come.

Entering the Virginia militia as a young officer, Washington distinguished himself in combat during the French and Indian Wars. The campaigns in which he served included the Battle of the Monongahela, fought on July 9, 1755. In this action the British forces under General Edward Braddock were decimated, with the commander himself being killed. Fifteen years after this battle, Washington and his lifelong friend Dr. Craik were exploring and surveying the wilderness territory in the Western Reserve. Near the junction of the Kanawha and Ohio Rivers, a band of Indians came to them with an interpreter. The leader of the band was an old and venerable chief who wished to have words with Washington. A council fire was kindled, and this is what the chief said:

> I am a chief and ruler over my tribes. My influence extends to the waters of the great lakes, and to the far blue mountains. I have traveled a long and weary path, that I might see the young warrior of the great battle. It was on the day when the white man's blood mixed with the streams of our forest, that I first beheld this chief. I called to my young men and said, "Mark yon tall and daring warrior? He is not of the red-coat tribe—he hath an Indian's wisdom, and his warriors fight as we do—himself alone is exposed. Quick let your aim be certain, and he dies." Our rifles were leveled, rifles which, but for him, knew not how to miss. . . . 'Twas all in vain; a power mightier far than we shielded him from harm. He cannot die in battle. I am old, and soon shall be gathered to the great council fire of my fathers in the land of shades, but ere I go, there is something that bids me speak in the voice of prophecy: Listen! The Great Spirit protects that man, and guides his destinies—he will become the chief of nations, and a people yet unborn will hail him as the founder of a mighty empire.[23]

Confirmation of this episode can be found in Bancroft's multi-volume definitive nineteenth-century history of the United States. At that same battle, according to other sources as well as Washington's journal, the twenty-three-year-old colonel had two horses shot out from under him and four musket balls pass through his coat.[24] There was nothing wrong with the Indians' marksmanship.

"Death," wrote Washington to his brother, Jack, "was leveling my companions on every side of me, but by the all-powerful dispensations of Providence, I have been protected."[25] This conviction was further shared by Samuel Davies, the famous Virginia Presbyterian evangelist, who wrote, "To the public I point out that heroic youth [Washington] . . . whom I cannot but hope Providence has preserved in so signal a manner for some important service to his country." Indeed, such was Washington's fame that across the ocean, Lord Halifax was to ask, "Who is Mr. Washington? I know nothing of him, but that they say he behaved in Braddock's action as bravely as if he really loved the whistling of bullets."

This was God's man, chosen for America's hour of greatest crisis.

General George Washington rode hard for Cambridge that June of 1775, compelled by a sense of urgency. God's Spirit was urging him on, for while he was not yet aware of it, America's intoxication from the wine of victory had slid from tipsy self-confidence into boastful arrogance. Arnold and Allen, who had taken Fort Ticonderoga, now wanted to take all of Canada. Each was convinced that he was the man to do it, and Congress, caught up in the exuberance of successive victories, reversed its policy of only defense and gave its approval.

With America about to undertake its first campaign of territorial acquisition, responsible and God-fearing leadership of the army was needed immediately.

21

"GIVE 'EM WATTS, BOYS!"

*I*t took George Washington only seven days to ride from Philadelphia to Cambridge, Massachusetts—nearly as fast as an express rider could make it. When he arrived on July 2, 1775, it had been raining torrentially for three straight days. The camp was a quagmire of mud, yet in no way did it dampen the enthusiasm of the troops for their new Commander in Chief. His earlier military exploits had made Washington something of a legend; the troops over whom he now assumed command were about to find that the legend was grounded on bedrock.

On his part, the General was stunned by the utter lack of discipline among the thirteen thousand troops casually encamped around Boston. Companies of militia had arrived from all over the colonies, and more were coming in all the time. These were brave men, Washington knew, and eager to serve. They were also woods-savvy, physically fit, and expert marksmen.

Just how expert had been demonstrated by the First Maryland Rifles at Fredericktown, where they paused on their way to Cambridge. A number of the backwoodsmen displayed their skill by repeatedly hitting a piece of paper the size of a silver dollar at a distance of up to thirty yards. As for fitness, on their way to Cambridge, the Virginia Rifles covered the six hundred miles in three weeks without losing a man.[1] (That is an average of twenty-nine miles a day—every day!)

But they did not have any concept of soldiering, and neither did their officers. Indeed, Washington swiftly concluded that the officers were the greatest problem. Almost all the militia companies were comprised of hometown units serving under their own officers. It was easy to see that an officer who had grown up with his men—who had farmed with them and hunted with them and drunk with them—was not likely to cut across old, deep friendships for the sake of enforcing discipline. Consequently, serious offenses received mild rebukes, and minor offenses were ignored. The resultant atmosphere at Cambridge was more like that of a jamboree than a military establishment.

Washington was shocked. He had not sought this assignment. He had accepted it only because his colleagues had pressed it upon him, and he had felt it his duty to respond. In private letters he freely confessed to his wife, Martha, or his brother Jack that he would like to leave it all and go and live on his land in the Western Reserve.

But leaving was impossible, and Washington knew it. For he was a man under authority—God's and country's—and his life was not his own.

Because he had spent his life under authority, Washington knew first-hand the value of discipline and obedience. He had been disciplining himself for years, and now, by the example he set, it was clear that he expected his officers to do the same. And while he did not require them to rise at 4:30 a.m. as he sometimes did, they were expected to be present at all inspections, assemblies, meals, and other functions—on time and in correct uniform.

One result of Washington's insistence upon proper military conduct was that a number of officers were court-martialed that summer for conduct unbecoming. Many were broken in rank, and more than a few were cashiered out of the army. Nor was he any more lenient on the generals. Washington had requested and had been granted the authority to handpick the four major-generals and four brigadiers who would be his immediate subordinates. Where possible, he filled these positions with men of experience who had proven their reliability and resourcefulness under the pressures of combat. Washington had a healthy appreciation of what it could cost to have the wrong person in a key position at a time of crisis. To have a commander on one's flank who was paralyzed by the fear of being wrong or who was emotionally unstable and prone to panic was to court disaster.

But there were nearly two dozen soldiers in Cambridge already possessing ranks of brigadier and above, veterans of the French and Indian Wars or leading the militias of their various colonies. A few of these were on Washington's list of eight; most were not. Washington was no people-pleaser; he did not hesitate to jump capable junior officers over those of far greater seniority. He did this with the full knowledge these men had influential friends in Congress and might spend the rest of their careers doing their best to undercut him (as several did). But he was willing to do whatever it took to build a capable army, regardless of what it might cost him in reputation or popularity.

The change in the attitude of the Continental Army that summer of 1775 was radical and rapid. William Emerson, pastor of the church on Harvard Square, in whose house Washington first stayed, wrote to a friend: "There is great overturning in the camp, as to order and regularity. New lords, new laws. The Generals Washington and [his adjutant, Charles] Lee are upon the lines every day. New orders from His Excellency are read to the respective regiments every morning after prayers."[2]

The day after Washington formally took command, the following General Order was issued:

> The General most earnestly requires and expects a due observance of those articles of war established for the government of the army, which forbid profane cursing, swearing and drunkenness. And in like manner, he requires and expects of all officers and soldiers not engaged in actual duty, a punctual attendance of Divine services, to implore the blessing of Heaven upon the means used for our safety and defense.[3]

Both of the concerns in this General Order—the requirement to attend worship services and the prohibition of cursing and swearing—would recur often in General Washington's messages to his troops. And both of them stemmed from his Christian faith. While it seems to have become fashionable of late among secular historians who have not conducted much research into their subject's character to accuse Washington of using foul language himself, nothing could be further from the truth.

His senior officers would personally experience the General's attitude toward cursing during the Continental Army's brief stay in New York City the following summer. Some were dining with him when an officer distinctly uttered an oath. Washington promptly dropped his fork on the table—loudly—and an embarrassed silence swept the room. The Commander in Chief surveyed the gathering, saying only, "I thought that we all supposed ourselves gentlemen."[4] Officers thereafter never swore or used foul language in Washington's presence.

Why did this matter so much to Washington? Partly because the vastly outnumbered, out-supplied, and out-generaled American armies could never expect to defeat the armed might of Great Britain without divine intervention on their behalf. He knew that because God does not bless immorality, a superior morality was required of his soldiers. One aspect of this was a strict watch on their language.

He would issue a General Order on August 3, 1776:

> The General is sorry to be informed that the foolish and wicked practice of profane cursing and swearing (a vice heretofore little known in an American Army) is growing into fashion; he hopes the officers will, by example, as well as influence, endeavor to check it, and that both they and the men will reflect that we can have little hopes of the blessing of Heaven on our arms, if we insult it by our impiety and folly; added to this, it is a vice so mean and low . . . that every man of sense and character despises it.[5]

Discipline and more discipline—that was the rule.

Another of the General Orders stated:

> The General orders this day [July 20, the first national fast day] to be religiously observed by the forces under his Command, exactly in manner directed by the Continental Congress. It is therefore strictly enjoined on all officers and soldiers to attend Divine service. And it is expected that all those who go to worship do take their arms, ammunition and accoutrements, and are prepared for immediate action, if called upon.[6]

They were to be like Gideon's men in the Old Testament, drinking water while keeping watch for the enemy, or like the Pilgrims, marching to their Sunday service with muskets shouldered.

The soldiers learned how to march and drill, but more importantly, they learned to obey. And gradually an astonishing transformation took place: the Continental Army began to become an army in fact as well as in name. And all the troops (with the exception of a few passed-over senior officers whose egos could never forgive him or who lusted after his position) gave the credit to Washington. He, in turn, was quick to ascribe it to God's providential watch over the American cause.

Others did also. Throughout America certain ministers were reminding their congregations that it was only through God's continuing mercy that America had fared as well as she had, and that repentance, not strength of arms, would decide the outcome. Typical was the very strong message that William Gordon, pastor of the Third Church of Roxbury, Massachusetts, preached to the Continental Congress on the day before the national fast:

> "Our degeneracies, we must conclude from the light of nature and revelation, have contributed to bring us under the present calamities. . . . We are now in an unusual way called upon to wash ourselves, to make ourselves clean, to put away the evil of our doings from before our eyes, to cease to do evil, to learn to do well, and to seek every kind of judgment."[7]

In most of these sermons there was not only a strong emphasis on the need for individual repentance before God but also a clear call for Americans to renew their covenant commitment to one another. The covenant theology of the Puritans was still very much in operation in New England.

Increasingly, reference was being made to the curse on the city of Meroz (Judg. 5:23 KJV): "Curse ye Meroz, said the angel of the LORD, curse ye bitterly the inhabitants thereof; because they came not to the help of the LORD, to the help of the LORD against the mighty."

Preaching after the battles of Lexington and Concord, William Stearns had said:

We trust that all whose circumstance will admit of it will go, that none of such will refuse to enlist in defense of his country. When God, in His providence, calls to take the sword, if any refuse to obey, Heaven's dread artillery is leveled against them, as you may see. . . . *Cursed be he that keepeth back his sword from blood!* (Jeremiah 48:10). Cursed is the sneaking coward who neglects the sinking state, when called to its defense—O then flee this dire curse—let America's valorous sons put on the harness, nor take it off till peace shall be to Israel.[8]

Nor were the exhortations of their ministers confined to words. These preachers did not hesitate to put their own lives on the line. On the same day as the battles of Lexington and Concord, Chelsea's minister, Philips Payson, led a band of men from his church in the capture of two British supply wagons.[9] Stephen Farrar of New Ipswich, New Hampshire, brought nintey-seven men from his church to the army assembling at Boston. David Avery of Windsor, Vermont, started his march with twenty-seven men, but his preaching collected more on the way. John Craighead raised a company of militia from his parish and led them to join Washington in New Jersey, where it was recorded that he "fought and preached alternately."[10]

So numerous, in fact, were the fighting pastors that the Tories began referring to them as "the black regiment," blaming them for much of the resurging zeal of the colonial troops. One of the most colorful examples is what happened in a staid Lutheran church in the Shenandoah Valley of Virginia one Sunday morning in 1775. The thirty-year-old pastor, Peter Muhlenberg, delivered a rousing sermon on the text "For everything there is a season, and a time for every matter under heaven" (Eccles. 3:1).

Reaching the end of his sermon, he said a solemn prayer—and continued to speak. "In the language of the Holy Writ, there is a time for all things. There is a time to preach and a time to fight." He paused and then threw off his pulpit robe to reveal the uniform of a colonel in the Continental Army. "And now is the time to fight!" he thundered, followed by his cry, "Roll the drums for recruits!" The drums rolled, and that same afternoon he marched off at the head of a column of three hundred men. His regiment was to earn fame as the 8th Virginia, and Muhlenberg was to distinguish himself in a number of battles, rising to the rank of brigadier general, in charge of Washington's first light infantry brigade.[11]

For sheer poignancy, one example of a Patriot pastor stands out. Early in June of 1780, in support of a British advance, Hessian General Wilhelm von Knyphausen crossed from Staten Island to New Jersey with five thousand men. At the little village of Springfield, just west of Union, he encountered unexpected resistance and was forced to withdraw. In the course of this action, the wife of the Reverend James Caldwell, a mother of nine, was shot in her home while her husband was away. Whether or not it was intentional (Caldwell had a price on his head, and later that same day his house was burned to the ground), the incident inflamed the townspeople.

When von Knyphausen's force returned two weeks later, even though reinforced by British General Clinton himself, he was again stopped, this time in furious action. At the height of the shooting, the Patriots, taking cover behind a fence that was adjacent to Caldwell's church, ran out of the paper wadding needed to hold powder and ball in place in their muskets. Caldwell gathered up all the copies of *Watts Psalms and Hymns* he could carry and rushed out to the crouching riflemen. Tearing pages out of the hymnals, he passed them out, shouting, "Put Watts into 'em, boys! Give 'em Watts!"[12]

As the fall of 1775 drew on, spirits remained high outside Boston. Within the city, however, spirits could hardly be lower. The Redcoats' memory of Bunker Hill was too searing to be easily forgotten, not just of the devastation of that afternoon, but in the streets of the city afterward. So filled were the streets with wounded crying out in agony that the city itself became an open-air field hospital. No transport was available to move the wounded to what little medical help existed, which meant that hundreds died unattended. There were so many funerals that General Gage ordered that the church bells not be tolled.

The British army garrisoned in Boston was under a veritable state of siege, reduced to eating salt pork, dried peas, and whatever the marauding British warships might be able to commandeer. Gage had been recalled in disgrace, and overall command was turned over to General Howe. But even with their losses replaced and their numbers increased by another thousand reinforcements, the British were still outnumbered nearly two to one. Against such odds, Howe felt that offensive operations were out of the question.

Across the Charles River, despite the high morale in the American ranks, Washington was frustrated by a Congress that seemed insensitive to his army's most basic needs: gunpowder and cannon. He had enough powder for only nine rounds per soldier, which would provide for about fifteen minutes of heavy combat. This was hardly sufficient to launch an offensive against Boston, and there was no artillery to batter down the British defenses, even if he could obtain more powder.

In addition, although he outnumbered the British, his lines were so long that it was almost impossible to assemble a sufficient strike force in one place and still protect his flanks. As a result, the General, who had been assured that he would have twenty-two thousand men (but who would never at any time during the war have more than fourteen thousand on the rolls), was left with only one option: to provoke the British into sallying forth.

In the meantime, the preliminary stages of the invasion of Canada were well under way. The main body of the attack force, under General Philip Schuyler, was at Fort Ticonderoga, with his field commander, Colonel Richard Montgomery, and under him, Ethan Allen. From the beginning, America's first campaign of territorial conquest seemed dogged with misfortune. Everything went wrong. The forces were supposed to have been halfway to Montreal by mid-October, but General Schuyler's illness had forced him to turn over command to Montgomery. In addition, short supplies, torrential rains, and endless debates over the meaning of Montgomery's orders had slowed their progress to a crawl.[13]

On the other prong of the attack things were going even worse. Benedict Arnold was leading a column of a thousand soldiers up the Kennebec River, straight into the heart of Maine's vast wilderness as the first frosts of winter were already setting in. He had persuaded Washington to let him plan and carry out a daring surprise attack on Quebec from a direction they would never expect. But a written request from Arnold to a friend in Quebec asking for information was intercepted before they had even reached the halfway point. From then on, the British knew when the Americans were coming, and where.

On the Kennebec, the men on the trek hardly cared because the operation had been reduced to a grinding ordeal. Their bateaux, or river boats, had been made hurriedly out of green wood, and the consequent leaking had ruined large quantities of provisions and ammunition. Vicious, icy rapids took a steady toll of the bateaux, and grueling portages delayed them still further. On October 18 the last team of oxen was slaughtered for meat, and some of the men were eating their candles to stay alive.

The next morning, the weather, which had never been good, became horrendous. Four successive days and nights of driving downpour had raised the river ten feet and turned it into a raging malevolent torrent. More bateaux and supplies were lost, and what had been a difficult and dangerous route before turned into a nightmare from which there was no awakening.

On October 25 the rain turned to snow and brought the bedraggled army to a halt. Mutiny now shifted from an ominous possibility to a stark reality. The officers of the Connecticut troops forced Roger Enos, their commander, to withdraw them from the folly and take them back to Cambridge.[14] His effective force now reduced by a third, Arnold struggled on.

But the worst was yet to come.

The frightening thing about the vast Maine wilderness is how easily one can get lost in it. When they reached Lake Mégantic, much of Arnold's remaining force, misled by inaccurate maps, became disoriented and close to panic in endless swamps that seemed hopelessly similar. For three days and nights, four companies of soldiers stumbled aimlessly through the frozen wastes with nothing to eat. As Dr. Isaac Senter, the army's physician, recorded, "We wandered through hideous swamps . . . with the conjoint addition of cold, wet and hunger, not to mention our fatigue—with the terrible apprehension of famishing in this desert. . . . We proceeded with as little knowledge of where we were, or where we should get to, as if we had been in the unknown interior of Africa or the deserts of Arabia."[15]

Many died, often from sheer exhaustion. George Morrison of the Pennsylvania Rifles wrote: "At length the wretches raise themselves up . . . wade through the mire to the foot of the next steep and gaze up at its summit, contemplating what they must suffer before they reach it. They attempt it, catching at every twig and shrub they can lay hold of—their feet fly from them—they fall down—to rise no more."[16]

During the first few days of November, along the Chaudière River there were more smashed bateaux, drowned riflemen, and starvation. The company dogs were eaten, and then the shaving soap. Lip salve, leather boots, and cartridge boxes soon followed. Finally, on November 8, the 650 remaining men of Arnold's column reached Point Lévis, opposite Quebec on the Saint Lawrence River. They were as exhausted as if they had experienced eight weeks of unbroken combat—and the British had yet to be encountered.

By this time, their whereabouts were well known to the brilliant British General Guy Carleton, who had ample opportunity to strengthen Quebec's defenses. He was expecting the attack, and he was ready. Arnold got his men across the river on November 13, the day Montreal fell to Montgomery's column. But it took nineteen more days before Montgomery was able to join Arnold, and he brought only three hundred soldiers. Moreover, the enlistment time of most of his men was about to run out. They had to attack quickly, but they felt they needed a stormy night to cover their maneuvers up the precipices of Quebec. On December 30 they got their cover in the form of a blinding snowstorm.

Montgomery and Arnold attacked from two different directions. In the first fusillade at close quarters, Montgomery and all his senior officers were killed outright. This left his force without effective leadership, and the commissary officer, who suddenly found that he was the only senior officer present, promptly ordered a retreat.

Meanwhile, Arnold and his soldiers, having heard nothing, continued their attack alone. Arnold's indomitable will made him a brilliant but erratic commander, and urging his men forward in their first skirmish, he was badly wounded and taken back to camp. His men, confused and lost in the storm, fought on gamely in small groups. But they were finally forced to surrender, and the fiasco of the Canadian invasion was mercifully over.

In the space of a few moments, all the weeks of sacrifice and agony had come to nothing. The Americans suffered thirty dead, forty-two wounded, and more than four hundred taken prisoner. The British counted seven dead and eleven wounded.

Arnold and the other survivors held out on the south bank of the Saint Lawrence until spring, even though their ranks were further decimated by an outbreak of smallpox. With the coming of spring and the arrival of two British warships, they finally gave up and started south for Lake Champlain. Back on American soil, wracked with dysentery and smallpox, they staggered into Fort Ticonderoga.

The story of the invasion of Canada is a grim and heartbreaking tragedy. These men had given everything in total, unhesitating commitment— and for nothing. Did it occur to them the reason might have been that, no matter how noble it appeared or how total their commitment, it was entirely out of God's will?

During the Canadian expedition, the blessing of Divine Providence seems to have been bestowed—or withheld—in relationship to whether individuals or groups were operating according to God's will. As Abraham Lincoln would respond, during another period of grave national crisis, "Sir, my concern is not whether God is on our side; my great concern is to be on God's side."[17]

The annexation of Canada was apparently not in God's plan for the United States. However, when the British for once pressed their advantage and came after the fleeing Americans in hot pursuit, divine providence once again seemed to favor the Patriot cause.

Down Lake Champlain came the Union Jack, flying in more than a score of makeshift gunboats, led by a flagship of eighteen guns that had been disassembled and transported overland. Nothing stood between them and Fort Ticonderoga—nothing except a ragtag fleet of bateaux and sailboats that Arnold had improvised in a desperate attempt to check the British advance. If they were not stopped, they could take the fort and carry on down the Hudson River, effectively splitting New England off from the other colonies.

Trading fire with them as both fleets sailed down the lake, the little American fleet fought on until their last bateau was destroyed. Arnold and a few of his men managed to make it to shore and get back to the fort.

Technically, America had lost its first naval engagement. But the unexpected stiff resistance that Arnold's makeshift navy had put up elicited the more typical British response of putting caution before zeal. General Carleton decided that control of Lake Champlain would require building a proper fleet, and because winter was coming on, construction was postponed until the following spring. Arnold's daring and courageous counterstroke purchased an entire winter, during which America was able to strengthen her Northern defenses.

How abruptly the tide had turned as soon as the battered Patriot remnant was back on American soil and defending it! It was as if God had a different plan for Canada. That endless Northern wilderness, which had been so dearly bought and paid for by the blood of French martyrs, had a destiny separate and distinct from His plan for America, which quite obviously did not include territorial acquisition to the north. Through the lifting of His grace, God delivered a strong rebuke, not merely to Arnold and the others involved, but to the nation that had sent them with its blessings.

With the winter of 1775–76 coming on, the outlook around Boston seemed nearly as bleak as that within. Due to the almost total lack of gunpowder and cannon, Washington was powerless to attempt even minor sorties, let alone launch any kind of major offensive. Indeed, he could do little more than sit and watch his army drain away, like sand running out of an hourglass. The problem was not desertion, which Washington had chosen to handle with the threat of disgrace rather than by the British method. The Redcoats had already hanged two men in Charlestown for desertion, although their customary penalty was a thousand lashes—which usually resulted in death long before the count was completed. Washington, however, prescribed thirty-nine lashes, to be followed by a general assembly to witness the deserter being drummed out of the army. The shame was lifelong.

The American problem was a hopeless mishmash of short-term provincial enlistments, some of which ran for only a month's duration. In

December, Connecticut troops, who had enlisted for only eight months, marched home a month early. Other troops followed, with so many of them taking the muskets the army had issued to them that there were not enough left for any new recruits that might arrive.

Washington's mood hit bottom. On January 14 he wrote to Joseph Reed that if he had known what lay ahead of him when he took command of the army, he never would have accepted the assignment. He had sent many officers back to their respective colonies to recruit a new army, based on one-year enlistments to begin January 1. But initial indications were that this program was going to fall far short of its projected quotas. As always for Washington, there was only one source of hope. To Reed he confessed: "If I shall be able to rise superior to these, and many other difficulties which might be enumerated, I shall most religiously believe that the finger of Providence is in it."[18]

Thankfully, the finger of Providence was soon in evidence. Thousands of New Hampshire and Massachusetts militiamen began to show up in the American camps around Boston. Even though they only intended short terms of service, they brought their own muskets, and they swelled the army's ranks to slightly less than ten thousand. And now powder was finally beginning to come in, though still only at a trickle.

Washington felt a compelling urgency that some sort of significant action had to take place soon while he had the manpower to achieve it. Yet even though he had the men and the powder he needed, without cannon to prepare and support an engagement—and specifically to smash down the British defenses on Boston Neck—there was no hope of taking the city.

But the Continental Army and its praying general were about to be favored by one of the most dramatic interventions of Divine Providence in the entire war.

In the course of one of the countless discussions of the need for artillery—"If only we had a dozen howitzers, or a dozen mortars, or a dozen twelve-pounders, or a dozen anything!"—someone remembered the guns at Fort Ticonderoga, recalling that Arnold had once proposed bringing them to Cambridge. But that had been back in April when the roads were dry. It was the dead of winter now; the roads were either muddy sinks or covered with ice. Yet sensing that God's leading might be in the suggestion, Washington turned the scheme over to Henry Knox. It was farfetched, but if anyone could make it work, Knox could.

Henry Knox was a rotund, twenty-five-year-old amateur engineer, who had learned what he knew of gunnery from books in the Boston bookstore he once owned. On the face of it, his youth and lack of any firsthand experience with artillery made him a most unlikely candidate. But once again Washington heeded his inspired intuition. In the early months of the war he had come to rely on Knox, a deft and skillful improviser, for solutions to his thornier problems.

There were upwards of fifty pieces of artillery at Ticonderoga. Knox's assignment: bring them to Cambridge as quickly as possible. His solution was a novel one—sleds! The one thing lacking was several inches of fresh snow—which Divine Providence, on cue and in response to fervent prayer, provided.

When Henry Knox and his bizarre caravan arrived in Cambridge on January 18, Washington was overjoyed. Having disregarded the unanimous counsel of his generals, he had set his will on taking and fortifying the heights on the Dorchester peninsula—the only site, other than Bunker Hill, from which Boston and the Royal Navy anchored in the harbor could be brought under effective bombardment.

Provided that enough gunpowder could ever be collected, only one obstacle remained: the ground was frozen so hard that it was impossible to dig any fortifications. And if they lacked protection, the first cannonade from the fleet would blow the defenders off the summit like flicking sweat off a brow.

Here again, God's hand could be seen in the solution. Later on the same night on which Washington had presented the problem to some of his officers, young Rufus Putnam, another amateur engineer, happened to be passing Brigadier General William Heath's quarters. The thought came to him to pay a visit. He did, and while he was there, he spied a book on field engineering among Heath's volumes. Thumbing through the book, Putnam noticed a diagram and description of a "chandelier"—a piece of French equipment new to him. It was a sectional wooden framework, designed to hold in place "fascines"—large, tightly bound bundles of sticks. Joined with other chandeliers, it made an above-ground barrier as effective as a trench. Voilà! As the magnitude of his discovery registered, he ran to tell General Washington.

At once the General gave the command to start constructing hundreds of chandeliers and fascines. Then was added an ingenious—purely Yankee—touch: barrels full of stones, to be laid end to end in front of the chandeliers and chocked in place. As the British lines came up the hill, the chocks would be knocked loose, and the barrels sent trundling down into their ranks with devastating effect.

Powder was now the only lacking ingredient, but supplies gradually came in to the point where there was enough for thirty cartridges per soldier. It was barely half the standard British combat issue, but Washington decided that it would have to suffice. Accordingly, on the night of March 2 the Americans commenced a heavy bombardment of the British lines with Henry Knox's cannon and mortars, to which the British began responding in kind the next morning. The exchange continued off and on for several days without much damage being done, but the attention of the British was diverted away from the Americans' feverish preparations for what was about to take place on Dorchester Heights.

The Continental Army could have waited a year and not experienced more ideal weather conditions than those that occurred on the night of March 4: a ground mist completely covered their operations at the base of Dorchester Heights, while the weather was perfectly clear on the top of the hill, well lit by a nearly full moon. The final touch was a breeze blowing inland to carry the noise of their work away from the British. Some eight hundred soldiers labored to place the preassembled chandeliers in position and load them with fascines, all of which were brought up the hill by three hundred amazingly quiet teams and drovers. Silently these soldiers worked hour after hour in the moonlit darkness, following plans that Knox had laid out with such precision that the whole line fit together as if it had been set up that way many times before.

The greatest evidence of how much the grace of God was involved, was the fact that nothing went wrong. No chance slip of the tongue, no wandering Tory passerby, and no lowing ox or breaking cart spoiled the perfect surprise.

At dawn the reaction of the British was stunned incredulity. Captain Charles Stuart wrote that the fortifications "appeared more like magic than the work of human beings." And the Royal Army's chief engineer, Captain Archibald Robertson, called it "a most astonishing night's work that must have employed from 15,000 to 20,000 men." Vice-Admiral Molyneux Shuldham informed General Howe that he "could not possibly remain in the harbor under the fire of the batteries from Dorchester Neck." And Howe himself could only say, "The rebels have done more in one night than my whole army would have done in months."[19]

The honor of the British Army demanded an immediate attack on the new rebel position, and accordingly Howe called a council of war. He gave orders for two forces of two thousand men each to be assembled for embarkation on the next tide, and down to the longboats went the files of red-coated infantry.

But as they waited for the tide, a storm came up out of nowhere. It was no ordinary storm: "A wind more violent than any I had ever heard," wrote one British soldier.[20] Approaching near-hurricane velocity, it drove thick snow laterally across the water, rendering any amphibious operation out of the question.

The storm continued all night. As it died away in the morning, Howe (greatly relieved) could now declare that the rebels had thus been given too much time to strengthen and solidify their positions, so a frontal attack would be nothing but foolhardy.

For the British, Boston was no longer tenable. A fortnight later, after the Americans had also fortified and set up a battery on Nob Hill, Dorchester's nearest promontory, the British abruptly evacuated Boston, giving up the city they had held for a year and a half.

Washington readily recognized that the storm represented "a remarkable interposition of Providence. . . . But . . . I can scarce forbear lamenting the disappointment."[21] For that first morning he had three thousand soldiers atop Dorchester Heights, far more than had defended Bunker Hill. And this time they had all the powder they could use.

In addition, the General had prepared a surprise for Howe: the moment the British troops were committed on Dorchester Heights, with two-thirds of their effective force out of the city, Washington planned to land an additional four thousand soldiers on Boston itself. His plan was that this body was to have raced to the heavily defended neck. Taking the defenders from behind, this force was to have broken open a passage, letting in another force that would have been waiting beyond. In this single stroke, the British would have been finished. In sum, it would appear that Washington had good cause to lament.

Yet as it worked out, the city of Boston was turned over to the Americans without the loss of a single life on either side.

As the Americans poured into Boston and the citizens cheered their welcome, they discovered to their shock something that confirmed a point their ministers had been emphasizing all along: the battle that they were fighting was basically a spiritual one. The British had wantonly and calculatedly desecrated Old South Church in retaliation for the times it had hosted meetings defying the king. "Gentleman Johnny" Burgoyne had turned it into a riding academy for the cavalry of his regiment. "The pulpit and all the pews were taken away and burned for fuel, and many hundred loads of dirt and gravel were carted in and spread upon the floor. The south door was closed, and a bar was fixed, over which the cavalry were taught to leap their horses at full speed. A grog shop was erected in the gallery."[22]

Nor was this an isolated incident. Throughout the Northern colonies, dissident (i.e., non-Anglican—especially Congregational and Presbyterian) churches were systematically abused, in a spontaneous manifestation of anti-Christian feeling. For example, the Presbyterian church at Newtown, Long Island, had its steeple sawed off, and the building was used as a prison and guardhouse. Later it was torn down completely, and its boards were used for the construction of soldiers' huts. In New Jersey the church at Princeton was stripped of its pews and gallery for fuel, and the churches at Elizabeth and Mount Holly were burned. In New York City the Presbyterian churches were made into prisons or were used by British officers for stabling their horses. All told, more than fifty churches throughout the country were totally destroyed, and dozens of others were damaged or otherwise misused.[23] There could be little doubt that the struggle against Britain was fundamentally a spiritual one.

After the Continental Army had reoccupied Boston with zero loss of life, prayers of thanksgiving had risen toward heaven, as had American morale, which hit a new high. But along with the enthusiasm, a dangerous spiritual condition of pride and self-confidence was permeating the colonies. Sensing it, many ministers called for repentance. Incredible as it may seem today, the Congress acknowledged that the war against our powerful enemy could be won only through a continuing willingness to face up to and deal with sin, both personal and national. Hence, throughout the eight-year conflict they continually called for days of fasting, humiliation, and prayer (or thanksgiving, if events warranted)—sixteen of them in all.

In light of the modern controversy regarding separation of Church and State, it is striking to note that these prayers often used explicitly Christian language. For example, the proclamation dated November 27, 1779, includes the phrases "our gracious Redeemer," the "light of the Gospel," "the light of Christian knowledge," and the "Holy Spirit."

As winter turned to spring in 1776, Congress declared a fast day for May 17 that would prove critical in its timing and importance. When the national day of repentance arrived, strong sermons were preached from every pulpit in the country. Perhaps the most widely reprinted was that of Dr. John Witherspoon, president of the College of New Jersey (Princeton):

> While we give praise to God, the supreme disposer of all events, for His interposition on our behalf, let us guard against the dangerous error of trusting in, or boasting of, an arm of flesh. . . . I look upon ostentation and confidence to be a sort of outrage upon Providence, and when it becomes general, and infuses itself into the spirit of a people, it is a forerunner of destruction. . . . but observe that if your cause is just, if your principles are pure, and if your conduct is prudent, you need not fear the multitude of opposing hosts.
>
> What follows from this? That he is the best friend to American liberty, who is most sincere and active in promoting true and undefiled religion, and who sets himself with the greatest firmness to bear down on profanity and immorality of every kind. Whoever is an avowed enemy of God, I scruple not to call him an enemy to his country.[24]

Throughout the war, committed ministers remained acutely aware of the need to guard against "trusting in the arm of flesh." As Samuel West, Dartmouth's minister, would preach in Boston two months later:

> Our cause is so just and good that nothing can prevent our success but only our sins. Could I see a spirit of repentance and reformation prevail throughout the land, I should not have the least apprehension or fear of being brought under the iron rod of slavery, even though all the powers of the globe were combined against us. And though I confess that the irreligion and profaneness which are so common among us gives something of a damp to my spirits, yet I cannot help hoping, and even believing, that Providence has designed this continent for to be the asylum of liberty and true religion.[25]

In the sessions of Congress that spring and early summer of 1776, the spiritual aspect of the struggle with Great Britain was at the heart of their debates. If America was to be "the asylum of liberty and true religion," what exactly did that mean? Should she seek to retain the security of her earlier relationship with the mother country? Should she put her trust in the vaunted "rights of Englishmen"? Should she continue to seek reconciliation and return to the peace of former years at whatever price?

22

"We Have Restored the Sovereign"

*Y*es, we should seek reconciliation with Great Britain, was the opinion that prevailed in Philadelphia, where an almost fantasy-like refusal to accept the reality of what had already taken place seems to have held the colonial representatives firmly in its thrall. So strong was it that they spent much time carefully drafting a conciliatory appeal (the Olive Branch Petition) addressed directly to King George. When it was presented to him, he disdained to even look at it.

The situation was reminiscent of the Israelites in the wilderness, convinced that they had been better off in Egypt and growing daily more certain that the only thing to do was to go back. Out in the wilderness they were facing the unknown and were forced to put their entire trust in God because there was no one else to trust. Forgotten was all memory of the slave pits and the grinding, hopeless existence they knew before the Lord God of Hosts delivered them. All they could remember now was that their bellies had been full, and they had known where their next meal was coming from, even if it was only stale crusts.

It may well have been the unknown—of having to trust in God because there was nowhere else to turn—that was causing many delegates to Congress in 1776 to wistfully turn their thoughts back to less perilous times.

There were, however, delegates in Congress who were not lingering in unreality about the possibilities of reconciliation with Britain, such as John and Samuel Adams, Patrick Henry, and the others from Virginia. John Adams, often the most persevering of the realists, had the benefit of having a wife with an extraordinary awareness of exactly what was at stake. As Abigail wrote to him on June 18:

> I feel no anxiety at the large armament designed against us. The remarkable interpositions of heaven in our favor cannot be too gratefully acknowledged. He who fed the Israelites in the wilderness, who clothes the lilies of the field and who feeds the young ravens when they cry, will not forsake a people engaged in so righteous a cause, if we remember His loving kindness.[1]

Adams and the other realists saw clearly that events had progressed beyond the point of no return; to go back now would be to go back under England's terms—under a far-from-benevolent dictatorship. For despite the support of eloquent and high-minded members of Parliament, the prevailing sentiment there reflected the King's own intransigence (as well it might, since George III's personal patronage had bought the majority of the seats). In the King's eyes, the only way to deal with rebellion was to crush it. To show even the slightest mercy was to invite a recurrence in the future.

When hearts are thus hardened, the most compelling persuasion in the world cannot move them. Nine plagues in swift succession had failed to soften Pharaoh's heart, and the comparison between him and George III was now being made in sermons throughout the colonies. Nevertheless, great Parliamentarians like Pitt, Burke, and Fox, in speaking out for the cause of America, reached heights of oratory seldom heard since the days of Rome.

The Bishop of Saint Asaph had summed up the position of the pro-American minority and set the tone when he said:

My Lords, I look upon North America as the only great nursery of free-dom now left on the face of the earth. . . . we seem not to be sensible of the high and important trust which Providence has committed to our charge. The most precious remains of civil liberty that the world can now boast of are lodged in our hands, and God forbid that we should violate so sacred a deposit. [2]

Pitt, England's great former Prime Minister, put it in strictly civil terms:

The spirit which now resists your taxation in America is the same which formerly . . . established the great fundamental, essential maxim of your liberties—that no subject of England shall be taxed but by his own consent. This glorious spirit . . . animates three millions in America, who prefer poverty with liberty, to gilded chains and sordid affluence, and who will die in deference of their rights as men, as freemen.

When your lordships look at the papers transmitted us from America, when you consider their decency, firmness and wisdom, you cannot but respect their cause, and wish to make it your own. For myself, I must declare and avow that in all my reading and observation . . . for solidity of reasoning, force of sagacity, and wisdom of conclusion, under such a complication of difficult circumstances, no nation or body of men can stand in preference to the general Congress at Philadelphia.

That was the considered opinion of the foremost British statesman of the eighteenth century. Did it make any impression on King George? He dismissed it contemptuously, calling Pitt "a trumpet of sedition."

The debate over the fate of America was hardly confined to Parliament. All of England, to say nothing of Scotland and Ireland, seemed to feel more intensely about it than anything since the Glorious Revolution in the previous century. Some of the highest officers in both the Royal Army and Royal Navy resigned their commission rather than serve. Lord Jeffrey Amherst, the Crown's greatest general in the French and Indian Wars, repeatedly rejected the King's offers of an active command. And General Henry Conway, only slightly less famous, not only refused to take any part in the war but openly opposed it at every point.

The same held true at the bottom of the military establishment. By his willingness to enlist, the British commoner traditionally expressed his approval or disapproval of his nation's wars, and in the case of the American rebellion, it was the latter. Never in all Britannia's history had she experienced such difficulty in raising an army. During the Seven Years' War with Spain, three-hundred thousand Britons had responded to the call of the recruiting drum; now she could not raise even fifty thousand. Recruiting officers were stoned in Ireland, tarred and feathered in Wales. Even the extensive use of press-gangs, who kidnapped able-bodied seamen wherever they could find them, could not meet the Royal Navy's needs.

In the end, a furious George III was forced to hire mercenaries from abroad. Even here he was rebuffed. Catherine of Russia did not bother to reply to the King's request, written in his own hand. Frederick the Great of Prussia curtly refused him. Johan Derk van der Capellen of Holland let George III know exactly where he stood, as he expressed his opinion to his fellow countrymen: "But above all, it must appear superlatively detestable to me, who think the Americans worthy of every man's esteem and look upon them as a brave people, defending in a becoming, manly and religious manner those rights which, as men, they derive from God, not from the legislature of Great Britain."[3]

In England, there were those not protected by the immunity of Parliament who spoke out at great risk. The Lord Mayor and Aldermen of London were so bold as to petition the king:

> As we would not suffer any man, or body of men, to establish arbitrary power over us, we cannot acquiesce in any attempt to force it upon any part of our fellow subjects. We are persuaded that, by the sacred, unalterable rights of human nature, as well as by every principle of the constitution, the Americans ought to enjoy peace, liberty and safety, [and] that whatever power invades these rights ought to be resisted. We hold such resistance, in vindication of their constitutional rights, to be their indispensable duty to God, from whom those rights are derived to themselves.[4]

George III was finally able to locate, among the lesser princes of Germany, three who would sell him the use of their soldiers—three princes who, in the words of Edmund Burke, "sniffed the cadaverous taint of lucrative war."[5] Altogether, he was able to buy the services of thirty thousand German mercenaries, which comprised more than half his total expeditionary force.

Of those in sympathy with the American cause, the most impressive address came not from the House of Lords but from the House of Commons. There, Mr. George Johnstone spoke in terms so ringing that he might have been standing alongside Samuel Adams or Patrick Henry:

> I maintain that the sense of the best and wisest men in this country are on the side of the Americans, that three to one in Ireland are on their side, that the soldiers and sailors feel an unwillingness to serve. . . . I speak it to the credit of the fleet and army: they do not like to butcher men whom the greatest characters in this country consider as contending in the glorious cause of preserving those institutions which are necessary to the happiness, security and elevation of the human mind. . . .
>
> To a mind who loves to contemplate the glorious spirit of freedom, no spectacle can be more affecting than the action on Bunker Hill. To see an irregular peasantry commanded by a physician [he was referring to Patriot leader Dr. Joseph Warren, killed as one of the last defenders], inferior in number, opposed by every circumstance of cannon and bombs that could terrify timid minds, calmly waiting the attack of the gallant Howe leading on the best troops in the world, with an excellent train of artillery, and twice repulsing those very troops who had often chased the chosen battalions of France, and at last retiring for want of ammunition, but in so respectable a manner that they were not even pursued—who can reflect on such scenes and not adore the constitution of government which could breed such men! Who is there that can dismiss all doubts on the justice of the cause which can inspire such conscious rectitude?
>
> The conduct of the people of New England for wisdom, courage, temperance, fortitude and all those qualities that can command the admiration of noble minds, is not surpassed in the history of any nation under the sun. Instead of wreaking our vengeance against that colony, their heroism alone should plead their forgiveness.[6]

Neither the King nor any of his ministers nor any of his bought members of Parliament had ears to hear. That same day George III publicly announced his decision to crush the rebellion by force of arms, including the use of mercenaries. When the ensuing debate was finally over, the

House of Lords voted in favor of the king's address, 76 to 33, and Commons voted 278 to 108 in favor. England declared war.

For eleven years the colonies had repeatedly sought reconciliation with the mother country, only to have their peaceful entreaties met with armed force. The Patriots had felt Biblically justified in taking up arms to defend their homes and families because they had not sought war and had never fired the first shot—not in the Boston Massacre of 1770, not at Lexington and Concord, and not at Breed's Hill. Their understanding of Biblical teaching was that God condones defensive wars, not offensive ones.

And now, King George III had decided to send a large invasion army against his own subjects—to forcibly enter their homes, take their property, and imprison them without trial—all in complete violation of British common law, the English Bill of Rights, and the Magna Carta.[7]

It is not surprising, then, that Samuel Adams would declare to British officials in the midst of the war:

> There is One above us who will take exemplary vengeance for every insult upon His majesty. You know that the cause of America is just. You know that she contends for that freedom to which all men are entitled—that she contends against oppression, rapine, and more than savage barbarity. The blood of the innocent is upon your hands, and all the waters of the ocean will not wash it away. We again make our solemn appeal to the God of heaven to decide between you and us. And we pray that, in the doubtful scale of battle, we may be successful as we have justice on our side, and that the merciful Savior of the world may forgive our oppressors.[8]

As the first week of June 1776 drew to a close, with the invasion fleet on its way to subdue the Patriots in the American colonies, the majority of delegates to the Congress in Philadelphia were hoping against hope that some eleventh-hour formula for reconciliation might be found. They were aware of what it would mean and how much it might personally cost them if they were to cast their votes with those who were now calling for an open declaration of independence. Such a move would close the door forever to any possibility of rapprochement with the Crown. And with the full might on both land and sea of the greatest military power on earth about to come down on them, even if the colonies were truly united, they could not hope to stand up to such a force for long.

But all their debates over the past weeks had indicated how utterly separated and individualistic these thirteen colonies actually still were. It would take a miracle of God to bring them into unity. Dare they cut the final ties to Britain and commit the colonies they represented to such peril?

Though none of the delegates openly spoke of their personal jeopardy, it was surely on the mind of more than a few. Those who signed such a declaration would, in the quite probable event of America's defeat, be held personally responsible. And throughout the British Empire, the penalty for instigating rebellion against the Crown was death. As Ben Franklin put it wryly, "Gentlemen, we must indeed all hang together, or most assuredly we will all be hanged separately."[9]

The yearning to be free and stay free was gaining momentum. On May 10, town meetings all over Massachusetts had unanimously voted in favor of independence.[10] On May 15, the Virginia Convention voted for independence. And on June 7, documented evidence arrived of the treaties that George III had made with the German princes, purchasing the use of their mercenaries in America.

In the face of that, Richard Henry Lee of Virginia formally proposed that Congress make a declaration of independence, stating that these united colonies are, and of a right ought to be, free and independent states. John Adams immediately seconded the proposal. After a day's debate, Congress adjourned for three weeks to let the doubtful representatives of the middle colonies go home to sound out the will of their constituents.

In the meantime, Franklin, Adams, Sherman of Connecticut, Livingston of New York, and young Jefferson of Virginia hurried to draw up a draft of the proposed declaration.

We hold these truths to be self-evident, that all men are created equal. . . . We, therefore, the Representatives of the United States of America, in General Congress, Assembled, appealing to the Supreme Judge of the world for the rectitude of our intentions, do, in the Name, and by Authority of the good People of these Colonies, solemnly publish and declare, That these United Colonies are, and of Right ought to be Free and Independent

States. . . . And for the support of this Declaration, with a firm reliance on the protection of Divine Providence, we mutually pledge to each other our Lives, our Fortunes and our sacred Honor.

Jefferson did most of the final composing, borrowing heavily from the popular phraseology of the day—except for the two phrases, "appealing to the Supreme Judge of the world for the rectitude of our intentions" and "with a firm reliance on the protection of Divine Providence." Congress insisted upon including these phrases, over Jefferson's vehement objection, for he was a confirmed "enlightened rationalist," soon to become privately a Unitarian.[11] (So resentful was Jefferson at their tampering with his prose, that he sent copies of his original draft to his friends, so they might better appreciate his unedited effort.)

June 28: The convention of Maryland voted for independence. Word reached Philadelphia that New Jersey had dismissed its old delegates and was sending new ones, who were instructed to vote for independence.

July 1: Congress entered what John Adams called "the greatest debate of all." Dickinson of Pennsylvania spoke eloquently and at length against independence. When he had finished, there was a long and thoughtful silence. Adams kept hoping that someone "less obnoxious" than himself, who was "believed to be the author of all the mischief," would rise to answer. But none did, and so, with great reluctance, Adams rose. And he spoke with such quiet power and conviction that not a man present remained unmoved, especially as he reached his conclusion:

Before God, I believe the hour has come. My judgment approves this measure, and my whole heart is in it. All that I have, and all that I am, and all that I hope in this life, I am now ready here to stake upon it. And I leave off as I began, that live or die, survive or perish, I am for the Declaration. It is my living sentiment, and by the blessing of God it shall be my dying sentiment, Independence now, and Independence for ever![12]

No one spoke. Just then, the door swung open and in strode a mud-spattered figure with two others behind him. It was Dr. John Witherspoon, at the head of the New Jersey delegation. Apologizing for being late, he said that although he had not heard the debate, he had not lacked sources of information on the various issues. "Gentlemen, New Jersey is ready to vote for independence. In our judgment, the country is not only ripe for independence, but we are in danger of becoming rotten for the want of it, if we delay any longer."[13]

The Congress proceeded to the vote, and eight of the thirteen colonies voted with New Jersey that day: Pennsylvania and South Carolina voted no, and New York abstained. Delaware was split, one delegate to one.

Since Congress was, in effect, acting as a committee on behalf of the whole country, the delegates had agreed that any decision on the declaration would have to be unanimous. It was decided that debate would resume the next morning, to be followed by another vote. In the meantime, an express rider was dispatched to Dover to fetch Delaware's third delegate, Caesar Rodney. He would be needed to resolve the delegation's deadlock, which could well determine the outcome.

A Patriot of deep conviction, Rodney had been summoned home on urgent business. But the express rider arrived at his farm at two in the morning, bearing word that debate would resume in less than seven hours, after which the final vote would be taken. Quickly getting dressed and saddling his best horse, Rodney galloped off into the pitch black, stormy night. It was eighty-nine miles to Philadelphia, over stretches of road that were difficult under the best of conditions, and this night the conditions could hardly have been worse. Streams that were normally fordable with ease had become swollen torrents, and the rain had turned one portion of the road into a quagmire so deep that Rodney had to dismount and lead his horse through it to avoid its being crippled.

Unable to obtain a fresh change of horses until dawn, Rodney nevertheless arrived at the State House by 1:00 p.m. just as the final vote was being taken. Half-carried into the assembly room, he was barely able to speak: "As I believe the voice of my constituents and of all sensible and honest men is in favor of independence, my own judgment concurs with them. I vote for independence."

Few knew the circumstances surrounding Rodney's vote.[14] Caesar Rodney had cancer of the face, which was so advanced that he had taken to wearing a scarf around his neck to hide the disfigurement of his jaw. He had been planning a trip to England because he had heard of a doctor in London who might be able to help him. But he, and every person in that room, was well aware that if they declared independence, Britain would immediately declare war on America and invade the colonies. Caesar Rodney knew that he might never see England before he died of cancer. Nonetheless, without a moment's hesitation, he voted "aye" for independence.

The last line of the document he had just voted to approve says: "with a firm reliance on the protection of Divine Providence, we mutually pledge to each other our Lives, our Fortunes and our sacred Honor."

With his vote Rodney literally pledged his life—and gave us the Declaration. Had he voted "nay," Delaware's vote would have been "nay," for the other two delegates had once again split their vote. Lacking a unanimous vote, the issue would have been tabled.

As it was, the vote was unanimous—twelve to none, with New York abstaining.[15] The thirteen colonies had just become the United States of America.

In the silence that followed the announcement of the vote, the afternoon sun cast its soft rays through the tall windows—on a brass candlestick standing on a green felt table covering, a carved eagle over the door, a pair of steel-rimmed spectacles lying on a polished desk.

The magnitude of what they had done began to weigh upon them, and they realized that they and their countrymen were no longer citizens of England but citizens of a fledging nation barely a few minutes old. Many stared out the window. Some had tears in their eyes. A few, like Witherspoon, bowed their heads and closed their eyes in prayer.

Two days later, as president of the Continental Congress, John Hancock would legalize the Declaration by placing his famous signature on it. He broke the silence: "Gentlemen, the price on my head has just been doubled!"

A month after the vote was taken, delegates who wished to sign the Declaration of Independence began gathering in Philadelphia on August 1. That evening, Samuel Adams spoke to those who had arrived, putting into sharp spiritual focus what they had accomplished: "We have this day restored the Sovereign, to Whom alone men ought to be obedient. He reigns in heaven and . . . from the rising to the setting sun, may his Kingdom come."[16]

23

CRUCIBLE OF FREEDOM

*A*s news of the Declaration of Independence spread throughout the newborn nation, Americans everywhere were delirious with joy—cheering, waving, ringing church bells, wasting gunpowder. Samuel Adams wrote: "The people, I am told, recognize the resolution as though it were a decree promulgated from heaven."[1] And John Adams was so elated that he wrote to Abigail twice on the same day. In the first letter, he took a sobering look at the reality of what lay immediately ahead:

> It is the will of heaven that the two countries should be sundered forever. It may be the will of heaven that America shall suffer calamities still more wasting and distresses yet more dreadful. If this is to be the case, it will have this good effect, at least: it will inspire us with many virtues which we have not, and correct many errors, follies and vices, which threaten to disturb, dishonor and destroy us. . . . The furnace of affliction produces refinements in states, as well as individuals.[2]

In his second letter, however, he looked prophetically into the future of the newborn nation, saying that the day on which the Declaration was signed, the fouth of July,

> will be the most memorable . . . in the history of America. I am apt to believe that it will be celebrated by succeeding generations, as the great anniversary festival. It ought to be commemorated, as the Day of Deliverance, by solemn acts of devotion to God Almighty. It ought to be solemnized with pomp and parade, with shows, games, sports, guns, bells, bonfires and illuminations, from one end of this continent to the other, from this time forward forevermore.
>
> You will think me transported with enthusiasm, but I am not. I am well aware of the toil and blood and treasure that it will cost to maintain this Declaration, and support and defend these States. Yet through all the gloom I can see the rays of ravishing light and glory. I can see that the end is worth more than all the means.

Throughout the struggle for America's independence, the signers of the Declaration would have been dismayed at the accusation that they were in rebellion against God. On the contrary, by revolting against tyranny they were restoring God's plan for American government. Thomas Jefferson would adopt for his personal motto the famous quote from John Bradshaw, President of the high court that had tried King Charles I for treason in 1649: "Resistance to tyranny is obedience to God."

At the same time that the Founding Fathers were declaring independence from Great Britain, they were declaring dependence upon God. John Adams would give voice to this attitude in the dark days of the winter of 1777, when he was asked by Pennsylvania's Benjamin Rush "if he thought we should succeed in our struggle with Great Britain. After a moment's pause, he answered, 'Yes—if we fear God and repent of our sins.'"[3]

America's euphoria over the Declaration died away quickly enough. On the same day that it was passed in Philadelphia, the new commander of the British expeditionary forces in America, Sir William Howe, landed on Staten Island with the first of what would ultimately amount to an occupying army of fifty-five thousand troops. American recruiters doubled their efforts, and soon farmers and tradesmen began to sign up for a whole year, once word of what had happened on the coast of South Carolina reached the Northern states.

On the morning of June 28, a combined British land and sea assault was launched to seal off the South's principal seaport, Charleston, and provide the British with an ideal Southern base for future operations. But "luck" was running against them. Fort Sullivan, guarding the entrance to Charleston's harbor, hardly deserved the designation fort. It was an earthworks-and-palmetto-stake affair with a great morass of mud in its middle.

These humble ingredients nonetheless worked mightily in the defenders' favor when the British warships drew closer and opened fire. Cannonballs that hit the sixteen-foot-thick earthworks made little impression on them, and the shells that landed inside disappeared into the mud without exploding. Overcharging their mortars for greater range, the British overdid it—and blew them up. The gap of water behind the fort proved narrower than General Clinton's reconnaissance team had indicated. A British ship tried to negotiate it and ran aground, with all hands having to abandon ship.

All day long and on into the darkness, the fleet pounded the fort, and the fort pounded the fleet—until around 9:30 in the evening the guns finally ceased firing. Having weighed the situation, Admiral Parker and General Clinton elected to disengage.

Dawn revealed that although the fort was badly battered, the fleet had fared worse. HMS *Bristol* and HMS *Experiment* each lost upward of a hundred men killed or wounded. Two other ships were sunk, and numerous others were severely damaged. (American casualties: twelve killed and twenty-four wounded.)[4] By the manifold grace of God, an outgunned and outnumbered American force had again stood its ground against seemingly overwhelming odds.

The British fleet, with the Royal Army units on board, sailed north to join the main body of British on Staten Island. There, during the next two months, thirty-two thousand troops gathered under General William Howe, including a Hessian contingent of nine thousand mercenaries. As Washington had anticipated, the British considered control of New York

City—and thereby the Hudson River—pivotal to suppressing the uprising. Control of the gateway to the north would effectively cut New England off from the other states.

Only one obstacle stood in the enemy's path: the American-held town of Brooklyn at the western end of Long Island.

On August 22, fifteen thousand British troops were landed without opposition on the southeast shore of Brooklyn. Three days later they were reinforced by an additional five thousand Hessians. Facing them were barely eight thousand Americans under Washington, half of them untrained. In fact, only three weeks before, there had been less than five thousand. But in response to a sincere appeal from Washington, revealing how desperate the American plight was, Connecticut's Governor Jonathan Trumbull had called for nine more regiments of volunteers, in addition to the five that Connecticut had already sent. "Be roused and alarmed to stand forth in our just and glorious cause. Join . . . march on; this shall be your warrant: play the man for God, and for the cities of our God! May the Lord of Hosts, the God of the armies of Israel, be your leader."[5]

Five days later, the British had nearly surrounded the Americans, just north of the Flatbush region. The order for attack was given. The Americans left and center were overwhelmed and fell back to the final defensive perimeter around the northern tip of Brooklyn. The right, under William Alexander (affectionately known as Lord Stirling because of his Scottish ancestry), was cut off and trapped. While Stirling and the men from Delaware held a ridge, their colors flying, five times the Marylanders flung themselves at Cornwallis's lines, trying to break through to rescue them. The last time they almost succeeded. Fresh British reinforcements stopped them, though the British reported that Stirling, personally leading his men, "fought like a wolf."[6]

Washington and his generals had observed the entire action through field telescopes. Several of his generals had speculated that Stirling would give up his hopeless position without a fight. When it was over, according to an eyewitness, General Washington cried out in anguish, "Good God, what brave fellows I must this day lose!"

All afternoon the Americans held their breath, waiting for the British assault that would surely finish them. Outnumbered more than three to one and low on powder (as always), they would soon have the British fleet in the mouth of the East River at their back. Dark thoughts must have gone through the minds of many of them: *it had been a noble, even glorious revolution, for there had been days of glory. No matter what happened in the next few hours, the British could never take away the memory of Lexington and Concord, of Bunker Hill, of Fort Sullivan. Freedom—it had been a cause worth fighting and dying for.*

But now they had to face the reality of how great were the odds stacked against them. "Put your trust in God," their ministers had said. "He is with us. He will see us through." Well, where was He now?

And so they waited and waited. They never knew that God was with them all the time. General Howe, against all military logic, was once again failing to take advantage of the situation and deliver the death blow. And this was not a dull general. His surrounding maneuver had been brilliantly conceived and flawlessly executed, taking the Americans by surprise. As afternoon became evening and the night wore on silently and peacefully, it became apparent that Howe was not going to attack. Unbelievable! It was a miracle, a few would begin to say. Yet Howe's unaccountable delay was only the opening curtain on what would be one of the most amazing episodes of divine intervention in the Revolutionary War.

The morning of August 29 dawned overcast and threatening—but quiet; there was still no movement from the British positions. All that day the Americans, tense and exhausted, continued to wait for the inevitable barrage that would precede the final action. But the British guns remained silent. In the late afternoon, a cold pelting rain began to fall and kept on falling into the night, soaking the tentless, lightly clothed, and hungry Americans. But the rain came on a northeast wind, and that wind prevented Howe's fleet from entering the East River.

And now Washington had a plan. Actually, it did not deserve to be called a plan, because it depended on the cooperation of many variables over which he had no control. To call it a desperate gamble would be closer to the truth. But surrender was out of the question, and anything was better than the suicidal defense that awaited them in the morning. If only God's grace would continue to favor them.

Washington called a council of war and informed his senior officers that he had decided to take the entire army down from Brooklyn Heights and across the East River by small boats. Once across, they would proceed down Manhattan to its southern tip, where the main body of American forces (some twelve thousand soldiers) were waiting behind Knox's major batteries.

Immediately his generals pointed out that it was a full mile across the East River. Once the British fleet got a glimpse of a flotilla of small boats filled with infantry, they would pulverize it. Better to die in the trenches; at least there they could sell themselves dearly.

Washington listened, hearing each one out, and then informed them that he had made up his mind. In his heart he must have been praying earnestly, for only God could prevent the enemy from discovering what they were up to.

The first thing they needed was boats and men who could handle them. By "coincidence," the last reinforcements to have come over from Manhattan were John Glover's company of Marbleheaders. Every one of them was an expert oarsman, who had grown up in small boats on the shores of Massachusetts Bay. The general now ordered them to locate the small boats they would need, and they were soon joined by the 27th Massachusetts—Salem men with the same skills.

With every seaworthy boat they could locate, all night long these men made the two-mile round trip. At first, they had to deal with the wind and the storm-tossed chop. But a little after midnight the wind died away, and soon they faced a different challenge—to glide as quietly as possible through the now-still waters. Dipping their oars deftly and silently into the water, they pulled them through without a wash and raised them out clean, ready for another stroke.

While the flat calm enabled them to take more men—the gunwales were barely above the water now—they faced a greater danger. There was no storm, no wind or rain to cover any accidental noise. Now they could ill afford the squabbles that had broken out earlier in the evening as the men had waited in line to be taken off the beach. The officers were vigilant to shut off any argument in its earliest stages, and the impossible evacuation (reminiscent of the miracle of Dunkirk) continued.

The clearing of the night sky now created another problem. It became crucial to maintain a screen of men in the front trenches, so the British would not suspect that a wholesale evacuation was under way. Shortly after two in the morning, however, the two Pennsylvania battalions under newly promoted Brigadier General Thomas Mifflin received orders, apparently from Washington, to quit their posts and proceed to the boats forthwith. Obediently they had done that, when their withdrawal happened to be discovered by the one man who could have known for certain that there had been a mistake: Washington himself. All night long he had been riding along the lines and the shore, and now he quickly redressed the situation and got the Pennsylvanians back into position. Perhaps a full half hour had passed during which there had been not a single defender visible anywhere on the American lines, and the night was so clear and well lit by moonlight that the enemy could be clearly seen, extending their trenches toward the American lines. The British must have been blind.

Now came the greatest peril of all: dawn. As the first wash of pink began to illumine the eastern horizon, the embarkation was far from over. At least three more hours would be needed to get all the men across, and the sky above was cloudless. August 30 would be a dazzlingly clear day. All American eyes were fixed on the eastern sky as it began to redden and the darkness above shrank westward. Though the men remained perfectly silent, one could sense their anxiety mounting, particularly the ones who would be the last to leave.

What happened next should be recounted by one who witnessed it. "As the dawn of the next day approached," Major Ben Tallmadge would write,

> those of us who remained in the trenches became very anxious for our own safety, and when the dawn appeared, there were several regiments still on duty. At this time a very dense fog began to rise [out of the ground and off the river], and it seemed to settle in a peculiar manner over both encampments. I recollect this peculiar providential occurrence perfectly well, and so very dense was the atmosphere that I could scarcely discern

a man at six yards distance. . . . we tarried until the sun had risen, but the fog remained as dense as ever.[7]

It remained intact, until the very last boat, with the general himself in it, had departed. Then the fog lifted. Shocked British officers and troops ran to the shore and started firing after them, but the musket balls fell into the water fifty to eighty yards astern.

Without the loss of a single life, nearly eight thousand men had been extricated from certain death or imprisonment. The Continental Army had suffered a severe defeat, with some fifteen hundred casualties. Yet, thanks to a storm, a wind, a fog, and what the General referred to as "Providence," there still was a Continental Army.

Once again, Howe inexplicably waited before crossing to Manhattan, this time giving the Americans a precious gift of two full weeks in which to recuperate, replenish supplies, and reposition themselves. Washington had learned the invaluable lesson of withdrawal before vastly superior forces, and it was a lesson that would earn him the grudging respect of the enemy, who would refer to him as a cunning fox. But he still had much to learn about tactics and the strategic placement of troops.

Washington had divided his forces. The main body was stretched in a line across upper Manhattan, along the Harlem Heights. But he had left Knox and his best artillery, along with four thousand men under Putnam, in the Battery, their heavily fortified position at the foot of the island. The east side of Manhattan Island, opposite which there was increasing British activity, was thinly held by local militia. When the British attack came, it came there. The militia broke and ran, scrambling north for the safety of the main lines.

The British landed with comparative ease at Kip's Bay, their officers proceeding to Murray Hill. As the British had been proceeding up the east side of Manhattan, Putnam and Knox had been making their own way up the west side, without either column being aware of the other. At one point, they were even on the same road, headed toward one another. Dr. James Thacher, surgeon with the Continental Army, describes what happened:

Most fortunately, the British generals, seeing no prospect of engaging our troops, halted their own and repaired to the house of Mr. Robert Murray, a Quaker and a friend of our cause. Mrs. Murray treated them with cake and wine, and they were induced to tarry two hours or more, Governor Tryon frequently joking her about her American friends. By this happy incident, General Putnam, by continuing his march, escaped an encounter with a vastly superior force, which must have proved fatal to his whole party. One half-hour, it is said, would have been sufficient for the enemy to have secured the road at the turn, and entirely cut off General Putnam's retreat. It has since become almost a common saying among our officers that Mrs. Murray saved this part of the American army.[8]

God works in mysterious ways, His wonders to perform.

The pattern of Washington tarrying but Howe tarrying even longer was to repeat itself a number of times that fall. The Continental Army withdrew from Manhattan and began a long retreat down the length of New Jersey, finally forming a thin line on the far side of the Delaware. Cornwallis had bragged that he would catch Washington in New Jersey "as a hunter bags a fox."[9] But the fox proved more elusive than he had anticipated. A British officer described the campaign: "As we go forward into the country, the rebels fly before us. And when we come back, they always follow us. 'Tis almost impossible to catch them. They will neither fight, nor totally run away, but they keep at such a distance that we are always a day's march from them. We seem to be playing at Bo-Peep."

The game ended on Christmas night, 1776. Once again, Washington faced the imminent prospect of a vanishing army. Most of the men sent from New York to reinforce him had not reenlisted, and their terms of enlistment were up at the end of the year. If Washington was going to make a bold stroke and take the offensive, it would have to be before then. A bold stroke was desperately needed: the nation's morale had never been so low. Key representatives in Congress, with no appreciation of Washington's brilliant husbanding of every soldier, bullet, and ounce of gun powder, were frustrated at an army that refused a "manly" fight. There had even been a conspiracy of jealous generals and congressmen afoot, to replace Washington with his second in command, General Charles Lee. A vastly overrated egocentric, Lee had just recently (and providentially) been captured by the enemy while going for a ride in front of the American lines.

The stroke was to be a surprise attack on Trenton. Once again, the Americans had the unseen aid of their strongest Ally. Rapidly developing the shrewd discernment for which he would become famous, Washington decided to attack in the predawn hours of December 26. The Hessian garrison in winter quarters there could be counted upon to be most heavily asleep, particularly if the schnapps had flowed as liberally as was their custom on Christmastide. As Washington's troops loaded into the small boats at three different places on their side of the Delaware, a violent snowstorm and hailstorm suddenly came up, reducing visibility to near zero. The thick ice floes on the river prevented two of his three battle groups from crossing, and when Washington's remaining troops finally got under way, the march was four hours behind schedule.

As the night wore on, the storm grew even more violent. In the words of Boston fifer John Greenwood, "it alternately hailed, rained, snowed and blew tremendously."[10] But by the mercy of God, the Americans lost only two men, who froze to death after becoming weary and dropping out of the line of march.

About five miles from Trenton, Washington divided his forces, planning a simultaneous attack from both the south and north ends of town. The troops were still several miles away from their objective when the coming of daylight threatened to erase any possibility of surprise. But the storm continued long after sunrise, keeping the sun obscured behind thick clouds.

The Hessians were not unprepared—an unauthorized American raid the night before had kept their outposts on full alert. But at the moment of attack, a sudden snow squall covered both of the advancing parties, north and south, enabling the Americans to catch the enemy entirely by surprise.

The Hessians fought bravely, but the ferocity of the attack, the weather, and a flawlessly executed battle plan made for a complete rout. Henry Knox was there, and as he described it in a letter to his wife, "The hurry, fright and confusion of the enemy was not unlike that which will be when the last trump will sound."[11]

In forty-five minutes of fighting, almost a thousand prisoners were taken. American casualties? Aside from the two unfortunates who had fallen out and frozen to death on the march, only three soldiers were wounded. The news electrified the young nation. Washington, having finally taken the offensive, had won a stunning victory. "Never were men in higher spirits than our whole army is," wrote Thomas Rodney, and he spoke for much of the rest of America as well.

Was it a fluke, as Washington's detractors, themselves now in disfavor, muttered? Or was it, as Knox wrote, that "Providence seemed to have smiled upon every part of this enterprise"?

Cornwallis, in charge of the British campaign in New Jersey, had been convinced that the front had stabilized for the winter and was about to sail for England to see his ailing wife, when news came that Trenton was lost. He was ordered south with heavy reinforcements. When he reached Trenton on January 2, he rejected the advice of his officers to attack Washington at once, observing that he could just as well "bag the fox" the next morning. His quartermaster general retorted, "My Lord, if you trust those people tonight, you will see nothing of them in the morning."[12]

Leaving his campfires burning and muffling his artillery wheels, Washington slipped away to Princeton. While driving back a support column that was on its way to join Cornwallis, he sought to steady his force of wavering recruits by spurring his large gray sorrel, which he had named Nelson, to a spot in front of his troops, within thirty yards of the British line. At six foot, three inches, Washington stood a full head above the average Continental soldier—an inviting target. Yet miraculously he survived the first volley. At the sight of him, the Americans rallied and went on to take the town and hold it until the General learned that Cornwallis was approaching.

This victory, following so closely on Trenton, made up the minds of those Americans still wondering about whether or not to volunteer. As Nicholas Cresswell, the caustic British gentleman traveler, would note, "Volunteer companies are collecting in every county on the continent, and in a few months the rascals will be stronger than ever. Even the parsons, some of them, have turned out as volunteers, and pulpit drums—or thunder, which you please to call it—summon all to arms in this cursed babble. Damn them all!"

With the coming of summer, the game of Bo-Peep resumed. Never having enough troops to launch a major offensive, Washington nonetheless continued to wear down and frustrate the British. It was a race against time, for once again America's patience with the General was wearing thin.

It wore a lot thinner with the loss of Fort Ticonderoga on July 8. The fort fell to Burgoyne, who was pushing down from Canada, planning a union with the forces that Howe was supposed to have dispatched up the Hudson from New York. But General Howe had now developed another strategy. In an effort to deal a heavy blow to the rebels, he struck out for Philadelphia, their largest city and the seat of government. Once again, he moved with ponderous slowness, badgered by Washington all the way.

As the summer faded into fall, up in northern New York, Burgoyne, without the aid of an attacking force coming up to meet him, was left to force his way through the wilderness. It went as badly for him as it had gone for Arnold, when the latter had attempted to take Canada. In the end, finding himself outmaneuvered and surrounded, he was finally defeated at the Battle of Saratoga on October 17—mainly by the heroic leadership of none other than Arnold himself. Gentleman Johnny Burgoyne and seven thousand troops surrendered in the Continentals' greatest single victory of the war.

But the solitary bright moment soon passed, and gloom returned to enshroud the American cause. A month earlier, the Continental Army had been mauled at Brandywine, as it had tried in vain to stop the British march toward Philadelphia. Saratoga may have cost the British seven thousand troops, but more than twice that number had arrived to replace them. America's chief city had now become an armed British camp. Liberty and independence, once almost within grasp, were a fading dream. For the first time, Americans were confronted with the hard facts of their circumstances. Locked in a desperate struggle for survival, they were slowly being backed toward the precipice of surrender by a more powerful adversary. Though they contested every inch of ground, there was now a real question as to how long America's will to resist would hold firm.

Such thoughts may have weighed heavily on Washington's mind as he sat astride Nelson and watched his troops file silently past on that cold and dismal afternoon of December 19. They were on their way into Valley Forge, the site the General had chosen for their winter encampment, because Trenton was too dangerous and Wilmington, Lancaster, or Reading would have afforded the British access to too much uncontested territory. Valley Forge was barely fifteen miles from Philadelphia; situated in the fork where Valley Creek ran into the Schuylkill River. It was easily defensible, and with open fields nearby for drilling and ample wood for fuel and shelter, a better strategic location could not have been found.[13]

Few of the men who shuffled past him through the snow had ever heard of Valley Forge. Nor did they care; they were exhausted, hungry, freezing—and had long ago given up hope of meat for supper, a warm bed, and a dry pair of stockings. Many did not have a pair of stockings left. Their footgear consisted of strips of blanket wound around their feet. All too quickly the blanket would wear through, and they would be walking through the snow barefoot, many of them leaving behind bloody footprints. In the dwindling army of eleven thousand, few were properly equipped for the terrible winter that lay ahead.

As they passed by, their heads bowed against the icy wind, no drumbeat marked the cadence of their steps, nor did the General attempt to encourage them. They knew he was there, and that was enough.

Though he did not speak, the tall figure on horseback was concerned for his men. For now would come their time of testing. The Refiner's fire would bring the dross to the surface, where it would be skimmed away.

Valley Forge would be America's crucible of freedom.

The rest of December was cold, with the daily temperatures varying between a high of thirty-seven degrees and a low of six.[14] And when January brought persistent snow and rain, the need for hard shelter became a matter of desperate urgency.

Washington himself had designed the log huts they would sleep in—eighteen feet long, sixteen feet wide, and six feet high. They would be easy to heat and could shelter a dozen men on four triple-decker bunks. With shake shingles, no windows, no flooring, and holes under the eaves for ventilation, they were so simple that they could be gotten up quickly by soldiers not possessing carpentry skills.

Every able-bodied man at Valley Forge was put to work on them, and upward of seven hundred cabins were erected in less than a month. Not until the last soldier was thus quartered did Washington quit his own patched and leaking field tent for the relative comfort of Isaac Potts's stone house, which had been rented for his headquarters. Doctor Thacher and the General's staff must have been immensely relieved at this move, having dreaded to think what would become of the army—and the nation—were their leader to be felled by influenza. Disease was taking a fearful toll that winter; they would lose more than one in four to flu, camp fever, smallpox, typhus, and exposure.

In this pitched battle between life and death, the General's wife, Martha, became a ministering angel. Every day that was free from rain or snow saw her making her way from hut to hut, bringing comfort and care to the sick and needy.

On one occasion she brought with her a young sixteen-year-old neighbor girl, who later remembered entering the hut of a dying sergeant who was attended by his wife. "His case seemed to particularly touch the heart of the good lady [Martha], and after she had given him some wholesome food she had prepared with her own hands, she knelt down by his straw pallet and prayed earnestly for him and his wife."[15]

Although the General spent most of his waking hours writing urgent letters to Congress and various governors, desperately trying to obtain food and supplies for his soldiers, he would often ride from one regiment to the next, talking with the men. As Dr. Thacher commented, "The army . . . was not without consolation, for his excellency, the Commander in Chief . . . manifested a fatherly concern and fellow-feeling for their sufferings and made every exertion in his power to remedy the evil and to administer the much-desired relief."[16]

Yet there was precious little that even the General could do beyond writing letters and praying. Congress, comfortably ensconced some ninety miles to the west in York, no longer benefited from the leadership of men like Adams, Franklin, Jay, Hancock, and Livingston, who were all vitally employed elsewhere. Their places had been filled by people of lesser talent and vision. Consumed with petty bickering and prone to jealousy of Washington, they convinced one another that his needs were exaggerated. Instead of sending the wagons of victuals and winter clothing for which he pleaded, they would merely print more Continental dollars. With these he was supposed to pay his troops and purchase what he needed. They chose to remain oblivious to the reality of the situation, which was that after several months of both armies feeding off the land, the countryside was exhausted. Many local farmers hid their wagons and livestock in the woods to avoid having to surrender them to the Valley Forge foraging parties in exchange for promissory notes or worthless paper dollars— hence the expression "not worth a Continental." What scant provender remained was finding its way into Philadelphia, where the British paid in silver and gold.

From the beginning, life in Valley Forge was grim. The huts were smoky and dark, and the newest men in each hut were given the bottom bunks closest to the door—the ones that got cold first when the night fire burned low. In the morning the men took turns fetching buckets of cooking water from the frozen creek. Meal after meal, their food consisted of "fire-cake"—wheat or cornmeal poured into a kettle of water, mixed, and ladled out on a big stone in the middle of an open fire, where it baked. Sometimes there was a bit of salt pork, too, or beef or dried fish, when the wagons got through. As for winter clothing, it was in such scarce supply that Washington had to issue a General Order threatening punishment to anyone cutting up a tent to make a coat out of it, for they would need every tent next summer.

As the winter wore on and the list of sick and dead mounted, life in Valley Forge became a nightmare. Now there were men who were almost naked, without coats and their clothes in tatters. A committee from Congress (finally sent in the middle of February) was shocked to find how many "feet and legs froze till they became black, and it was often necessary to amputate them."[17] Exposure to the elements combined with a woefully inadequate diet to create optimum conditions for the diseases that now ravaged the camp.

Washington himself, throughout his life given to understatement, wrote:

No history now extant can furnish an instance of an army's suffering such uncommon hardships as ours has done, and bearing them with the same patience and fortitude. To see men without clothes to cover their naked-ness, without blankets to lie on, without shoes, by which their marches might be traced by the blood from their feet, and almost as often without provisions as with; marching through frost and snow, and at Christmas taking up their winter quarters within a day's march of the enemy, with-out a house or hut to cover them till they could be built and submitting to it without a murmur, is a mark of patience and obedience which in my opinion can scarce be paralleled.[18]

The nightmare grew worse. When the entire camp was down to its last twenty-five barrels of flour in mid-February, Washington wrote: "I am now convinced beyond a doubt that unless some great and capital change suddenly takes place . . . this army must inevitably be reduced to one or other of these three things: starve, dissolve, or disperse, in order to obtain subsistence."[19]

And on February 16, a civilian named John Joseph Stoudt would write in his diary:

For some days there has been little less than a famine in the camp. . . . Naked and starving as they are, we cannot enough admire the incompa-rable patience and fidelity of the soldiery, that they have not been excited ere this by their suffering, to a general mutiny and dispersion. Indeed, the distress of this army for want of provisions is perhaps beyond anything you can conceive.[20]

This, then, was the miracle of Valley Forge. That the soldiers endured was truly amazing to all who knew of their circumstances. But the reason they endured—the reason they believed in God's eventual deliverance—was simple: they could believe because the General believed.

While Washington was quite reticent about expressing his Christian faith, he occasionally referred to it openly.* In May 1778, a General Order issued at Valley Forge called for divine services every Sunday and included this statement: "To the distinguished character of a Patriot, it should be our highest glory to add the more distinguished character of a Christian."[21]

*For further evidence of Washington's Christianity see Appendix Two.

Henry Muhlenberg, the pastor of a nearby Lutheran church, noted the General's faith with approval:

> I heard a fine example today, namely, that His Excellency General Washington rode around among his army yesterday and admonished each and every one to fear God, to put away the wickedness that has set in and become so general, and to practice the Christian virtues. From all appearances, this gentleman does not belong to the so-called world of society, for he respects God's Word, believes in the atonement through Christ, and bears himself in humility and gentleness. Therefore, the Lord God has also singularly, yea, marvelously, preserved him from harm in the midst of countless perils, ambuscades, fatigues, etc., and has hitherto graciously held him in His hand as a chosen vessel.[22]

When it came to prayer, Washington must have prayed earnestly and often that winter, but because he preferred to pray in private, there is only one supposedly eyewitness story of someone discovering him in prayer at Valley Forge. It concerns the General's winter landlord, Isaac Potts, and because there are several differing accounts, some modern historians are inclined to doubt its veracity. However, Potts's biographer, Mrs. Thomas Potts James, felt strongly that Potts's daughter Ruth-Anna's handwritten and signed version of the story (which James obtained from Potts's granddaughter) was authentic. Presbyterian minister Dr. N. R. Snowden also related the incident, claiming that he got it from Isaac Potts himself. Though the accounts differ in some details, they agree on the facts of the event.

Potts was a Quaker and a pacifist, who one day noticed Washington's horse tethered by a secluded grove of trees, not far from his headquarters. Hearing a voice, he approached quietly and saw the General on his knees at prayer. Not wanting to be discovered, he stood motionless until Washington had finished and returned to his headquarters.

Potts then hurriedly returned to his house and told his wife Sarah, "If George Washington be not a man of God, I am greatly deceived—and still more shall I be deceived, if God do not, through him, work out a great salvation for America."[23]

Something else happened that winter which says much about the quality of Washington's faith. A turncoat collaborator named Michael Widman was captured, and at his trial it was proven that he had given the British invaluable assistance on numerous occasions. He was found guilty of spying and was sentenced to death by hanging. On the evening before the execution, an old man with white hair asked to see Washington, giving his name as Peter Miller. Miller had joined the pacifist German Seventh Day Baptists and had become a member of their Ephrata Cloister. He was ushered in without delay, for these Ephrata "Dunkers" were giving hospital care to the army's sick and wounded, including soldiers from Valley Forge who had come down with camp fever. Miller now had a favor to ask of the General, who nodded agreeably.

"I've come to ask you to pardon Michael Widman."

Washington was taken aback. "Impossible! Widman has done all in his power to betray us, even offering to join the British and help destroy us." He shook his head. "In these times we cannot be lenient with traitors; and for that reason I cannot pardon your friend."

"Friend? He's no friend of mine; he is my bitterest enemy. He has persecuted me for years. He has even beaten me and spit in my face, knowing full well that I would not strike back. Michael Widman is no friend of mine!"

Washington was puzzled. "And you still wish me to pardon him?"

"I do. I ask it of you as a great personal favor."

"Why?"

"I ask it because Jesus did as much for me."

Washington turned away and walked into the next room. Soon he returned with a paper on which was written the pardon of Michael Widman. "My dear friend," he said, placing the paper in the old man's hand, "I thank you for this."[24]

Such charity did not weaken him in the army's eyes; the troops loved him for it, as did the officers. No one who had served with him could understand why there were generals and congressmen who wanted to see him replaced. But then, the public did not know how it was at Valley Forge. "The greatest difficulty," said the young Marquis de Lafayette, "was that, in order to conceal misfortunes from the enemy, it was necessary to conceal them from the nation also."[25]

Despite the necessity for secrecy, across the nation pastors were beginning to sense the tremendous spiritual struggle being waged at Valley Forge. More and more sermons were likening Washington to Moses. There were the obvious parallels, of course, but there was also the similarity in his choosing to partake of the same hardships as his men: "By faith Moses, when he was come to years, refused to be called the son of Pharaoh's daughter; Choosing rather to suffer affliction with the people of God, than to enjoy the pleasures of sin for a season; Esteeming the reproach of Christ greater riches than the treasures in Egypt" (Heb. 11:24–26 KJV). Thus did Washington covenant himself with his men in the suffering of Valley Forge, while a day's ride away, the British sat warm and full-bellied, enjoying after-dinner brandy by the fireside.

In the crucible of freedom, God was forging the iron of the Continental Army into steel. And now there was a new strength and determination in the camp, as revealed in this comment by an anonymous Valley Forge soldier, which appeared in the *Pennsylvania Packet*: "Our attention is now drawn to one point: the enemy grows weaker every day, and we are growing stronger. Our work is almost done, and with the blessing of heaven, and the valor of our worthy General, we shall soon drive these plunderers out of our country!"[26]

The soldiers at Valley Forge were being tempered into the carbon-steel core around which an army could be built.

24

"The World Turned Upside Down"

To aid in the tempering process, God sent as unlikely an agent as Squanto had been to the Pilgrims—a ruddy-cheeked, short, stout, bemedaled German with a passion for drill and a twinkle in his eye. This was Friedrich Wilhelm Augustus Baron von Steuben, a former captain in the Prussian army and a staff officer of Frederick the Great. Well recommended by Ben Franklin in Paris, von Steuben volunteered his services to the American cause.

General Washington must have sighed. How many European officers, caught between wars with time on their hands, had been sent to him by well-meaning friends? They had trouble fitting in and expected to be treated deferentially, which did not happen in the young Republic's army.

But unlike others, Franklin was wise enough not to send him fools. The young Marquis de Lafayette had proven invaluable. And this roly-poly Prussian just might be, as well. They would soon see; the General assigned him the task of making a professional army out of the Continentals.[1]

Von Steuben proceeded with typical Prussian thoroughness. Because there was no drill instruction manual, he set about writing one and had it translated into English. Then he worked with one company of soldiers until they responded with crisp precision to the most complex commands. Right oblique, counter-march, flank left, wheel right. . . . When they did exactly what he wanted, exactly the way he wanted them to—forming, breaking, and re-forming on the double—he was able to use this company to show the others what was possible. Soon the noncommissioned officers were able to take over, and by April whole regiments could be moved quickly and efficiently anywhere on the battlefield.

In musketry, von Steuben's memorized precision was badly needed. When it came to firing volleys, it had often taken the Continental Army more than a minute to fire, reload, and be ready to fire again. But hours of practice began to cut the time between shots. "Prime firing pans . . . charge muskets . . . remove ramrods "—there were twelve steps to firing a musket, and if, in the heat of battle, one step was overlooked, there would be a gap in the volley. (There were instances of soldiers forgetting to remove their ramrods from their barrels and actually firing them at the enemy. Although a flying ramrod had been known to kill a man, the soldier's musket was useless after that.) By the time spring came, von Steuben had drilled the troops to the point where they could produce a tight volley every fifteen seconds.

Arising at 3:00 a.m. and appearing on the parade ground by sunrise, the Prussian was a demanding drillmaster. He had a saving sense of humor, however, and his oaths were frequently punctuated by laughter. When driven to distraction by the repeated mistakes of one company or another, he would swear at them in German till he was out of breath and then call on his interpreter to carry on in English.

His perseverance bore fruit. As March turned into April, the Continental army began to march as one. The General could not have been more pleased. Before von Steuben, it must have felt as if he was playing chess with only pawns—good for digging in and holding ground but unable to parry and thrust. Now he had a full assortment of moving pieces with which he could counter any maneuver the enemy cared to make. And the soldiers began to take pride in their newly acquired

411

skills; indeed, that was more than a little responsible for their steadily improving morale.

From this time forth, Washington never needed to worry about another year-end enlistment lag; volunteers were now signing up for three-year tours. Regardless of the contracted length of their tour, the veterans of Valley Forge were in for the duration of the war and would not think of leaving until the job was done. And in coming years, when the hardest assignments came—the frontal attacks, the bayonet charges, the advance flanker details—the Valley Forge survivors were the ones invariably chosen.

On the first of May, intelligence reached the American camp that France, at last convinced that the Continental Army could stand up to the full might of the British military establishment, was coming into the war on the side of America. The dark night was over; the French now were allies. With that news, volunteers and supplies began pouring in from all over the country. And now, thanks to Valley Forge, there was an army—a real army—to receive them.

Historians generally credit Washington's strong leadership as having held the army together at Valley Forge. But Washington himself, knowing it was a miracle that they were still intact, credited God. In announcing the French decision to his joyous troops, he declared:

> It having pleased the Almighty Ruler of the universe propitiously to de-
> fend the cause of the United American States, and finally by raising us up
> a powerful friend among the princes of the earth, to establish our liberty
> and independence upon lasting foundations, it becomes us to set apart a
> day for gratefully acknowledging the Divine goodness, and celebrating the
> important event which we owe to His benign interposition. [2]

In Philadelphia, less than two weeks later, a farewell party was held for General Howe—now Sir William, as like his brother, he too had been knighted. He had asked to be recalled and had turned his command over to Sir Henry Clinton. It was a costume fête, and in extravagance it rivaled the court of Louis XIV, showing more imagination than the entire British Expeditionary Force had exhibited at any time since coming to America.

It was followed by new orders from London, returning Clinton to New York. Because the few ships available were crammed with Tory refugees, Clinton's troops and artillery would have to go by land, back up through New Jersey. That meant a long, strung-out column with exposed flanks.

It was an attack-commander's dream: to hit from the side, with a sharp, compacted force. The damage they could inflict was incalculable. They could cut communications and supply lines, and in the chaos and confusion—known today as the fog of war—they could hit again and again before the British column could re-form. It would be the retreat from Concord all over again, but on a much broader scale. And now they would be ready.

But when the British commenced their march on the morning of June 18, there was dissension in Washington's war council. His second in command, General Charles Lee (recently returned in a prisoner exchange), was "passionately opposed" to an attack on Clinton. To Lee, who at every opportunity cut Washington down behind his back, it was appalling naïveté to believe that Americans could stand up to British regulars. The thing to do, he repeatedly counseled, was to do nothing, just stay where they were and see what developed. And some junior and even senior officers came under the spell of this seasoned professional.

Washington then turned to ask the opinion of a young and fiercely loyal brigadier general who had been with him all through New Jersey and Valley Forge. "Fight, sir!" was Anthony Wayne's reply; and Nathanael Greene, Lafayette, and John Cadwalader all closed ranks behind their Commander in Chief. But five precious days would pass before Washington would shake off the hypnotic grip of Lee's prestige and inform the officer corps that they were going into action immediately.

The opportunity for a staggering, even killing, blow from the flank was gone, but they could still catch the Redcoats and deliver an attack to the rear of their column if they moved quickly. Once again their unseen Ally seemed to be doing His part; the weather suddenly turned almost tropical, with hundred-degree heat and sudden downpours, which only increased the humidity. The British column was strung out over twelve miles and was barely dragging along, because all the wells along the way had been filled and the bridges blown in anticipation of their return to New York.

Military etiquette dictated that Charles Lee be given field command of the attack force—which he spurned as unworthy of him. Vastly relieved, Washington gratefully turned the command over to Lafayette and Wayne, whom he knew he could count on to press the attack. And at last the Continental Army swung out of Valley Forge and onto the trail of the British.

This was a different army than had come down that road six months before, leaving a trail of bloody footprints in the snow. Now there was a sharpness to the beat of the field drums and a bite to the music of the fifes, which added an inch or two to each stride—and an extra half-mile to the distance covered in an hour. And when the pipers played "Yankee Doodle," the soldiers grinned and their grips tightened on the stocks of long-barreled rifles. As the sergeants called out marching orders and counted cadence, there was a fresh snap to the response. The Americans were an army now. In training and toughness they could go toe to toe with the Redcoats, or anyone else, as they were about to demonstrate.

They caught the British at Monmouth, and Charles Lee, who had changed his mind and now demanded that he be given the field command after all, permitted Wayne to engage the enemy. But the moment the British turned to fight, Lee ordered a general retreat.

Furious, Washington spurred to the front of the column, relieved Lee of command, and rescued his forces from impending disaster. Back and forth he rode on Nelson, calmly urging the men to re-form, giving them the example of his own bravery under fire. No soldier could look at him and not take heart. The troops stopped, turned, and fought the British to a standstill, causing them to grudgingly fall back. There was no clear-cut victory at Monmouth that day, but from that time forth, the British never again made the mistake of underestimating their opponents.

In the wake of the British withdrawal, the military command of Philadelphia was turned over to Arnold. The name of Benedict Arnold has become synonymous with the depths of betrayal and infamy, as familiar to Americans as the name of Judas Iscariot. Yet with the exception of

Washington himself, Arnold was the most courageous and intrepid field commander in American uniform, which only makes the well-known tale the more tragic.

Part of Arnold's story is pertinent to the role that Divine intervention played in the Revolutionary scheme of things. Arnold's secret liaison with the British was Clinton's adjutant, Major John André. Disguised as a civilian (and hence, by military definition, a spy), André had the bad "luck" to encounter an American patrol as he was about to reenter the British lines above New York. Mistaking the patrol for British, André let slip that he was a British officer. He was immediately searched, and in the heel of his shoe were discovered secret plans for the fortifications of West Point, along with a pass signed by Arnold, the commander of the fort.

The officer in charge, failing to put two and two together, sent André under guard to explain to Arnold just how he happened to be in possession of the pass and the plans. At this point, Major Ben Tallmadge, Washington's chief of intelligence, by "coincidence" happened to be in the area and heard about the capture of the apparent spy. He *did* put two and two together, for he had been privately concerned about Arnold for some time. Although he was too late to stop the news from getting to Arnold, he did have his men hold the spy, and when he interrogated him, it all came out.

Arnold narrowly escaped, but West Point was saved. Had the patrol not met André, had he not mistaken them for British soldiers, had the one man most likely to comprehend quickly the enormity of the plot not been in precisely the right place at the right time, the outcome could have been quite different.

In announcing the discovery of Arnold's infamy to the army, Washington said: "Treason of the blackest dye was yesterday discovered. . . . The providential train of circumstances which led to it affords the most convincing proofs that the liberties of America are the object of Divine protection."[3] A poignant epilogue to this sad narrative is that Arnold's last request, as he lay dying in England, was to be dressed in his American uniform.

Monmouth marked the last time that the two main bodies of the British and American armies would be within striking distance of one another. For the next two years, the actions would mostly involve detachments and would often be indecisive—fluid campaigns that swept the South and involved such places as Cowpens, King's Mountain, and Guilford Courthouse. It was a frustrating war for both sides, since there never seemed to be enough time or troops or supplies to decide the issue. The Americans were usually outnumbered and therefore in the familiar role of drawing the enemy ever further from their bases of supply.

Of all of the instances of Divine intervention during the war, one of the most dramatic occurred after the battle of Cowpens in South Carolina. On January 17, 1781, Colonel Banastre Tarleton's large detachment from Lord Cornwallis's army had been soundly defeated by General Daniel Morgan, who took about five hundred British prisoners. Morgan immediately began to withdraw toward the Catawba River to join up with General Nathanael Greene's division. Their ultimate goal was to get across the Dan River into friendly Virginia territory. But they were facing a winter march across more than two hundred miles of Carolina countryside, which was honeycombed with rain-swollen creeks and two major rivers—the Catawba and the Yadkin. There were no bridges, so they were dependent on finding sufficiently shallow fords.

News of Tarleton's defeat sent Lord Cornwallis into a fury. Destroying his heavy baggage, he set out in hot pursuit of Morgan's small army, hoping to catch them at the ford of the Catawba. But he arrived at sunset, two hours too late. Confident that he could easily destroy the Americans in the morning, he decided to delay crossing until daylight.

During the night, however, a heavy rain swelled the water level to flood stage, rendering it impassable. Forty-eight hours would pass before the river subsided, allowing him to get across. Had the river's rise occurred a few hours earlier, Morgan would have been trapped and his army annihilated.

And that was only the first of the river miracles.

Both armies pushed hard for the Yadkin River in North Carolina. The Continentals reached the western bank of the Yadkin late in the evening of February 2. But rather than halt his entire army for the night, as the pursuing Cornwallis had done, Morgan pushed his horsemen across the river at midnight. The rest of his small army followed in boats at dawn, apparently aided by an overnight drop in the water level.

When Lord Cornwallis's advance units reached the river bank a few hours later, they could plainly see General Morgan's troops forming up on the opposite bank to march off. But in the brief interval between the last of Morgan's boats crossing and Cornwallis's arrival, the waters had once again risen so fast that the fords were impassable, and the Americans had taken all the available boats.[4]

Sir Henry Clinton, Cornwallis's second in command, would later express the British frustration in his memoirs: "Here the Royal Army was again stopped by a sudden rise of the waters, which had only just fallen [almost miraculously] to let the enemy over, who could not else have eluded Lord Cornwallis' grasp, so close was he up to their rear."[5]

Marching rapidly up his side of the Yadkin, Cornwallis finally found a shallow ford and got his army across. This maneuver actually put his army closer to the final fords of the Dan River than Morgan's. If he could get there first, he could prevent the American army from reaching safety in Virginia.

Meanwhile, Daniel Morgan had become so worn down by rheumatism and exhaustion that he resigned his command, and General Greene replaced him with Maryland officer of the line O. H. Williams, who proved more than capable.

The two armies raced for the Dan, moving in parallel forced marches, sometimes at the incredible rate of about thirty miles a day. Williams allowed his men only six hours sleep every two days, and the Americans met the challenge, gradually pulling ahead of the British.

At one point, the British altered their route of march, and their advance unit closed to only four miles behind the American army's rear. Only a gallant delaying action by "Light Horse Harry" Lee's cavalry enabled the small army to escape. After three more days of skirmishes and desperate marches, the American army reached the banks of the Dan just before sunset on February 13. Normally fordable here, the river was again much too high. But by the grace of God, advance riders had gathered all available boats, and by midnight every last soldier and horse had been ferried across to the safety of Virginia.

Blocked for the third time by a flooded river in his path, with all boats on the far shore, a disgusted Lord Cornwallis finally abandoned the pursuit and turned his army back toward Hillsborough, North Carolina.[6]

Even when the British were able to inflict defeats on the Americans, which happened fairly often, the problem was that the Patriots refused to stay defeated. General Greene summed up the war: "We fight, get beat, rise and fight again."[7] The fact that they kept rising to fight again finally began to take the heart out of the British war effort. The Americans gave every indication that they were prepared to go on fighting, and getting beat, and rising and fighting again until the Lord returned.

That kind of perseverance wore the British down, and they began to make mistakes. The biggest one was an accumulation of misjudgments, human errors, and the handiwork of God.

In the fall of 1781, hoping to be evacuated by the British fleet under Admiral Graves and transported in New York to rejoin Clinton, Cornwallis had brought his Southern campaign to a close. He had fought well, and his six thousand troops had done all that could be expected of them. Yet now he was here in Yorktown, and the fox he was going to bag five summers before had him under siege. No matter, the Royal Navy would soon be taking them off.

But Graves exhibited the same shortcoming that so often characterized the British throughout the War for Independence: tardiness. Slow in getting under way, Graves arrived at Chesapeake Bay to evacuate Cornwallis's army—one day too late. The French fleet under de Grasse had gotten there first and had put the cork in Cornwallis's bottle. Graves immediately formed a line of battle, and the French came out to meet him rather than risk being trapped in the bay.

As they sailed out of the Chesapeake, beating into an offshore headwind, they were easy targets for the British. But Graves failed to press his advantage and allowed the French time to form their own battle line. As they closed, there was confusion in the signals along the British line, with the result that the French were able to outmaneuver them and inflict substantial damage. Graves finally decided to break off and return to New York, to refit his ships—thereby sealing Cornwallis's fate.

The end was now inevitable, and both sides knew it. The Americans brought their heaviest artillery to bear on Yorktown and the British lines.

On the night of October 14, 1781, four hundred Frenchmen stormed Redoubt #9, and four hundred Americans simultaneously stormed Redoubt #10. (The charge was led by one of Washington's staff officers, a young lieutenant colonel named Alexander Hamilton.) In fifteen minutes of furious hand-to-hand fighting, it was over. The Americans made these two British outposts the right anchor of their new siege line, which brought their cannon into nearly point-blank range.

To escape the ever-tightening American noose, Cornwallis had one last, desperate gambit. He would employ the same surprise tactic that Washington had used to extricate the Continental Army from Brooklyn Heights. On the night of October 16, under cover of darkness, he began ferrying his troops across the York River in small boats. But now, instead of being favored by the elements, this small-boat evacuation was disrupted by them.

Cornwallis had actually succeeded in getting a third of his army across undetected when a sudden violent storm came out of nowhere, driving the boats downriver and making further passage impossible. By the time it subsided, too many hours had been lost to complete the evacuation, so Cornwallis ordered the troops on the far side of the river to be brought back. As the last boats returned at daybreak, they came under the heaviest American artillery fire yet. As Tarleton put it, "Thus expired the last hope of the British Army."[8]

That morning as the sun rose, the newly dug forward batteries opened fire with a relentless bombardment. Cornwallis raised the white flag before noon.

Doctor Thacher was there:

> The whole of our works are now mounted with cannon and mortars. Not less than one hundred pieces of heavy ordnance have been in continual operation during the last twenty-four hours. The whole peninsula trembles under the incessant thunderings of our infernal machines. We have leveled some of their works in ruins and silenced their guns. They have almost ceased firing. We are so near as to have a distinct view of the dreadful havoc and destruction of their works.[9]

Although in other theaters the war would drag on for another two years, Washington and Cornwallis both sensed that it was now essentially over. Formal surrender was set for two o'clock on the afternoon of the nineteenth. In an open field behind Yorktown, the American and French forces formed two long lines, down the middle of which the British were to march in a column of fours. The French, with fresh uniforms and new, black leather leggings, looked resplendent in the soft October sunlight of a warm fall day. The Americans, in buckskins, homespun shirts or faded blue-and-white Continentals, seemed more like a militia than an army, except that their lines were just as straight, their posture as erect.

Silence hung over the field as a gentle breeze stirred leaves that were just beginning to turn color. In the distance came the sound of the British field drums—slurred, erratic, not at all sharp, as they had once been. The drummers, like many of the other soldiers, had prepared themselves with rum. The officers came first, on horseback.

Cornwallis, it turned out, could not bring himself to turn over his sword to Washington in person and so had pleaded "indisposition" and instructed his deputy to do so. Washington refused to deal with Cornwallis's deputy and sent Benjamin Lincoln, his deputy of comparable rank, to accept the sword.

When the soldiers came, it was to the popular tune of "The World Turned Upside Down" (as indeed it was). Down the files they came, some angry, some weeping; the Americans said not a word but looked straight ahead. Six years seemed to pass with the slow tread of the infantry and grenadiers. Lexington, Concord, Bunker Hill, Dorchester Heights, Brooklyn Heights, Trenton, Princeton, Saratoga, Valley Forge, Monmouth, the Southern Campaign, Yorktown . . . It seemed longer, a lifetime at least.

"Ground muskets!" each British officer commanded his soldiers when they reached the end of the file, and they did so sullenly, flinging their Brown Besses on the pile of discarded weapons in front of them. Some of the British were seen to crack the butts of their muskets on the ground as they threw them on a pile. Some of the regimental musicians staved in the heads of their drums.

When it was finally finished, a tremendous roar of joy went up from the Americans—a roar that would be heard throughout the country and around the world. There were prayers that day, too—not as loud perhaps, but which carried much farther.

Washington ordered a thanksgiving service to be held the day after the surrender: "The Commander in Chief earnestly recommends that the troops not on duty should universally attend with that seriousness of deportment and gratitude of heart which the recognition of such reiterated and astonishing interposition of Providence demands of us."[10]

This was a theme that would be very much on his mind in later days. As he would write to Brigadier Nelson, "The hand of Providence has been so conspicuous in all this, that he must be worse than an infidel that lacks faith, and more than wicked, that has not gratitude enough to acknowledge his obligations." Then his sense of humor slipped out: "But, it will be time enough for me to turn preacher, when my present appointment ceases; and therefore, I shall add no more on the Doctrine of Providence."[11]

The most fitting word on Yorktown was spoken by one of the most famous ministers of that day, Timothy Dwight. In a sermon "occasioned by the capture of the British Army under the command of Earl Cornwallis," he preached on Isaiah 59:18–19: "According to their deeds, accordingly he will repay, fury to his adversaries . . . to the islands he will repay recompence. So shall they fear the name of the LORD from the west, and his glory from the rising of the sun. When the enemy shall come in like a flood, the Spirit of the LORD shall lift up a standard against him" (KJV).

In the sermon itself, he said:

> Who, but must remember with hymns of the most fervent praise, how God judged our enemies, when we had no might against the great company that came against us, neither knew we what to do? But our eyes were upon Him. Who, but must give glory to the infinite Name, when he calls to mind that our most important successes, in almost every instance, have happened when we were peculiarly weak and distressed? While we mark the Divine hand in the illustrious event we are now contemplating, can we fail to cry out, "Praise the Lord, for He is good, for His mercy endureth forever."[12]

Two years later, with news of the peace treaty finally arrived, the time had come for Washington's senior officers to bid farewell to their Commander in Chief. They gathered at Fraunce's Tavern in lower Manhattan ten days after General Clinton and the Royal Army had quit the city. The senior officers of the Continental Army, dressed in the best uniforms that they could manage, seemed to have no interest in the sumptuous fare on the gleaming white tablecloth before them. There was a heaviness in the room, and halfhearted conversations died away into silence. They were awaiting the General, and Ben Tallmadge, now a lieutenant colonel, recorded the details.

The General arrived, prompt as always, and from his face, he was as deeply moved as any of them. Most of them had been with him since Valley Forge, and a few, like Henry Knox, had been with him from the beginning. But now it was over; this was the last time they would be together like this again.

Looking around and noticing that no one had approached the elegant buffet, with its several wines and choice of succulent meats, puddings, and pies, the General took a plate and absently helped himself to a small portion. Taking a glass of wine, he encouraged the others to do likewise. One or two moved to do as he had bid them, and then the General spoke to what was so heavy on all their hearts.

"With a heart full of gratitude," he began, his voice breaking, "I now take leave of you." He made a maximum effort to control his emotions. "I most devoutly wish that our latter days be as prosperous and happy as your former ones have been glorious and honorable." He raised his glass, and one or two made a faltering attempt at a reply.

The General, his eyes glistening, spoke again. "I cannot come to each of you, but shall feel obliged if each of you will come and take me by the hand."

The first to come to him was Henry Knox. The two men looked at one another and said nothing. The tears streaming down their faces said it all. They shook hands and parted. One by one, the remaining officers, among them old von Steuben, shook their Commander in Chief's hand and silently parted.

Tallmadge wrote:

Such a scene of sorrow and weeping I had never before witnessed, and hope I may never be called to witness again. . . . Not a word was uttered to break the solemn silence . . . or to interrupt the tenderness of the scene. The simple thought that we were then about to part from the man who had conducted us through a long and bloody war, and under whose conduct the glory and independence of our country had been achieved, and that we would see his face no more in this world, seemed to me to be utterly unsupportable.[13]

The moment their farewells were completed, the General begged leave, and he departed, passing through a corps of light infantry at attention. He walked to the waterfront, where a barge waited to take him to the Jersey shore, and his officers followed behind him in saddened silence. A large crowd had gathered to wish him good-bye, and one wondered if his mind cast back to that bright June morning in Philadelphia in 1775 when a throng had gathered to wish Godspeed to the new Commander in Chief. As soon as he was seated, the barge cast off, and the tall figure in its stern raised his hat in a final farewell.

But the General's ordeal of honor was not over. One more parting was required: the formal resignation of his commission before Congress. The government was now temporarily headquartered at Annapolis, Maryland (which fortunately was on his way to Mount Vernon). Thomas Mifflin, the same brigadier who had inadvertently withdrawn his covering troops from the line at Brooklyn Heights, was now President of Congress. He addressed the General with respect born of the awareness of the moment: "Sir, the United States, in Congress assembled, are prepared to receive your communications."

The General rose and bowed to the members. From his pocket he drew a paper, which shook noticeably in his hand. He congratulated Congress, and then, speaking of the war, commended to them the officers who had served him so faithfully and well. At this point, he recalled some of the individuals who had performed with unusual distinction—Nathanael Greene, Daniel Morgan, Henry Lee, and of course his own staff.

He paused, and his emotions again threatened to overwhelm him. He now held the paper in front of him with both hands to quiet its trembling. "I consider it an indispensable duty to close this last solemn act of my official life by commending the interests of our dearest country to the protection of Almighty God, and of those who have superintendence of them to His holy keeping."

The General's voice caught, and there were many who could scarcely see the tall speaker through their own tears. "Having now finished the work assigned me, I retire from the great theatre of action, and bidding affectionate farewell to this august body under whose orders I have so long acted, I here offer my commission and take my leave of all the employments of public life."

And so saying, from the inside breast pocket of his uniform coat, he drew forth his commission and handed it to President Mifflin. At last, nothing stood between him and Mount Vernon, far from the demands and pressures of public life.

25

"Except the Lord Build the House . . ."

*T*he search was almost over. We had seen how miraculously God would intervene to preserve and protect His covenanted people. And He continued to do so, even though they did not always live up to their end of the covenant. We saw how He brought them by His grace to final victory. At last, all that God had purposed for His "New Israel" seemed to be within reach. America was now free to be the "city on a hill" that John Winthrop had envisioned.

But instead, a sad trend toward a de-emphasis of the Covenant Way had already begun. Even as the newborn republic was everywhere proclaiming its trust in God, that trust was lessening. For the first time in more than a century and a half, America's ministers were no longer its most influential leaders. We needed to find out why.

We did find out. And in the process we discovered something else: that despite the spiritual decline, God made certain that those same covenant promises that He had made to our ancestors when He brought them here would always be a viable possibility in the United States of America.

We saw how He ensured that, no matter what happened in intervening generations, we Americans would still be able to avail ourselves of those promises and reenter a covenant relationship with Him as a nation.

The state of the nation was one of exhilaration. For the United States of America was truly a nation—totally free and independent for the first time in the nearly two centuries since the first English ships had sailed up the James River to settle Jamestown and the three centuries since Columbus had glimpsed the low coastline of San Salvador.

"Great indeed is the salvation He hath shown! And great the obligations we are under to praise!" preached George Duffield in Philadelphia, reflecting the sentiment of the majority of the nation's ministers. For Duffield, the destiny of the Redeemer Nation, of the City set on a Hill, was now fulfilled. God's "New Israel" was now established.

> With Israel of old, we take up our song: "Blessed be the Lord, who gave us not as a prey to their teeth. Blessed be the Lord, the snare is broken and we are escaped." . . . Here also shall our Jesus go forth conquering and to conquer, and the heathen be given Him for an inheritance, and these uttermost parts for a possession. The pure and undefiled religion of our blessed Redeemer—here shall it reign in triumph over all opposition![1]

But Duffield's words were premature. While this promise was indeed bright, it had not happened yet. And David Tappan, in his pulpit at Newbury, Massachusetts, was one of the first of the minority to sound a more cautionary note. He reminded his hearers that God had delivered America in spite of her national traits—not because of them.

> Let us beware that we do not impute these signal divine appearances in our favor to any peculiar excellence in our national character. Alas, the moral face of our country effectually confutes such a vainglorious statement. Crimes of the blackest hue, countless multitudes of abominations, mark the visible character of this great, this highly favored community, and still provoke the great displeasure of heaven. . . . Let us remember that for His own sake, He hath done these great things, not for any righteousness in us.

. . . But that His own name might be exalted, that His own great designs . . . extending the Kingdom of His Son, may be carried into effect.[2]

John Rodgers, in New York, preached a whole sermon on the remarkable instances of Divine Providence in the war just concluded. Among other things, he pointed out that if the British had first struck in the South rather than at Boston, three colonies—Georgia and the two Carolinas—in all likelihood would not have joined the war. He speculated on what would have happened had a lesser man assumed the generalship of the army and on the unlikelihood of such total surprise as that which accompanied the attacks on Trenton and Princeton. He noted the extraordinary timing of the arrivals of de Grasse and Washington at Yorktown, which sealed Cornwallis's fate.

> Lastly, God has done great things for us, by that honorable, and may I add, glorious peace, by which He has terminated the late unnatural war. . . . There is not an instance in history, within my recollection, of so great a revolution being effected in so short a time, and with so little loss of life and property, as that in which we this day rejoice.[3]

With few exceptions, it seemed to the ministers of America that the Light, which had been brought by the first Christ-bearers, had at last been joined by the glory of his Kingdom come—or soon coming. The most outspoken was Timothy Dwight, grandson of Jonathan Edwards. This candid and persuasive clergyman was shortly to become President of Yale College and the leading advocate of his age for evangelical Christianity. Dwight was looking for the imminent arrival of God's kingdom:

> God brought His little flock hither and placed it in this wilderness, for the great purpose of establishing permanently the Church of Christ in these vast regions of idolatry and sin, and commencing here the glorious work of salvation. This great continent is soon to be filled with the praise and piety of the Millennium. But here is the seed, from which this last harvest is to spring.[4]

Dwight was convinced that a return to Puritan ideals and priorities was the only thing that would ensure the coming of the Kingdom that

God had clearly intended to create here. And one of the themes that he repeatedly hit upon was the need for a reestablishment of the covenant relationship that their forebears had entered into with God and with one another. He was not averse (as were most of his colleagues) to looking at the duality of the Old Testament concept of covenant—at what would happen if they did *not* keep their end of the bargain.

"Nothing obstructs the deliverance of America," he had preached in 1777, "but the crimes of its inhabitants." Only if America honored the vertical and horizontal aspects of the covenant would "independence and happiness [be] fixed upon the most lasting foundations, and that Kingdom of the Redeemer . . . [be] highly exalted and durably established on the ruins of the Kingdom of Satan."[5]

So there it was, once again back to the same basic truth: the glory that could be America's depended on her living up to the light that she had been given. Nothing had changed since leaders like William Bradford and John Winthrop and Thomas Hooker had heeded God's calls on their lives and given definition to the corporate call on God's people. As far as God was concerned (if Dwight was hearing him correctly), the covenant was still in effect.

Dwight was not the only one gravely concerned about the need for a spiritual binding together. Washington wrote to the governor of each of the thirteen states upon his disbanding of the army:

> I now make it my earnest prayer that God . . . would incline the hearts of the citizens . . . to entertain a brotherly affection for one another, for their fellow-citizens of the United States at large, and particularly for their brethren who have served in the field. And finally that He would most graciously be pleased to dispose us all to do justice, to love mercy, and to demean ourselves, with that charity, humility and pacific temper of mind, which were the characteristics of the Divine Author of our religion, and without an humble imitation of whose example in these things we can never hope to be a happy nation.[6]

Just how united were the United States? The dire peril of the war that had threatened them all had forced a semblance of the covenant on the states. For there could have been no suing for peace, no conditional surrender; it had to have been either victory or subjection of the most ruthless sort. That was how Great Britain traditionally dealt with uprisings—with the gibbet or the headsman's axe.

America had known this in her heart. So, when Boston's harbor had been shut down, all the colonies had responded spontaneously; after the Battle of Lexington, riflemen from Virginia and Maryland had marched to Cambridge. And when Cornwallis had cut into the heart of Virginia, there were many soldiers from Massachusetts who had come down to avenge her. For eight years the states had fought and bled and cared for one another, almost as if they had covenanted before to do so.

Yet even with all the prayer and the sacrifice, Congress still had to beg the states for money to support the war effort. Nor was it empowered to impose a draft, with the result that the Continental Army was trying to attract recruits at the same time that soldiers were going for several months without getting paid.

But what really belied any covenant attitude among them—what proved that the horizontal aspect of the covenant was not possible outside of Christ—was what happened as soon as the war was over and the pressure lifted. Fallen humanity's utter selfishness came roaring back with a vengeance. States that had throughout the war avoided contributing their fair share now simply refused to pay at all. Massachusetts wound up paying more of the war's expenses than any other state—about as much as Pennsylvania, New York, Virginia, and Maryland combined—though her population was only 13 percent of America's total.[7]

The disputes between the states accelerated and deepened with a rapidity that was disheartening, to say the least. Some states were willing to cede their western holdings to Congress; others refused to do so. Some states had worked hard to pay off their war debts; others wanted Congress to assume them. The Articles of Confederation—an emergency, stopgap solution intended to provide some form of unified, legal government— were woefully inadequate. They provided for no executive or judicial branches and no national power to compel. The only power Congress had was the power to make war and peace, draft treaties, and maintain a postal service. Yet some of the states thought that even this was too much and refused to ratify the Articles.

Quarrels between the states finally grew deep-seated and vindictive, with each state raising or lowering tariffs and coining its own money. Several states even sent their own ambassadors abroad to make trade agreements in competition with one another and with the United States government. In a word, the Union was a mess. And many of the most responsible, realistic leaders in America were seriously beginning to question whether it would work at all.

George Washington, who passionately wanted no more of public life, now felt compelled to do all he could to save the Union. He started a letter-writing campaign to the people who were in a position to most shape opinions in America. Pleading from deep conviction and with great dignity for the salvation of the nation and exerting all of his own considerable influence, he declared that "something must be done, or the fabric will fall, for it is certainly tottering."[8]

That "something" turned out to be the Constitutional Convention in Philadelphia in May 1787. Originally convened to patch up the holes in the Articles of Confederation, it was soon redirected to the framing of a whole new constitution. Washington was hoping that he would not have to go, but the state of Virginia insisted that he be among her delegates. And once he got to Philadelphia, he was the unanimous choice to chair what should have been an awesome and momentous occasion. For it was the first time in history that people had ever had the opportunity to freely write a new constitution for their own representative government.

It started out, instead, to be an extremely stormy convention. The Northern states insisted that representation be apportioned on the basis of population; the Southern states (less densely populated) felt it should be on the basis of land under cultivation. And the small states feared a ganging up by the larger states, both Northern and Southern. There was a great deal of heat and very little light being generated; in fact, historians are in general agreement that it was only the dignity of Washington's presence and demeanor that preserved the convention at all. God's placing of the right person in the right role at the most critical moments in American history is a thing of never-failing astonishment.

In his superb two-volume history, *A New Age Now Begins,* Page Smith offers this appraisal of Washington:

His genius was the ability to endure, to maintain his equilibrium in the midst of endless frustrations, disappointments, setbacks and defeats. . . . George Washington became the symbol of the [American colonists'] determination to endure. He was bound to create and sustain a Continental Army and in the process to destroy or at least mute the deep-rooted parochialism of the states. So he not only symbolized the will of the Americans to persevere in the cause of liberty, he symbolized the unity of the states; he embodied the states united, or the United States. . . . If Washington's army had disintegrated, as it seemed so often on the verge of doing, Congress might well have followed suit. . . . If Congress had disbanded, the problem of creating a viable nation out of thirteen disparate and jealous provinces would have been infinitely more difficult. Above all, if Washington had not, in his splendid erectness . . . and his presence, *embodied* the union, it is doubtful that unification could have been accomplished on the practical political level. . . .

In a sense it was Washington's restraint, more than Washington's actions, that determined his greatness. . . . Greatness consists, as we have said before, in being appropriate to the requirements of the hour. By this measure Washington, as Commander in Chief of the Continental Army and perhaps even more as the first President of the United States, was a very great man.[9]

Smith does not comment on the source of Washington's remarkable ability to endure, but Washington himself commented on it often enough, giving the credit to God and expressing his own needs through prayer. As for his restraint, which is another word for self-denial, never did it bear more fruit than at the Constitutional Convention of 1787. As deeply as he felt about the issues at hand, he would not permit himself to enter into the debate. He remained scrupulously impartial in the manner in which he presided, and he restricted himself to sharing his beliefs in between the floor sessions.

Nevertheless, the mood eventually reached an ugly pitch, and it became painfully apparent to all present that the convention and the Union were about to break up. "And thy neighbor as thyself"—the horizontal aspect of the covenant, which Timothy Dwight and a few others were calling for—seemed to be nowhere in evidence. What was now being required of the states was the same relinquishing of self-interest and individual rights that the Pilgrims and Puritans had chosen when they entered into covenant with God and one another. But the states were unwilling to give up enough of their "sovereign rights" to form the nation that God intended.

With debate over representation now hopelessly deadlocked and growing increasingly bitter (part of the New York delegation had already gone home in disgust, and others were preparing to follow), God once again had mercy on the affairs of America. This time he used perhaps an unlikely (and therefore quite arresting) vehicle—the eighty-one-year-old *philosophe* who had, some forty years before, good-naturedly rejected the efforts of his friend George Whitefield to convert him.

At this crucial moment, when there was not a person present who had any real hope of finding an effective solution, Ben Franklin rose to speak on June 28. This elder statesman, who was also one of the most prominent physicists of his age, quietly said:

> In the beginning of the contest with Britain, when we were sensible of danger, we had daily prayers in this room for Divine protection. Our prayers, Sir, were heard, and they were graciously answered. All of us who were engaged in the struggle must have observed frequent instances of a superintending Providence in our favor. . . . And have we now forgotten this powerful Friend? Or do we imagine we no longer need His assistance?
>
> I have lived, Sir, a long time, and the longer I live, the more convincing proofs I see of this truth: "that God governs in the affairs of man." And if a sparrow cannot fall to the ground without His notice, is it probable that an empire can rise without His aid?
>
> We have been assured, Sir, in the Sacred Writings that except the Lord build the house, they labor in vain that build it. I firmly believe this. I also believe that, without His concurring aid, we shall succeed in this political building no better than the builders of Babel; we shall be divided by our little, partial local interests; our projects will be confounded; and we ourselves shall become a reproach and a byword down to future ages. And what is worse, mankind may hereafter, from this unfortunate instance, despair of establishing government by human wisdom and leave it to chance, war, or conquest.
>
> I therefore beg leave to move that, henceforth, prayers imploring the assistance of Heaven and its blessing on our deliberation be held in this assembly every morning before we proceed to business.[10]

Franklin's motion failed because someone pointed out that the convention had no money to pay a chaplain. But a motion by Edmund Randolph of Virginia that "a sermon be preached at the request of the Convention on the Fourth of July" went through quickly. During the three-day recess many of the delegates, including Washington, went to a special service at the Calvinist church. After the oration by a young law student, the minister of the church, the Reverend William Rogers, prayed for the delegates that God would "be their wisdom and strength [and] enable them to devise such measures as may prove happy instruments in healing all divisions."[11]

Rogers' prayers were answered, for under Washington's careful shepherding, the convention soon thereafter reached the harmonious compromises that gave us the Constitution of the United States. The Union was assured.

James Madison, not given to Christian exuberance, wrote to Thomas Jefferson in Paris that "it is impossible to conceive the degree of concord which ultimately prevailed, as less than a miracle."[12] The following year he and New Yorkers Alexander Hamilton and John Jay would author the *Federalist Papers*, explaining the new Constitution to the people of New York State in an attempt to persuade them to ratify it. Remarking on the astonishing resolution of the convention's conflicts, Madison wrote: "It is impossible for the man of pious reflection not to perceive in it [the Constitution] a finger of the Almighty hand which has been so frequently and signally extended to our relief in the critical stages of the Revolution."

"We the People of the United States . . ." Thus begins what has become the oldest written constitution still in effect today. William Gladstone, one of Britain's great prime ministers, called it "the most wonderful work ever struck off at a given time by the brain and purpose of man."[13] Legal minds of more than two centuries have continued to marvel at it as being almost beyond the scope and dimension of human wisdom. When one stops to consider the enormous problems the Constitution of the United States of America somehow anticipated and the challenges and tests it foresaw, that statement appears more understated than exaggerated. Not even the combined collective genius of the fledgling nation could claim credit for the fantastic strength, resilience, balance, and timelessness of the Constitution. And most of them knew it.

The proof of its magnitude is how well it works—better than its framers ever dared hope. In a number of recent controversies, the world has seen just how well the intricate system of built-in checks and balances—and its awesome self-cleansing ability—works. Through due process of law, the body politic purges itself—so smoothly and effectively that many of us take it for granted.

Why does it work so well? Aside from the Divine origin of its inspiration, the Constitution was the culmination of nearly two hundred years of Puritan political thought. The earliest church covenants started with the basic, underlying assumption central to their faith: the sinfulness of humanity's fallen nature, in which "dwells no good thing." That may appear depressingly negative to anyone who wants to believe in the innate goodness of man. But the fact is, it is only depressing to someone who has not yet learned the full reality of the truth that Jesus Christ came to save sinners and that only He can be our righteousness.

As we have seen, the Puritans were anything but joyless, no matter how certain modernists would like to paint them. They were, nonetheless, absolute realists about the sinful nature of human beings when they are not allowing the Spirit of Christ to operate within them. The Puritans calmly anticipated the possibility of the very worst happening in their church and civil governments, and they planned accordingly, so that when the worst occasionally did occur, the blockage, rather than the system, would be eliminated.

The Constitution was conceived and framed on exactly this principle. The *Federalist Papers* revealed that the Constitution was based on the assumption that "the primary political motive of man was self-interest, and that men, whether acting individually or collectively, were selfish and only imperfectly rational."[14]

In *Paper #10* Madison focused on the chief obstacle inherent in the democratic system—"a factious spirit":

> There are two methods of curing the mischief of faction: the one, by removing the causes; the other by controlling its effects.

434

There are again two methods of removing the causes of faction: the one, by destroying the liberty which is essential to its existence; the other, by giving to every citizen the same opinions, the same passions, and the same interests.

It could never be more truly said than of the first remedy that it was worse than the disease. Liberty is to faction what air is to fire, an element without which it instantly expires. But it could not be less folly to abolish liberty, which is essential to political life, because it nourishes faction, than it would be to wish the annihilation of air, which is essential to animal life, because it imparts to fire its destructive agency.

The second expedient is as impracticable as the first would be unwise. As long as the reason of man continues fallible, and he is at liberty to exercise it, different opinions will be formed. As long as the connection subsists between his reason and his self-love, his opinions and his passions will have a reciprocal influence on each other. . . . The latent causes of faction are thus sown in the nature of man.[15]

The alternative to removing the causes of faction was to control its effects, and this was what the Constitution was all about. In contrast, all totalitarian governments—whether Nazi, Communist, or Islamic—always attempt to remove the causes of faction by removing liberty and, as much as possible, freedom of thought. And through intensive indoctrination of the young, they also attempt to impose a sameness of opinion.

In American life in the early seventeenth century, the cause of faction was much reduced because so many people sincerely wanted the will of God to prevail. A community of people trying to find God's will tended to create agreement among themselves. Hence there was the dynamic tension of a general uniformity of opinion, while at the same time the liberty always existed to choose one's independence over the will of God.

The Constitution, this institutionalizing of the covenant's legacy, was constructed on the realistic and scriptural assumption that the natural self-interest and self-love of man had to be checked. The checks and balances were ingenious: there would be three separate branches of government—legislative, executive, and judicial. The legislative branch would make the laws, but the executive branch had the power to veto. The executive branch appointed the members of the Supreme Court, but the appointments were subject to the approval of the legislative branch. On the other hand, these appointments were for life, where the other two branches were subject to frequent elections.

There are many more examples, but the amazing thing is how smoothly such an elaborately interwoven and interdependent system works. And (aside from God's grace and inspiration) it works for one reason: it begins with an acceptance of what the Puritans termed "the utter depravity of man."

By contrast, less than two years later another revolution would take place, this one also by a people desiring to rule their own lives in a free and democratic society. The difference was that the French Revolution was based on the "enlightened" philosophy of the Age of Reason. Popularized by Voltaire and Rousseau, who emphasized the supposed innate goodness of man, it correspondingly de-emphasized the need for dependence on God or the redemption of Christ.

And what did the French Revolution produce? A democracy, to be sure—in the beginning. But it almost immediately devolved into a Reign of Terror, the likes of which for sheer rapaciousness and cruelty, has seldom been seen in the history of man.

In recent times it has become commonplace to hear America referred to as a democracy. We are not a democracy—or government by the ma- jority—we are a republic. America's system of government is based not on the whims and passions of men, unchecked by law, but on constitutional laws that protect the rights of individuals and minorities.

The Founding Fathers were clear-eyed about the dangers of "moboc- racy," as they called it. John Adams spoke for all of them when he said: "Democracy will soon degenerate into . . . such an anarchy that every man will do what is right in his own eyes, and no man's life or property or reputation or liberty will be secure. . . . Democracy never lasts long. It soon wastes, exhausts, and murders itself. There never was a democracy yet that did not commit suicide."[16]

But to agnostics and atheists who have no Redeemer, no Savior, no Comforter, no source of grace or forgiveness or Providential intervention, the concept of utter depravity is so threatening that they have to believe in the basic goodness of man—or go into despair. Such people simply blind themselves to the bankruptcy of their philosophy and go through life carefully avoiding a head-on confrontation with reality, all the while affirming the nobility of "the Brotherhood of Man."

Such a person was Thomas Jefferson, who was so blind to the forces being unleashed by the French Revolution that in a letter from France he would glowingly write, "The mass possesses such a degree of good sense as to enable them to decide well." In this he was diametrically opposed by the realist Alexander Hamilton, who said, "Take mankind in general, they are vicious."[17]

The new Rationalism, or Enlightenment, of the Age of Reason soon found its way into the most fashionable salons on this side of the Atlantic, and preachers such as Dwight and Witherspoon became gravely concerned, particularly since the epidemic seemed to be gaining a foothold on their respective campuses. But many other ministers were actually duped by its subtle blandishments, as it flattered the ego by exalting the intellect.

Why did the explosion of this false light progress so rapidly? Puritan tradition in America had put great emphasis on the importance of a well-trained and disciplined mind—albeit as a tool to be placed at God's disposal and totally submitted to His will and glory. The first two colleges in America, Harvard and Yale, were founded in order to give future American ministers an education equal to those hitherto obtainable only at Oxford and Cambridge. The ministers were further encouraged to continue their studies after college, for the one thing the Puritans despised was a "dumb dog" of a clergyman in the pulpit.

But without the strong awareness of the dangers of self-righteousness, the intellect can easily become an instrument for the glorification of self, not God. Many ministers began to be led astray into Enlightenment thinking. Indeed, things got to the point that in some ministerial circles it became rather naïve and even primitive to think of God in such intensely intimate and personal terms as had been the case in the Great Awakening prior to the War for Independence. The "French Infidelity" caught on quickly, and a number of ministers became the unwitting progenitors of rational Deism. They had forgotten what the Puritans had known so well: that ultimately it was not the mind but the will that mattered—the willingness to put down one's own will for God's will.

And so, for the first time, the ministers lost touch with the people. For the better part of two centuries they had provided the spiritual, moral, and intellectual leadership for the nation. Now that mantle had passed to statesmen, politicians, educators, publishers, and prominent laymen. The nation was spiritually adrift, and the ministers had no one to blame but themselves.

The people, however, still retained enough of a relationship with the Lord to know when their hearts were not being reached. And the people stayed away from church in droves. In 1788 when the ministers of Connecticut published a rebuke to the people for the neglect of their worship, the newspapers spoke some strong truth to the ministers in a reply on their editorial pages. "We have heard your animadversions upon our absence from Sabbath meetings," said the New Haven *Gazette*, "and we humbly conceive that if you wish our attendance there, you would make it worth our while to give it. To miss a sermon of the present growth, what is it but to miss an opiate? And can the loss of a nap expose our souls to eternal perdition?"[18]

This attitude was symptomatic of the general feeling throughout the land. There were still many sermons about the Kingdom of God being established in America, but relatively few were dealing bluntly with what that Kingdom was going to cost personally. The problem was that the ministers themselves were no longer willing to pay the price. At the moment when the Light that had overcome the darkness in America should have been at its brightest, ready to burst into glory, it was beginning to dim. America had been complacent before—or affluent or self-reliant or greedy—but never had she been so adrift from her spiritual moorings.

The Constitution, however, was her safeguard. For the surprising truth about it is that it is nothing less than the institutional guardian of the covenant way of life for the nation as a whole. More than two centuries later, it still guarantees the possibility of reentering our covenant with God as a nation, whenever we might choose to do so. As long as the Constitution with its attendant Bill of Rights (for example, Article I: "Congress shall make no law respecting an establishment of religion, or prohibiting the free exercise thereof") remains the law of the land, the choice will still be there.

The Constitution is the finest contract ever drawn by man for his own self-government. But as precious as the Constitution is, it is nonetheless a secularizing of the spiritual reality of the covenant. It can thus never be the substitute for a national covenant life under the lordship of God. There is an enormous difference between the two, as Richard Niebuhr points out: "Contract always implies limited [commitment], covenant unlimited commitment. Contract is entered into for the sake of mutual advantages; covenant implies the presence of a cause to which all advantages may need to be sacrificed."[19]

With the Constitution in place, America was ready to consider who should be her first President. The obvious candidate was already so popular that even those who jealously sought to tear him down dared not provoke the public's wrath by saying much against him. When the electors from the thirteen states gathered, only one name commanded the respect of the States-Rightists as well as the Federalists. It mattered not to them that he sincerely did not want the honor and only wanted to be left in peace. No other name was put forward, and an express rider was sent to Mount Vernon to request George Washington's presence.

A visit to Mount Vernon at the end of April when the dogwoods are in full bloom is a memorable experience. It is a beautiful and well-cared-for estate, with outbuildings in good repair, pointing up the traditional conservative lines of the main house. But from the moment one sets foot on the long brick walk, one is struck by the incredible sense of peace about the place. If it is possible to tell anything of a someone's personality from the feel of his home, then this was the home of a someone who was perfectly at rest in his inner self.

Spacious and graceful, it is complete with a small formal garden and a greenhouse for experiments with growing oranges and peppers and other exotic plants. Blending harmoniously as it does with its natural surroundings, Mount Vernon reflects a heart in tune with its Creator. Standing on the porch with its tall colonnade, gazing out over the smooth green lawn and the swaying willows to the peaceful Potomac, one might conclude that this was God's gift to an obedient servant and that Washington appreciated it as such.

But "to whom much is given, of him much will be required" (Luke 12:48). When the messenger from the Electoral College arrived, Washington sighed and went in to pack the appropriate attire.

He reached New York in time to be inaugurated on April 30, 1789. Prior to the ceremony he had requested that a Bible be obtained for the swearing-in. Now, stepping out onto the outdoor balcony of Federal Hall in full view of the assembled multitude, he placed his right hand on the open book and took the oath of office. Then, embarrassed at the thunderous ovation that followed, the pealing church bells, and the roaring of artillery, the new President went inside to deliver his Inaugural Address to Congress.

Speaking with a gravity befitting the heavy responsibility he had just undertaken, he stressed the role of God in the birth of the nation:

> It would be peculiarly improper to omit, in this first official act, my fervent supplication to that Almighty Being, who rules over the universe, who presides in the councils of nations, and whose providential aids can supply every human defect, that His benediction may consecrate to the liberties and happiness of the people of the United States. . . . No people can be bound to acknowledge and adore the invisible hand which conducts the affairs of men more than the people of the United States. Every step by which they have advanced to the character of an independent nation seems to have been distinguished by some token of providential agency. . . . We ought to be no less persuaded that the propitious smiles of Heaven can never be expected on a nation that disregards the eternal rules of order and right, which Heaven itself has ordained.[20]

The next eight years saw the sober, prayerful judgment of this leader imparted to the beginnings of the new nation. Thanks to God, the United States was getting off on the right step.

But there was another spirit rising in those first eight years, a spirit which was a further refinement of the new rationalism. It held that while Christianity had certainly played its part, it was most definitely not the sole wellspring of morality that devout Christians claimed. Indeed, it had exerted entirely too much influence on the running of the country and the affairs of its citizens. When this spirit cried out for the separation of Church and State (which were already separated), what it was really calling for was a drastic deemphasis of religion's public influence in national life. Orthodox Christianity was no longer regarded as advisable or necessary, for it called people to believe in myths, and thus it had no right to a major role in the shaping of their lives. If some people wanted to indulge in it, that was their own business, but other people should not have to be exposed to it.

The person who came to personify this attitude also came from Virginia, from an estate three days' ride from Mount Vernon. It was an estate which was also beautiful in its way—an exquisite monument to the intellect of its owner, Thomas Jefferson. As Washington's Secretary of State and later as President, Jefferson was careful to conceal his rationalism and never commit himself publicly on the subject of Christianity, beyond stating that in his opinion Christ was the greatest moralist who had ever lived. For, as modern historian Russell Kirk points out, "were his rejection of Christ as supernatural Redeemer fully known, he and his party would be in deep difficulty with popular opinion."[21]

It was what Jefferson did not say that gave his position away. Those ministers who were still in close touch with the Lord and still had an appreciation of His call upon the nation were incensed that Jefferson would be given such national responsibility. None was more outspoken than Timothy Dwight, whom Jefferson's inner circle sarcastically referred to as "the pope in New Haven."

The battle lines were drawn: throughout the country there were religious leaders who believed with Dwight that "where there is no religion [meaning Christianity], there is no morality" and that "with the loss of religion . . . the ultimate foundation of confidence is blown up, and the security of life, liberty and property buried in ruins."[22]

On the other hand, the movement around Jefferson maintained that human beings had progressed to the point where they could be responsible for their own morality, without the benefit of an intrusive, restrictive, narrow-minded religion. The rationalists would affect a posture of marvelous toleration. As Puritan Nathaniel Ward said,

"Nothing is easier than to tolerate when you do not seriously believe that differences matter."[23]

Jefferson's true feelings finally came to light with the posthumous publication of his personal correspondence. Here he revealed himself to be a private champion of Unitarianism, who, during his term in the office of President, compiled the "Jefferson Bible." This was a retelling of the story of Jesus, pointedly leaving out every reference to the miraculous or the divine origin of the Savior. His purpose:

> The establishment of the innocent and genuine character of this benevolent moralist, and the rescuing it from the imputation of imposture, which has resulted from artificial systems invented by ultra-Christian sects, e.g., the immaculate conception of Jesus, his deification, the creation of the world by him, his miraculous powers, his resurrection and visible ascension, his corporal presence in the Eucharist, the Trinity, original sin, atonement, regeneration, election, orders of Hierarchy, etc.[24]

Since such a list includes practically every tenet of the Christian faith, what Jefferson was really calling for was an end to orthodox Christianity.

Unitarianism was just coming into being, and as he confidentially wrote to Benjamin Waterhouse, "That doctrine [Unitarianism] has not yet been preached here to us [in Charlottesville], but the breeze begins to be felt which precedes the storm, and fanaticism is all in a bustle, shutting its doors to keep it out." In Boston, however, Jefferson would write to Thomas Cooper, "Unitarianism has advanced to so great strength as now to humble this haughtiest of all religious sects [Presbyterianism]." And finally, in one of his last letters, he would write to Waterhouse: "I rejoice that in this blessed country of free inquiry and belief, which has surrendered its creed and conscience to neither kings nor priests, the genuine doctrine of only one God is reviving, and I trust there is not a young man now living in the United States who will not die a Unitarian."

Why such concern about describing exactly where Jefferson really stood? Because he was greatly responsible for initiating the de-emphasis of religion in public life that has gained much momentum in our time. For Jefferson's refusal to accept that morality not only stems from Christianity but cannot long exist without it—is reflected with mirrorlike verisimilitude today.

The conflict finally embroiled even Washington. For eight years our first President had been led to preserve the dignity of his office by refusing to get entangled in the gut-level fighting that was going on, permitting himself to comment on it only upon the occasion of his leaving office. In his farewell address, Washington said: "Of all the dispositions and habits which lead to political prosperity, Religion and Morality are indispensable supports. . . . And let us with caution indulge the supposition that morality can be maintained without religion. . . . reason and experience both forbid us to expect that national morality can prevail in exclusion of religious principle."[25]

Washington's successor to the Presidency, John Adams, would go on record with a clear statement about the importance of religion and morality to American life. In an address to the Massachusetts militia in 1798, he warned: "We have no government capable of contending with human passions unbridled by morality and religion. Avarice, ambition, revenge . . . would break the strongest cords of our Constitution as a whale goes through a net. Our Constitution was made for only a moral and religious people. It is wholly inadequate to the government of any other."[26]

A generation later, the great French historian Alexis de Tocqueville would spend a year traveling in the United States and would confirm Adams's statement with this observation: "I do not know whether all Americans have a sincere faith in their religion—for who can search the human heart—but I am certain that they hold it to be indispensable to the maintenance of republican institutions."[27]

George Washington's last day in office did not involve the ordeal of public ceremonies that was required at his leave-taking as Commander in Chief of the Continental Army; nonetheless, it was a day of honor for the retiring President. For he was voluntarily laying down the reins of power—an immensely honorable gesture of self-denial. Like the Roman hero Cincinnatus, to whom he was often compared, he had saved the republic in war and was now finally retiring to his farm.

It would have been easy for Washington to continue on into a third term; many had begged him to do it, and the people would certainly have re-elected him. But he was sixty-four years old now and tired. The Presidency had taken a tremendous physical and emotional toll. Perhaps he also sensed that his Maker would soon be calling him home, and he wanted to see one more spring and summer come to his beloved estate on the Potomac.

He had just come from the swearing-in ceremonies at Congress Hall, where John Adams had taken the oath of office and then delivered a moving Inaugural Address. Washington had stopped by his quarters to clear his desk before paying the new President a visit at his rooms in the Francis Hotel. There is no account of these last moments at his desk, but from what we know of the man and the circumstances surrounding his departure, it is not difficult to imagine them.

On his desk were drafts of the last two personal letters he had written as President—to Henry Knox, offering his condolences on the death of three of his children, and to his friend Jonathan Trumbull who, as Governor of Connecticut, had once raised nine companies of riflemen in response to the General's urgent personal appeal. Also on his desk was a large pile of letters from friends and well-wishers and some clipped-out editorials. Most of them were full of praise, except for a vitriolic attack by Tom Paine, who had done his best to smear the reputation of the departing President and hence the Federalists, which Washington and Adams and Hamilton had led.

It was only politics, Washington might have told himself. But Paine's comments hurt, as they were intended to, and the General knew that there was more to them than just politics. Paine had privately asked him for the job of Postmaster General, and when Washington, after much consideration, had turned him down as not sufficiently qualified, Paine had flown into a rage, calling him "treacherous in private friendship and a hypocrite in public life."[28] The public did not know that and would not, unless Washington chose to reveal it. If he were to expose what lay behind Paine's vicious personal attack on him, the latter's career as a pamphleteer and editorialist might well be finished.

Washington merely shook his head and looked out the window. In another month the dogwoods would be out at Mount Vernon, he might have mused. Or perhaps he prayed and commended the nation into the hands of the God who had shepherded them so amazingly to this point. Then, slowly and stiffly, he got up from the familiar desk, gathered the papers into a letter case, took a last look around, and left.

Outside he did not seem to notice the handful of people, waiting at a respectful distance, as he turned and headed down Chestnut Street toward the Francis Hotel. The people followed discreetly behind him without speaking. Others joined them as they recognized the tall, slightly bent figure, until by the time he reached his destination, there was a sizable throng assembled. On the steps of the hotel, he turned and took note of them standing there, from all trades and all walks of life. They said not a word, but as he noted how many eyes were glistening with tears, his own suddenly brimmed. He bowed silently and quickly went inside.[29]

"Good-bye, Mr. President," someone called after him. "God bless you!"

THE SEARCH ENDS

Two years after Washington assumed the Presidency, a Southern Method-ist preacher named Francis Aspinwall made a pilgrimage to New England, where the groundwork of God's "New Israel" had first been laid.

> I rode over rocks and hills, and came to Wilton. . . . My horse is very small, and my carriage inconvenient in such rocky, uneven, jolting ways. . . . We are now in Connecticut, and never out of sight of a house. . . . I do feel as if there had been religion in this country once, and I apprehend there a little form and theory left. There may have been a praying ministry and people there, but I fear they are now dead.[1]

"America, America, God shed His grace on thee." From the very be-ginning God did abundantly answer this nineteenth-century prayer that we have sung so often. There is no way to measure how much the grace that God has poured out on this nation is a direct result of the obedience and sacrifice of those first Franciscan and Dominican missionaries, the Jesuit martyrs, and the earliest generations of nameless Americans who chose the Covenant Way.

Yet even as God's grace continued, spiritual sloth began to encase our hearts, to the point where we took His grace so much for granted that we made a joke of it: "God looks after fools, drunks, and the United States." In the face of such callous indifference, God could not go on blessing us indefinitely, and now the grace has begun to lift. Francis Aspinwall's summation of Connecticut in 1791 could well apply to the nation today.

The opening pages of this book mentioned some social indicators of the lifting of God's grace—the holocaust of abortion, the rapidly decaying moral fabric of our public and private lives, the attacks on traditional marriage, and the disintegration of the American family. The recent increase and intensity of natural disasters seem to bear further witness to it. Earthquakes, floods, droughts, hurricanes, tornadoes, and raging forest fires—if one were to view them with the benefit of time-lapse photography, it would be difficult not to conclude that God had a controversy with all humankind, and especially America.

Since the first Christian settlers entered into covenant with Him, God has called the people of this country to be "a City set on a Hill." Due to our repeated betrayal of this covenant, it should hardly come as a surprise that His dealings with America have now become more severe. Yet even in the midst of judgment, God shows His mercy. For while He does deal with His people more strictly than with others, He does not reject them. When He enters a covenant, it is forever. The promises that He made to the early comers to this "New Israel" remain intact and unmodified, though a far greater amendment of our lives is now required to fulfill our end of the bargain.

For a whole nation to return to the Covenant Way seems impossible. But it is not impossible; it has been done before. We have the Old Testament example of Nineveh to prove it. The biggest and most powerful city of its age had reached such a state of corruption that God was on the verge of destroying it, as He had Sodom and Gomorrah. But through His reluctant prophet Jonah, He gave the people of Nineveh one last chance. If they would repent, God would stay His hand. The Ninevehites believed Jonah and repented. The entire city, from its simplest inhabitants to its most sophisticated, left their old ways—and were spared.

We are not saying that America has arrived at the Nineveh point—yet. Indeed, our demise may be a more gradual, drawn-out affair, to allow us as much time as possible to repent. Or it may not. If God continues to lift His grace, it will not be long before we will be in a state of chaos very much of our own making. Whether the end comes with a bang or a whimper, we seem to be approaching a national point of no return, beyond which it will be too late for America to turn back.

Yet such is God's mercy that He does not require the whole nation to repent. It is enough if only the Christians, those who truly know Him, will do this. Most of us are well familiar with His admonition in 2 Chronicles 7:14: "if my people who are called by my name humble themselves, and pray and seek my face, and turn from their wicked ways, then I will hear from heaven, and will forgive their sin and heal their land." We are so familiar, in fact, that we do not really hear its meaning. Many of us believe that we are already living according to its dictates. Yet do we take them to the deepest level? Are we battling pride, self, and ego, as the early Pilgrims and Puritans did when they strove to go the Covenant Way?

Consider this possible amplification from God's perspective:

> If my people—those in covenant with me—will humble themselves, then it will not be necessary for me to humble them.
>
> If they will pray—from the depths of their heart, truly wanting to find me—then I will hear them.
>
> If they will seek my face—not glory and rewards for themselves—then they shall find me.
>
> If they will then turn from their wicked ways—the public ones and the hidden ones—then I will forgive their sin.
>
> But I cannot forgive that which is not repented of, so each of you must allow me to search the darkest corners of your heart.
>
> Only in this way will I heal your land.

Many had hoped that electing a Christian President would do the job. But as Dwight Eisenhower once said, "Never let yourself be persuaded that any one Great Man, any one leader, is necessary to the salvation of America. When America consists of one leader and 158 million followers, it will no longer be America."[2] We are now well over 300 million, so Eisenhower's point is even stronger. It is the most dangerous kind of corporate self-delusion to think that a President, regardless of how much he or she heeds God, can reverse the bent of the national will once it is set in a certain direction. And when it becomes apparent that a single person cannot do so, that person and that person's faith will become the scapegoat.

All of which seems to put the responsibility squarely upon each of us who has a personal relationship with our Savior, even though we would prefer to blame the immorality of others for the precipitous rate of decline. The responsibility is ours, and it always has been. When Solomon Stoddard once challenged Increase Mather on this very point, pointing out that the covenanted Christians in seventeenth-century New England were only a fraction of the population, Mather retorted that, nonetheless, that fraction was sufficient to "stand for the entire land" and "redeem the whole."[3]

There is a new move of the Spirit of God abroad in our land now, full of promise and encouragement and new life in Christ. In response to it, Christian roots of excitement and enthusiasm are shooting out laterally in all directions. Yet while these feeder roots are vital to rapid growth, what is now desperately needed is a simultaneous deepening of the taproot. For without it, the first great storms of tribulation are going to wreak a terrible destruction.

Jesus said, "I am the way, and the truth, and the life" (John 14:6). The Christian walk begins with the discovery that He *is* the way. Through Bible study and good teaching, the believer next learns that He is the truth. Yet our Lord does not intend us to stop there but to move on into the third phase of our walk, the daily experience of Him as our life. This third phase, which so many Christians are loath to enter into, is the one that develops the taproot.

Why do many Christians resist moving into a deeper relationship with Christ? Because deepening our life in Christ means going the Way of the Cross: the way of self-denial—of unconditional surrender of one's own will to God's will and of true covenant commitment to one another. This is the way to which He has called all serious Christians: "If any man would come after me, let him deny himself and take up his cross daily and follow me" (Luke 9:23). From everything that our Christian experience teaches us, it is the only way to spiritual maturity.

It also is the only way that we Christians can yet fulfill our nation's call. Individually—and corporately—we need to reenter the covenant relationship that our forebears had with God and one another.

As we have seen, the vertical aspect of the Covenant Way requires that we all consider ourselves to be soldiers in Christ's army, to be deployed when and where He directs, for whatever purpose He might have.

Our ancestors, from the Pilgrims and Puritans to those who resisted the tyranny of George III, understood that the call on our nation was a call to both personal and corporate freedom in Christ. "For freedom Christ has set us free; stand fast therefore, and do not submit again to a yoke of slavery" (Gal. 5:1). They also understood that this freedom was not license to do as they pleased but freedom to do as God pleased. In short, they chose to live by what we, their modern descendants, have tended to ignore—Paul's strong warning to the Galatians a dozen verses further on: "Do not use your freedom as an opportunity for the flesh, but through love be servants of one another. For the whole law is fulfilled in one word, 'You shall love your neighbor as yourself'" (Gal. 5:13–14).

In other words, the true measure of our commitment to Christ is demonstrated in the horizontal aspect of our covenant: How willing are we Christians to be servants of one another? Enough to become deeply involved in others' lives? To have them involved in ours? How much do we really care about our neighbors—at home, at work, or at church?

Sad to say, most of us do not care that much. Even where our fellow Christians are involved, we prize our personal independence too much to truly get involved with them. And yet, if we are ever to break out of our self-centeredness and become Christ-centered members of one body, this is what we must do. We must covenant with one another in a practical way—husband and wife, prayer partners, co-workers—to be open and honest with one another and to care enough for one another to help each other grow out of self and mature in Christ.

For in Christ, we are called to be our brothers' and sisters' keepers—to walk and live in openness and honesty with one another. As the Apostle John said, "If we say we have fellowship with Him, while we walk in darkness, we lie and do not live according to the truth; but if we walk in the light as He is in the light, we have fellowship with one another, and the blood of Jesus his Son cleanses us from all sin" (1 John 1:6–7).

The Pilgrims knew the value of becoming one body. With the Mayflower Compact they chose to relinquish their individual independence. As a covenanted people, they not only survived but established our basic American spiritual and civil institutions. The first Puritans knew it, too; the very survival of their little towns depended upon the depth of their covenant relationship with one another. And surely this was what God was doing at Valley Forge when He forged an army out of a disintegrating band of independent individuals.

In our hearts we, too, know that God has called us Christians to a horizontal as well as vertical covenant. But the price—of turning from our independent ways, of being willing to hear God speak to us through the lips of others, of exposing the hidden sins of attitude or thought, of humbling ourselves by admitting where we are wrong—is more than most of us care to pay.

Thus it was for many of the second-generation Pilgrims, too, as they broke covenant and moved away—and deeply wounded Governor Bradford's heart in the process. Later, many of the Half-Way Covenanted Puritans were forcibly reminded by King Philip's War of how far they had strayed from their commitment. And a century later, the states' refusal to relinquish their independence nearly aborted the birth of our national republic.

"United we stand" is one of our nation's mottos, and "Out of many, one" is another. They ring with truth, only because the first Americans were willing to pay the price.

So we modern Christians must humble ourselves and renew the horizontal as well as the vertical aspect of our covenant with God. If we do this, He will hear, and forgive our sins, and heal our land.

It can still happen. Our forebears have broken trail for us and shown the way. Their call is our call. If just a fraction of us Americans choose to go the Covenant Way, it will suffice. Then each of our lives will be filled with the Light of Him who said, "I am the light of the world." And if the candlepower of each covenanted Christian will be joined to the whole, the result will truly be the blaze of glory that John Adams foresaw.

APPENDIX ONE

THE MYSTERY OF
THE LOST COLONY

*T*he actual fate of the Roanoke Colony remains one of America's enduring mysteries. Counting the three men who were abandoned when Sir Francis Drake took Ralph Lane's settlers home, the fifteen-man garrison that Sir Richard Grenville left on Roanoke, and the colonists who remained behind when John White sailed for England in 1587, more than 120 English men, women, and children had been deposited on the wild, windswept shores of North Carolina.

In 1605 Ben Johnson's play *Eastward Hoe* (see chapter 6) opened in London. Speaking of those left behind, one character declares: "A whole country of English is there, bred of those who were left. They had intermarried with the Indians and make them bring forth as beautiful faces as any have in England."[1] While there were only rumors to support this conjecture, the mystery has been kept alive for four centuries by tantalizing scraps of information.

The intermarriage theory gained credence when George Percy, who had come to Jamestown with Newport in 1607, reported that he had caught a glimpse of "a savage boy, about the age of ten years, which had a head of hair of a perfect yellow and a reasonably white skin, which is a miracle amongst savages."[2]

If we can believe the stories of Captain John Smith, the most plausible explanation about the fate of the lost colonists was related by the wily old chief Powhatan, which Smith in turn privately relayed to King James, omitting it from his *True Relation*. According to Powhatan, not long after John White had departed, the remaining Roanoke settlers moved north, to the southern shores of Chesapeake Bay, near the Indian village of Skicoac. The Chesapeake Indians, the only tribe in those parts that had not submitted to Powhatan, welcomed them as allies in their ongoing struggles with that chief, and for twenty years they lived at peace among them.

There is, however, a problem with Powhatan's story. If it is true, why was CROATOAN carved in the tree?

Powhatan apparently also admitted to Smith that he had ordered his men to slaughter the Chesapeake and the English shortly before Newport's landing in the spring of 1607. Though Smith was never able to ascertain exactly what had happened to the settlers, he was shown "a musket barrel and a bronze mortar and certain pieces of iron which had been theirs."

As possible corroboration, several years later Colonial Secretary William Strachey discovered after his arrival at Jamestown in 1609 that "the men, women and children of the first plantation at Roanoke were by practice and commandment of Powhatan . . . miserably slaughtered without any offence given him."[3]

The English were later able to date the attack within a few days of Newport's arrival on April 27, 1607; indeed, it may well have been the sighting of his approaching sails that triggered the massacre. Powhatan's priests had previously told him "that from the Chesapeake Bay a nation should arise which should dissolve and give end to his empire." Perhaps Powhatan concluded that he should attack and destroy the Chesapeake Indians and their English friends before the arriving English could land enough reinforcements to fulfill the prophecy. As Strachey put it, "he destroyed and put to the sword all such who might lie under any doubtful construction of the said prophecy."[4]

Some of the English must have escaped, however, because the Virginia Company's 1608 pamphlet, *A True and Sincere Declaration*, claimed that "some of our nation, planted by Sir Walter Ralegh, [are] yet alive, within fifty miles of our fort." The first search party from Jamestown may have come close to finding them, but it was stopped by Indians. "Though denied by the savages speech with them, [they] found crosses and letters, the characters and assured testimonies of Christians cut in the barks of trees."[5]

Rumors of survivors persisted in England, for the Company's 1609 instructions to Sir Thomas Gates included the information that at a village called Pakerikanick, near the Chowan River, "you will find four of the English alive, left by Sir Walter Rawley, which escaped from the slaughter of Powhatan." They were held captive by "a weroance named Gepanocon, by whose consent you will never recover them," because the chief had discovered a source of copper and was forcing the English prisoners to help him forge it into weapons and utensils.[6]

By the time Gates finally arrived at Jamestown in 1610, the colony's situation had grown so desperate that the information was never acted upon. A later search party into the interior, consisting of one Indian chief and two Englishmen, was told that there were "four men clothed" that had originally come from Roanoke, but the search was broken off before they could find anything.

Strachey, who arrived at Jamestown in 1609, had diligently tried to track down the rumors. A friendly Indian named Machumps assured him that there were indeed survivors from Roanoke, and that Indians southwest of Chesapeake Bay had timbered houses built with stone walls, one story above another, "so taught them by those English." He added that in addition to the four massacre survivors held by Gepanocon there were others. "At Ritanoe the weroance Eyanoco preserved seven of the English alive, four men, two boys and one young maid, escaped and fled up the river of Choanoke, to beat his copper, of which he hath certain mines at the said Ritanoe."[7]

Few subsequent attempts were made, none to any avail, as the main preoccupation was now the sheer survival of the Jamestown colony. In

1622 John Smith seemed to write the epitaph for the search attempts when he wrote that thirty-five years after John White left Roanoke, "we left seeking our colony, that was never any of them found, nor seen to this day."[8]

There it rested until 1701. While visiting the Outer Banks, a naturalist by the name of John Lawson related that coastal Indians had told him that "several of their ancestors were white people and could talk in a book [read], as we do; the truth of which is confirmed by gray eyes being found frequently amongst these Indians, and no others."[9]

In the latter part of the nineteenth century, North Carolinians noted that many Indians in the southeastern part of the state were light-skinned with pale eyes and bore surnames matching those of the Roanoke colonists. The state legislature designated them as Croatan Indians in 1885 and afforded them slightly better status than other nonwhites.[10]

No definitive information has emerged since then, but just when most historians were thinking that the case was closed, in 1998 an Elizabethan gold signet ring was dug up in the soil near the site of Manteo's village. The mystery of the Lost Colony is still unsolved.

APPENDIX TWO

THE CHRISTIAN FAITH
OF GEORGE WASHINGTON

*T*hree decades of subsequent research into the spirituality of America's first President have confirmed our original conclusion: George Washington was not a Deist but a practicing and thoroughly orthodox Christian. This brief appendix is intended merely to offer additional evidence of his Christianity to that already noted in the text.

Washington's Christianity is not easily discerned—not only because he was a typically restrained eighteenth-century Virginia Anglican but also because of his intense desire not to speak openly about himself on any subject.

His mother, Mary Ball Washington, was a devout Christian who read the Bible to her son and taught him by example and word the importance and efficacy of prayer.

In the first edition of this book, the authors quoted from prayers supposedly written by Washington in his own handwriting, entitled "Daily Sacrifice." They had turned up in Philadelphia in 1891, among various items offered for auction by Washington's descendants. These prayers, written in orthodox Christian language, seemed to offer proof of Washington's Christianity, since Deists did not adhere to the Biblical beliefs expressed in them. Historians have subsequently proved, however, that Washington could not have written these particular prayers, since neither the handwriting nor the writing style matches his.[1] So the authors have not included them in this second edition.

The fact that George Washington didn't write those prayers has no bearing on the question of whether he was a man of prayer. He was. There are more than a hundred written prayers in his public and private letters. And although a certain number of the public prayers were drafted by aides, Washington would never have signed or uttered any of them unless he agreed with their sentiments, which were often explicitly Christian.

Moreover, Washington often added prayers to the letters drawn up by his aides. Alexander Hamilton's draft of a letter for Washington's signature to the Comte de Rochambeau on February 26, 1781, stated: "This repetition of advices justifies a confidence in their truth." To which the General added, "which I pray God may be confirmed in its greatest extent."[2]

A reliable testimony to Washington's personal prayer life comes from a letter from General Lewis of Augusta County, Virginia, dated December 14, 1855, relating a conversation with former Continental Army General Robert Porterfield shortly before his death. In recounting some of his experiences during the New Jersey campaign and the army's crucible of suffering at Valley Forge, Porterfield said that his duties as a brigade inspector brought him in frequent contact with General Washington. In an emergency he had once gone directly to Washington's lodgings and found him on his knees in prayer. When he mentioned this to Alexander Hamilton, the General's aide replied that "such was his constant habit."[3]

This was a habit that Washington acquired early in his life. E. C. M'Guire's early 1800s biography of Washington, written when some of his sources were still alive, quotes the recollections of Colonel B. Temple, an aide to Washington during the French and Indian War. Temple told M'Guire that in the absence of a chaplain, Washington would read the Bible to his troops and lead in prayer, adding that "on sudden and unexpected visits into his [Washington's] marquee, he has, more than once, found him on his knees at his devotions."[4]

Washington's extensive knowledge of the Bible and his frequent use of Biblical phrases are strong evidence of his Christianity. In a personal letter to the Marquis de Lafayette (whom Washington loved as a son), he made seven separate references to Biblical passages. This was pure Washington— no aide wrote it. Another letter, this one to the Hebrew Congregation of Newport, Rhode Island, employs nine Biblical allusions.

The Father of His Country was a voluminous writer. His papers contain over two hundred different Biblical phrases or allusions to Biblical passages.[5] Some he quoted often, like his favorite Bible verse, Micah 4:4:

> But they shall sit every man under his vine and under his fig tree,
> and none shall make them afraid;
> for the mouth of the LORD of hosts hath spoken.

Further, Washington referred to the Bible as only a Christian would—as the Word of God. In April 1789 he said: "The blessed Religion revealed in the Word of God will remain an eternal and awful monument to prove that the best Institutions may be abused by human depravity."[6] Deists neither believed that the Bible was the Word of God, nor accepted the doctrine of human depravity.

In one of his best-known letters, his *Circular to the States*, written after the end of the War for Independence, there is a lengthy list of blessings for America that ends: "and above all, the pure and benign light of Revelation."[7] In Washington's time the word *Revelation* generally referred to the Bible, and more specifically to the gospel of Christ revealed in the New Testament. Deists did not believe in the revelation of Holy Scripture and never would have referred to the Bible as Revelation with a capital *R*.

When our first President took the oath of office, he revealed his reverence for the Bible by kissing it. Also, he added the words "So help me God" at the end of the oath of office. This precedent fell into disuse, but in modern times it was renewed by Franklin Roosevelt and has subsequently been followed by every President.

Those skeptical of Washington's Christian faith sometimes raise the question of his church attendance, pointing to the fact that in the years before the War for Independence, the Washington family probably attended church on the average of about once a month. It should be remembered that they had to travel about nine miles over wilderness roads to get to Pohick Church, the nearest Anglican congregation to Mount Vernon, a rural parish at which available ministers would show up only about once a month.

Before and after the War for Independence, Washington had close relationships with many ministers of the gospel—corresponding with or entertaining at his home more than a hundred of them.[8] He always observed the Sabbath, never working on Sunday, save for writing letters to friends. He always gave his staff and his servants the day off to attend church. Any Sunday the family did not go to church, Washington would lead in devotions and read aloud one of the sermons that he had collected.

As we have seen, during the war, the General insisted on his soldiers attending Divine Services. His first General Order, issued when he took command of the Continental Army and dated July 4, 1775, states:

> The General most earnestly requires, and expects, a due observance of those articles of war, established for the Government of the army, which forbid profane cursing, swearing and drunkenness [the first of a number of orders he would issue concerning this]; And in like manner requires and expects, of all Officers, and Soldiers, not engaged on actual duty, a punctual attendance on divine Service, to implore the blessings of heaven upon the means used for our safety and defense.[9]

When there was no church service in the camp, he was not always able to get to church himself, but apparently he made efforts to do so. Biographer E. C. M'Guire reported that "one of his secretaries, Judge Harrison, has often been heard to say, that 'whenever the General could be spared from camp, on the Sabbath, he never failed riding out to some neighboring church, to join those who were publicly worshipping the Great Creator.'"[10]

During his Presidency, George Washington often attended church with his wife, Martha, on Sunday morning. Tobias Lear, Washington's secretary, wrote: "While President, Washington followed an invariable routine on Sundays. The day was passed very quietly, no company being invited to the house. After breakfast, the President read aloud a chapter from the Bible, then the whole family attended church together." In the afternoon Washington tended to his personal correspondence, "while Mrs. Washington frequently went to church again, often taking the children with her. In the evening, Lear read aloud to the family some sermon or extracts from a book of a religious nature and everyone went to bed at an early hour."[11]

After he retired to Mount Vernon, there was a year when the Washingtons apparently did not attend services. Christ Church in Alexandria was by this time having weekly services, so they switched their attendance to that church. Nelly Custis, the Washington's adopted granddaughter, testified: "He [Washington] attended the church at Alexandria when the weather and roads permitted a ride of ten miles. In New York and Philadelphia [when he was President] he never omitted attendance at church in the morning, unless detained by indisposition. . . . No one in church attended to the service with more reverential respect. My grandmother, who was eminently pious, never deviated from her early habits. She always knelt. The General, as was then the custom, stood during the devotional parts of the service."[12]

Accusations that George Washington never took Holy Communion began to be leveled not many years after his death and became a common part of the controversy over his religious belief. The initial point is that the custom in colonial Virginia was to offer the sacrament only at Christmas, Easter, and Whitsuntide (Pentecost Sunday), so many Anglicans received it only once a year. In addition, as Bishop William Meade pointed out, "there was a mistaken notion, too prevalent both in England and America, that it was not so necessary in the professors of religion to communicate [receive Communion] at all times, but that in this respect persons might be regulated by their feelings. . . . Into this error of opinion and practice General Washington may have fallen."[13]

Support for this comes from his granddaughter Nelly Custis, who wrote of her childhood at Mount Vernon: "On Communion Sundays he [Washington] left the church with me, after the blessing, and returned home, and we sent the carriage back for my grandmother"[14] (Martha

Washington). Since at that time the Communion Services were as long as the service they had just attended, it was not unusual for two-thirds of the congregation to leave before the Communion Service began. Washington's practice, though regrettable, was common for believers in his day.

In addition, there are several testimonies of those who observed him take Holy Communion during the war. General S. H. Lewis of Augusta County, Virginia, in a letter dated December 14, 1855, quoted General Robert Porterfield as saying that "he had known General Washington personally for many years. . . . I saw him myself on his knees receive the Sacrament of the Lord's Supper."[15] There is also a story that Washington took Communion in the Presbyterian church while the Continental Army was at Morristown, New Jersey, for the winter of 1778–79. Dr. James Richards, who followed Rev. Timothy Johnes, the pastor when Washington was in Morristown, noted that "the report that Washington did actually receive the Communion from the hands of Dr. Johnes was universally current during that period, and so far as I know, never contradicted. I have often heard it from the members of Dr. Johnes' family, while they added that a note was addressed by Washington to their father, requesting the privilege."[16]

Further, there is a credible account from the pen of the Reverend Alexander Hamilton, great-grandson of Washington's aide, recounting the events of a Hamilton family reunion held in New York City in 1854. By that time, Hamilton's widow, who was Continental Army General Phillip Schuyler's daughter, was a woman of ninety-six.

But she made a special effort to take her seven-year-old great-grandson and other family members to visit St. Paul's Church because, she said, she had something important to tell the boy that she wanted him to always remember. When they got to the church, she said that she had been present in the church on George Washington's Inauguration Day in 1789, when he had received Holy Communion. She impressed on her great-grandson that she wanted him to know that she had personally witnessed Washington receiving the sacrament, so he could tell others. Rev. Hamilton recollected that her words were: "If anyone ever tells you that George Washington was not a communicant of the Church, you say that your great-grandmother told you to say that she had knelt at this chancel rail at his side and received with him the Holy Communion."[17]

Finally, there is the question of Washington's use of the word *Providence*. Although there are at least 270 recorded instances when George Washington used the term *Providence* to refer indirectly to God, it is quite clear in his writings that for him the word did not denote some vague sort of celestial deity. In Washington's view God was the God of the Bible, who often intervened personally on behalf of the American cause, just as He had in ancient Israel. When Washington used the word *Providence,* he was usually thinking in those terms. From his letter to the Hebrew congregation of Savannah, Georgia:

"May the same wonder-working Deity, who long since delivering the Hebrews from their Egyptian Oppressors planted them in the promised land—whose Providential Agency has lately been conspicuous in establishing these United States as an independent Nation—still continue to water them with the dews of Heaven and to make the inhabitants of every denomination participate in the temporal and spiritual blessings of that people whose God is Jehovah."[18]

Further, in his letter to Major-General Israel Putnam, dated October 19, 1777, just after the American victory at Saratoga, he wrote, "Should Providence be pleased to crown our arms in the course of the campaign with one more fortunate stroke . . . I trust all will be well in His good time."[19]

In Peter Lillback's well-researched work on Washington's spirituality, he quotes Mary Thompson, a research specialist at Mount Vernon: "I would think that God and Providence are synonymous in Washington's mind. When you look at a number of the letters, it becomes obvious that he feels that Providence . . . is involved in what happens in the world. . . . What I found [in researching Washington's religious beliefs] . . . was that this was a man who believed that God took an active role in the founding of the United States, a man who believed that God took an active interest in people's lives . . . and that's not the belief of a Deist."[20]

Although his religious views and practice were strongly influenced by his eighteenth-century Virginia Anglican culture, it seems clear that our first President was an orthodox Christian believer.

APPENDIX THREE

THE CHRISTIAN FAITH OF
OTHER FOUNDING FATHERS

*A*n appendix can hardly do justice to the Christian faith of the approximately two hundred people who deserve the title Founding Father.* This brief sampling will cite sufficient evidence of orthodox Christian belief to refute the absurd (and endlessly repeated) untruths that they were all Deists or that they were not Christians. For a few of these leaders, the additional evidence of their Christian faith provided here will supplement that found in the text.

Samuel Adams—Massachusetts

Substantial material revealing the strong Christian faith of the man historians call the Father of the American Revolution appears in the text

*The term Founding Fathers includes members of the First and Second Continental Congress, the Constitutional Convention, the First Congress of the United States, the first Supreme Court, the first Governors of the states, and the early Presidents of the United States.

of this book. But there are several other points of interest. As one of the most outspoken Christians among the Founding Fathers, Adams was disgusted by Thomas Paine's *The Age of Reason*, a Deistic attack on the Christian faith, the first part of which was published in 1794. When Paine returned to America in 1802, after a fourteen-year absence, rumor had it that he had more to write against Christianity. Adams finally took pen in hand:

> When I heard you had turned your mind to a defense of infidelity, I felt myself much astonished and more grieved, that you had attempted a measure so injurious to the feelings and so repugnant to the true interest of so great a part of the citizens of the United States.... Do you think that your pen ... can unchristianize the mass of our citizens, or have you hopes of converting a few of them to assist you in so bad a cause?[1]

Eighteenth-century Americans often took the occasion of making out their wills to express their Christian convictions to their children and others who would read the document after they were gone. In his, Samuel Adams left no doubts about his faith: "Principally, first of all, I recommend my soul to that Almighty Being who gave it, and my body I commit to the dust, relying upon the merits of Jesus Christ for a pardon of all my sins."[2]

Elias Boudinot—New Jersey

Born in 1740, Boudinot studied law under Richard Stockton and became devoted to the Patriot cause. Elected to the Continental Congress in 1777, he served until 1779, and again from 1781 to 1784. One of the most influential members of Congress, he served on more than thirty committees, usually as chairman. In November of 1782 he was chosen as the President of Congress, and as such signed both the treaty of alliance with France and the peace treaty with Great Britain. A strong Federalist, he helped ratify the new Constitution in New Jersey, and the people of that state elected him to the first three Federal Congresses. President Washington appointed him as director of the mint in 1795.[3]

Boudinot's correspondence with his daughter Susan reveals a strong Christian faith. His letter of October 30, 1782, written while listening to a debate in the Continental Congress, was occasioned by his fatherly concern that before long she would be leaving home. (Indeed, she would be married two years later). He wrote: "May the God of your parents for many generations past seal instruction to your soul and lead you to Himself through the blood of His too generally despised Son, who, notwithstanding, is still reclaiming the world to God through that blood, not imputing to them their sins, to him be Glory forever."[4]

After the second part of Thomas Paine's *The Age of Reason* appeared in 1795, Boudinot also took pen in hand and wrote a refutation entitled *The Age of Revelation, or the Age of Reason Shown to be An Age of Infidelity,* which took the form of a pamphlet written to his daughter. In it he wrote:

> May that God, who delighteth in the meek and humble temper which trembleth at His word, lead you to the Cross of Christ; and there, by His Holy Spirit, direct you into all truth. May He instruct you in His holy Word, which is able to make you wise unto salvation. . . . In short, were you to ask me to recommend the most valuable book in the world, I should fix on the Bible as the most instructive, both to the wise and ignorant.[5]

A lifelong Christian, Boudinot helped to found the American Bible Society in 1816 and served as its first President. His involvement in the Bible society was not unique among the Founding Fathers. A strong indicator of their reverence for the Word of God is the fact that about 40 percent of the Founding Fathers were not just members but officeholders in various Bible societies—local, state, or national.

Charles Carroll—Maryland

Elected to the Second Continental Congress on July 4, 1776, Carroll signed the Declaration with other delegates on August 2 in Philadelphia. He worked hard for the adoption of the Constitution after independence and as a member of the Federalist Party was elected as one of Maryland's senators in 1789. Educated in Jesuit schools in Maryland and in France, he once declared: "On the mercy of my Redeemer I rely for salvation and on His merits; not on the works I have done in obedience to His precepts."[6]

John Dickinson—Pennsylvania

Few Patriots argued the case for American rights in the conflict with Great Britain as eloquently as John Dickinson. His *Letters from a Farmer in Pennsylvania* earned him the title Penman of the Revolution and led to his election to the both the First and Second Continental Congresses.

In response to the Stamp Acts, he wrote:

> Kings or parliaments could not give the rights essential to happiness. . . . We claim them from a higher source—from the King of kings, and Lord of all the earth. They are not annexed to us by parchments or seals. They are created in us by the decrees of Providence, which establish the laws of our nature. They are born with us; exist with us; and cannot be taken from us by any human power, without taking our lives. . . . It would be an insult on the divine Majesty to say that He has given or allowed any man or body of men a right to make me miserable.[7]

With Thomas Jefferson he wrote the *Declaration of the Causes and Necessity of Taking Up Arms*, though he maintained to the end the hope of reconciliation with the mother country and helped to write the last-ditch *Olive Branch Petition* appeal to the King of England. Dickinson refused to vote for the Declaration and was the only member of Congress who did not sign the document. But he enlisted in the Pennsylvania militia and fought for the cause of independence.

In spite of being Delaware's largest slaveholder, Dickinson became convinced of the immorality of slavery and freed his slaves during the war. In 1779 Delaware appointed him to the Continental Congress, and while there he signed the Articles of Confederation, the original draft of which he had written. Two years later the Delaware Assembly elected him president of Delaware, with the only dissenting vote being cast by Dickinson himself. In 1782, because Pennsylvania and Delaware had until recently shared the same governor, he was elected President of Pennsylvania while technically still President of Delaware. He held the office for the constitutional limit of three years. Four years later, Delaware sent him to the Constitutional Convention, and after helping to create the Constitution, he wrote nine essays urging its adoption under the pen name of Fabius.[8]

As was not uncommon for Christian leaders of the Founding Fathers' era, John Dickinson wrote a pamphlet entitled "Religious Instruction for Youth," in which he paraphrased 2 Timothy 3:15: "The Holy Scriptures are able to make us wise unto salvation through Faith which is in Jesus Christ."[9]

In his will Dickinson stated: "Rendering thanks to my Creator for my existence and station among His works, for my birth in a country enlightened by the Gospel and enjoying Freedom, and for all His other kindnesses, to Him I resign myself, humbly confiding in His goodness, and in His mercy through Jesus Christ, for the events of eternity."

Benjamin Franklin

Americans of the Founding Fathers' generation considered Franklin to be our nation's greatest homegrown philosopher, and his counsel on matters both personal and public was deemed practical and sagacious. In France he was celebrated as the quintessential American, but he was just as famous at home as a statesman, writer, printer, inventor, scientist, musician, and all-around genius.

As to his religious views, while it would be impossible to characterize him as a professing Christian, he was nonetheless quite supportive of the Christian faith. In 1747 he wrote a prayer proclamation for Pennsylvania and two years later recommended that Christianity be taught in the colony's schools.[10] Not only did he promote increased church attendance in Pennsylvania,[11] but he also hoped to start a model colony in Ohio with his good friend George Whitefield "to facilitate the introduction of pure religion among the heathen." The intent was to show the Indians "a better sample of Christians than they commonly see in our Indian traders." About this dream he wrote to Whitefield: "In such an enterprise I could spend the remainder of life with pleasure, and I firmly believe God would bless us with success."[12]

Franklin remained ambiguous about his personal relationship with Christ, as revealed by his comment on Whitefield's efforts to convert him: "He used, indeed, sometimes to pray for my conversion, but never had the satisfaction of believing that his prayers were heard."

It seems that late in his life Franklin still had doubts about the divinity of Jesus, but it should be noted that while he was America's ambassador to France he wrote, "He who shall introduce into public affairs the principles of primitive Christianity will change the face of the world."[13]

Patrick Henry—Virginia

As previously noted in the text, Patrick Henry was a devoted Christian. His daughter Sarah said that the children's first contact with their father every morning was his cheery "good morrow" to them from the dining room, where he would sit and read his Bible before breakfast. And every Sunday evening he would read to the family from his penciled study notes on the truths of the Christian faith, after which they would play sacred music together while he accompanied them on the violin.[14]

After Henry's death when his will was opened, there was found a copy of his famous resolutions against the hated Stamp Act, dated May 29, 1765. These were sealed and addressed to the executors of his estate, indicating that he valued these most among all the acts of his life of public service. He had written an introduction to the resolutions, describing how they were presented and adopted, at the end of which were found these words:

> Whether this will prove a blessing or a curse, will depend upon the use our people make of the blessings which a gracious God hath bestowed on us. If they are wise, they will be great and happy. If they are of a contrary character, they will be miserable. Righteousness alone can exalt them as a nation. Reader! whoever thou art, remember this; and in thy sphere practice virtue thyself, and encourage it in others.[15]

In composing his will, after parceling out his estate, Patrick Henry was brief and to the point: "This is all the inheritance I can give to my dear family. The religion of Christ can give them one which will make them rich indeed."[16]

Francis Hopkinson—New Jersey

A musician, composer, and member of the New Jersey delegation to the Continental Congress, Hopkinson signed the Declaration of Independence. After independence he submitted a design for the first American flag remarkably similar to today's, and assisted in the design for the Great Seal of the United States. He was appointed by President Washington to the office of Judge of the United States for the District of Pennsylvania.

Prior to the War for Independence, Francis Hopkinson was a church choir director and editor of a 1767 hymnal. He took the psalms of the Old Testament and set them to music, producing one of the first American hymnals.[17]

John Jay—New York

Few Americans have had a more illustrious career of public service than John Jay. His law practice ended when New York sent him to both the First and Second Continental Congresses. He guided the writing of his state's constitution and then served as the Chief Justice of New York while helping to organize the antislavery movement in the state.

Jay, along with John Adams and Ben Franklin, negotiated the 1783 peace treaty with Britain that ended the War for Independence, and he was one of the three authors (with Madison and Hamilton) of the *Federalist Papers*, urging ratification of the new Constitution. President George Washington appointed him as the first Chief Justice of the United States, and he negotiated the Jay Treaty of 1794, which settled problems with Britain that remained from the older treaty. Returning to New York State, he was elected to several terms as Governor.[18]

A devout Christian, Jay was insistent on regular devotions to begin and end each day at the family home at Bedford, New York. Every morning before breakfast the entire household was summoned to prayers, and they were summoned again every evening promptly at nine o'clock, when Jay would read aloud a chapter in the Bible and then conclude with prayer.[19]

Not only was he a member of the American Board of Commissioners for Foreign Missions, but he was one of the original officers of the American Bible Society and served terms as both its Vice President and President. Among his papers was found this prayer in his own handwriting:

> O most merciful Father! who desireth not the death of a sinner, but will have all men to be saved and to come to the knowledge of the truth, give me grace so to draw nigh unto Thee as that Thou wilt condescend to draw nigh unto me. . . . Above all, I thank Thee for Thy mercy to our fallen race, as declared in Thy holy Gospel by Thy beloved Son, "who gave Himself as a ransom for all." . . . Let Thy Holy Spirit purify and unite me to my Savior for ever, and enable me to cleave unto Him as unto my very life, as indeed He is. Perfect and confirm my faith, my trust, and hope of salvation in Him and in Him only.[20]

In his will, he declared: "Unto Him, who is the author and giver of all good, I render sincere and humble thanks for His manifold and unmerited blessings, and especially for our redemption and salvation by His beloved Son . . . blessed be His holy name."[21]

As John Jay lay dying, with the family gathered about his bed, someone asked him if he had anything further to say to his children. He replied: "No, they have the Book!"

Thomas McKean—Delaware

An avid promoter of American independence, Thomas McKean was the other Delaware delegate who voted for the Declaration with Caesar Rodney on July 2, 1776. He signed the document and fought as a militia officer in the resulting war. McKean was one of the authors of the Articles of Confederation and served as the second President of the Continental Congress during the Confederation period. Later he served as the Chief Justice of the Pennsylvania Supreme Court for twelve years and as Governor of Pennsylvania for nine years after that.

As Chief Justice of Pennsylvania, McKean presided over the case of *Republica v. John Roberts*, in which Roberts was convicted of treason and sentenced to death. After the sentence was pronounced, McKean preached a Gospel message to Roberts, exhorting him to accept Christ as Savior before his execution.[22]

Robert Treat Paine—Massachusetts

A member of the Massachusetts delegation to the Second Continental Congress and a signer of the Declaration of Independence, Paine was the prosecuting attorney for the colony when the British soldiers who had fired on unarmed civilians in the Boston Massacre of 1770 were put on trial. They were defended by none other than John Adams.

Twenty-one years earlier, while a student at Harvard, Robert Treat Paine had made a confession of faith in Jesus Christ: "God has opened mine eyes . . . to see that out of Christ there was no hope of salvation for me and has been inclining me to accept of Christ as for the pardon of my sins. . . . I believe the Bible to be the written Word of God and to contain in it the whole rule of faith and manners; I consent to the Assembly's Shorter Catechism [the Westminster Shorter Catechism of 1647] as being agreeable to the revealed will of God and to contain in it the doctrines that are according to godliness."[23]

By the time of his death on May 11, 1814, the passage of years had not dimmed his Christian convictions. His will reads: "I am constrained to express my adoration of the Supreme Being, the Author of my existence, in full belief of his Providential Goodness and His forgiving mercy revealed to the world through Jesus Christ, through whom I hope for never ending happiness in a future state."[24]

Benjamin Rush—Pennsylvania

At the time of his death in 1813, Dr. Benjamin Rush was considered by Americans to be as prominent a Founding Father as George Washington or Ben Franklin. A signer of the Declaration of Independence, he was a medical doctor and an influential Christian educator. The list of institutions he founded or helped start is impressive. He assisted Presbyterians in starting Dickinson College in 1783 and served as one of its trustees; he founded the Philadelphia School of Medicine, which later became the medical school at the University of Pennsylvania; he created the First Day Society, a precursor of today's Sunday schools; he started America's first Bible society—the Bible Society of Philadelphia; and in 1774 he helped to organize the Pennsylvania Society for Promoting the Abolition of Slavery.

In July 1776 he became a member of the Continental Congress, and he was appointed Surgeon General of the Armies of the Middle Department. At Valley Forge he helped to vaccinate the army against smallpox.[25]

At various times he was a member of both the Episcopal and Presbyterian Churches. Though he leaned toward Universalism, he was thoroughly orthodox in regard to his own salvation. In his autobiography he wrote: "My only hope of salvation is in the infinite transcendent love of God manifested to the world by the death of His Son upon the Cross. Nothing but His blood will wash away my sins. I rely exclusively upon it. Come, Lord Jesus! come quickly![26]

Roger Sherman—Connecticut

In addition to signing both the Declaration and the Constitution, Roger Sherman was the only Founding Father to also sign the other founding documents of the Republic—the Articles of Association of 1774 and the Articles of Confederation following independence. Sherman belonged to the conservative wing of the Patriots, but along with Jefferson, James Wilson, and George Wythe, he was one of the first ones to deny that Parliament had any jurisdiction in the colonies. Elected to the Continental Congress in 1774, he served until 1781 and was a member of the committee appointed to draft the Declaration. He served in Congress again in 1783 and 1784.

One of the chief framers of both the Articles of Confederation and the Constitution, he also served as a judge on Connecticut's Supreme Court, a Congressman, and a U.S. Senator.

A strong and unwavering Christian, he was referred to by John Adams as "an old Puritan, as honest as an angel and as firm in the cause of American Independence as Mount Atlas."

As a Congregationalist, his patriotism was boosted by his legitimate fears that the British were bent on establishing Anglican episcopacy in all the colonies.[27]

Roger Sherman's Christianity was practical and down-to-earth, but he loved theology, and in his own handwriting wrote a confession of faith for the White Haven Church in New Haven when it changed its creed in 1788: "I believe that there is one only living and true God, existing in three persons, the Father, the Son, and the Holy Ghost . . . that God did send His own Son to become man, die . . .in the stead of sinners, and thus to lay a foundation for the offer of pardon and salvation to all mankind . . . that at the end of this world there will be a resurrection of the dead, and a final judgment of all mankind."[28] The following year he published in New Haven a pamphlet entitled "*A Short Sermon on the Duty of Self-Examination Preparatory to Receiving the Lord's Supper.*"[29]

Yale College President Timothy Dwight spoke of Sherman as "profoundly versed in theology" and said that he "held firmly the doctrines of the Reformation," which in Dwight's view probably meant that Sherman was a staunch Calvinist. In fact, he was, and he was so concerned about correct Biblical doctrine that he got into a written debate with theologian Samuel Hopkins over the finer points of Calvinism.[30]

Richard Stockton—New Jersey

A signer of the Declaration of Independence, Richard Stockton was a brilliant lawyer who mentored Founding Fathers Joseph Reed, William Paterson, and Elias Boudinot. During the early years of the struggle with Britain he was a moderate, but when the Stamp Act was passed, he maintained that Parliament had no authority over the colonies.

The people of New Jersey elected Stockton to the Continental Congress on June 22, 1776, and six days later he arrived in Philadelphia in time to attend the last two days of debate on the Declaration. At first he was unsure about the merits of declaring independence, but after listening intently to the speeches, and particularly the conclusive arguments of John Adams, his doubts were resolved, and joining his voice to those urging independence, he voted for the Declaration.

A few months later he received an equal number of votes as Robert Livingston in the election for Governor of New Jersey, but Livingston was chosen. Turning down an immediate election as Chief Justice of the state, he continued to actively represent New Jersey in the Congress, serving on important committees.

When the British army swept down New Jersey, Stockton moved his family to a friend's house about thirty miles from his home, but there he was captured. His magnificent library was burned, and all his personal property, animals, and estate were either plundered or destroyed. Worse, because he was a signer of the Declaration, the British treated him so abusively in prison that his health was broken. Stockton never recovered, and he died in February 1781. He was fifty-one.[31]

His will reads:

> As my children will have frequent occasion of perusing this instrument, and may probably be particularly impressed with the last words of their father, I think it proper here not only to subscribe to the entire belief of the great and leading doctrines of the Christian religion, such as the Being of God, the universal defection and depravity of human nature, the divinity of the person and the completeness of the redemption purchased by the blessed Savior, the necessity of the operations of the divine Spirit; of divine faith, accompanied with an habitual virtuous life, and the universality of the divine Providence; but also, in the bowels of a father's affection, to exhort and charge them, that the fear of God is the beginning of wisdom, that the way of life held up in the Christian system, is calculated for the most complete happiness that can be enjoyed in this mortal state.[32]

Charles Thomson—Pennsylvania

Called by John Adams "the Samuel Adams of Philadelphia," Charles Thomson served as the Secretary of the Continental Congress for its entire fifteen years. His signature on the Declaration of Independence, along with that of John Hancock, legalized the document on July 4, 1776, which is why we celebrate independence on that day. Greatly influential in foreign affairs, he was dubbed the Prime Minister of America. He and

William Barton designed the Great Seal of the United States, which appears on the back of our dollar bills.

What is less well known is that Presbyterian Charles Thomson spent most of the last years of his life creating the first translation of the Greek Septuagint version of the Bible into English. It took him nineteen years.[33]

Dr. John Witherspoon—New Jersey

The sixth President of the College of New Jersey (later Princeton University), this Scottish emigrant and Presbyterian minister had a profound effect on the founding of our Republic. As an active teacher of political philosophy and civil government while he was president of the college, Witherspoon personally educated thirty-seven future judges (of whom three made it to the Supreme Court), ten Cabinet officers, twelve members of the Continental Congress, twenty-eight U.S. senators, forty-nine U.S. congressmen, one Vice President (Aaron Burr), and one President (James Madison).

He represented New Jersey in the Continental Congress and was a tireless worker, serving on over one hundred committees. He was the only clergyman to sign the Declaration of Independence. Witherspoon helped to draft the Articles of Confederation, served twice in the New Jersey legislature, and strongly supported the Constitution's adoption by his state.

As an evangelical minister, Witherspoon was always emphatically clear in his preaching. In an address entitled "*The Absolute Necessity of Salvation through Christ,*" he exhorted:

> I shall now conclude my discourse by preaching this Savior to all who hear me, and entreating you, in the most earnest manner, to believe in Jesus Christ, for "there is no salvation in any other." . . . But whether you acknowledge it or not, I bear from God Himself this message to you all . . . if you are not reconciled to God through Jesus Christ, if you are not clothed with the spotless robe of His righteousness, you must for ever perish.[34]

SOURCE NOTES

A Generation Later . . .

1. Samuel Adams, *Writings,* vol. 4, 124. Complete publication data for all works cited can be found in the bibliography.

2. John Adams, *Works,* vol. 9, 401, 636.

3. William Wirt Henry, *Patrick Henry,* 592.

The Search Begins

1. Columbus's *Book of Prophecies* is largely a compilation of a number of the teachings and prophecies in the Bible on the subject of the earth, distant lands, population movements, and undiscovered tribes, as well as similarly pertinent writings of the ancient Church fathers. Much of this work was originally translated by the late August J. Kling, who quoted these excerpts in an article in *The Presbyterian Layman,* October 1971.

2. Sacvan Bercovitch, *The Puritan Origins of the American Self,* 28.

3. Sacvan Bercovitch, *Typology and Early American Literature,* 76.

4. Cotton Mather, *Magnalia Christi Americana,* vol. 1, 7–11.

5. Ibid., 52.

6. Daniel Webster, *Writings and Speeches,* vol. 13, 492.

Chapter 1: Christ-bearer

1. The original journal of Christopher Columbus has been lost, but much of it was retold by Bishop Bartolomé de Las Casas, a sixteenth-century historian who was with Columbus in Española on his third voyage. This passage is from the translation by Cecil Jane, *The Voyages of Christopher Columbus,* 146, 147.

2. As recorded by Oviedo, official chronicler of the court of Ferdinand and Isabella, from subsequent interviews with the participants. However, the exact details are a matter of conjecture. Since comparatively little source material on Columbus is available in English, we

found we had to rely greatly on his two major modern biographers, Samuel Eliot Morison and Björn Landström, for the narrative details of his life. To these two discerning scholars we acknowledge our debt and our gratitude. This incident was referred to in Morison's *Admiral of the Ocean Sea*, 285–91.

3. These figures are from the first four chapters of Björn Landström's *Columbus*. An ocean sailor himself, Landström brings his own navigational expertise to bear in his evaluation.

4. Morison, *Admiral of the Ocean Sea*, 57–60.

5. Landström, *Columbus*, 37, 38.

6. Samuel Eliot Morison, *European Discovery of America*, 40.

7. Delno C. West and August Kling, *The Libro de las Profecias of Christopher Columbus*, 111.

8. Ibid., 55.

9. Ibid., 60–63.

10. Ibid., 53. (The authors have given the literal Latin translation in the text.)

11. Morison, *Admiral*, 172.

Chapter 2: In Peril on the Sea

1. This quote and those to follow are from Landström, *Columbus*, 66–75.

2. Quoted in West and Kling, *Libro*, 65.

Chapter 3: "If Gold Be Your Almighty"

1. Landström, *Columbus*, 103.

2. Ibid.

3. Ibid., 106.

4. Christopher Columbus, *His Own Book of Privileges* (1893), facsimile edition of manuscripts in the Foreign Office in Paris. (This copy in the Beinecke Rare Book Library, Yale University, New Haven, Conn.)

5. Morison, *Admiral*, 404–5.

6. This unbridled lust and rape was to receive its own uniquely fitting punishment. Many of the women were carriers of a strange and deadly disease that would become known as syphilis, and the men thus infected were sentenced to a lingering, excruciatingly painful insanity and death. The sailors returning from this voyage introduced this new plague to Spain, and from there it was shared with the rest of the civilized world.

7. Landström, *Columbus*, 133.

8. Morison, *Admiral*, 523–26.

9. Landström, *Columbus*, 152.

10. This quote and the following one are from Morison, *Admiral*, 617–19.

11. This quote and the following one are from Jane, *The Voyages*, 299, 304.

Chapter 4: Blessed Be the Martyrs

1. Luther Weigle, *The Pageant of America*. (The author was for many years dean of the Yale Divinity School and was the Chairman of the committee responsible for the Revised Standard Version of the Bible.)

2. An ethnological study in Southern California indicated (from aerial surveys and extensive examination of ancient growing fields and watering systems) that the population of northern Latin America at the beginning of the sixteenth century was between 85 and 115 million. A

reliable census, taken a century later by Spain's administrators in the New World, fixes the population at 10 million. If the study is accurate, this means that the Conquistadors and their successors were responsible for the greatest demographic annihilation in history.

3. Henry Morton Robinson, *Stout Cortez: A Biography of the Spanish Conquest*, 47–48.

4. Landström, *Columbus*, 133.

5. This quote and the four that follow are from Weigle, *Pageant*, 24–30.

6. Charles E. Kistler, *This Nation Under God*, 18.

7. Weigle, *Pageant*, 28.

Chapter 5: The Lost Colony

1. Giles Milton, *Big Chief Elizabeth*, 42.

2. Ibid., 43.

3. This quote and the previous one are from Captain John Smith, *Writings*, 820.

4. Ibid., 822.

5. Milton, *Elizabeth*, 58. The Elizabethan spelling was Algonkian.

6. This may well mark the beginning of the fur trade, which would eventually bring far more wealth to England than any gold or silver mines.

7. Smith, *Writings*, 826.

8. Milton, *Elizabeth*, 78.

9. Smith, *Writings*, 900.

10. Quoted in Milton, *Elizabeth*, 154–55.

11. There has been scholarly speculation that Fernandez may have been secretly in the employ of Sir Francis Walsingham, Elizabeth's Secretary of State, who was one of the courtiers determined to bring Raleigh down. This would explain his repeated efforts to derail the expedition. See Lee Miller's *Roanoke: Solving the Mystery of the Lost Colony* (Arcade, 2001).

12. Smith, *Writings*, 915.

13. Milton, *Elizabeth*, 237. He would later write this in a letter to Richard Hakluyt.

Chapter 6: Garboil

1. This quote and the following one are from the Virginia Company's pamphlet: *A True and Sincere Declaration of the Purpose and Ends of the Plantation begun in Virginia*, published in London in 1610.

2. Smith, *Writings*, 42.

3. Ibid., 923–24.

4. Quote from von Buseck article.

5. Smith, *Writings*, 930.

6. Ibid., 933.

7. Ibid., 47–48.

8. Ibid., 809.

9. Ibid., 47.

10. Ibid., 8.

11. Ibid., 8–9.

12. Ibid., 1086.

13. The authenticity of this famous story is murky. The question is, why did Smith not include it in his *A True Relation* account (1608) of his encounter with Powhatan but wait until his 1624 *Generall Historie* to print the story? Some historians have speculated that since the Virginia Company Partners heavily edited his *Relation*, perhaps they censored it. Others have

suspected that he made it all up or that he simply plagiarized a similar tale by Juan Ortiz, the Spaniard captured by natives in Florida, who became De Soto's translator.

14. Smith *Writings*, 323.
15. Ibid., 404.
16. Ibid., 328.
17. John Smith, *Travels and Works*, vol. 1, 152; and Barbour, *Jamestown Voyages*, vol. 2, 44, as quoted in Morgan, *American Slavery*, 73.
18. Smith, *Writings*, 328–29.
19. Ibid., 330.
20. Alexander Brown, *The Genesis of the United States*, vol. 1, 256.
21. Ibid., 369.
22. Ibid., 4.

Chapter 7: "Damn Your Souls! Make Tobacco!"

1. Smith, *Writings*, 357–58.
2. Milton, *Elizabeth*, 341–42.
3. Smith, *Writings*, 84–86.
4. Ibid., 374.
5. George F. Willison, *Behold Virginia!*, 112.
6. Brown,*Genesis,* 339.
7. Smith, *Writings*, 782–83.
8. Ibid., 1100.
9. Ibid., 1014.
10. Ibid., 413.
11. George Bancroft, *Bancroft's History of the United States*, vol. 1, 141.
12. Smith *Writings*, 414–15.
13. Ibid., 416.
14. Ibid., 1164.
15. Willison, *Behold Virginia!* 345.

Chapter 8: To the Promised Land

1. Cotton Mather, *Magnalia Christi Americana*, 1855 edition, 110.
2. William Bradford, *Of Plimoth Plantation*, Wright and Potter edition, 3. While there are several modern editions of this classic available, anyone seriously interested should be sure to get an unexpurgated edition, for at least one modern edition we know of has elected to leave out "irrelevant theological meditations."
3. Ibid., 13.
4. Ibid., 36.
5. Fleming, *One Small Candle*, 31.
6. Bradford, *Plimoth*, Wright and Potter edition, 34, 35.
7. Jesper Rosenmeier, "Bradford's of Plymouth Plantation," in *Typology and Early American Literature*, Sacvan Bercovitch, ed., 76.
8. Bradford, *Plimoth*, Wright and Potter edition, 41, 42.
9. Fleming, *Candle,* 36.
10. Bradford, *Plimoth*, Wright and Potter edition, 72.
11. This quote and the following ones from Robinson's letter are from Bradford, *Plimoth*, Wright and Potter edition, 76, 79–81.
12. Perry Miller and Thomas H. Johnson, *The Puritans*, vol. 1, 246.

13. This quote and the ones to follow, including Cushman's letter, are all from Bradford, *Plimoth*, Wright and Potter edition, 85–89.

14. From a photograph of the original in Kate Caffrey's *The Mayflower*, 115.

15. This quote and the ones to follow are from Bradford, *Plimoth*, Wright and Potter edition, 94–96.

Chapter 9: "God Our Maker Doth Provide"

1. This quote and the following story are from Bradford, *Plimouth*, Wright and Potter edition, 101, 103.

2. From Bradford and Winslow's *Morte's Relation*, as quoted in Alexander Young's *Chronicles of the Pilgrim Fathers*, 158, 159.

3. Fleming, *One Small Candle*, 133.

4. Bradford, *Plimoth*, Wright and Potter edition, 106.

5. Fleming, *Candle*, 136.

6. This quote and the following one are from Bradford, *Plimoth*, Wright and Potter edition, 113, 114.

7. Ibid., 492.

8. For many of the specific details of this remarkable story, we are indebted to Stanley E. Goodman's "Squanto" in *They Knew They Were Pilgrims*, L. D. Geller, ed., 25–31.

9. Bradford, *Plimoth*, Wright and Potter edition, 117.

10. For the following details we are indebted to Fleming, *Candle*, 208–13.

11. Bradford, *Plimoth*, Wright and Potter edition, 129.

12. From the original sermon, the first American sermon ever published. Robert Cushman, "The Sin and Danger of Self-Love," 33.

13. Bradford, *Plimoth*, Wright and Potter edition, 162.

14. Bradford, *Of Plymouth Plantation*, Samuel Eliot Morison, ed., 114.

15. Ibid., 120–21.

16. This quote and the following one are from Edward Winslow, quoted in Young's *Chronicles*, 347–50.

17. Bradford, *Plimoth*, Wright and Potter edition, 171.

18. Young, *Chronicles*, 350.

19. "Emmanuel Altham to Sir Edward Altham," quoted in Sydney V. James, Jr.'s *Three Visitors to Early Plymouth*, 23ff.

20. Fleming, *Candle*, 218.

Chapter 10: Thy Kingdom Come

1. Fleming, *Candle*, 22.

2. Bercovitch, *Puritan Origins*, 17.

3. Ibid., 18.

4. This quote and the two to follow are from the *Winthrop Papers*, Massachusetts Historical Society, vol. 1, 196, 201.

5. Francis J. Bremer, *John Winthrop: America's Forgotten Founding Father*, 173–74.

6. Ibid., 103.

7. Ibid., 115.

8. William Warren Sweet, *The Story of Religion in America*, 48.

9. *Winthrop Papers*, vol. 2, 138–43.

10. Edmund S. Morgan, *The Puritan Dilemma*, 47.

11. Bremer, *Winthrop*, 161.

12. *Winthrop Papers*, vol. 2, 152.

13. Perry Miller, *Errand into the Wilderness*, 11.

14. This quote and the following one are from Morison, "John Winthrop and the Founding of New England" in *Colonial America*, edited by David R. B. Ross, Alden T. Vaughan, and John B. Duff, 25.

Chapter 11: A City upon a Hill

1. Morgan, *Dilemma*, 54.

2. J. Franklin Jameson, ed., *Johnson's Wonder-Working Providence 1628-1651*, 61.

3. Bremer, *Winthrop*, 169.

4. *Winthrop Papers*, vol. 2, 160, 161.

5. Bremer, *Winthrop*, 200.

6. Ibid., 192.

7. *Winthrop Papers*, vol. 2, 292–95. Oddly, for a document that has been referred to as the "Ur-text of American literature," we do not know exactly when Winthrop preached his *Model of Christian Charity* to the emigrants, and the timing of it is not mentioned in either Cotton Mather's *Magnalia Christi Americana* or in Edward Johnson's *Wonder-Working Providence*.

8. Edward Johnson, *Providence*, 46, 47.

9. Cotton Mather, *Magnalia Christi Americana*, vol. 2, as quoted in Bercovitch, *Puritan Origins*, 1.

10. Bremer, *Winthrop*, 193.

11. Ibid., 194.

12. Ibid., 193.

Chapter 12: The Puritan Way

1. Morgan, *Dilemma*, xi. In this quote the author was also speaking against the popular negative image of the Puritans.

2. Miller and Johnson, *Puritans*, vol. 1, 284.

3. Edmund S. Morgan, *The Puritan Family*, 10.

4. This quote and the following one are from John Demos, ed., *Remarkable Providences*, 222–39.

5. Winthrop, *History of New England*, vol. 2, 12–13.

6. This quote and those immediately following are from Barrett Wendell, *Cotton Mather*, 119, 198.

7. *Winthrop Papers*, vol. 3, 223, 224.

8. This quote and the two following are from Morgan, *Family*, 7, 19, 143.

9. Bremer, *Winthrop*, 194.

10. W. De Loss Love Jr., *The Fast and Thanksgiving Days of New England*, 104.

11. Edward Johnson, *Wonder-Working Providence*, 77, 78.

12. Morgan, *Dilemma*, 60.

13. This quote and the following one are from Love, *Fast and Thanksgiving Days*, 105, 106.

14. Quoted in Sanford H. Cobb, *The Rise of Religious Liberty in America*, 162.

15. Alice Morse Earle, *The Sabbath in Puritan New England*, 68.

16. Ibid., 315.

17. This quote and the following one are from Sweet, *The Story of Religion*, 57, 58.

18. Earle, *Sabbath*, 275–78.

Chapter 13: The Pruning of the Lord's Vineyard

1. Mather, *Magnalia*, vol. 2, 430.
2. Morgan, *Dilemma*, 116.
3. Roger Williams, *The Complete Writings of Roger Williams*, vol. 7, 37, as quoted in Bercovitch, *Puritan Origins*, 110.
4. Bradford, *Plimouth*, Wright and Potter edition, 370.
5. *The Complete Writings of Roger Williams*, John Russell Bartlett, ed., vol. 6, 141.
6. Clifford Shipton, "Puritanism and Modern Democracy," *New England Historical and Genealogical Register*, July 1947, 189.
7. Roger Williams, *Writings*, vol. 6, 350.
8. Morgan, *Dilemma*, 152.
9. Winthrop, *History*, vol. 1, 313–16.
10. Thomas Hooker, *The Christian's Two Chief Lessons*.
11. Miller and Johnson, *The Puritans*, 188.
12. Perry Miller, *Errand*, 44.
13. Clinton Rossiter, "Thomas Hooker," *New England Quarterly*, vol. 25, 479–81.
14. John C. Miller, *The Colonial Image*, 25.

Chapter 14: God's Controversy with New England

1. Mather, *Magnalia*, vol. 2, 306.
2. Winthrop, *History*, vol. 1, 119, 120.
3. Mather, *Magnalia*, vol. 2, 295, 296.
4. Ibid., 300.
5. Winthrop, *History*, vol. 1, 126.
6. Mather, *Magnalia*, vol. 2, 356.
7. Bradford, *Plimouth*, Morrison edition, 253–54.
8. Bradford, *Plimouth*, Wright and Potter edition, 508, 509.
9. Mather, vol. 1, 63, as quoted in Stephen Foster, *Their Solitary Way*, 121.
10. This quote and the following one are from Foster, *Way*, 124, 132.
11. Winthrop, *History*, vol. 2, 277.
12. Love, *Fast and Thanksgiving Days*, 181.
13. Johnson, *Providences*, 253.
14. This quote and the following one are from Rosenmeier in *Typology*, Bercovitch, ed., 104.
15. Foster, *Way*, 58.
16. Mather, *Magnalia*, vol. 1, 7, 8.
17. Love, *Fast and Thanksgiving Days*, 191.

Chapter 15: As a Roaring Lion

1. Winthrop, *History*, vol. 1, 387, 388.
2. For the sequence of these events we are much indebted to Douglas Edward Leach's excellent work, *Flintlock and Tomahawk*.
3. Although our scene is imagined, the place and the approximate date of Philip's opening attack can be ascertained from John Fiske's *The Beginnings of New England*, 214.
4. George N. Williams, *Wilderness and Paradise in Christian Thought*, 112.
5. *Old Sudbury*, 23.
6. Demos, *Providences*, 287.

7. John Miller, *The Colonial Image*, 260–62.

8. This quote and the following one are from Leach, *Flintlock and Tomahawk*, 195, 198.

9. Demos, *Providences*, 305.

10. John Miller, *Image*, 289.

11. This quote and the following one are from Mather, *Magnalia*, vol. 2, 392–403.

12. John Miller, *Image*, 185, 186.

13. Eve LaPlante, *Salem Witch Judge*, 136.

14. Ibid., 156.

15. Ibid., 138–39.

16. Sweet, *The Story of Religion*, 61. The author gives the figure of half a million witches executed in Europe from the fourteenth century to the eighteenth.

17. LaPlante, *Judge*, 175.

18. Ibid., 180.

19. Ibid., 193.

20. Ibid., 196.

21. John Miller, *Image*, 190.

Chapter 16: A Sunburst of Light

1. H. Richard Niebuhr, *The Kingdom of God in America*, 126.

2. Jonathan Edwards, *The Works of President Edwards*, Isaiah Thomas, ed., vol. 3, 14–19.

3. This quote and the following one are from John Pollock, *George Whitefield and the Great Awakening*, 18, 19.

4. John Wesley, *Journal*, 64.

5. Thomas Hobbes, *Leviathan*, part 1, chapter 8.

6. This quote and the facts in the following two paragraphs are from Pollock, *Whitefield*, 83, 112, 115.

7. This quote and the following two quotes are from Russell T. Hitt, *Heroic Colonial Christians*, 171, 198.

8. Pollock, *Whitefield*, 164.

9. These references to Whitefield's visit to Philadelphia are from Pollock, *Whitefield*, 117–21.

10. Ibid., 156.

11. From Whitefield's journal, as quoted by Peter Gomes in "George Whitefield in the Old Colony: 1740," in L. D. Geller, ed., *They Knew They Were Pilgrims*, 93.

12. Pollock, *Whitefield*, 162.

13. Whitefield's journal, quoted in Gomes, *They Knew They Were Pilgrims*, 93.

14. Pollock, *Whitefield*, 250.

15. Ibid., 246.

16. Ibid., 248.

17. This quote and the following quotes are all from Pollock, *Whitefield*, 268–70.

Chapter 17: When Kings Become Tyrants

1. Perry Miller, *Orthodoxy in Massachusetts*, 220.

2. Fiske, *Beginnings*, 247.

3. Wendell, *Cotton Mather*, 46.

4. This quote and the following one are from David Lovejoy, *The Glorious Revolution in America*, 154, 155.

5. Ibid., 176.

6. This is the famous quote of John Bradshaw, President of the high court that had tried Charles I in 1649 (*Encyclopaedia Britannica*, vol. 4, 60) as quoted in Foster, *Their Solitary Way*, 165.

7. John Wingate Thornton, *The Pulpit of the American Revolution*, 74.

Chapter 18: "No King but King Jesus!"

1. Printed in the Maryland *Gazette*, September 29, 1774, and quoted in Hezekiah Niles, *Principles and Acts of the Revolution in America*, 164.

2. Thornton, *Pulpit*, 73, 74.

3. This quote and the following one are from Clinton Rossiter, *Seedtime of the Republic*, 241–45.

4. Mather, *Magnalia*, vol. 1, 26, as quoted in A. W. Plumstead, *The Wall and the Garden*, 28.

5. Bancroft, *History*, vol. 6, 102.

6. This quote and the two following quotes are from Bancroft, vol. 6, 140–42.

7. Ibid., 195.

8. Edmund Morgan, "The Puritan Ethic and the American Revolution," *William & Mary Quarterly*, vol. 24, no. 1, 17.

9. This quote and the following one are from Bancroft, *History*, vol. 6, 440–42.

10. Kistler, *This Nation*, 56.

11. Niles, *Principles and Acts of the Revolution in America*, 198.

12. Cushing Stout, *The New Heavens and the New Earth*, 59.

13. William V. Wells, *Life and Public Services of Samuel Adams*, vol. 3, 504.

14. John Adams, *Diary and Autobiography*, vol. 1, 270–71.

15. Quoted in Pauline Maier, *The Old Revolutionaries*, 37.

16. James K. Hosmer, *American Statesman: Samuel Adams*, 271.

17. Bancroft, *History*, vol. 7, 73, 74. One eighteenth-century pound sterling equaled sixteen ounces of silver, currently worth around $18.00 per ounce.

18. Ibid., 99.

19. B. J. Lossing, *Biographical Sketches of the Lives of the Signers of the Declaration*, 35.

20. John R. Musick, *Great Americans of History: John Hancock*, 156.

21. Dennis Fradin, *Samuel Adams: the Father of American Independence*, 90.

22. Charles Francis Adams, *Familiar Letters of John Adams and His Wife Abigail Adams, During the Revolution*, 87–88.

23. Thornton, *Pulpit*, 195–96.

24. Bancroft, *History*, vol. 7, 229.

25. William Wirt Henry, *Patrick Henry: Life, Correspondence, and Speeches*, vol. 1, 125.

26. Henry Mayer, *A Son of Thunder*, 160.

27. Henry, *Patrick Henry*, vol. 1, 83.

28. Henry, *Patrick Henry*, vol. 2, 261, 264, 267.

29. Ibid., 262–70. Though Patrick Henry may have prepared this speech ahead of time, there is no mention of his using notes. This famous speech by one of America's greatest orators (which American schoolchildren were once required to memorize) was apparently delivered under the inspiration of the moment.

30. Ibid., 270–71. Edward Carrington, who later served as a colonel in the Continental Army, was unable to get into the church because of the crowd. Relegated to a window view of Patrick Henry, he was so overcome by the power of the speech that he declared, "Let me be buried at this spot!" His wish was granted.

Chapter 19: "If They Want to Have a War . . ."

1. For the events of the night of April 18–19, 1775, we are indebted to David Hackett Fischer, *Paul Revere's Ride,* 108–12, 174–79.

2. Revere saw Adams and Hancock safely out of Lexington and then dashed back into the town to rescue (with a Patriot named John Lowell) a heavy trunk of incriminating papers that Adams and Hancock had left behind at Buckman Tavern. They were lugging the heavy trunk across the Common behind the militia just before the shooting began. But somehow they were unseen by the British, and they managed to carry the heavy trunk to a hiding place in a nearby wood, where they waited until the Redcoats had left the town.

3. For the events of April 19, 1775, we are indebted to *The Boston Globe's* special section "The Lexington-Concord Alarm," March 9, 1975, 39–71.

4. David Hackett Fischer, *Paul Revere's Ride,* 257.

5. Fischer, *Revere's Ride,* 205.

6. Franklin P. Cole, *They Preached Liberty,* 38.

7. *The Boston Globe,* "The Battle of Bunker Hill," June 8, 1975, 15, 16.

8. Page Smith, *A New Age Now Begins,* 508.

9. Samuel Langdon, sermon reprinted in Plumstead, *The Wall,* 364–73.

Chapter 20: "The Great Spirit Protects That Man!"

1. For the story of the Battle of Bunker Hill, we are indebted to *The Boston Globe,* "Bunker Hill," 20–39.

2. Winston S. Churchill, *A History of the English-Speaking Peoples,* vol. 3, 152.

3. *The Boston Globe,* "Bunker Hill," 30.

4. Ibid., 35.

5. Ibid., 38.

6. This quote and the following one are from *The Spirit of '76,* Henry Steele Commager and Richard B. Morris, eds., 122–24.

7. George F. Scheer and Hugh F. Rankin, *Rebels and Redcoats,* 62.

8. Ibid., 62, 63.

9. *The Boston Globe,* "Bunker Hill," 39.

10. This quote and the following one are from *The Boston Globe,* "Washington's First Victory," March 7, 1976, 5.

11. This quote and the following two quotes are from Richard Brookhiser, *Founding Father,* 107, 109, 111.

12. Ibid., 110.

13. Quoted in Peter Lillback, *George Washington's Sacred Fire,* 577–78.

14. George Washington, *Writings of George Washington,* vol. 37, John C. Fitzpatrick, ed., 526.

15. The other members of this illustrious committee were Robert Carter Nicolas, John Randolph, Richard Bland, Benjamin Harrison, and Edmund Pendleton. With the exception of Nicolas and the addition of Peyton Randolph, these men would comprise the Virginia delegation to the First Continental Congress five years later.

16. Lillback, *Sacred Fire,* 292.

17. Ibid., 55–57.

18. Michael Novak and Jana Novak, *Washington's God,* 11–12.

19. This quote and the one following from Lillback, *Sacred Fire,* 137.

20. Novak and Novak, *Washington's God,* 17.

21. Lillback, *Sacred Fire,* 139.

22. William Johnson, *George Washington, the Christian*, 36.

23. Ibid., 41– 42.

24. Kistler, *This Nation*, 54.

25. This quote and the following two quotes are all from Bancroft, *History*, vol. 4, 190.

Chapter 21: "Give 'Em Watts, Boys!"

1. Smith, *A New Age*, 572.

2. Johnson, *George Washington*, 69–70.

3. Washington, *Writings*, vol. 3, 309.

4. Johnson, *George Washington*, 209.

5. Washington, *Writings*, vol. 5, 367.

6. Ibid., vol. 3, 341.

7. From the original printed sermon, Boston, 1775.

8. Philip Davidson, *Propaganda and the American Revolution*, 205, 206.

9. Bancroft, *History*, vol. 7, 307.

10. W. P. Breed, *Presbyterians and the Revolution*, 85.

11. From the fourth installment of George Cornell's series, "The Founding Faith," Associated Press, April 16, 1976.

12. Breed, *Presbyterians*, 80–82.

13. Bruce Lancaster and J. H. Plumb, *The American Heritage Book of the Revolution*, 119, 120.

14. *The Boston Globe*, "Washington's First Victory," March 7, 1976, 34.

15. Ibid., 35.

16. Lancaster and Plumb, *American Heritage Book*, 123.

17. Frank S. Mead, ed., *The Encyclopedia of Religious Quotations*, 265.

18. *The Papers of George Washington: Revolutionary War Series*, vol. 3, Philander D. Chase, ed., 89.

19. *The Boston Globe*, "Washington's First Victory," 65.

20. James Thomas Flexner, "Providence Rides a Storm," *American Heritage* 19 (December 1967), 17.

21. Ibid., 98.

22. H. Niles, *Principles and Acts*, 480.

23. J. Franklin Jameson, *The American Revolution Considered as a Social Movement*, 91, 92.

24. From the original sermon, Princeton, May 17, 1776.

25. Thornton, *Pulpit*, 311.

Chapter 22: "We Have Restored the Sovereign"

1. L. H. Butterfield, ed., *Adams Family Correspondence*, vol. 2, 16.

2. This quote and the following one are from Commager and Morris, *The Spirit*, 230–33.

3. Ibid., 265–66.

4. Ibid., 241.

5. Ibid., 265.

6. Ibid., 260–61.

7. David Barton, pamphlet entitled "Was the American Revolution a Biblically Justified Act?" 4.

8. Samuel Adams, *Writings*, vol. 4, 38. Letter to the Earl of Carlisle, Lord Viscount Howe, Sir William Howe, William Eden and George Johnstone, printed in the *Massachusetts Spy*, July 16, 1778.

9. *Annals of America*, vol. 2, *Encyclopaedia Britannica*, 1968, 276.

10. Actually, the first Americans to declare their independence were the citizens of Mecklenburg County, North Carolina, in May 1775.

11. Russell Kirk, *The Roots of American Order*, 342–43, 404.

12. Dan Smoot, *America's Promise*, 6.

13. Edward Frank Humphrey, *Nationalism and Religion*, 85.

14. For the details of this story we are indebted to Robert E. Lewis, *Pace Magazine*, July/August 1976, 25.

15. The New York delegates supported independence, but they had pledged not to vote until they received instructions from their constituents. The instructions had not yet arrived.

16. Kistler, *This Nation*, 71.

Chapter 23: Crucible of Freedom

1. Kistler, *This Nation*, 73.

2. This quote and the following one are from *Adams Family Correspondence*, vol. 2, 28, 30–31.

3. Butterfield, ed., *Letters of Benjamin Rush*, vol. 1, 534.

4. Richard Wheeler, ed., *Voices of 1776*, 144–50.

5. Bancroft, *History*, vol. 9, 79.

6. Scheer and Rankin, *Rebels and Redcoats*, 167.

7. Ibid., 171.

8. Commager and Morris, *The Spirit*, 464.

9. Ibid., 495–96, for this quote and the following one.

10. David Hackett Fischer, *Washington's Crossing*, 227.

11. This quote and the following two are from Commager and Morris, *The Spirit*, 513.

12. Ibid., 518–19 for this quote and the following one.

13. For these facts and much of the description that follows we are indebted to Henry Armitt Brown, *The Valley Forge Oration*, 1878, as reprinted in Verna M. Hall's *The Christian History of the American Revolution*, 56–59, and John W. Jackson, *Valley Forge: Pinnacle of Courage*.

14. Jackson, *Valley Forge*, 43.

15. Ibid., 56.

16. Wheeler, *Voices*, 288.

17. Hall, *Revolution*, 61–62.

18. Washington, *Writings*, vol. 2, 291–92.

19. Ibid., vol. 10, 192.

20. John Joseph Stoudt, *Ordeal at Valley Forge*, 135.

21. Washington, *Writings*, vol. 2, 343.

22. Henry Melchior Muhlenberg, *Notebook of a Colonial Clergyman*, 195.

23. Mason Weems in William Johnson, *George Washington*, 103.

24. Lillback, *Sacred Fire*, 629–38. Although some historians have challenged the accuracy of this story, Lillback's argument for its authenticity seems convincing to the authors.

25. Wheeler, *Voices*, 287.

26. Stoudt, *Ordeal*, 146.

Chapter 24: "The World Turned Upside Down"

1. For these details and the ones to follow, we are indebted to Page Smith, *A New Age*, 1008–13.
2. Washington, *Writings*, vol. 11, 354.
3. Washington, *Writings*, vol. 20, 95.
4. Benson J. Lossing, *The Pictorial Field-Book of the Revolution*, vol. 2, 596–605, and Benson J. Lossing, *Our Country*, vol. 4, 1068–69.
5. Sir Henry Clinton, *The American Rebellion*, 261.
6. Lossing, *Pictorial Field-Book*, 601–4.
7. Lancaster and Plumb, *The American Heritage*, 320.
8. Page Smith, *New Age*, 1704.
9. Wheeler, *Voices*, 454.
10. Washington, *Writings*, vol. 23, 247.
11. Washington, *Writings*, vol. 12, 343.
12. From the original sermon.
13. This quote and the following ones are from Scheer and Rankin, *Rebels and Redcoats*, 504, 506, 507.

Chapter 25: "Except the Lord Build the House . . ."

1. Frank Moore, ed., *The Patriot Preachers of the American Revolution*, 358–60.
2. Ibid., 305–6.
3. Ibid., 334–35.
4. From the original sermon, Boston, 1813.
5. Quoted in Stephen E. Berk, *Calvinism Versus Democracy*, 24.
6. Washington, *Writings*, vol. 26, 496.
7. Daniel Wait Howe, *The Puritan Republic of the Massachusetts Bay in New England*, 397.
8. Allan Nevins on Washington, in the *Encyclopaedia Britannica*, vol. 23, 1970 edition, 243.
9. Page Smith, *New Age*, 1792–97.
10. Norman Cousins, ed., *In God We Trust*, 42.
11. David Barton, *Original Intent*, 111–12.
12. This quote and the following one are from James Madison, *Papers*, vol. 10, 208 (letter to Thomas Jefferson, October 24, 1787); and James Madison (writing under Publius), *The Federalist Papers*, Mary E. Webster, ed., 37.
13. *Annals of America*, Britannica, vol. 3, 122.
14. Cecelia Marie Kenyon in the *Encyclopaedia Britannica*, vol. 9, 1970 edition, 138.
15. *The Federalist Papers*, as quoted in *Annals of America*, vol. 3, 216, 217.
16. These two quotes are from John Adams, *Papers*, vol. 1, 83; and John Adams, *Works*, vol. 6, 484.
17. *Time* magazine, special issue, "The New Nation, September 26, 1789," 14.
18. July 31, 1788, as quoted in Esmond Wright, *Causes and Consequences of the American Revolution*, 183.
19. Richard Niebuhr, "The Idea of Covenant and American Democracy," in *Church History*, vol. 23, 134.
20. Washington, *Writings*, vol. 30, 292–93.
21. Kirk, *The Roots of American Order*, 343.
22. Charles Roy Keller, *The Second Great Awakening*, 36.
23. Quoted in Cushing Stout, *The New Heavens and New Earth*, 79.

24. This quote and the following three quotes are from Cousins, *In God We Trust,* 149, 161–63.

25. Washington, *Writings*, vol. 35, 229.

26. John Adams, *Works,* vol. 9, 229.

27. Alexis de Tocqueville, *Democracy in America*, vol. 1, 391.

28. *Guideposts*, "A Letter from the President of the United States," May 1975, 16–18.

29. J. A. Carroll and M. W. Ashworth, *George Washington*, vol. 7 of the Douglas Southall Freeman biography, 438.

The Search Ends

1. Chard Powers Smith, *Yankees and God*, 289, 290.

2. *National Courier*, September 3, 1976, 20.

3. Bercovitch, *Puritan Origins*, 95, 96.

Appendix One: The Mystery of the Lost Colony

1. Horwitz, *A Voyage Long and Strange*, 314.

2. Smith, *Writings*, 930.

3. Ibid., 1072–73.

4. Ibid., 1085.

5. Milton, *Elizabeth*, 341.

6. Ibid.

7. Ibid., 342.

8. Ibid.

9. Horwitz, *Voyage*, 314.

10. Ibid., 314–15.

Appendix Two: The Christian Faith of George Washington

1. Lillback, *Sacred Fire*, 801–13.

2. Washington, *Writings,* vol. 21, letter dated February 26,1781.

3. Lillback, *Fire*, 352.

4. Ibid., 333.

5. Ibid., 305.

6. Washington, *Writings,* vol. 30, entry of April 1789.

7. Ibid., vol. 26, letter dated June 8, 1783.

8. Lillback, *Fire*, 264.

9. Washington, *Writings,* vol. 3, order for July 4, 1775.

10. Lillback, *Fire*, 268–69.

11. Ibid., 1051.

12. Ibid., 721.

13. Ibid., 424.

14. Ibid.

15. Ibid., 410–11.

16. Ibid., 415–16.

17. Ibid., 420–21.

18. Ibid., 577–78.

19. Washington, *Writings,* vol. 9, letter dated October 19, 1777.

20. Lillback, *Fire*, 578.

Appendix Three: The Christian Faith of Other Founding Fathers

1. William V. Wells, *The Life and Public Services of Samuel Adams*, vol. 3, 372–73.

2. From the Last Will & Testament of Samuel Adams, attested December 29, 1790.

3. Dumas Malone, *Dictionary of American Biography*, vol. 2, 477–78; *Appleton's Cyclopedia of American Biography*, vol. 1, James Grant Wilson and John Fiske, ed., 327–28.

4. *The Life, Public Services, Addresses and Letters of Elias Boudinot*, vol. 1, J. J. Boudinot, ed., 261–62.

5. Elias Boudinot, *The Age of Revelation, or The Age of Reason Shown to be An Age of Infidelity*, xv.

6. Letter from Charles Carroll to Charles W. Wharton Esq., September 27, 1825.

7. *The Political Writings of John Dickinson*, vol. 1, 111–12.

8. Dumas Malone, *Dictionary of American Biography*, 299–300.

9. Quoted in James H. Hutson, *The Founders on Religion*, 24.

10. Benjamin Franklin, *Papers*, vol. 3, 226–27, "Proclamation for a General Fast on December 9, 1747"; Benjamin Franklin, *Proposals Relating to the Education of Youth in Pennsylvania*, Philadelphia, 1749, 22.

11. Jared Sparks, *Life of Benjamin Franklin, Containing the Autobiography, with Notes*, 352; see also Franklin, *Works* (1840), vol. 10, 208–9n, to Granville Sharp on July 5, 1785.

12. Benjamin Franklin, *Papers*, (1963), vol. 6, 469, to George Whitefield on July 2, 1756.

13. Kistler, *This Nation*, 83.

14. William Wirt Henry, *Patrick Henry*, vol. 2, 519.

15. Ibid., 632.

16. Ibid., 631.

17. David Barton, *The Role of Pastors and Christians in Civil Government*, 26.

18. Malone, *Dictionary*, vol. 10, 5–9.

19. William Jay, *The Life of John Jay*, vol. 1, 443.

20. Henry Johnston, *The Correspondence and Public Papers of John Jay*, vol. 1, (digital edition), 515–17.

21. Jay, *The Life of John Jay*, vol. 1, 519–20.

22. William B. Reed, *Life and Correspondence of Joseph Reed*, vol. 2, 35–37.

23. Robert Treat Paine, *Papers*, vol. 1, Stephen T. Riley and Edward W. Hanson, ed., 49.

24. From the Last Will & Testament of Robert Treat Paine, attested May 11, 1814.

25. Malone, *Dictionary*, vol. 16, 227–30.

26. Benjamin Rush, *The Autobiography of Benjamin Rush*, George W. Corner, ed., 166.

27. Malone, *Dictionary*, vol. 17, 88–90; Sanderson, *Biography of the Signers*, 250–76.

28. Lewis Henry Boutell, *The Life of Roger Sherman*, 272–73.

29. Roger Sherman Boardman, *Roger Sherman, Signer and Statesman*, 320.

30. Correspondence between Roger Sherman and Samuel Hopkins, Proceedings of the American Antiquarian Society, October 22, 1888, 2–27.

31. Malone, *Dictionary*, vol. 18, 45–46; B. J. Lossing, *Biographical Sketches of the Signers*, 77–80; Sanderson, *Biography of the Signers*, 86–103.

32. From the Last Will & Testament of Richard Stockton, attested May 20, 1780.

33. Barton, *Pastors & Christians*, 25.

34. John Witherspoon, *The Works of John Witherspoon*, 276–79.

BIBLIOGRAPHY

Adams, Amos. "A Concise Historical View of the Difficulties, Hardships and Perils which Attended the Planting and Progressive Improvements of New England." First Church of Roxbury, 1770.

Adams, Charles Francis. *Familiar Letters of John Adams and His Wife Abigail Adams, During the Revolution.* Boston: Houghton Mifflin, 1898.

Adams, John. *Diary and Autobiography of John Adams.* Vol. 1. Edited by L. H. Butterfield. Cambridge, MA: Belknap Press, 1962.

———. *The Papers of John Adams.* Vol. 1. Edited by Robert J. Taylor. Cambridge, MA: Belknap Press, 1977.

———. *The Works of John Adams, Second President of the United States.* Vols. 6 and 9. Edited by Charles Francis Adams. Boston: Little, Brown, 1850.

Adams, Samuel. *The Rights of the Colonists.* Boston: Old South Leaflets, vol. 7.

———. *The Writings of Samuel Adams.* Vol. 4. Edited by Harry Alonzo Cushing. New York: G. P. Putman's Sons, 1904. Reprinted New York: Octagon Books, 1968.

Ahlstrom, Sydney E. *A Religious History of the American People.* New Haven: Yale University Press, 1972.

American Heritage History of the Thirteen Colonies. New York: American Heritage, 1967.

Andrews, Charles M. *The Rise and Fall of the New Haven Colony*. New Haven: Yale University Press, 1936.

Angle, Paul M. *The American Reader*. New York: Rand McNally, 1958.

Balch, Thomas. "Calvinism and American Independence." *Presbyterian Quarterly*, July 1876.

Baldwin, Alice M. *The New England Clergy and the American Revolution*. New York: Frederic Ungar, 1958.

Bancroft, George. *Bancroft's History of the United States*. 3rd ed. Vol. 1–10. Boston: Little, Brown, 1838.

Bartlett, Robert Merrill. *The Pilgrim Way*. Philadelphia: United Church Press, 1971.

Barton, David. *Original Intent*. Aledo, TX: Wallbuilders Press, 2000.

———. *The Role of Pastors and Christians in Civil Government*. Aledo, TX: Wallbuilders Press, 2003.

Bercovitch, Sacvan. *The Puritan Origins of the American Self*. New Haven: Yale University Press, 1975.

———, ed. *Typology and Early American Literature*. Cambridge, MA: University of Massachusetts Press, 1972.

Berger, Josef, and Dorothy Berger, eds. *Diary of America*. New York: Simon & Schuster, 1957.

Berk, Stephen E. *Calvinism Versus Democracy*. Hamden, CT: Shoestring Press, 1974.

Blodgett, John Taggard. "Political Theory of the Mayflower Compact." Publica-

tion of the Colonial Society of Massachusetts, vol. 12, January, 1909.

Boardman, Roger Sherman. *Roger Sherman, Signer and Statesman*. Philadelphia: University of Pennsylvania Press, 1938.

Boller, Paul F., Jr. *George Washington and Religion*. Dallas: Southern Methodist University Press, 1963.

Boni, Albert, and Charles Boni. *Journal of First Voyage to America* by Christopher Columbus. New York, 1924.

Boorstin, Daniel J. *The Americans: The Colonial Experience*. New York: Vintage Books, 1958.

Boudinot, Elias. *The Age of Revelation, or The Age of Reason Shown to be An Age of Infidelity*. Philadelphia: Asbury Dickins, 1801.

Boudinot, J. J., ed. *The Life, Public Services, Addresses and Letters of Elias Boudinot*. Vol. 1. Cambridge, MA: Houghton Mifflin, 1896.

Boutell, Lewis Henry. *The Life of Roger Sherman*. Chicago: A.C. McClurg, 1896.

Bradford, William. *Of Plimouth Plantation*. Boston: Wright & Potter, 1901.

———. *Of Plymouth Plantation*. Edited by Samuel Eliot Morrison. New York: Alfred A. Knopf, 2002.

Branscomb, Harvie. "The Contribution of Moral and Spiritual Ideas to the Making of the American Way of Life." Madison: University of Wisconsin, 1952.

Brauer, Jerald C. "The Rule of the Saints in American Politics." Church History, vol. 27. Indiana: The American Society of Church History, 1958.

Breed, Rev. W. P. *Presbyterians and the Revolution.* Philadelphia: Presbyterian Board of Publication, 1876.

Breen, T. H. *The Character of the Good Ruler.* New Haven: Yale University Press, 1970.

Bremer, Francis J. *John Winthrop: America's Forgotten Founding Father.* New York: Oxford University Press, 2003.

Brewer, David J. *The United States as a Christian Nation.* Philadelphia: John C. Winston, 1905.

Bridenbaugh, Carl. *Vexed and Troubled Englishmen, 1590–1642.* New York: Oxford University Press, 1968.

Brookhiser, Richard. *Founding Father.* New York: The Free Press, 1996.

Brown, Alexander. *The First Republic in America.* Boston: Houghton Mifflin, 1898.

———. *The Genesis of the United States.* Vols. 1 and 2. Boston: Houghton Mifflin, 1890–91.

Bumgardner, Georgia B., ed. *American Broadsides.* Barre, MA: Imprint Society, 1971.

Butterfield, L. H., ed. *Adams Family Correspondence.* Vol. 2. Cambridge: Harvard University Press, 1963.

Caffrey, Kate. *The Mayflower.* New York: Stein and Day, 1974.

Calder, Isabel MacBeath. *The New Haven Colony.* New Haven: Yale University Press, 1934.

Carroll, Peter N. *Puritanism and the Wilderness.* New York: Columbia University Press, 1969.

Cheever, George B. *The Journal of the Pilgrims at Plymouth in New England in 1620.* New York: John Wiley, 1848.

Churchill, Winston S. *A History of the English-Speaking Peoples.* Vol. 3. New York: Bantam Books, 1963.

Clark, Jonas. *The Battle of Lexington, A Sermon and Eyewitness Narrative.* Ventura, CA: Nordskog Publishing, 2007.

Clebsch, William A. *From Sacred to Profane America.* New York: Harper & Row, 1968.

Clinton, Sir Henry. *The American Rebellion.* Edited by William B. Willcox. New Haven: Yale University Press, 1954.

Cobb, Sanford H. *The Rise of Religious Liberty in America.* New York: Macmillan, 1902.

Cohen, J. M., ed. and trans. *The Four Voyages of Christopher Columbus.* Baltimore: Penguin Books, 1969.

Cole, Franklin P. *They Preached Liberty.* Fort Lauderdale: Coral Ridge Ministries, n.d.

Columbus, Christopher. *His Own Book of Privileges.* London: Chiswick Press, 1893.

Commager, Henry Steele, and Richard B. Morris, eds. *The Spirit of Seventy-Six.* New York: Bobbs-Merrill Co., 1958.

Cooke Samuel. "A Sermon Preached at Cambridge, May 30, 1770." Boston, 1770.

Cornelison, Isaac S. *The Relation of Religion to Civil Government in the United States of America.* New York: De Capo Press, 1970.

Cornell, George W. "The Founding Faith." *The Daily Item* (Sunbury, PA), April 16, 1976.

Cotton, John. "God's Promise to His Plantations." Old South Leaflets, vol. 3. Boston: Directors of the Old South Work, Old South Meeting House, n.d.

Cousins, Norman. *In God We Trust.* New York: Harper & Bros., 1958.

Crouse, Nellie M. "Causes of the Great Migration 1630–1640." *New England Quarterly* 5 (1932).

Cushman, Robert. *The First Sermon Ever Preached in New England, 1621.* New York: J. E. D. Comstock, 1858.

Davidson, Philip. *Propaganda and the American Revolution.* Chapel Hill: University of North Carolina Press, 1941.

Demos, John, ed. *Remarkable Providences.* New York: George Braziller, 1972.

Dickinson, John. *The Political Writings of John Dickinson.* Vol. 1. Wilmington: Bonsal & Niles, 1801.

Dillon, Francis. *The Pilgrims.* Garden City, NY: Doubleday, 1975.

Dulles, John Foster. "The Power of Moral Forces." General Foreign Policy Series 84. Washington, DC: U.S. Dept. of State, 1954.

Dwight, Timothy. *The Conquest of Canaan.* New York: AMS Press, 1971.

———. "A Discourse in Two Parts, on the Public Fast." Boston, July 23, 1812.

———. "A Discourse on Some Events of the Last Century." New Haven, January 7, 1801.

———. *Greenfield Hill.* New York, 1794.

———. "Sermon Preached at Northampton on November 28th, 1781," Lamont Library Basement Microtexts, Harvard University.

———. "Virtuous Rulers a National Blessing." A sermon preached at the General Election, Hartford, May 12, 1791.

Earle, Alice Morse. *The Sabbath in Puritan New England.* New York: Scribner, 1891.

Eddy, Sherwood. *The Kingdom of God and the American Dream.* New York: Harper & Bros., 1941.

Edwards, Jonathan. *Thoughts on the Revival of Religion in New England.* New York: American Tract Society, 1740.

Eliot, John. *The Christian Commonwealth or the Civil Policy: or The Rising Kingdom of Jesus Christ.* Reprint of 1659 edition. New York: Arno Press, 1972.

Ellis, Joseph J. *His Excellency George Washington.* New York: Alfred A. Knopf, 2004.

Encyclopaedia Britannica, The Annals of America. Vols. 2 and 3, 1784–1796. Chicago, 1968.

Fischer, David Hackett. *Paul Revere's Ride.* New York: Oxford University Press, 1994.

———. *Washington's Crossing.* New York: Oxford University Press, 2004.

Fiske, John. *The Beginnings of New England or the Puritan Theocracy in Its Relations to Civil & Religious Liberty.* Cambridge, MA: Houghton Mifflin, 1900.

Fleming, Thomas J. *One Small Candle: The Pilgrims' First Year in America.* New York: W. W. Norton, 1963.

Flexner, James Thomas. "Providence Rides a Storm." *American Heritage* 19 (December 1967).

———. *Washington The Indispensable Man.* New York: New American Library, 1984.

Ford, Paul Leicester, ed. *Writings of Christopher Columbus.* New York, 1892.

Foster, Stephen. *Their Solitary Way.* New Haven: Yale University Press, 1971.

Fradin, Dennis B. *Samuel Adams: The Father of American Independence.* New York: Clarion Books, 1998.

Franklin, Benjamin. *Papers.* Vols. 3 and 6. New Haven: Yale University Press, 1961, 1963.

———. *Proposals Relating to the Education of Youth in Pennsylvania.* Philadelphia, 1749.

———. *Works.* Boston: Hillard, Gray & Company, 1840.

Freeman, Douglas S. *George Washington, A Biography.* Vols. 1–7. New York: Scribner, 1948.

Geller, L. D., ed. *They Knew They Were Pilgrims: Essays in Plymouth History.* New York: Poseidon Books, 1971.

Gordon, William. "Sermon to the Third Church of Roxbury." July 19, 1775.

Gray, Stanley. "The Political Thought of John Winthrop." *New England Quarterly* 3 (1930).

Guideposts Magazine. "A Letter from the President of the United States." May 1975.

Gutman, Judith Mara. *The Colonial Venture.* New York: Basic Books, 1966.

Hall, David D. *The Faithful Shepherd: A History of the New England Ministry in the Seventeenth Century.* Chapel Hill: University of North Carolina Press, 1972.

Hall, Verna M. *The Christian History of the American Revolution.* San Francisco: Foundation for American Christian Education, 1976.

———. *The Christian History of the Constitution of the United States of America.* San Francisco: Foundation for American Christian Education, 1975.

Halliday, E. M. "Nature's God and the Founding Fathers." *American Heritage* 14 (October 1963).

Hansen, Marcus Lee. *The Atlantic Migration 1607–1860.* Cambridge: Harvard University Press, 1940.

Harris, John. "Battle of Bunker Hill." *The Boston Globe,* June 8, 1975.

———. "Lexington-Concord Alarm." *The Boston Globe,* March 9, 1975.

———. "Washington's First Victory." *The Boston Globe,* March 7, 1976.

Hart, Albert Bushnell, ed. *American History Told by Contemporaries.* New York: Macmillan. Vol. 1. *Era of Colonization 1492–1689.* 1900. Vol. 2. *Building of the Republic 1689–1783.* 1899.

Heimert, Alan. "Puritanism, the Wilderness and the Frontier." *New England Quarterly* 26 (September 1953).

———. *Religion and the American Mind.* Cambridge: Harvard University Press, 1966.

Henry, William Wirt. *Patrick Henry: Life, Correspondence and Speeches.* Vols. 1 and 2. New York: Scribner, 1891.

Hill, Douglas. *The English to New England.* New York: Clarkson N. Potter, 1925.

Hitt, Russell T., ed. *Heroic Colonial Christians.* Philadelphia: J. B. Lippincott, 1966.

Hooker, Thomas. *The Christian's Two Lessons, Self-Denial and Self-Trial.* London: Printed by T. B. for P. Stephens and C. Meredith, at the Golden Lion in St. Paul's Churchyard, 1640.

Horwitz, Tony. *A Voyage Long and Strange.* New York: Henry Holt, 2008.

Hosmer, James K. *American Statesman: Samuel Adams.* Boston: Houghton Mifflin, 1898.

———. ed. *Winthrop's Journal "History of New England."* Vol. 2, 1630–1649. New York: Barnes & Noble, 1908.

Howe, Daniel Wait. *The Puritan Republic of the Massachusetts Bay in New England.* Indianapolis: Bowen-Merrill, 1899.

Humphrey, Edward Frank. *Nationalism and Religion.* Boston: Chipman Law Publishing, 1924.

Hutson, James H., ed. *The Founders on Religion.* Princeton, NJ: Princeton University Press, 2005.

Irvin, Benjamin H. *Samuel Adams.* New York: Oxford University Press, 2002.

Jackson, John W. *Valley Forge: Pinnacle of Courage.* Gettysburg, PA: Thomas Publications, 1992.

James, Sydney V., Jr., ed.. *Three Visitors to Early Plymouth.* Plymouth, MA: Plimoth Plantation, Inc., 1963.

Jameson, J. Franklin. *The American Revolution Considered as a Social Movement.* Princeton, NJ: Princeton University Press, 1926.

———. ed. *Johnson's Wonder-Working Providence 1628–1651.* New York: Barnes & Noble, 1910.

Jane, Cecil, trans. and ed. *The Voyages of Christopher Columbus.* London: Argonaut Press, 1930.

Jay, William. *The Life of John Jay.* Vol. 1. New York: J. & J. Harper, 1833.

Johnson, William J. *George Washington, the Christian.* Nashville: Abingdon, 1919.

Johnston, Henry P. *The Correspondence and Public Papers of John Jay.* Vol. 1 (digital edition). New York: Burt Franklin, 1970.

Jones, Alonzo T. *Civil Government and Religion or Christianity and the American Constitution.* Chicago: American Sentinel, 1889.

Jones, Rufus M. *The Quakers in the American Colonies.* New York: Russell & Russell, 1962.

Keller, Charles Roy. *The Second Great Awakening in Connecticut.* New Haven: Yale University Press, 1942.

Kirk, Russell. *The Roots of American Order.* LaSalle, IL: Open Court, 1974.

Kistler, Charles E. *This Nation Under God.* Boston: Richard G. Badger, The Gorham Press, 1924.

Kling, August J. "Columbus—A Layman 'Christ-bearer' to Uncharted Isles." *Presbyterian Layman,* October 1971.

Lancaster, Bruce, and J. H. Plumb. *The American Heritage Book of the Revolution.* New York: Dell, 1958.

Landström, Björn. *Columbus.* New York: Macmillan, 1966.

LaPlante, Eve. *Salem Witch Judge.* New York: Harper One, 2007.

Leach, Douglas Edward. *Flintlock and Tomahawk.* New York: Macmillan, 1958.

Lewis, Robert E. "Listen My Children and You Shall Hear. . . ." *Pace Magazine,* July/August 1976.

Lossing, Benson J. *Biographical Sketches of the Lives of the Signers of the Declaration of American Independence.* Glendale, NY: Benchmark, 1970.

———. *Our Country: A Household History of the United States.* Vol. 4. New York: James A. Bailey, 1895.

———. *The Pictorial Field-Book of the Revolution.* Vol. 2. New York: Harper & Bros., 1852.

Love, W. DeLoss, Jr. *The Fast and Thanksgiving Days of New England.* Boston: Houghton Mifflin, 1895.

Lovejoy, David S. *The Glorious Revolution in America.* New York: Harper & Row, 1972.

Madison, James. *The Papers of James Madison.* Vol. 10. Edited by Robert A. Rutland et al. Chicago: University of Chicago Press, 1977.

Maier, Pauline. *The Old Revolutionaries.* New York: Random House, 1980.

Malone, Dumas. *Dictionary of American Biography.* Vol. 2. New York: Scribner, 1932.

Marty, Martin E. *Righteous Empire: The Protestant Experience in America.* New York: Dial Press, 1970.

Mather, Cotton. *A Faithful Account of the Discipline Professed and Practised in the Churches of New England.* Boston: S. Gerrish, 1726.

———. *Magnalia Christi Americana: or the Ecclesiastical History of New England*. Vols. 1 and 2. Hartford, CT: Silas Andrus, 1820. Also 1855 edition.

———. "The Present State of New England," lecture in Boston, 1690. New York: Haskell House, 1972.

Mather, Increase. "An Earnest Exhortation to the Inhabitants of New England." Boston, 1676.

———. *Remarkable Providences*. London: John Russell Smith, 1856.

Mayer, Henry. *A Son of Thunder*. Charlottesville, VA: University Press of Virginia, 1991.

McLaughlin, Andrew C. *Foundations of American Constitutionalism*. New York: New York University Press, 1932.

Mead, Frank S., ed. *The Encyclopedia of Religious Quotations*. Westwood, NJ: Revell, 1965.

Mead, Sidney E. *The Lively Experiment, The Shaping of Christianity in America*. New York: Harper & Row, 1963.

Miller, John C., ed. *The Colonial Image*. New York: George Braziller, 1962.

Miller, Perry. *Errand into the Wilderness*. Cambridge: Belknap Press of Harvard University Press, 1956.

———. "The Garden of Eden and the Deacon's Meadow." *American Heritage* 7 (December 1955).

———. "The Marrow of Puritan Divinity." *Colonial Society of Massachusetts Publications* 32 (February 1935).

———. *Nature's Nation*. Cambridge: Harvard University Press, 1967.

———. *The New England Mind*. New York: Macmillan, 1939.

———. *Orthodoxy in Massachusetts 1630–1650*. Boston: Beacon Press, 1959.

———. "The Religious Impulse in the Founding of Virginia: Religion and Society in the Early Literature." *The William & Mary Quarterly*, 3rd series, vol. 5. Williamsburg: Institute of Early American History & Culture, 1948.

Miller, Perry, and Thomas H. Johnson, eds. *The Puritans*. Vol. 1. New York: Harper & Row, 1963.

Milton, Giles. *Big Chief Elizabeth*. New York: Farrar, Straus & Giroux, 2000.

Mode, Peter G. *Source Book and Bibliographic Guide for American Church History*. Menasha, WI: George Banta, 1920.

Moehlman, Conrad Henry. *The American Constitutions and Religion*. Barre, IN, 1938.

Monsma, John Clover. *What Calvinism Has Done for America*. Chicago: Rand, McNally , 1919.

Moore, Frank, ed. *The Patriot Preachers of the American Revolution*. New York, 1860.

Morgan, Edmund S. *American Slavery—American Freedom*. New York: W. W. Norton, 1975.

———. *The Puritan Dilemma*. Boston: Little, Brown, 1958.

———. "The Puritan Ethic and the American Revolution." *William & Mary Quarterly*, 3rd series, vol. 24, no. 1.

———. *The Puritan Family*. New York: Harper & Row, 1944.

———. *Visible Saints: The History of a Puritan Idea*. New York: New York University Press, 1962.

Morison, Samuel Eliot. *Admiral of the Ocean Sea*. Boston: Little, Brown, 1942.

———. *The European Discovery of America*. New York: Oxford University Press, 1974.

Morris, B. F. *Christian Life and Character of the Civil Institutions of the United States*. Philadelphia: George W. Childs, 1864.

Muhlenberg, Henry Melchior. *The Notebook of a Colonial Clergyman*. Translated and edited by Theodore G. Tappert and John W. Doberstern. Philadelphia: Fortress Press, 1975.

Musick, John R. *Great Americans of History: John Hancock*. Chicago: Union School Furnishing Company, 1898.

Newman, Paul S. *In God We Trust*. Norwalk, CT: C. R. Gibson Co., 1973.

Niebuhr, H. Richard. "The Idea of Covenant and American Democracy." Paper presented at the American Studies section of the American Historical Association, Chicago, December 28, 1953.

———. *The Kingdom of God in America*. New York: Harper & Bros., 1959.

Niles, H. *Principles and Acts of the Revolution in America*. Baltimore, 1822. Old Sudbury, Boston: Pinkham Press, 1929.

Novak, Michael, and Jana Novak. *Washington's God*. New York: Basic Books, 2006.

Olasky, Marvin. *Fighting for Liberty and Virtue*. Wheaton: Crossway, 1995.

Park, Edward A. *The Works of Samuel Hopkins*. Vol. 1. Boston: Doctrinal Tract & Book Society, 1854.

Pellman, Hubert Ray. *Thomas Hooker: A Study in Puritan Ideals*. Philadelphia: University of Pennsylvania Press, 1958.

Perry, Ralph Barton. *Puritanism and Democracy*. New York: Vanguard Press, 1944.

Plumstead, A.W., ed. *The Wall and the Garden, Selected Massachusetts Election Sermons, 1670–1775*. Minneapolis: University of Minnesota Press, 1968.

Pollock, John. *George Whitefield and the Great Awakening*. Garden City, NY: Doubleday, 1972.

Pope, Liston. "Religion as a Social Force in America." Lecture at Smith College.

Priestly, Herbert Ingram. *The Coming of the White Man 1492–1848*. Volume 1 of *A History of American Life*. New York: Macmillan, 1929.

Reed, William B. *Life and Correspondence of Joseph Reed*. Vol. 2. Philadelphia: Lindsay and Blakiston, 1847.

Richey, Russell E. *American Civil Religion*. New York: Harper & Row, 1974.

Riley, Stephen T., and Edward W. Hanson, eds. *Papers of Robert Treat Paine*. Vol. 1. Boston: Massachusetts Historical Society, 1992.

Robinson, Henry Morton. *Stout Cortez: A Biography of the Spanish Conquest*. New York: Century, 1931.

Robinson, Stewart M. *And . . . We Mutually Pledge*. New Canaan, CT: The Long House, 1964.

Ross, David R. B., Alden T. Vaughan, and John B. Duff, eds. *Colonial America: 1607–1763*. New York: Thomas Y. Crowell, 1970.

Rossiter, Clinton. *Seedtime of the Republic*. New York: Harcourt, Brace & World, 1953.

———. "Thomas Hooker." *New England Quarterly*, vol. 25.

Rush, Benjamin. *The Autobiography of Benjamin Rush*. Edited by George W. Corner. Princeton, NJ: Princeton University Press, 1948.

———. *Letters*. Edited by L. H. Butterfield. Princeton, NJ: Princeton University Press, 1951.

Russell, Francis. "Apostle to the Indians." In *A Treasury of American Heritage*. New York: Simon & Schuster, 1954–60.

Sanderson, John. *Biography of the Signers to the Declaration of Independence*. Philadelphia: R. W. Pomeroy, 1823.

Savage, James, ed. *A Review of Winthrop's Journal*. Boston: Dutton & Wentworth, 1854.

Scheer, George F., and Hugh F. Rankin. *Rebels and Redcoats*. New York: The World Publishing Co., 1957.

Shaw, Mark R. "The Spirit of 1740." *Christianity Today*, January 2, 1976.

Sherman, Roger. *Correspondence between Roger Sherman and Samuel Hopkins, Proceedings of the American Antiquarian Society, October 22, 1888*. Worcester, MA: Charles Hamilton, 1889.

Shipton, Clifford K. "Puritanism and Modern Democracy." *New England Historical and Genealogical Register*, July 1947.

Simpson, Alan. *Puritanism in Old and New England*. Chicago: University of Chicago Press, 1955.

Smith, Chard Powers. *Yankees and God*. New York: Hermitage House, 1954.

Smith, James Ward, and A. Leland Jamison, eds. 4 vols. *Religion in American Life*. Princeton, NJ: Princeton University Press, 1961.

Smith, John. *Writings with Other Narratives of Roanoke, Jamestown, and the First English Settlement of America*. New York: The Library of America, 2007.

Smith, Page. *A New Age Now Begins*. 2 vols. New York: McGraw-Hill, 1976.

Smith, William. *A Sermon on the Present Situation of American Affairs*. Philadelphia: James Humphreys Jr., 1775.

Smoot, Dan. *America's Promise*. Dallas: The Dan Smoot Report, 1960.

Sparks, Jared. *Life of Benjamin Franklin, Containing the Autobiography, with Notes*. Boston: Tappan & Dennet, 1844.

Stiles, Ezra. "Sermon Preached at the Anniversary Election May 8, 1783." New Haven: Thomas & Samuel Green, 1783.

Stoddard, Solomon. "The Way for a People to Live Long in the Land That God Hath Given Them" (Sermon). Boston: Bartholomew Green, 1703.

Stoudt, John Joseph. *Ordeal at Valley Forge*. Philadelphia: University of Pennsylvania Press, 1963.

Stout, Cushing. *The New Heavens and New Earth*. New York: Harper & Row, 1974.

Sweet, William Warren. *The Story of Religion in America*. New York: Harper & Bros., 1950.

Thomas, Elbert D. *This Nation Under God*. New York: Harper & Bros., 1950.

Thomas, Isaiah. *Works of President Edwards*. Vol. 2. Worcester, 1808.

Thornton, John Wingate. *The Pulpit of the American Revolution*. Boston: D. Lothrop & Co., 1876.

Time magazine, special issue. "Independence, July 4, 1776." July 4, 1976.

Time magazine, special issue. "The New Nation, September 26, 1789."

Tocqueville, Alexis de. *Democracy in America*. 2nd ed. Translated by Henry Reeve. Edited by Francis Bowen. 2 vols. Cambridge, 1863.

Tuveson, Earnest Lee. *Redeemer Nation*. Chicago: University of Chicago Press, 1974.

Vaughan, Alden T. *American Genesis: Captain John Smith and the Founding of Virginia*. Boston: Little, Brown, 1975.

———. ed. *The Puritan Tradition in America 1620–1730*, Columbia, SC: University of South Carolina Press, 1972.

Washington, George. "The Invisible Hand." *Decision*, February 1976.

———. *Papers: Revolutionary War Series*. Vol. 3. Edited by Philander D. Chase. Charlottesville, VA: University Press of Virginia, 1988.

———. *The Writings Of*. Edited by John C. Fitzpatrick. Washington, DC: Government Printing Office, 1931–1939.

Webster, Daniel. *The Writings and Speeches of Daniel Webster*. Vol. 13. Boston: Little, Brown, 1903.

Webster, Mary E., ed. *The Federalist Papers in Modern Language*. Bellevue, WA: Merril Press, 1999.

Weigle, Luther A. *The Pageant of America*. New Haven: Yale University Press, 1928.

Wells, William V. *Life and Public Services of Samuel Adams*. Vol. 3. Boston: Little, Brown, 1865.

Wendell, Barrett. *Cotton Mather*. New York: Dodd, Mead, 1891.

Wesley, John. *Journal*. Edited by Percy Livingstone Parker. Chicago: Moody Press, 1974.

West, Delno C., and August Kling. *The Libro de las Profecias of Christopher Columbus*. Gainesville, FL: University of Florida Press, 1991.

Wheeler, Richard. *Voices of 1776*. Greenwich, CT: Fawcett Premier Book, 1972.

Whitefield, George. *The Two First Parts of His Life, With His Journals*. London: W. Strahan, 1756.

Whittelsey, Chauncy. Speech to the General Assembly of the State of Connecticut, May 14, 1778.

Williams, George H. "Christian Attitudes toward Nature." *Christian Scholar's Review* 2 (Fall 1971).

———. *Wilderness and Paradise in Christian Thought*. New York: Harper & Bros., 1962.

Williams, Roger. *Complete Writings of Roger Williams*. New York: Russell & Russell.

———. Vol. 1. Edited by Reuben Aldridge Guild. 1963.

———. Vol. 2. Edited by Rev. J. Lewis Diman and Reuben Aldridge Guild. 1963.

———. Vol. 3. Edited by Samuel L. Caldwell. 1963.

———. Vol. 6. Edited by John Russell Bartlett. 1963.

———. Vol. 7. Edited by Perry Miller. 1963.

Willison, George F. *Behold Virginia!* New York: Harcourt, Brace, 1952.

———. *Saints and Strangers*. New York: Reynal & Hitchcock, 1945.

Wilson, James Grant, and John Fiske, eds. *Appleton's Cyclopedia of American Biography*. Vol. 1. New York: D. Appleton, 1888.

Winslow, Ola Elizabeth. *Meetinghouse Hill 1630–1783*. New York: Macmillan, 1952.

Winthrop, John. *The History of New England from 1630 to 1649*. Edited by James Savage. Boston: Little, Brown, 1853.

The Winthrop Papers. Boston: Massachusetts Historical Society:

———. Vol. 1, 1598–1628. 1929.

———. Vol. 2, 1623–1630. 1931.

———. Vol. 3, 1631–1637. 1943.

———. Vol. 4, 1638–1644. 1944.

———. Vol. 5, 1645–1649. 1947.

Witherspoon, John. "Sermon Preached at Princeton on May 17, 1776." Philadelphia: R. Aitken.

———. *The Works of John Witherspoon, D.D.* Edinburgh: J. Ogle, Parliament Square, 1815.

Woolman, John. *The Journal of John Woolman*. Cambridge, MA: Riverside Press, 1871.

Wright, Esmond. *Causes and Consequences of the American Revolution*. New York: Quandrangel Books, 1966.

Wright, Louis B. *The Atlantic Frontier: Colonial American Civilization (1607–1763)*. New York: Alfred A. Knopf, 1947.

———. *The Colonial Civilization of North America 1607–1763*. London: Eyre & Spottiswoode, 1949.

———. *Religion and Empire*. Chapel Hill: University of North Carolina Press, 1943.

Young, Alexander. *Chronicles of the Pilgrim Fathers*. Boston: Little, Brown, 1841.

Zintl, Terry. "Love Didn't Make the World Go Round 200 Years Ago." *Miami Herald*, February 7, 1976.

INDEX

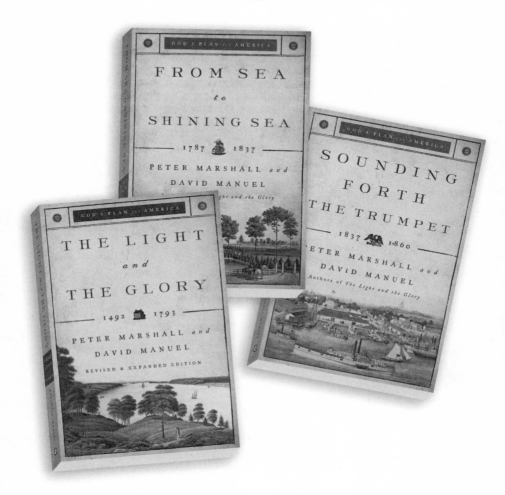

Beautiful repackages of the *God's Plan for America* series

Revell
a division of Baker Publishing Group
www.RevellBooks.com